READINGS IN WESTERN CIVILIZATION

—VOLUME FOUR—

THIRD EDITION

Spring 2006

PROVIDENCE COLLEGE

Development of Western Civilization Program

Tapestry Press, Ltd.
Littleton, MA 01720

Front Cover: Edward Hopper, *Nighthawks* (1942). Courtesy of Art Institute of Chicago.

All possible effort has been made to locate the copyright owner or holder of the copyrighted material included in this book. If any rights have been inadvertently infringed upon, the publisher asks to be excused, and agrees to make corrections to any subsequent editions or reprintings.

Acknowledgments:

Pp. 20–27: From *The Collected Poems of Wallace Stevens* by Wallace Stevens, copyright © 1954 by Wallace Stevens and renewed 1982 by Holly Stevens. Used by permission of Alfred A. Knopf, a division of Random House, Inc.

Pp. 63–66: "A Clean, Well-Lighted Place" by Ernest Hemingway. Reprinted with permission of Scribner, an imprint of Simon & Schuster Adult Publishing Group, from *The Short Stories of Ernest Hemingway*. Copyright © 1933 by Charles Scribner's Sons. Copyright renewed © 1961 by Mary Hemingway.

Pp. 67–75: "Requiem" by Anna Akhmatova. From *Selected Poems of Anna Akhmatova*, translated by Robin Kemball, Ardis, 1976. All rights reserved.

Pp. 76–94: "Shooting an Elephant" and "Politics and the English Language" from *Shooting an Elephant and Other Essays* by George Orwell, copyright © 1950 by Sonia Brownell Orwell and renewed 1978 by Sonia Pitt-Rivers, reprinted by permission of Harcourt, Inc.

Pp. 95–129: "No Exit" by Jean-Paul Sartre from *No Exit and the Flies* by Jean-Paul Sartre, translated by Stuart Gilbert, copyright © 1946 by Stuart Gilbert. Copyright renewed 1974, 1975 by Maris Agnes Mathilde Gilbert. Used by permission of Alfred A. Knopf, a division of Random House.

Pp. 130–139: "Zaabalawi" by Naguib Mahfouz. From *Modern Arabic Short Stories*, edited by Denys Johnson Davies. Translation copyright © 1967 by Denys Johnson Davies. All rights reserved.

Pp. 140–160: From *Invisible Man* by Ralph Ellison, copyright © 1947, 1948, 1952 by Ralph Ellison. Copyright renewed 1975, 1976, 1980 by Ralph Ellison. Used by permission of Random House, Inc.

Pp. 161–170: From *The Collected Poems of Langston Hughes* by Langston Hughes, copyright © 1994 by The Estate of Langston Hughes. Used by permission of Alfred A. Knopf, a division of Random House.

Pp. 174–179: "Yet Do I Marvel," "Heritage," and "Incident" by Countee Cullen from *My Soul's High Song: The Collected Writings of Countee Cullen, Voice of the Harlem Renaissance*. Countee Cullen Papers, Amistad Research Center at Tulane University. Reprinted by permission.

Pp. 180–194: "Sweat" and "Spunk" as taken from *The Complete Stories* by Zora Neale Hurston. Introduction copyright © 1995 by Henry Louis Gates, Jr. and Sieglinde Lemke. Compilation copyright © 1995 by Vivian Bowden, Lois J. Hurston Gaston, Clifford Hurston, Lucy Ann Hurston, Winifred Hurston Clark, Zora Mack Goins, Edgar Hurston, Sr., and Barbara Hurston Lewis. Afterword and Bibliography copyright © 1995 by Henry Louis Gates. Reprinted by permission of HarperCollins Publishers.

Pp. 204–209: "Those Winter Sundays," copyright © 1966 by Robert Hayden; "Middle Passage" copyright © 1962, 1966 by Robert Hayden, from *Collected Poems of Robert Hayden* by Robert Hayden, edited by Frederick Glaysher. Used by permission of Liveright Publishing Corporation.

Pp. 210–217: "A Worn Path" by Eudora Welty. From *A Curtain of Green and Other Stories*, copyright © 1941 and renewed 1969 by Eudora Welty. Reprinted by permission of Harcourt, Inc.

Pp. 218–231: "A Good Man Is Hard to Find" by Flannery O'Connor. From *A Good Man Is Hard to Find and Other Stories*, copyright © 1953 by Flannery O'Connor and renewed 1981 by Regina O'Connor. Reprinted by permission of Harcourt, Inc.

Pp. 232–264: "Matryona's House" by Alexander Solzhenitsyn from *Stories and Prose Poems* by Alexander Solzhenitsyn, translated by Michael Glenny. Translation copyright © 1971 by Michael Glenny. Reprinted by permission of Farrar, Straus, and Giroux, LLC.

Pp. 279–286: All text from "Death Constant Beyond Love" from *Innocent Erendira and Other Stories* by Gabriel Garcia Marquez. Translated from the Spanish by Gregory Rabassa. English translation copyright © 1978 by Harper & Row, Publishers, Inc. Reprinted by permission of HarperCollins Publishers.

Pp. 287–293: "Bogland," "Casualty," and "Death of a Naturalist" by Seamus Heaney from *Opened Ground: Selected Poems 1996–1998* by Seamus Heaney. Copyright © 1998 by Seamus Heaney. Reprinted by permission of Farrar, Straus, and Giroux, LLC.

Pp. 294–297: All lines from "Daddy" from *Ariel* by Sylvia Plath. Copyright © 1963 by Ted Hughes. Reprinted by permission of HarperCollins Publishers. All lines from "Metaphors" from *Crossing the Water* by Sylvia Plath. Copyright © by Ted Hughes. Reprinted by permission of HarperCollins Publishers. "The Colossus" by Sylvia Plath from *The Colossus and Other Poems* by Sylvia Plath, copyright © 1962 by Sylvia Plath. Used by permission of Alfred A. Knopf, a division of Random House, Inc.

Pp. 298–304: "Diving into the Wreck," copyright © 2002 by Adrienne Rich, copyright © 1973 by W.W. Norton & Company, Inc., "Aunt Jennifer's Tigers," copyright © 2002, 1951 by Adrienne Rich, and "Living in Sin," copyright © 2002, 1955 by Adrienne Rich from *The Fact of a Doorframe: Selected Poems 1950–2001* by Adrienne Rich. Used by permission of W.W. Norton & Company, Inc. "Toward the Solstice" from *The Dream of a Common Language: Poems 1974–1977* by Adrienne Rich. Copyright © 1978 by W.W. Norton & Company, Inc. Used by permission of W.W. Norton & Company, Inc.

Pp. 305–308: "In the Secular Night" by Margaret Atwood from *Morning in the Burned House: New Poems* by Margaret Atwood. Copyright © 1995 by Margaret Atwood. Reprinted by permission of Houghton Mifflin Company. All rights reserved. "This Is a Photograph of Me" by Margaret Atwood from *Selected Poems, 1965–1975* by Margaret Atwood. Copyright © 1976 by Margaret Atwood. Reprinted by permission of Houghton Miffling Company. All rights reserved.

Pp. 309–310: "On the Subway" by Sharon Olds from *The Gold Cell* by Sharon Olds, copyright © 1987 by Sharon Olds. Used by permission of Alfred A. Knopf, a division of Random House, Inc.

Pp. 311–315: From *The Shawl* by Cynthia Ozick, copyright © 1980, 1983 by Cynthia Ozick. Used by permission of Alfred A. Knopf, a division of Random House, Inc.

Pp. 316: "No-Name Woman" by Maxine Hong Kingston from *The Woman Warrior* by Maxine Hong Kingston, copyright © 1975, 1976 by Maxine Hong Kingston. Used by permission of Alfred A. Knopf, a division of Random House, Inc.

Contents

PROLOGUE

Readings in Western Civilization, volume four, third edition, provides selections for the literature component of Providence College's Development of Western Civilization Program. It is for use in the program's second year which runs, roughly, from France in the middle of the Seventeenth Century with Louis XIV and Descartes, to the present time. The two semesters of the academic year break around 1880. In literature that means that traditionally we end the Fall semester with Dostoevsky and begin the Spring semester with Tolstoy. The course integrates literature with history, theology, philosophy, and the fine arts, so literary works are studied in their historical and intellectual context.

For the most part, *Readings in Western Civilization* consists of shorter pieces and is designed to be supplemented by paperbacks of such fundamental works as *Tartuffe*, *Gulliver's Travels, Candide* and so on. The western focus of the program, partial as it is, reflects a conscious effort to provide a coherent view of the various western heritages by which we in the modern west have been historically shaped—regardless of our race, ethnicity, or national origin. The program traces that historical development, including its expansion towards greater appreciation of non-western achievements and influences as the past moves to the present and cultural influences are no longer contained in or by geography.

Brian Barbour

1. WILLIAM BUTLER YEATS

Yeats (1865–1939) was an Irishman at a time when hatred of England and of colonialism boiled over. His poetry expresses both admiration for and disgust with politics and political obsessiveness. His own vision tended more toward a mystical-historicism and, in his great work, a symbolism controlled by tight, tense rhythms. His sense of history as moving through vast cycles competed with his nearer sense of the value of a functioning landed aristocracy. The disappearance of much that he held dear resulted in some of Yeats' greatest poems. And in one line from "The Second Coming" he caught the essence of his age: "Things fall apart; the centre cannot hold."

EASTER 1916

I have met them at close of day
Coming with vivid faces
From counter or desk among grey
Eighteenth-century houses.
5   I have passed with a nod of the head
Or polite meaningless words,
Or have lingered awhile and said
Polite meaningless words,
And thought before I had done
10   Of a mocking tale or a gibe
To please a companion
Around the fire at the club,
Being certain that they and I
But lived where motley is worn:
15   All changed, changed utterly:
A terrible beauty is born.

That woman's[1] days were spent
In ignorant good-will,
Her nights in argument
20   Until her voice grew shrill.
What voice more sweet than hers
When, young and beautiful,
She rode to harriers?

---

[1]Constance Gore-Booth

This man[2] had kept a school
25 And rode our wingèd horse;
This other[3] his helper and friend
Was coming into his force;
He might have won fame in the end,
So sensitive his nature seemed,
30 So daring and sweet his thought.
This other man[4] I had dreamed
A drunken, vainglorious lout.
He had done most bitter wrong
To some who are near my heart,[5]
35 Yet I remember him in the song;
He too has resigned his part
In the casual comedy;
He, too, has been changed in his turn,
Transformed utterly:
40 A terrible beauty is born.

Hearts with one purpose alone
Through summer and winter seem
Enchanted to a stone
To trouble the living stream.
45 The horse that comes from the road,
The rider, the birds that range
From cloud to tumbling cloud,
Minute by minute they change;
A shadow of cloud on the stream
50 Changes minute by minute;
A horse-hoof slides on the brim,
And a horse plashes within it;
The long-legged moor-hens dive,
And hens to moor-cocks call;
55 Minute by minute they live:
The stone's in the midst of them all.

Too long a sacrifice
Can make a stone of the heart.
O when may it suffice?
60 That is Heaven's part, our part
To murmur name upon name

---

[2]Patrick Pearse

[3]Thomas MacDonagh

[4]John MacBride

[5]Maude Gonne. Yeats loved her but she married MacBride, who abused her and separated from her.

As a mother names her child
When sleep at last has come
On limbs that had run wild,
65   What is it but nightfall?
No, not night but death;
Was it needless death after all?
For England may keep faith
For all that is done and said.
70   We know their dream; enough
To know they dreamed and are dead;
And what if excess of love
Bewildered them till they died?
I write it out in a verse—
75   MacDonagh and MacBride
And Connolly and Pearse
Now and time to be,
Wherever green is worn,
Are changed, changed utterly:
80   A terrible beauty is born.   1916

THE SECOND COMING

Turning and turning in the widening gyre
The falcon cannot hear the falconer;
Things fall apart; the centre cannot hold;
Mere anarchy is loosed upon the world,
5   The blood-dimmed tide is loosed, and everywhere
The ceremony of innocence is drowned;
The best lack all conviction, while the worst
Are full of passionate intensity.

Surely some revelation is at hand;
10   Surely the Second Coming is at hand.
The Second Coming! Hardly are those words out
When a vast image out of *Spiritus Mundi*
Troubles my sight: somewhere in sands of the desert
A shape with lion body and the head of a man,
15   A gaze blank and pitiless as the sun,
Is moving its slow thighs, while all about it
Reel shadows of the indignant desert birds.
The darkness drops again; but now I know
That twenty centuries of stony sleep
20   Were vexed to nightmare by a rocking cradle
And what rough beast, its hour come round at last,
Slouches towards Bethlehem to be born?   1921

A PRAYER FOR MY DAUGHTER

Once more the storm is howling, and half hid
Under this cradle-hood and coverlid
My child sleeps on. There is no obstacle
But Gregory's wood and one bare hill
5   Whereby the haystack- and roof-levelling wind,
Bred on the Atlantic, can be stayed;
And for an hour I have walked and prayed
Because of the great gloom that is in my mind.

I have walked and prayed for this young child an hour
10   And heard the sea-wind scream upon the tower,
And under the arches of the bridge, and scream
In the elms above the flooded stream;
Imagining in excited reverie
That the future years had come,
15   Dancing to a frenzied drum,
Out of the murderous innocence of the sea.

May she be granted beauty and yet not
Beauty to make a stranger's eye distraught,
Or hers before a looking-glass, for such,
20   Being made beautiful overmuch,
Consider beauty a sufficient end,
Lose natural kindness and maybe
The heart-revealing intimacy
That chooses right, and never find a friend.

25   Helen being chosen found life flat and dull
And later had much trouble from a fool,
While that great Queen, that rose out of the spray,
Being fatherless could have her way
Yet chose a bandy-leggèd smith for man.
30   It's certain that fine women eat
A crazy salad with their meat
Whereby the Horn of Plenty is undone.

In courtesy I'd have her chiefly learned;
Hearts are not had as a gift but hearts are earned
35   By those that are not entirely beautiful;
Yet many, that have played the fool
For beauty's very self, has charm made wise,
And many a poor man that has roved,
Loved and thought himself beloved,
40   From a glad kindness cannot take his eyes.

1. William Butler Yeats

May she become a flourishing hidden tree
That all her thoughts may like the linnet be,
And have no business but dispensing round
Their magnanimities of sound,
45   Not but in merriment begin a chase,
Nor but in merriment a quarrel.
O may she live like some green laurel
Rooted in one dear perpetual place.

My mind, because the minds that I have loved,
50   The sort of beauty that I have approved,
Prosper but little, has dried up of late,
Yet knows that to be choked with hate
May well be of all evil chances chief.
If there's no hatred in a mind
55   Assault and battery of the wind
Can never tear the linnet from the leaf.

An intellectual hatred is the worst,
So let her think opinions are accursed.
Have I not seen the loveliest woman born
60   Out of the mouth of Plenty's horn,
Because of her opinionated mind
Barter that horn and every good
By quiet natures understood
For an old bellows full of angry wind?

65   Considering that, all hatred driven hence,
The soul recovers radical innocence
And learns at last that it is self-delighting,
Self-appeasing, self-affrighting,
And that its own sweet will is Heaven's will;
70   She can, though every face should scowl
And every windy quarter howl
Or every bellows burst, be happy still.

And may her bridegroom bring her to a house
Where all's accustomed, ceremonious;
75   For arrogance and hatred are the wares
Peddled in the thoroughfares.
How but in custom and in ceremony
Are innocence and beauty born?
Ceremony's a name for the rich horn,
80   And custom for the spreading laurel tree.   1921

SAILING TO BYZANTIUM

1

That is no country for old men. The young
In one another's arms, birds in the trees
—Those dying generations—at their song,
The salmon-falls, the mackerel-crowded seas,
5   Fish, flesh, or fowl, commend all summer long
Whatever is begotten, born, and dies.
Caught in that sensual music all neglect
Monuments of unageing intellect.

2

An aged man is but a paltry thing,
10   A tattered coat upon a stick, unless
Soul clap its hands and sing, and louder sing
For every tatter in its mortal dress,
Nor is there singing school but studying
Monuments of its own magnificence;
15   And therefore I have sailed the seas and come
To the holy city of Byzantium.

3

O sages standing in God's holy fire
As in the gold mosaic of a wall,
Come from the holy fire, perne in a gyre,
20   And be the singing-masters of my soul.
Consume my heart away; sick with desire
And fastened to a dying animal
It knows not what it is; and gather me
Into the artifice of eternity.

4

25   Once out of nature I shall never take
My bodily form from any natural thing,
But such a form as Grecian goldsmiths make
Of hammered gold and gold enamelling
To keep a drowsy Emperor awake;
30   Or set upon a golden bough to sing
To lords and ladies of Byzantium
Of what is past, or passing, or to come.   1927

LEDA AND THE SWAN

A sudden blow: the great wings beating still
Above the staggering girl, her thighs caressed
By the dark webs, her nape caught in his bill,
He holds her helpless breast upon his breast.
5   How can those terrified vague fingers push
The feathered glory from her loosening thighs?
And how can body, laid in that white rush,
But feel the strange heart beating where it lies?
A shudder in the loins engenders there
10   The broken wall, the burning roof and tower
And Agamemnon dead.
                Being so caught up,
So mastered by the brute blood of the air,
Did she put on his knowledge with his power
15   Before the indifferent beak could let her drop?   1924

2. THOMAS HARDY

Thomas Hardy (1840–1928) was an English novelist and poet, born in Dorsetshire, which would serve as the model for the Wessex of his many novels, including Far from the Madding Crowd *(1876),* The Return of the Native *(1879),* Tess of the D'Urbervilles *(1897) and* Jude the Obscure *(1897). After Jude, Hardy abandoned fiction writing, and turned exclusively to poetry, of which he became a prolific writer until the end of his life.*

Hardy's world view is bleak; both his poems and novels tend to focus on protagonists who stand powerless against a cruel—or worse, indifferent—universe governed by an almost mechanical chance. He was very aware of his position "between" two worlds, the fading world of the nineteenth century and the intimidating, impersonal world of twentieth century modernity; his great poem "The Darkling Thrush" (1900) bids farewell to the nineteenth century and looks forward, with some anxiety, to the new world being born.

HAP

If but some vengeful god would call to me
From up the sky, and laugh: 'Thou suffering thing,
Know that thy sorrow is my ecstasy,
That thy love's loss is my hate's profiting!'

5   Then would I bear it, clench myself, and die,
Steeled by the sense of ire unmerited;
Half-eased in that a Powerfuller than I
Had willed and meted me the tears I shed.

But not so. How arrives it joy lies slain,
10   And why unblooms the best hope ever sown?
—Crass Casualty obstructs the sun and rain,
And dicing Time for gladness casts a moan . . .
These purblind Doomsters had as readily strown
Blisses about my pilgrimage as pain.

NEUTRAL TONES

We stood by a pond that winter day,
And the sun was white, as though chidden of God,
And a few leaves lay on the starving sod;
—They had fallen from an ash, and were gray.

5   Your eyes on me were as eyes that rove
Over tedious riddles of years ago;
And some words played between us to and fro
On which lost the more by our love.

The smile on your mouth was the deadest thing
10   Alive enough to have strength to die;
And a grin of bitterness swept thereby
Like an ominous bird a-wing . . .

Since then, keen lessons that love deceives,
And wrings with wrong, have shaped to me
15   Your face, and the God-curst sun, and a tree,
And a pond edged with grayish leaves.

THE DARKLING THRUSH

I leant upon a coppice gate
When Frost was spectre-gray,
And Winter's dregs made desolate
The weakening eye of day.
5   The tangled bine-stems scored the sky
Like strings of broken lyres,
And all mankind that haunted nigh
Had sought their household fires.

The land's sharp features seemed to be
10   The Century's corpse outleant,
His crypt the cloudy canopy,
        The wind his death-lament.
The ancient pulse of germ and birth
        Was shrunken hard and dry,
15   And every spirit upon earth
Seemed fervourless as I.

At once a voice arose among
The bleak twigs overhead
In a full-hearted evensong

20   Of joy illimited;
      An aged thrush, frail, gaunt, and small,
      In blast-beruffled plume,
      Had chosen thus to fling his soul
      Upon the growing gloom.

25   So little cause for carolings
      Of such ecstatic sound
      Was written on terrestrial things
      Afar or nigh around,
      That I could think there trembled through
30   His happy good-night air
      Some blessed Hope, whereof he knew
      And I was unaware.

3. THE WAR POETS

British poetry of The Great War generally falls into two categories, divided by the Battle of the Somme. The early poems are straightforward expressions of an innocent patriotism untouched by the horrendous experience of the war itself, illustrating the illusion that it would be a short and glory-filled war. On the first day of the battle, July 1, 1916, the British lost 54,000 men, yet they kept up the offensive until the first week of November, by which time the total casualties (on both sides) were well over a million. Post-Somme poems are aggressively anti-poetic, as their authors struggle to articulate the realities of war to a civilian audience conditioned by the pro-war propaganda of the time, with its empty, high-sounding abstractions.

LETTER FROM HENRY JAMES TO HOWARD STURGIS
(AUGUST 5TH, 1914)

HENRY JAMES

The taper went out last night, and I am afraid I now kindle it again to a very feeble ray—for it's vain to try to talk as if one weren't living in a nightmare of the deepest dye. How can what is going on not be to one as a huge horror of blackness? Of course that is what
5 it is to you, dearest Howard, even as it is to your infinitely sickened inditer of these lines. The plunge of civilization into this abyss of blood and darkness by the wanton feat of those two infamous autocrats is a thing that so gives away the whole long age during which we have supposed the world to be, with whatever abatement, grad-
10 ually bettering, that to have to take it all now for what the treacherous years were all the while really making for and *meaning* is too tragic for any words.

THE SOLDIER
RUPERT BROOKE

If I should die, think only this of me:
    That there's some corner of a foreign field
That is for ever England. There shall be
    In that rich earth, a richer dust concealed;
A dust whom England bore, shaped, made aware,
    Gave, once, her flowers to love, her ways to roam,
A body of England's, breathing English air,
    Washed by the rivers, blest by suns of home.
And think, this heart, all evil shed away,
10   A pulse in the eternal mind, no less
        Gives somewhere back the thoughts by England given;
Her sights and sounds; dreams happy as her day;
    And laughter, learnt of friends; and gentleness,
        In hearts at peace, under an English heaven.

November–December 1914

[handwritten: -enthusiastic -glorifies the war]

IN FLANDERS FIELDS
JOHN MCCRAE

In Flanders fields the poppies blow
Between the crosses, row on row,
    That mark our place; and in the sky
    The larks, still bravely singing, fly
5 Scarce heard amid the guns below.

We are the Dead. Short days ago
We lived, felt dawn, saw sunset glow,
    Loved and were loved, and now we lie
    In Flanders fields.

10 Take up our quarrel with the foe:
To you from failing hands we throw
    The torch; be yours to hold it high.
    If ye break faith with us who die
We shall not sleep, though poppies grow
15   In Flanders fields.

1915

COUNTER-ATTACK

SIEGFRIED SASSOON

We'd gained our first objective hours before
While dawn broke like a face with blinking eyes,
Pallid, unshaved and thirsty, blind with smoke.
Things seemed all right at first. We held their line,   → tentative
5 With bombers posted, Lewis guns well placed,
And clink of shovels deepening the shallow trench.
The place was rotten with dead; green clumsy legs
High-booted, sprawled and groveled along the saps
And trunks, face downward, in the sucking mud,
10 Wallowed like trodden sand-bags loosely filled;
And naked sodden buttocks, mats of hair,
Bulged, clotted heads slept in the plastering slime.
And then the rain began,—the jolly old rain!
A yawning soldier knelt against the bank,
15 Staring across the morning blear with fog;
He wondered when the Allemands would get busy;
And then, of course, they started with five-nines
Traversing, sure as fate, and never a dud.
Mute in the clamour of shells he watched them burst
20 Spouting dark earth and wire with gusts from hell,
While posturing giants dissolved in drifts of smoke.
He crouched and flinched, dizzy with galloping fear,
Sick for escape,—loathing the strangled horror
And butchered, frantic gestures of the dead.

25 An officer came blundering down the trench:
"Stand-to and man the fire-step!" On he went . . .
Gasping and bawling, "Fire-step . . . counter-attack!"
Then the haze lifted. Bombing on the right
Down the old sap: machine-guns on the left;
30 And stumbling figures looming out in front.
"O Christ, they're coming at us!" Bullets spat,
And he remembered his riflle . . . rapid fire . . .
And started blazing wildly . . . then a bang
Crumpled and spun him sideways, knocked him out
35 To grunt and wriggle: none heeded him; he choked
And fought the flapping veils of smothering gloom,
Lost in a blurred confusion of yells and groans . . .
Down, and down, and down, he sank and drowned,
Bleeding to death. The counter-attack had failed.   1916–1917

" "
. . .
poetic language
breaking down
under weight
of situation

GLORY OF WOMEN
Siegfried Sassoon

You love us when we're heroes, home on leave,
Or wounded in a mentionable place.
You worship decorations; you believe
That chivalry redeems the war's disgrace.
5   You make us shells. You listen with delight,
By tales of dirt and danger fondly thrilled.
You crown our distant ardours while we fight,
And mourn our laureled memories when we're killed.
You can't believe that British troops "retire"
10   When hell's last horror breaks them, and they run,
Trampling the terrible corpses—blind with blood.
    O German mother dreaming by the fire,
While you are knitting socks to send your son
His face is trodden deeper in the mud.   1917

REPRESSION OF WAR EXPERIENCE
Siegfried Sassoon

Now light the candles; one; two; there's a moth;
What silly beggars they are to blunder in
And scorch their wings with glory, liquid flame—
5   No, no, not that,—it's bad to think of war,
When thoughts you've gagged all day come back to scare you;
And it's been proved that soldiers don't go mad
Unless they lose control of ugly thoughts
That drive them out to jabber among the trees.

10   Now light your pipe; look, what a steady hand.
Draw a deep breath; stop thinking; count fifteen,
And you're as right as rain . . .
        Why won't it rain?. . .
I wish there'd be a thunder-storm to-night,
15   With bucketsful of water to sluice the dark,
And make the roses hang their dripping heads.

Books; what a jolly company they are,
Standing so quiet and patient on their shelves,
Dressed in dim brown, and black, and white, and green,
20   And every kind of colour. Which will you read?
Come on; O *do* read something; they're so wise.

20   I tell you all the wisdom of the world
    Is waiting for you on those shelves; and yet
    You sit and gnaw your nails, and let your pipe out,
    And listen to the silence: on the ceiling
    There's one big, dizzy moth that bumps and flutters;
25   And in the breathless air outside the house
    The garden waits for something that delays.
    There must be crowds of ghosts among the trees,—
    Not people killed in battle—they're in France—
    But horrible shapes in shrouds—old men who died
30   Slow, natural deaths—old men with ugly souls,
    Who wore their bodies out with nasty sins.

    You're quiet and peaceful, summering safe at home;
    You'd never think there was a bloody war on!. . .
    O yes, you would . . . why, you can hear the guns.
35   Hark! Thud, thud, thud,—quite soft . . . they never cease—
    Those whispering guns—O Christ, I want to go out
    And screech at them to stop—I'm going crazy;
    I'm going stark, staring mad because of the guns.

Weirleigh, July 1917

RAIN

EDWARD THOMAS

    Rain, midnight rain, nothing but the wild rain
    On this bleak hut, and solitude, and me
    Remembering again that I shall die
    And neither hear the rain nor give it thanks
5   For washing me cleaner than I have been
    Since I was born into this solitude.
    Blessed are the dead that the rain rains upon:
    But here I pray that none whom once I loved
    Is dying to-night or lying still awake
10   Solitary, listening to the rain,
    Either in pain or thus in sympathy
    Helpless among the living and the dead,
    Like a cold water among broken reeds,
    Myriads of broken reeds all still and stiff,
15   Like me who have no love which this wild rain
    Has not dissolved except the love of death,
    If love it be for what is perfect and
    Cannot, the tempest tells me, disappoint.

DULCE ET DECORUM EST
WILFRED OWEN

Bent double, like old beggars under sacks,
Knock-kneed, coughing like hags, we cursed through sludge,
Till on the haunting flares we turned our backs
And towards our distant rest began to trudge.
Men marched asleep. Many had lost their boots
But limped on, blood-shod. All went lame; all blind,
Drunk with fatigue; deaf even to the hoots
Of gas shells dropping softly behind.

5

"Gas! Gas! Quick, boys!"—An ecstasy of fumbling,
Fitting the clumsy helmets just in time;
But someone still was yelling out and stumbling,
And flound'ring like a man in fire or lime . . .
Dim through the misty panes and thick green light,

10   As under a green sea, I saw him drowning.

In all my dreams, before my helpless sight,
He plunges at me, guttering, choking, drowning.

If in some smothering dreams you too could pace

15   Behind the wagon that we flung him in,
And watch the white eyes writhing in his face,
His hanging face, like a devil's sick of sin;
If you could hear, at every jolt, the blood
Came gargling from the froth-corrupted lungs,
Obscene as cancer, bitter as the cud

20   Of vile, incurrable sores on innocent tongues,—
My friend, you would not tell with such high zest
To children ardent for some desperate glory,
The old Lie: *Dulce et decorum est*
Pro patria mori.

25

(After serving for four years, Wilfred Owen was killed
November 4, 1918, one week before the Armistice.)   1918

those not in the war have no idea

STRANGE MEETING
WILFRED OWEN

It seemed that out of battle I escaped
Down some profound dull tunnel, long since scooped
Through granites which titanic wars had groined.

Yet also there encumbered sleepers groaned,
5   Too fast in thought or death to be bestirred.
Then, as I probed them, one sprang up, and stared
With piteous recognition in fixed eyes,
Lifting distressed hands, as if to bless.
And by his smile, I knew that sullen hall,—
10   By his dead smile I knew we stood in Hell.

With a thousand pains that vision's face was grained;
Yet no blood reached there from the upper ground,
And no guns thumped, or down the flues made moan.
'Strange friend,' I said, 'here is no cause to mourn.'
15   'None,' said that other, 'save the undone years,
The hopelessness. Whatever hope is yours,
Was my life also; I went hunting wild
After the wildest beauty in the world,
Which lies not calm in eyes, or braided hair,
20   But mocks the steady running of the hour,
And if it grieves, grieves richlier than here.
For by my glee might many men have laughed,
And of my weeping something had been left
Which must die now. I mean the truth untold,
25   The pity of war, the pity war distilled.
Now men will go content with what we spoiled,
Or, discontent, boil bloody, and be spilled.
They will be swift with swiftness of the tigress.
None will break ranks, though nations trek from progress.
30   Courage was mine, and I had mystery,
Wisdom was mine, and I had mastery:
To miss the march of this retreating world
Into vain citadels that are not walled.
Then, when much blood had clogged their chariot-wheels,
35   I would go up and wash them from sweet wells,
Even with truths that lie too deep for taint.

LOUSE HUNTING
Isaac Rosenberg

Nudes—stark and glistening,
Yelling in lurid glee. Grinning faces
And raging limbs
Whirl over the floor one fire.
5   For a shirt verminously busy
Yon soldier tore from his throat, with oaths
Godhead might shrink at, but not the lice.
And soon the shirt was aflare
Over the candle he'd lit while we lay.

10   Then we all sprang up and stript
To hunt the verminous brood.
Soon like a demons' pantomime
The place was raging.
See the silhouettes agape,
15   See the gibbering shadows
Mixed with the battled arms on the wall.
See gargantuan hooked fingers
Pluck in supreme flesh
To smutch supreme littleness.
20   See the merry limbs in hot Highland fling
Because some wizard vermin
Charmed from the quiet this revel
When our ears were half lulled
By the dark music
25   Blown from Sleep's trumpet.

BREAK OF DAY IN THE TRENCHES
Isaac Rosenberg

The darkness crumbles away—
It is the same old druid Time as ever.
Only a live thing leaps my hand—
A queer sardonic rat—
5   As I pull the parapet's poppy
To stick behind my ear.
Droll rat, they would shoot you if they knew
Your cosmopolitan sympathies.
Now you have touched this English hand
10   You will do the same to a German—

3. The War Poets

Soon, no doubt, if it be your pleasure
To cross the sleeping green between.
It seems you inwardly grin as you pass
Strong eyes, fine limbs, haughty athletes
15 Less chanced than you for life,
Bonds to the whims of murder,
Sprawled in the bowels of the earth,
The torn fields of France.
What do you see in our eyes
20 At the shrieking iron and flame
Hurled through still heavens?
What quaver—what heart aghast?
Poppies whose roots are in man's veins
Drop, and are ever dropping;
25 But mine in my ear is safe,
Just a little white with the dust.

4. WALLACE STEVENS

Wallace Stevens (1879–1955) was an executive of the Hartford Insurance Company and one of the great poets of the century. His early work explores the condition of modern man in a world where "God is dead" ("Sunday Morning" is the great poem of modern unbelief) and where reality is a puzzle. Is reality merely The Rock—dead, lifeless matter, meaningless until transformed by the human imagination? Which then is real, The Rock or the idea made of it by the Imagination? Stevens' elegant, meditative verse endlessly explores this situation in its many formulations and possibilities. In the final months of his life, Stevens resolved the issue: reality was not an idea but was something objectively "there," independent of the imagining mind. Now The Rock took on a new signification, and Stevens completed his intellectual pilgrimage in a deathbed conversion to the Catholic Church.

THE SNOW MAN

One must have a mind of winter
To regard the frost and the boughs
Of the pine-trees crusted with snow;

And have been cold a long time
5   To behold the junipers shagged with ice,
The spruces rough in the distant glitter

Of the January sun; and not to think
Of any misery in the sound of the wind,
10   In the sound of a few leaves,

Which is the sound of the land
Full of the same wind
That is blowing in the same bare place

15   For the listener, who listens in the snow,
And, nothing himself, beholds
Nothing that is not there and the nothing that is.

THE EMPEROR OF ICE-CREAM

Call the roller of big cigars,
The muscular one, and bid him whip
In kitchen cups concupiscent curds.
Let the wenches dawdle in such dress
5   As they are used to wear, and let the boys
Bring flowers in last month's newspapers.
Let be be finale of seem.
The only emperor is the emperor of ice-cream.

10   Take from the dresser of deal,
Lacking the three glass knobs, that sheet
On which she embroidered fantails once
And spread it so as to cover her face.
If her horny feet protrude, they come
15   To show how cold she is, and dumb.
Let the lamp affix its beam.
The only emperor is the emperor of ice-cream.   1923

DISILLUSIONMENT OF TEN O'CLOCK

The houses are haunted
By white night-gowns
None are green,
Or purple with green rings,
5   Or green with yellow rings,
Or yellow with blue rings.
None of them are strange,
With socks of lace
And beaded ceintures.
10   People are not going
To dream of baboons and periwinkles.
Only, here and there, an old sailor,
Drunk and asleep in his boots,
Catches tigers
15   In red weather.   1923

SUNDAY MORNING

I

Complacencies of the peignoir, and late
Coffee and oranges in a sunny chair,
And the green freedom of a cockatoo
Upon a rug mingle to dissipate
5   The holy hush of ancient sacrifice.
She dreams a little, and she feels the dark
Encroachment of that old catastrophe,
As a calm darkens among water-lights.
The pungent oranges and bright, green wings
10   Seem things in some procession of the dead,
Winding across wide water, without sound.
The day is like wide water, without sound,
Stilled for the passing of her dreaming feet
Over the seas, to silent Palestine,
15   Dominion of the blood and sepulchre.

II

Why should she give her bounty to the dead?
What is divinity if it can come
Only in silent shadows and in dreams?
Shall she not find in comforts of the sun,
20   In pungent fruit and bright, green wings, or else
In any balm or beauty of the earth,
Things to be cherished like the thought of heaven?
Divinity must live within herself:
Passions of rain, or moods in falling snow;
25   Grievings in loneliness, or unsubdued
Elations when the forest blooms; gusty
Emotions on wet roads on autumn nights;
All pleasures and all pains, remembering
The bough of summer and the winter branch.
30   These are the measures destined for her soul.

III

Jove in the clouds had his inhuman birth.
No mother suckled him, no sweet land gave
Large-mannered motions to his mythy mind.
He moved among us, as a muttering king,
35   Magnificent, would move among his hinds,
Until our blood, commingling, virginal,

With heaven, brought such requital to desire
The very hinds discerned it, in a star.
Shall our blood fail? Or shall it come to be
40 The blood of paradise? And shall the earth
Seem all of paradise that we shall know?
The sky will be much friendlier then than now,
A part of labor and a part of pain,
And next in glory to enduring love,
45 Not this dividing and indifferent blue.

IV

She says, "I am content when wakened birds,
Before they fly, test the reality
Of misty fields, by their sweet questionings;
But when the birds are gone, and their warm fields
50 Return no more, where, then, is paradise?"
There is not any haunt of prophecy,
Nor any old chimera of the grave,
Neither the golden underground, nor isle
Melodious, where spirits gat them home,
55 Nor visionary south, nor cloudy palm
Remote on heaven's hill, that has endured
As April's green endures; or will endure
Like her remembrance of awakened birds,
Or her desire for June and evening, tipped
60 By the consummation of the swallow's wings.

V

She says, "But in contentment I still feel
The need of some imperishable bliss."
Death is the mother of beauty; hence from her,
Alone, shall come fulfilment to our dreams
65 And our desires. Although she strews the leaves
Of sure obliteration on our paths,
The path sick sorrow took, the many paths
Where triumph rang its brassy phrase, or love
Whispered a little out of tenderness,
70 She makes the willow shiver in the sun
For maidens who were wont to sit and gaze
Upon the grass, relinquished to their feet.
She causes boys to pile new plums and pears
On disregarded plate. The maidens taste
75 And stray impassioned in the littering leaves.

VI

Is there no change of death in paradise?
Does ripe fruit never fall? Or do the boughs
Hang always heavy in that perfect sky,
Unchanging, yet so like our perishing earth,
80   With rivers like our own that seek for seas
They never find, the same receding shores
That never touch with inarticulate pang?
Why set the pear upon those river-banks
Or spice the shores with odors of the plum?
85   Alas, that they should wear our colors there,
The silken weavings of our afternoons,
And pick the strings of our insipid lutes!
Death is the mother of beauty, mystical,
Within whose burning bosom we devise
90   Our earthly mothers waiting, sleeplessly.

VII

Supple and turbulent, a ring of men
Shall chant in orgy on a summer morn
Their boisterous devotion to the sun,
Not as a god, but as a god might be,
95   Naked among them, like a savage source.
Their chant shall be a chant of paradise,
Out of their blood, returning to the sky;
And in their chant shall enter, voice by voice,
The windy lake wherein their lord delights,
100   The trees, like serafin, and echoing hills,
That choir among themselves long afterward.
They shall know well the heavenly fellowship
Of men that perish and of summer morn.
And whence they came and whither they shall go
105   The dew upon their feet shall manifest.

VIII

She hears, upon that water without sound,
A voice that cries, "The tomb in Palestine
Is not the porch of spirits lingering.
It is the grave of Jesus, where he lay."
110   We live in an old chaos of the sun,
Or old dependency of day and night,
Or island solitude, unsponsored, free,
Of that wide water, inescapable.

Deer walk upon our mountains, and the quail
115   Whistle about us their spontaneous cries;
Sweet berries ripen in the wilderness;
And, in the isolation of the sky,
At evening, casual flocks of pigeons make
Ambiguous undulations as they sink,
120   Downward to darkness, on extended wings.   1923

THE MAN WHOSE
PHARYNX WAS BAD

The time of year has grown indifferent.
Mildew of summer and the deepening snow
Are both alike in the routine I know.
I am too dumbly in my being pent.

5   The wind attendant on the solstices
Blows on the shutters of the metropoles,
Stirring no poet in his sleep, and tolls
The grand ideas of the villages.

The malady of the quotidian. . . .
10   Perhaps, if winter once could penetrate
Through all its purples to the final slate,
Persisting bleakly in an icy haze,

One might in turn become less diffident,
Out of such mildew plucking neater mould
15   And spouting new orations of the cold.
One might. One might. But time will not relent.   1923

THE IDEA OF ORDER AT KEY WEST

She sang beyond the genius of the sea.
The water never formed to mind or voice,
Like a body wholly body, fluttering
Its empty sleeves; and yet its mimic motion
5   Made constant cry, caused constantly a cry,
That was not ours although we understood,
Inhuman, of the veritable ocean.

The sea was not a mask. No more was she.
The song and water were not medleyed sound
10   Even if what she sang was what she heard,
Since what she sang was uttered word by word.

It may be that in all her phrases stirred
The grinding water and the gasping wind;
But it was she and not the sea we heard.

15   For she was the maker of the song she sang.
The ever-hooded, tragic-gestured sea
Was merely a place by which she walked to sing.
Whose spirit is this? we said, because we knew
It was the spirit that we sought and knew
20   That we should ask this often as she sang.

If it was only the dark voice of the sea
That rose, or even colored by many waves;
If it was only the outer voice of sky
And cloud, of the sunken coral water-walled,
25   However clear, it would have been deep air,
The heaving speech of air, a summer sound
Repeated in a summer without end
And sound alone. But it was more than that,
More even than her voice, and ours, among
30   The meaningless plungings of water and the wind,
Theatrical distances, bronze shadows heaped
On high horizons, mountainous atmospheres
Of sky and sea.

            It was her voice that made
35   The sky acutest at its vanishing.
She measured to the hour its solitude.
She was the single artificer of the world
In which she sang. And when she sang, the sea,
Whatever self it had, became the self
40   That was her song, for she was the maker. Then we,
As we beheld her striding there alone,
Knew that there never was a world for her
Except the one she sang and, singing, made.

Ramon Fernandez, tell me, if you know,
45   Why, when the singing ended and we turned
Toward the town, tell why the glassy lights,
The lights in the fishing boats at anchor there,
As the night, descended, tilting in the air,
Mastered the night and portioned out the sea,
50   Fixing emblazoned zones and fiery poles,
Arranging, deepening, enchanting night.

Oh! Blessed rage for order, pale Ramon,
The maker's rage to order words of the sea,
Words of the fragrant portals, dimly-starred,
55   And of ourselves and of our origins,
In ghostlier demarcations, keener sounds.   1936

NOT IDEAS ABOUT THE THING
BUT THE THING ITSELF

At the earliest ending of winter,
In March, a scrawny cry from outside
Seemed like a sound in his mind.

He knew that he heard it,
5   A bird's cry, at daylight or before,
In the early March wind.

The sun was rising at six,
No longer a battered panache above the snow. . .
It would have been outside.

10   It was not from the vast ventriloquism
Of sleep's faded papier-mâché . . .
The sun was coming from outside.

That scrawny cry—it was
A chorister whose c preceded the choir.
15   It was part of the colossal sun,

Surrounded by its choral rings,
Still far away. It was like
A new knowledge of reality.   1954

5. EZRA POUND

Ezra Pound (1885–1972) was born in Idaho, but moved to Europe in his early twenties and spent the majority of his life as an expatriate in Paris, London, and Italy. In addition to his own poetic achievements, Pound was the great promoter of international modernism; more than any other figure, Pound defined the terms and created the mythology of the period, by writing critical manifestos and especially by editing, advising, and arranging publication for an astonishing range of writers including W. B. Yeats, James Joyce, T. S. Eliot, Robert Frost, Ernest Hemingway, Gertrude Stein, and Marianne Moore. In his early career, Pound was involved in a literary movement called Imagism, which drew on the influence of haiku in calling for poetry made of simple, spare, and concrete language, arranged around a powerful central image. Pound defined the 'image' as the presentation of "an intellectual and emotional complex in an instant of time." The short poem "In a Station of the Metro" exemplifies this crucial modernist style.

As Pound's career progressed, he became an increasingly controversial figure, embracing Italian fascism in the 1930s, recording vitriolic anti-American rants for radio broadcast during World War II, and espousing an ugly anti-Semitism; his reputation has been rightfully tarnished as a result. In 1945, he was arrested in Italy by American forces and tried for treason; he was judged insane and was committed to St. Elizabeth's Hospital in Washington, D.C., where he remained from 1946 to 1958.

For the last sixty years of his life, from the late 1910s to his death in 1972, Pound worked on a sprawling modern epic poem entitled the Cantos, a notoriously fragmented and disunified work; nevertheless, it contains some of Pound's most moving poetry, particularly the Pisan Cantos (see Canto LXXXI), which were written during Pound's imprisonment in Italy after his arrest in 1945. In its sheer ambition, in its moments of stunning lyric beauty, as well as in its fragmentary disorderliness, the Cantos (and Pound himself) exemplify modernism's many contradictions.

IN A STATION OF THE METRO

The apparition of these faces in the crowd;
Petals on a wet, black bough.

THE RIVER-MERCHANT'S WIFE:
A LETTER

While my hair was still cut straight across my forehead
I played about the front gate, pulling flowers.
You came by on bamboo stilts, playing horse.
You walked about my seat, playing with blue plums.
5   And we went on living in the village of Chokan:
Two small people, without dislike or suspicion.

At fourteen I married My Lord you.
I never laughed, being bashful.
Lowering my head, I looked at the wall.
10   Called to, a thousand times, I never looked back.

At fifteen I stopped scowling,
I desired my dust to be mingled with yours
Forever and forever, and forever.
Why should I climb the look out?

15   At sixteen you departed
You went into far Ku-to-en, by the river of swirling eddies,
And you have been gone five months.
The monkeys make sorrowful noise overhead.
You dragged your feet when you went out.
20   By the gate now, the moss is grown, the different mosses,
Too deep to clear them away!
The leaves fall early this autumn, in wind.
The paired butterflies are already yellow with August
Over the grass in the West garden;
25   'They hurt me.
I grow older.
If you are coming down through the narrows of the river Kiang,
Please let me know beforehand,
And I will come out to meet you
30   As far as Cho-fu-Sa.[1]   1915

---

[1]A beach several hundred miles upriver from the speaker's home in Chokan.

FROM THE CANTOS

I[2]

And then went down to the ship,
Set keel to breakers, forth on the godly sea, and
We set up mast and sail on that swart ship,
Bore sheep aboard her, and our bodies also
5   Heavy with weeping, and winds from sternward
Bore us out onward with bellying canvas,
Circe's this craft, the trim-coifed goddess.
Then sat we amidships, wind jamming the tiller,
Thus with stretched sail, we went over sea till day's end.
10   Sun to his slumber, shadows o'er all the ocean,·
Came we then to the bounds of deepest water,
To the Kimmerian lands, and peopled cities
Covered with close-webbed mist, unpierced ever
With glitter of sun-rays
15   Nor with stars stretched, nor looking back from heaven
Swartest night stretched over wretched men there.
The ocean flowing backward, came we then to the place
Aforesaid by Circe.
Here did they rites, Perimedes and Eurylochus,
20   And drawing sword from my hip
I dug the ell-square pitkin;[3]
Poured we libations unto each the dead,
First mead and then sweet wine, water mixed with white flour.
Then prayed I many a prayer to the sickly death's-heads;
25   As set in Ithaca, sterile bulls of the best
For sacrifice, heaping the pyre with goods,
A sheep to Tiresias only, black and a bell-sheep.
Dark blood flowed in the fosse,[4]
Souls out of Erebus, cadaverous dead, of brides
30   Of youths and of the old who had borne much;
Souls stained with recent tears, girls tender,
Men many, mauled with bronze lance heads,
Battle spoil, bearing yet dreory[5] arms,
These many crowded about me; with shouting,

---

[2]This Canto is a retelling of the opening of Book II of Homer's *Odyssey*. Pound uses the common modernist technique of referencing mythical sources in order to establish cultural parallels with earlier periods.

[3]A small pit.

[4]'ditch' (Latin)

35   Pallor upon me, cried to my men for more beasts;
        Slaughtered the herds, sheep slain of bronze;
        Poured ointment, cried to the gods,
        To Pluto the strong, and praised Proserpine;
        Unsheathed the narrow sword,
40   I sat to keep off the impetuous impotent dead,
        Till I should hear Tiresias.
        But first Elpenor came, our friend Elpenor,
        Unburied, cast on the wide earth,
        Limbs that we left in the house of Circe,
45   Unwept, unwrapped in sepulchre, since toils urged other.
        Pitiful spirit. And I cried in hurried speech:
        "Elpenor, how art thou come to this dark coast?"
        "Cam'st thou afoot, outstripping seamen?"
                        And he in heavy speech:
50   "Ill fate and abundant wine. I slept in Circe's ingle.
        "Going down the long ladder unguarded,
        "I fell against the buttress,
        "Shattered the nape-nerve, the soul sought Avernus.
        "But thou, O King, I bid remember me, unwept, unburied,
55   "Heap up mine arms, be tomb by sea-bord, and inscribed:
        "*A man of no fortune, and with a name to come.*
        "And set my oar up, that I swung mid fellows."

        And Anticlea came, whom I beat off, and then Tiresias Theban,
        Holding his golden wand, knew me, and spoke first:
60   "A second time? why? man of ill star,
        "Facing the sonless dead and this joyless region?
        "Stand from the fosse, leave me my bloody bever
        "For soothsay."
                        And I stepped back,
65   And he strong with the blood, said then: "Odysseus
        "Shalt return through spiteful Neptune, over dark seas,
        "Lose all companions." And then Anticlea came.
        Lie quiet Divus. I mean, that is Andreas Divus,
        In officina Wecheli, 1538, out of Homer.[6]
70   And he sailed, by Sirens and thence outward and away
        And unto Circe.

---

[6]Here, Pound acknowledges that his source for this retelling of the *Odyssey* is not Homer, but a medieval Latin translation of the poem, published by the office of Wechel, in Paris, in 1538. Notice that what we're reading, therefore, is a retelling of a retelling—a distant echo of a deeply remembered story.

Venerandam[7]

In the Cretan's phrase, with the golden crown, Aphrodite,
Cypri munimenta sortita est,[8] mirthful, orichalchi,[9] with golden
Girdles and breast bands, thou with dark eyelids
Bearing the golden bough of Argicida. So that:

75

1917, 1925

---

[7]'commanding reverence' (Latin)

[8]'The citadels of Cyprus were her appointed realm.' (Latin)

[9]Made of copper (Latin)

6. T. S. ELIOT

Although he was born in St. Louis, T. S. Eliot (1888–1965) eventually dominated modern British letters as the great poet-critic of his time. He had an extraordinarily rich education in languages, English and French literature, and philosophy (where he all but earned a Ph.D. from Harvard, never receiving the degree because World War I prevented him from returning to defend his thesis). Very early in his intellectual life Eliot came to recognize the great unspoken truth about the modern world: it was a world without love, a world without a soul. His studies brought him to connect this absence with the absence of God: modernity lacked any sense of transcendence and thus any sense of ultimate purpose. His early verse explores various dimensions of these themes in all their inner painfulness. Was there a way to redeem the time? (Shakespeare's phrase from 2 Henry IV haunted Eliot's thought-life.) The final section of "The Waste Land" explores the possibility of personal renewal on the basis of ascesis or self-discipline: "Shall I at least set my lands in order?" In 1927 Eliot was baptized and confirmed in the Church of England and connected his quest with the wider Christian body. His later poetry is formally Christian and explores the conditions of belief in the modern world.

THE LOVE SONG OF J. ALFRED PRUFROCK (1917)

S'io credessi che mia risposta fosse	If I believed that my reply were made
a persona che mai tornasse al mondo,	To one who could ever climb to the world again,
questa fiamma staria senza più scosse.	This flame would shake no more. But since no shade
Ma per ciò che giammai di questo fondo	Ever returned—if what I am told is true—
non tornò vivo alcun, s'i'odo il vero,	From this blind world into the living light,
senza tema d'infamia ti rispondo.	without fear of dishonor I answer you.

Dante, Inferno, XXVII, 61–66.

- figure in inferno willing to speak b/c no one will ever have to hear what he says

Let us go then, you and I,
When the evening is spread out against the sky
Like a patient etherised upon a table;
Let us go, through certain half-deserted streets,
The muttering retreats
Of restless nights in one-night cheap hotels
And sawdust restaurants with oyster-shells:
Streets that follow like a tedious argument
Of insidious intent
10 To lead you to an overwhelming question . . .
Oh, do not ask, "What is it?"
Let us go and make our visit.

          In the room the women come and go
Talking of Michelangelo.

15   The yellow fog that rubs its back upon the window-panes,
The yellow smoke that rubs its muzzle on the window-panes,
Licked its tongue into the corners of the evening,
Lingered upon the pools that stand in drains,
Let fall upon its back the soot that falls from chimneys,
20 Slipped by the terrace, made a sudden leap,
And seeing that it was a soft October night,
Curled once about the house, and fell asleep.

          And indeed there will be time
For the yellow smoke that slides along the street
25 Rubbing its back upon the window-panes;
There will be time, there will be time
To prepare a face to meet the faces that you meet;
There will be time to murder and create,
And time for all the works and days of hands
30 That lift and drop a question on your plate;
Time for you and time for me,
And time yet for a hundred indecisions,
And for a hundred visions and revisions,
Before the taking of a toast and tea.

35   In the room the women come and go
Talking of Michelangelo.

          And indeed there will be time
To wonder, "Do I dare?" and, "Do I dare?"
Time to turn back and descend the stair,
40 With a bald spot in the middle of my hair—
(They will say: "How his hair is growing thin!")

6. T. S. Eliot

My morning coat, my collar mounting firmly to the chin,
My necktie rich and modest, but asserted by a simple pin— → *self-conscious*
(They will say: "But how his arms and legs are thin!")
45   Do I dare
Disturb the universe?
In a minute there is time
For decisions and revisions which a minute will reverse.

For I have known them all already, known them all—
50   Have known the evenings, mornings, afternoons,
I have measured out my life with coffee spoons;
I know the voices dying with a dying fall
Beneath the music from a farther room.
        So how should I presume?

55   And I have known the eyes already, known them all— *— Sense of*
The eyes that fix you in a formulated phrase,   *being under*
And when I am formulated, sprawling on a pin,   *such intense*
When I am pinned and wriggling on the wall,   *scrutiny*
Then how should I begin
60   To spit out all the butt-ends of my days and ways?
        And how should I presume?

And I have known the arms already, known them all— *details about*
Arms that are braceleted and white and bare   *the woman*
(But in the lamplight, downed with light brown hair!)
65   Is it perfume from a dress
That makes me so digress?
Arms that lie along a table, or wrap about a shawl.
And should I then presume?
And how should I begin?
70   * * * * *

Shall I say, I have gone at dusk through narrow streets
And watched the smoke that rises from the pipes
Of lonely men in shirt-sleeves, leaning out of windows? . . .
        I should have been a pair of ragged claws
75   Scuttling across the floors of silent seas.
                        * * * * *

And the afternoon, the evening, sleeps so peacefully!
Smoothed by long fingers,
Asleep . . . tired . . . or it malingers,
80   Stretched on the floor, here beside you and me.
Should I, after tea and cakes and ices,
Have the strength to force the moment to its crisis?

-35-

But though I have wept and fasted, wept and prayed,
Though I have seen my head (grown slightly bald) brought in
upon a platter,   ~ St. John the Baptist
I am no prophet—and here's no great matter;
I have seen the moment of my greatness flicker,
And I have seen the eternal Footman hold my coat, and snicker,
And in short, I was afraid.

[margin: moment has passed here 85]

90   And would it have been worth it, after all,
After the cups, the marmalade, the tea,
Among the porcelain, among some talk of you and me,
Would it have been worth while,
To have bitten off the matter with a smile,
95   To have squeezed the universe into a ball
To roll it towards some overwhelming question,
To say: "I am Lazarus, come from the dead,
Come back to tell you all, I shall tell you all"—
If one, settling a pillow by her head,
105   Should say: "That is not what I meant at all.
That is not it, at all."

[margin: the worst that could have happened 105]

And would it have been worth it, after all,
Would it have been worth while,
After the sunsets and the dooryards and the sprinkled streets,
110   After the novels, after the teacups, after the skirts that trail
along the floor—
And this, and so much more?—
It is impossible to say just what I mean!
But as if a magic lantern threw the nerves in patterns on a screen:
115   Would it have been worth while
If one, settling a pillow or throwing off a shawl,
And turning toward the window, should say:
"That is not it at all,
That is not what I meant at all."
120   * * * * *

[margin: Frustrated, emphatic, incommunicability of private experience 115]

No! I am not Prince Hamlet, nor was meant to be;
Am an attendant lord, one that will do
To swell a progress, start a scene or two,
Advise the prince; no doubt, an easy tool,
125   Deferential, glad to be of use,
Politic, cautious, and meticulous;
Full of high sentence, but a bit obtuse;
At times, indeed, almost ridiculous—
Almost, at times, the Fool.

[margin: —Not the star, not a major figure 125]
[margin: —held be an extra, but never the star]

130   I grow old . . . I grow old . . .
       I shall wear the bottoms of my trousers rolled.

[handwritten: sense of growing old, + how he'll pass the time remaining]

       Shall I part my hair behind? Do I dare to eat a peach?
       I shall wear white flannel trousers, and walk upon the beach.
       I have heard the mermaids singing, each to each.

135   I do not think that they will sing to me.
       I have seen them riding seaward on the waves
       Combing the white hair of the waves blown back
       When the wind blows the water white and black.

       We have lingered in the chambers of the sea
140   By sea-girls wreathed with seaweed red and brown
       Till human voices wake us, and we drown.

THE WASTE LAND (1922)

"Nam Sibyllam quidem Cumis ego ipse oculis meis vidi
in ampulla pendere, et cum illi pueri dicerent: ΣΊβυλλα
τΊ θΈλεις; respondebat illa: αποθαυειυ θΈλω."[1]

For Ezra Pound
il miglior fabbro.

[handwritten: Theme of hopelessness]

I. THE BURIAL OF THE DEAD

       April is the cruellest month, breeding[2]
       Lilacs out of the dead land, mixing
       Memory and desire, stirring
       Dull roots with spring rain.
5   Winter kept us warm, covering

[handwritten: April = spring, usually life, happiness, etc. IRONIC]

---

[1]"Once with my own eyes I saw the Sybil at Cumae hanging in a cage; and when the boys said to her, 'Sybil, what do you want?' she replied, 'I want to die.'" From Petronius, *Satyricon.*

Eliot himself provided notes for the poem when it was published as a separate book (the first publication had no notes). He began by saying, "Not only the title, but the plan and a good deal of the incidental symbolism of the poem were suggested by Miss Jessie L. Weston's book on the Grail legend: *From Ritual to Romance.*" Some of these notes are included here, but not all of them by any means. Ezra Pound called "The Waste Land" "the longest poem in the English language" because of the multilayered density of allusion packed into its 434 lines.

[2]The first eighteen lines both evoke and contrast the first eighteen lines of The General Prologue to Chaucer's *Canterbury Tales,* suggesting how far modern life is from medieval life with its fundamental sense of religious purpose (enacted in Pilgrimage).

[handwritten: ? life is flipped around — not from what it should be]

Earth in forgetful snow, feeding
A little life with dried tubers.
Summer surprised us, coming over the Starnbergersee
With a shower of rain; we stopped in the colonnade,
10 And went on in sunlight, into the Hofgarten,
And drank coffee, and talked for an hour.
Bin gar keine Russin, stamm' aus Litauen, echt deutsch.[3]
And when we were children, staying at the archduke's,
My cousin's, he took me out on a sled,
15 And I was frightened. He said, Marie,
Marie, hold on tight. And down we went.
In the mountains, there you feel free.
I read, much of the night, and go south in the winter.
  What are the roots that clutch, what branches grow
20 Out of this stony rubbish? Son of man,
You cannot say, or guess, for you know only
A heap of broken images, where the sun beats,
And the dead tree gives no shelter, the cricket no relief,
And the dry stone no sound of water. Only
25 There is shadow under this red rock,
(Come in under the shadow of this red rock),
And I will show you something different from either
Your shadow at morning striding behind you
Or your shadow at evening rising to meet you;
30 I will show you fear in a handful of dust.
    Frisch weht der Wind
    Der Heimat zu,
    Mein Irisch Kind,
    Wo weilest du?[4]
35 "You gave me hyacinths first a year ago;
"They called me the hyacinth girl."
—Yet when we came back, late, from the Hyacinth garden,
Your arms full, and your hair wet, I could not
Speak, and my eyes failed, I was neither
40 Living nor dead, and I knew nothing,
Looking into the heart of light, the silence.
Oed' und leer das Meer.[5]

---

[3]"I am no Russian; I come from Lithuania, a true German." The line should be imagined as overheard by the speaker (here a woman) as she drinks coffee in the Hofgarten in Munich before The Great War.

[4]"Fresh blows the wind to my homeland; my Irish child, where are you now?" These richly romantic lines are from Wagner, *Tristan and Isolde*, I: 5–8, evoking a love left behind by a man sailing away from Ireland.

[5]"The sea is blank and empty." Also from *Tristan and Isolde* but Act III: 24; these words are the antithesis to the earlier Wagnerian lines, for here all romantic hope has been lost and the feeling is of utter emptiness.

6. T. S. Eliot

Superstition

Madame Sosostris, famous clairvoyante,[6]
Had a bad cold, nevertheless

45   Is known to be the wisest woman in Europe,
With a wicked pack of cards. Here, said she,
Is your card, the drowned Phoenician Sailor,
(Those are pearls that were his eyes. Look!)
Here is Belladonna, the Lady of the Rocks,

50   The lady of situations.
Here is the man with three staves, and here the Wheel,
And here is the one-eyed merchant and this card,
Which is blank, is something he carries on his back,
Which I am forbidden to see. I do not find

55   The Hanged Man. Fear death by water.
I see crowds of people, walking round in a ring.
Thank you. If you see dear Mrs. Equitone,
Tell her I bring the horoscope myself:
One must be so careful these days.

60   Unreal City,
Under the brown fog of a winter dawn,
A crowd flowed over London Bridge, so many,[7]
I had not thought death had undone so many.
Sighs, short and infrequent, were exhaled,

65   And each man fixed his eyes before his feet.
Flowed up the hill and down King William Street,
To where Saint Mary Woolnoth kept the hours
With a dead sound on the final stroke of nine.
There I saw one I knew, and stopped him, crying: "Stetson!

70   "You who were with me in the ships at Mylae!
"That corpse you planted last year in your garden,
"Has it begun to sprout? Will it bloom this year?
"Or has the sudden frost disturbed its bed?
"Oh keep the Dog far hence, that's friend to men,

75   "Or with his nails he'll dig it up again!
"You! hypocrite lecteur!—mon semblable,—mon frère!"[8]

[handwritten: True wasteland = modern city]

[handwritten: Not happy people ghosts]

[handwritten: guarding the center of hell]

---

[6]In these lines Eliot is using the Tarot deck of cards employed by fortunetellers. The cards evoke other parts of the poem, and they suggest a key theme: with the loss of religious belief comes a grabbing after superstition as human beings attempt to understand their world.

[7]This line and the next draw on Dante: *Inferno*, III: 55–57 and IV: 25–27. The modern world is a kind of Hell.

[8]"You! hypocrite reader!—my twin,—my brother!" From Baudelaire, "Fleurs du Mal," the final line of the introductory poem.

II. A GAME OF CHESS[9]

The Chair she sat in, like a burnished throne,
Glowed on the marble, where the glass
Held up by standards wrought with fruited vines
80   From which a golden Cupidon peeped out
(Another hid his eyes behind his wing)
Doubled the flames of sevenbranched candelabra
Reflecting light upon the table as
The glitter of her jewels rose to meet it,
85   From satin cases poured in rich profusion;
In vials of ivory and coloured glass
Unstoppered, lurked her strange synthetic perfumes,
Unguent, powdered, or liquid—troubled, confused
And drowned the sense in odours; stirred by the air
90   That freshened from the window, these ascended
In fattening the prolonged candle-flames,
Flung their smoke into the laquearia,
Stirring the pattern on the coffered ceiling.
Huge sea-wood fed with copper
95   Burned green and orange, framed by the coloured stone,
In which sad light a carvèd dolphin swam.
Above the antique mantel was displayed
As though a window gave upon the sylvan scene
The change of Philomel, by the barbarous king[10]
100   So rudely forced; yet there the nightingale
Filled all the desert with inviolable voice
And still she cried, and still the world pursues,
"Jug Jug" to dirty ears.
And other withered stumps of time
105   Were told upon the walls; staring forms
Leaned out, leaning, hushing the room enclosed.
Footsteps shuffled on the stair.
Under the firelight, under the brush, her hair
Spread out in fiery points
110   Glowed into words, then would be savagely still.

---

[9]A Game of Chess is a metaphor for seduction in Thomas Middleton's play, *Women Beware Women*. In this section we are shown the reduction of love into lust in two different strata of society, the upper middle class and the working class.

[10]Philomel was raped by Tereus (her brother-in-law) then had her tongue cut out so she could not tell. She told anyway, by weaving the crime into a tapestry, and then was changed into the nightingale. Ovid, *Metamorphoses*, VI.

6. T. S. Eliot

"My nerves are bad to-night. Yes, bad. Stay with me.
"Speak to me. Why do you never speak. Speak.
"What are you thinking of? What thinking? What?
"I never know what you are thinking. Think."

115   I think we are in rats' alley
Where the dead men lost their bones.

"What is that noise?"
              The wind under the door.
"What is that noise now? What is the wind doing?"
120   Nothing again nothing.
                        "Do
"you know nothing? Do you see nothing? Do you remember
"Nothing?"

I remember
125   Those are pearls that were his eyes. *Tarrot Cards*
"Are you alive, or not? Is there nothing in your head?"
                        But

O O O O that Shakespeherian Rag—
It's so elegant
130   So intelligent
"What shall I do now? What shall I do?"
"I shall rush out as I am, and walk the street
"With my hair down, so. What shall we do to-morrow?
"What shall we ever do?"
135   The hot water at ten.
And if it rains, a closed car at four.
And we shall play a game of chess,
Pressing lidless eyes and waiting for a knock upon the door.

When Lil's husband got demobbed, I said—
140   I didn't mince my words, I said to her myself,
HURRY UP PLEASE ITS TIME[11]
Now Albert's coming back, make yourself a bit smart.
He'll want to know what you done with that money he gave you
To get yourself some teeth. He did, I was there.
145   You have them all out, Lil, and get a nice set,
He said, I swear, I can't bear to look at you.
And no more can't I, I said, and think of poor Albert,
He's been in the army four years, he wants a good time,

---

[11]These words can still be heard in English pubs telling customers to drink up because it is closing time.

Two Sides of Modern Sexuality (handwritten)

And if you don't give it him, there's others will, I said.
150 Oh is there, she said. Something o'that, I said.
Then I'll know who to thank, she said, and give me a straight look.
HURRY UP PLEASE ITS TIME
If you don't like it you can get on with it, I said,
Others can pick and choose if you can't.
155 But if Albert makes off, it won't be for lack of telling.
You ought to be ashamed, I said, to look so antique.
(And her only thirty-one.)
I can't help it, she said, pulling a long face,
It's them pills I took, to bring it off, she said.

Terminated Pregnancy (handwritten)
Marriage/Life as death (handwritten)

160 (She's had five already, and nearly died of young George.)
The chemist said it would be alright, but I've never been the same.
You are a proper fool, I said.
Well, if Albert won't leave you alone, there it is, I said,
What you get married for if you don't want children?
165 HURRY UP PLEASE ITS TIME
Well, that Sunday Albert was home, they had a hot gammon,
And they asked me in to dinner, to get the beauty of it hot—
HURRY UP PLEASE ITS TIME
HURRY UP PLEASE ITS TIME

Sense of urgency (handwritten)
you can't escape or stop time (handwritten)

170 Goonight Bill. Goonight Lou. Goonight May. Goonight.
Ta ta. Goonight. Goonight.
Good night, ladies, good night, sweet ladies, good night, good night.[12]

III. THE FIRE SERMON[13]

wasteland = cold, dry, barren (handwritten)

The river's tent is broken: the last fingers of leaf
Clutch and sink into the wet bank. The wind
175 Crosses the brown land, unheard. The nymphs are departed.
Sweet Thames, run softly, till I end my song.
The river bears no empty bottles, sandwich papers,
Silk handkerchiefs, cardboard boxes, cigarette ends
Or other testimony of summer nights. The nymphs are departed.

ugliness vs. sweet Thames (handwritten)

180 And their friends, the loitering heirs of city directors;
Departed, have left no addresses.
By the waters of Leman I sat down and wept . . .
Sweet Thames, run softly till I end my song,
Sweet Thames, run softly, for I speak not loud or long.
185 But at my back in a cold blast I hear
The rattle of the bones, and chuckle spread from ear to ear.

---

[12]Contrasting words are spoken by Ophelia (in Hamlet) just before she dies (by water).

[13]The Fire Sermon was preached by The Buddha against the fires of lust and other destructive passions.

↳ *we should give up earthly passions* (handwritten)

6. T. S. Eliot

A rat crept softly through the vegetation
Dragging its slimy belly on the bank
While I was fishing in the dull canal
190 On a winter evening round behind the gashouse
Musing upon the king my brother's wreck
And on the king my father's death before him.
White bodies naked on the low damp ground
And bones cast in a little low dry garret,
195 Rattled by the rat's foot only, year to year.
But at my back from time to time I hear
The sound of horns and motors, which shall bring
Sweeney to Mrs. Porter in the spring.
O the moon shone bright on Mrs. Porter
200 And on her daughter
They wash their feet in soda water
Et O ces voix d'enfants, chantant dans la coupole![14]

Twit twit twit
Jug jug jug jug jug jug
205 So rudely forc'd.
Tereu

Unreal City
Under the brown fog of a winter noon
Mr. Eugenides, the Smyrna merchant
210 Unshaven, with a pocket full of currants
C.i.f. London: documents at sight,
Asked me in demotic French
To luncheon at the Cannon Street Hotel
Followed by a weekend at the Metropole.

215 At the violet hour, when the eyes and back
Turn upward from the desk, when the human engine waits
Like a taxi throbbing waiting,
I Tiresias, though blind, throbbing between two lives,[15]
Old man with wrinkled female breasts, can see

[14]"And O these children's voices singing in the dome" (i.e., of a chapel). From Verlaine, "Parsifal," a poem that presents Parsifal resisting sexual temptation to keep himself pure for the pursuit of the Holy Grail.

[15]"Tiresias, although a mere spectator and not indeed a 'character,' is yet the most important personage in the poem, uniting all the rest. Just as the one-eyed merchant, seller of currants, melts into the Phoenician sailor, and the latter is not wholly distinct from Ferdinand Prince of Naples, so all the women are one woman, and the two sexes meet in Tiresias. What Tiresias sees, in fact, is the substance of the poem" [Eliot's note]. Tiresias is from Ovid, *Metamorphoses*.

-43-

220 At the violet hour, the evening hour that strives
Homeward, and brings the sailor home from sea,
The typist home at teatime, clears her breakfast, lights
Her stove, and lays out food in tins.
Out of the window perilously spread
225 Her drying combinations touched by the sun's last rays,
On the divan are piled (at night her bed)
Stockings, slippers, camisoles, and stays.
I Tiresias, old man with wrinkled dugs
Perceived the scene, and foretold the rest—
230 I too awaited the expected guest.
He, the young man carbuncular, arrives,
A small house agent's clerk, with one bold stare,
One of the low on whom assurance sits
As a silk hat on a Bradford millionaire.
235 The time is now propitious, as he guesses,
The meal is ended, she is bored and tired,
Endeavours to engage her in caresses
Which still are unreproved, if undesired.
Flushed and decided, he assaults at once;
240 Exploring hands encounter no defence;
His vanity requires no response,
And makes a welcome of indifference.
(And I Tiresias have foresuffered all
Enacted on this same divan or bed;
245 I who have sat by Thebes below the wall
And walked among the lowest of the dead.)
Bestows one final patronising kiss,
And gropes his way, finding the stairs unlit . . .

She turns and looks a moment in the glass,
250 Hardly aware of her departed lover;
Her brain allows one half-formed thought to pass:
"Well now that's done: and I'm glad it's over."
When lovely woman stoops to folly and
Paces about her room again, alone,
255 She smoothes her hair with automatic hand,
And puts a record on the gramophone.

"This music crept by me upon the waters"
And along the Strand, up Queen Victoria Street.
O City city, I can sometimes hear
260 Beside a public bar in Lower Thames Street,
The pleasant whining of a mandoline
And a clatter and a chatter from within

Where fishmen lounge at noon: where the walls
Of Magnus Martyr hold
265   Inexplicable splendour of Ionian white and gold.

    The river sweats
Oil and tar
The barges drift
With the turning tide
270   Red sails
Wide
To leeward, swing on the heavy spar.
The barges wash
Drifting logs
275   Down Greenwich reach
Past the Isle of Dogs.
Weialala leia
Wallala leialala

    Elizabeth and Leicester
280   Beating oars
The stem was formed
A gilded shell
Red and gold
The brisk swell
285   Rippled both shores
Southwest wind
Carried down stream
The peal of bells
White towers
290   Weialala leia
        Wallala leialala
"Trams and dusty trees.
Highbury bore me. Richmond and Kew
Undid me. By Richmond I raised my knees
295   Supine on the floor of a narrow canoe."

    "My feet are at Moorgate, and my heart
Under my feet. After the event
He wept. He promised 'a new start'
I made no comment. What should I resent?"

300   "On Margate Sands.
I can connect
Nothing with nothing.
The broken fingernails of dirty hands.

[handwritten annotations: "Stanzas get short, lines get short — peaceful"; "'Virgin Queen' — public sexuality"; "reminds me of stone-cutters"]

My people humble people who expect
305 Nothing."

        la la
To Carthage then I came[16]
Burning burning burning burning[17]
O Lord Thou pluckest me out
310 O Lord Thou pluckest[18]

    burning

IV. DEATH BY WATER

Phlebas the Phoenician, a fortnight dead,
Forgot the cry of gulls, and the deep sea swell
And the profit and loss.
315   A current under sea
Picked his bones in whispers. As he rose and fell
He passed the stages of his age and youth
Entering the whirlpool.
        Gentile or Jew
320 O you who turn the wheel and look to windward,
Consider Phlebas, who was once handsome and tall as you.

V. WHAT THE THUNDER SAID[19]

After the torchlight red on sweaty faces
After the frosty silence in the gardens
After the agony in stony places
325 The shouting and the crying
Prison and palace and reverberation
Of thunder of spring over distant mountains
He who was living is now dead
We who were living are now dying
330 With a little patience

Handwritten margin notes: "the Aneid", "the great sailor", "- Forgets worldly cares in his death", "- reject ideas of renewal", "- he just gets eaten + that's the end", "reflection of WWI", "sense of Time", "- Phoenician", "- fortnight", "- age + youth", "- Fulfills prophecy 'Fear death by water'", "hell", "Apocalypse"

---

[16]"See St. Augustine's *Confessions*: 'to Carthage then I came, where a cauldron of unholy loves sang all about my ears'" [Eliot].

[17]"The Buddha's Fire Sermon (which corresponds in importance to The Sermon on the Mount) [is the source] from which these words are taken" [Eliot].

[18]"From St. Augustine's *Confessions* again. The collocation of these two representatives of eastern and western asceticism, as the culmination of this part of the poem, is not an accident" [Eliot].

[19]"In the first part three themes are employed: the journey to Emmaus, the approach to the Chapel Perilous (see Miss Weston's book), and the present [Eliot means post-World War I] decay of eastern Europe" [Eliot].

6. T. S. Eliot

Here is no water but only rock
Rock and no water and the sandy road
The road winding above among the mountains
Which are mountains of rock without water
335 If there were water we should stop and drink
Amongst the rock one cannot stop or think
Sweat is dry and feet are in the sand
If there were only water amongst the rock
Dead mountain mouth of carious teeth that cannot spit
340 Here one can neither stand nor lie nor sit
There is not even silence in the mountains
But dry sterile thunder without rain
There is not even solitude in the mountains
But red sullen faces sneer and snarl
345 From doors of mudcracked houses
                    If there were water

        And no rock
        If there were rock
        And also water
350   And water
        A spring
        A pool among the rock
        If there were the sound of water only
        Not the cicada
355   And dry grass singing
        But sound of water over a rock
        Where the hermit-thrush sings in the pine trees
        Drip drop drip drop drop drop drop
        But there is no water

360 Who is the third who walks always beside you?
When I count, there are only you and I together
But when I look ahead up the white road
There is always another one walking beside you
Gliding wrapt in a brown mantle, hooded
365 I do not know whether a man or a woman
—But who is that on the other side of you?

        What is that sound high in the air
Murmur of maternal lamentation
Who are those hooded hordes swarming
370 Over endless plains, stumbling in cracked earth
Ringed by the flat horizon only

-47-

What is the city over the mountains
Cracks and reforms and bursts in the violet air
Falling towers
375 Jerusalem Athens Alexandria
Vienna London
Unreal

rejection of city life [handwritten annotation] → *symbol of modernity, ironic* [handwritten annotation]

A woman drew her long black hair out tight
And fiddled whisper music on those strings
380 And bats with baby faces in the violet light
Whistled, and beat their wings
And crawled head downward down a blackened wall
And upside down in air were towers
Tolling reminiscent bells, that kept the hours
385 And voices singing out of empty cisterns and exhausted wells.

In this decayed hole among the mountains
In the faint moonlight, the grass is singing
Over the tumbled graves, about the chapel
There is the empty chapel, only the wind's home.
390 It has no windows, and the door swings,
Dry bones can harm no one.
Only a cock stood on the rooftree
Co co rico co co rico
In a flash of lightning. Then a damp gust
395 Bringing rain

Ganga was sunken, and the limp leaves
Waited for rain, while the black clouds
Gathered far distant, over Himavant.
The jungle crouched, humped in silence.
400 Then spoke the thunder[20]
DA
Datta: what have we given?
My friend, blood shaking my heart
The awful daring of a moment's surrender
405 Which an age of prudence can never retract
By this, and this only, we have existed
Which is not to be found in our obituaries
Or in memories draped by the beneficent spider
Or under seals broken by the lean solicitor

[20]Datta: Give. Dyadhvam: Sympathize. Damyata: Control. "The fable of the meaning of the Thunder is found in the Brihadaranyaka—Upanishad, V, 1" [Eliot].

410   In our empty rooms
         DA
         Dayadhvam: I have heard the key[21]
         Turn in the door once and turn once only
         We think of the key, each in his prison
415   Thinking of the key, each confirms a prison
         Only at nightfall, aethereal rumours
         Revive for a moment a broken Coriolanus
         DA
         Damyata: The boat responded
420   Gaily, to the hand expert with sail and oar
         The sea was calm, your heart would have responded
         Gaily, when invited, beating obedient
         To controlling hands
                              I sat upon the shore
425   Fishing, with the arid plain behind me
          Shall I at least set my lands in order?
         London Bridge is falling down falling down falling down
         Poi s'ascose nel foco che gli affina[22]
         Quando fiam uti chelidon[23]—O swallow swallow
430   *Le Prince d'Aquitaine à la tour abolie*[24]
         These fragments I have shored against my ruins
         Why then Ile fit you. Hieronymo's mad againe.[25]
         Datta. Dayadhvam. Damyata.
         Shantih   shantih   shantih[26]

---

[21] After directing the reader to Dante, *Inferno*, XXXIII, 46, Eliot goes on: "Also F. H. Bradley, Appearance and Reality, p. 346. 'My external sensations are no less private to myself than are my thoughts or my feelings. In either case my experience falls within my own circle, a circle closed on the outside; and, with all its elements alike, every sphere is opaque to the others which surround it. . . . In brief, regarded as an existence which appears in a soul, the whole world for each is peculiar and private to that soul.'" Eliot had written his doctoral dissertation (in philosophy) on Bradley and the situation presented by Bradley's words here is exactly what Eliot is struggling against.

[22] "Then he hid himself within the fire." From Dante, Purgatorio, XXVI: 148. This note on refining fire is a hopeful sign; all the previous allusions to Dante have been to the Inferno.

[23] "When shall I be like the swallow?" From a late Latin poem the "Pervirgilium Veneris." The reference takes us back to Philomel (in Part II).

[24] "The Prince of Aquitaine is the ruined tower." Gerard de Nerval, *El Desdichado.*

[25] Thomas Kyd, *The Spanish Tragedy* (1594), one of the "fragments" the speaker is using to "shore up [his] ruins."

[26] "Shantih. Repeated as here, a formal ending to an Upanishad. 'The Peace which passeth understanding' is our equivalent word" [Eliot].

↳ not our culture

TRADITION AND THE
INDIVIDUAL TALENT

I

In English writing we seldom speak of tradition, though we occasionally apply its name in deploring its absence. We cannot refer to "the tradition" or to "a tradition"; at most, we employ the adjective in saying that the poetry of So-and-so is "traditional" or
5   even "too traditional." Seldom, perhaps, does the word appear except in a phrase of censure. If otherwise, it is vaguely approbative, with the implication, as to the work approved, of some pleasing archæological reconstruction. You can hardly make the word agreeable to English ears without this comfortable reference to the
10   reassuring science of archæology.

Certainly the word is not likely to appear in our appreciations of living or dead writers. Every nation, every race, has not only its own creative, but its own critical turn of mind; and is even more oblivious of the shortcomings and limitations of its critical habits
15   than of those of its creative genius. We know, or think we know, from the enormous mass of critical writing that has appeared in the French language the critical method or habit of the French; we only conclude (we are such unconscious people) that the French are "more critical" than we, and sometimes even plume ourselves a lit-
20   tle with the fact, as if the French were the less spontaneous. Perhaps they are; but we might remind ourselves that criticism is as inevitable as breathing, and that we should be none the worse for articulating what passes in our minds when we read a book and feel an emotion about it, for criticizing our own minds in their work of
25   criticism. One of the facts that might come to light in this process is our tendency to insist, when we praise a poet, upon those aspects of his work in which he least resembles anyone else. In these aspects or parts of his work we pretend to find what is individual, what is the peculiar essence of the man. We dwell with satisfaction upon the
30   poet's difference from his predecessors, especially his immediate predecessors; we endeavour to find something that can be isolated in order to be enjoyed. Whereas if we approach a poet without this prejudice we shall often find that not only the best, but the most individual parts of his work may be those in which the dead poets,
35   his ancestors, assert their immortality most vigorously. And I do not mean the impressionable period of adolescence, but the period of full maturity.

Yet if the only form of tradition, of handing down, consisted in following the ways of the immediate generation before us in a blind

or timid adherence to its successes, "tradition" should positively be
discouraged. We have seen many such simple currents soon lost in
the sand; and novelty is better than repetition. Tradition is a matter
of much wider significance. It cannot be inherited, and if you want
5   it you must obtain it by great labour. It involves, in the first place,
the historical sense, which we may call nearly indispensable to anyone who would continue to be a poet beyond his twenty-fifth year;
and the historical sense involves a perception, not only of the past-
ness of the past, but of its presence; the historical sense compels a
10   man to write not merely with his own generation in his bones, but
with a feeling that the whole of the literature of Europe from Homer
and within it the whole of the literature of his own country has a
simultaneous existence and composes a simultaneous order. This
historical sense, which is a sense of the timeless as well as of the
15   temporal and of the timeless and of the temporal together, is what
makes a writer traditional. And it is at the same time what makes a
writer most acutely conscious of his place in time, of his contempo-
raneity.

No poet, no artist of any art, has his complete meaning alone.
20   His significance, his appreciation is the appreciation of his relation
to the dead poets and artists. You cannot value him alone, you must
set him, for contrast and comparison, among the dead. I mean this
as a principle of æsthetic, not merely historical, criticism. The necessity that he shall conform, that he shall cohere, is not onesided; what
25   happens when a new work of art is created is something that happens simultaneously to all the works of art which preceded it. The
existing monuments form an ideal order among themselves, which
is modified by the introduction of the new (the really new) work of
art among them. The existing order is complete before the new
30   work arrives; for order to persist after the supervention of novelty,
the *whole* existing order must be, if ever so slightly, altered; and so
the relations, proportions, values of each work of art toward the
whole are readjusted; and this is conformity between the old and
the new. Whoever has approved this idea of order, of the form of
35   European, of English literature, will not find it preposterous that the
past should be altered by the present as much as the present is
directed by the past. And the poet who is aware of this will be aware
of great difficulties and responsibilities.

In a peculiar sense he will be aware also that he must inevitably
40   be judged by the standards of the past. I say judged, not amputat-
ed, by them; not judged to be as good as, or worse or better than,
the dead; and certainly not judged by the canons of dead critics. It
is a judgment, a comparison, in which two things are measured by
each other. To conform merely would be for the new work not real-
45   ly to conform at all; it would not be new, and would therefore not

be a work of art. And we do not quite say that the new is more valuable because it fits in; but its fitting in is a test of its value—a test, it
is true, which can only be slowly and cautiously applied, for we are
none of us infallible judges of conformity. We say: it appears to con-
5 form, and is perhaps individual, or it appears individual, and may
conform; but we are hardly likely to find that it is one and not the
other.

To proceed to a more intelligible exposition of the relation of
the poet to the past: he can neither take the past as a lump, an indis-
10 criminate bolus, nor can he form himself wholly on one or two private admirations, nor can he form himself wholly upon one preferred period. The first course is inadmissible, the second is an
important experience of youth, and the third is a pleasant and highly desirable supplement. The poet must be very conscious of the
15 main current, which does not at all flow invariably through the
most distinguished reputations. He must be quite aware of the obvious fact that art never improves, but that the material of art is never
quite the same. He must be aware that the mind of Europe—the
mind of his own country—a mind which he learns in time to be
20 much more important than his own private mind—is a mind which
changes, and that this change is a development which abandons
nothing *en route*, which does not superannuate either Shakespeare,
or Homer, or the rock drawing of the Magdalenian draughtsmen.
That this development, refinement perhaps, complication certainly,
25 is not, from the point of view of the artist, any improvement.
Perhaps not even an improvement from the point of view of the
psychologist or not to the extent which we imagine; perhaps only in
the end based upon a complication in economics and machinery.
But the difference between the present and the past is that the con-
30 scious present is an awareness of the past in a way and to an extent
which the past's awareness of itself cannot show.

Some one said: "The dead writers are remote from us because
we *know* so much more than they did." Precisely, and they are that
which we know.

35 I am alive to a usual objection to what is clearly part of my pro-
gramme for the *métier* of poetry. The objection is that the doctrine
requires a ridiculous amount of erudition (pedantry), a claim which
can be rejected by appeal to the lives of poets in any pantheon. It
will even be affirmed that much learning deadens or perverts poet-
40 ic sensibility. While, however, we persist in believing that a poet
ought to know as much as will not encroach upon his necessary
receptivity and necessary laziness, it is not desirable to confine
knowledge to whatever can be put into a useful shape for examina-
tions, drawing-rooms, or the still more pretentious modes of pub-
45 licity. Some can absorb knowledge, the more tardy must sweat for

it. Shakespeare acquired more essential history from Plutarch than most men could from the whole British Museum. What is to be insisted upon is that the poet must develop or procure the consciousness of the past and that he should continue to develop this
5   consciousness throughout his career.

What happens is a continual surrender of himself as he is at the moment to something which is more valuable. The progress of an artist is a continual self-sacrifice, a continual extinction of personality.
10   There remains to define this process of depersonalization and   *depersonalizat*
its relation to the sense of tradition. It is in this depersonalization that art may be said to approach the condition of science. I shall, therefore, invite you to consider, as a suggestive analogy, the action which takes place when a bit of finely filiated platinum is intro-
15   duced into a chamber containing oxygen and sulphur dioxide.

II

Honest criticism and sensitive appreciation is directed not upon the poet but upon the poetry. If we attend to the confused cries of the newspaper critics and the susurrus of popular repetition that follows, we shall hear the names of poets in great numbers; if
20   we seek not Blue-book knowledge but the enjoyment of poetry, and ask for a poem, we shall seldom find it. In the last article I tried to point out the importance of the relation of the poem to other poems by other authors, and suggested the conception of poetry as a living whole of all the poetry that has ever been written. The other aspect
25   of this Impersonal theory of poetry is the relation of the poem to its author. And I hinted, by an analogy, that the mind of the mature poet differs from that of the immature one not precisely in any valuation of "personality," not being necessarily more interesting, or having "more to say," but rather by being a more finely perfected
30   medium in which special, or very varied, feelings are at liberty to enter into new combinations.

The analogy was that of the catalyst. When the two gases previously mentioned are mixed in the presence of a filament of platinum, they form sulphurous acid. This combination takes place
35   only if the platinum is present; nevertheless the newly formed acid contains no trace of platinum, and the platinum itself is apparently unaffected; has remained inert, neutral, and unchanged. The mind of the poet is the shred of platinum. It may partly or exclusively operate upon the experience of the man himself ; but, the more per-
40   fect the artist, the more completely separate in him will be the man who suffers and the mind which creates; the more perfectly will the mind digest and transmute the passions which are its material.

The experience, you will notice, the elements which enter the presence of the transforming catalyst, are of two kinds: emotions and feelings. The effect of a work of art upon the person who enjoys it is an experience different in kind from any experience not of art.
5   It may be formed out of one emotion, or may be a combination of several; and various feelings, inhering for the writer in particular words or phrases or images, may be added to compose the final result. Or great poetry may be made without the direct use of any emotion whatever: composed out of feelings solely. Canto XV of the
10 *Inferno* (Brunetto Latini) is a working up of the emotion evident in the situation; but the effect, though single as that of any work of art, is obtained by considerable complexity of detail. The last quatrain gives an image, a feeling attaching to an image, which "came," which did not develop simply out of what precedes, but which was
15 probably in suspension in the poet's mind until the proper combination arrived for it to add itself to. The poet's mind is in fact a receptacle for seizing and storing up numberless feelings, phrases, images, which remain there until all the particles which can unite to form a new compound are present together.
20   If you compare several representative passages of the greatest poetry you see how great is the variety of types of combination, and also how completely any semi-ethical criterion of "sublimity" misses the mark. For it is not the "greatness," the intensity, of the emotions, the components, but the intensity of the artistic process, the
25 pressure, so to speak, under which the fusion takes place, that counts. The episode of Paolo and Francesca employs a definite emotion, but the intensity of the poetry is something quite different from whatever intensity in the supposed experience it may give the impression of. It is no more intense, furthermore, than Canto XXVI,
30 the voyage of Ulysses, which has not the direct dependence upon an emotion. Great variety is possible in the process of transmution of emotion: the murder of Agamemnon, or the agony of Othello, gives an artistic effect apparently closer to a possible original than the scenes from Dante. In the *Agamemnon*, the artistic emotion
35 approximates to the emotion of an actual spectator; in *Othello* to the emotion of the protagonist himself. But the difference between art and the event is always absolute; the combination which is the murder of Agamemnon is probably as complex as that which is the voyage of Ulysses. In either case there has been a fusion of elements.
40 The ode of Keats contains a number of feelings which have nothing particular to do with the nightingale, but which the nightingale, partly, perhaps, because of its attractive name, and partly because of its reputation, served to bring together.
        The point of view which I am struggling to attack is perhaps
45 related to the metaphysical theory of the substantial unity of the

soul: for my meaning is, that the poet has, not a "personality" to express, but a particular medium, which is only a medium and not a personality, in which impressions and experiences combine in peculiar and unexpected ways. Impressions and experiences which
5   are important for the man may take no place in the poetry, and those which become important in the poetry may play quite a negligible part in the man, the personality.

   I will quote a passage which is unfamiliar enough to be regarded with fresh attention in the light—or darkness—of these observa-
10 tions:

        And now methinks I could e'en chide myself
        For doating on her beauty, though her death
        Shall be revenged after no common action.
        Does the silkworm expend her yellow labours
15   For thee? For thee does she undo herself?
        Are lordships sold to maintain ladyships
        For the poor benefit of a bewildering minute?
        Why does yon fellow falsify highways,
        And put his life between the judge's lips,
20   To refine such a thing—keeps horse and men
        To beat their valours for her ? . . .

   In this passage (as is evident if it is taken in its context) there is a combination of positive and negative emotions: an intensely strong attraction toward beauty and an equally intense fascination
25 by the ugliness which is contrasted with it and which destroys it. This balance of contrasted emotion is in the dramatic situation to which the speech is pertinent, but that situation alone is inadequate to it. This is, so to speak, the structural emotion, provided by the drama. But the whole effect, the dominant tone, is due to the fact
30 that a number of floating feelings, having an affinity to this emotion by no means superficially evident, have combined with it to give us a new art emotion.

   It is not in his personal emotions, the emotions provoked by particular events in his life, that the poet is in any way remarkable
35 or interesting. His particular emotions may be simple, or crude, or flat. The emotion in his poetry will be a very complex thing, but not with the complexity of the emotions of people who have very complex or unusual emotions in life. One error, in fact, of eccentricity in poetry is to seek for new human emotions to express; and in this
40 search for novelty in the wrong place it discovers the perverse. The business of the poet is not to find new emotions, but to use the ordinary ones and, in working them up into poetry, to express feelings which are not in actual emotions at all. And emotions which he has never experienced will serve his turn as well as those familiar to
45 him. Consequently, we must believe that "emotion recollected in

tranquillity" is an inexact formula. For it is neither emotion, nor recollection, nor, without distortion of meaning, tranquillity. It is a concentration, and a new thing resulting from the concentration, of a
very great number of experiences which to the practical and active
5   person would not seem to be experiences at all; it is a concentration
which does not happen consciously or of deliberation. These experiences are not "recollected," and they finally unite in an atmosphere which is "tranquil" only in that it is a passive attending upon
the event. Of course this is not quite the whole story. There is a great
10 deal, in the writing of poetry, which must be conscious and deliber-
ate. In fact, the bad poet is usually unconscious where he ought to
be conscious, and conscious where he ought to be unconscious.
Both errors tend to make him "personal." Poetry is not a turning
loose of emotion, but an escape from emotion; it is not the expres-
15 sion of personality, but an escape from personality. But, of course,
only those who have personality and emotions know what it means
to want to escape from these things.

III

ὁ δὲ νοῦς ἴσως θειότερόν τι καὶ ἀπαθές ἐστιν [*]

This essay proposes to halt at the frontier of metaphysics or
20 mysticism, and confine itself to such practical conclusions as can be
applied by the responsible person interested in poetry. To divert
interest from the poet to the poetry is a laudable aim: for it would
conduce to a juster estimation of actual poetry, good and bad. There
are many people who appreciate the expression of sincere emotion
25 in verse, and there is a smaller number of people who can appreciate technical excellence. But very few know when there is expression of *significant* emotion, emotion which has its life in the poem
and not in the history of the poet. The emotion of art is impersonal.
And the poet cannot reach this impersonality without surrendering
30 himself wholly to the work to be done. And he is not likely to know
what is to be done unless he lives in what is not merely the present,
but the present moment of the past, unless he is conscious, not of
what is dead, but of what is already living.

---

[*]"Presumably the mind is something more divine, and is unaffected."
Aristotle, *De Anima*.

7. MARIANNE MOORE

Marianne Moore (1887–1972) was born in St. Louis, spent her childhood in Pennsylvania, and lived for most of her adult life in Brooklyn. She attended Bryn Mawr College, where she edited the literary magazine and studied biology; both of these interests would inform her literary activities throughout her career. As a poet, she is known for her scientist's eye, keen and scrupulous in the detail of its observations. She also became the editor of the Dial magazine, a literary journal that would publish many of the great writers of American modernism, including T. S. Eliot, Ezra Pound, William Carlos Williams, and Hart Crane.

Moore's poetic style is very distinctive; she is known for her use of syllabic meters, in which the length of a poetic line is determined simply by the number of syllables, not by sound or rhythmic accent. The result is a poetry that sounds, in some respects, like natural speech. In other ways, however, Moore's epigrammatic style and abstruse vocabulary make it impossible to mistake her voice for anyone else's. She peppers her work with quotations, which is a common modernist technique; but Moore is as likely to cite a newspaper account of a baseball game or an article from Life magazine as she is Shakespeare or Dante.

While many of the great works of literary modernism were produced by expatriates and exiles (like Pound, Eliot, Joyce, Stein, and Hemingway), Moore's is a distinctly American voice, grounded in practical observation and a fascination with the abundance of the American wilderness. Yet with her sense of poetry as a made thing, a sculpture in words, she is consistent with many of the other poets of the first half of the twentieth century.

IN THE DAYS OF PRISMATIC COLOUR

not in the days of Adam and Eve, but when Adam
    was alone; when there was no smoke and colour was
fine, not with the refinement
    of early civilization art, but because
5   of its originality; with nothing to modify it but the

mist that went up, obliqueness was a varia-
    tion of the perpendicular, plain to see and
to account for: it is no

longer that; nor did the blue-red-yellow band
10   of incandescence that was colour keep its stripe: it also is one of

those things into which much that is peculiar can be
read; complexity is not a crime, but carry
it to the point of murki-
. ness and nothing is plain. Complexity,
15   moreover, that has been committed to darkness, instead of
granting it-

self to be the pestilence that it is, moves all a-
bout as if to bewilder us with the dismal
fallacy that insistence
20   is the measure of achievement and that all
truth must be dark. Principally throat, sophistication is as it al-

ways has been—at the antipodes from the init-
ial great truths. 'Part of it was crawling, part of it
was about to crawl, the rest
25   was torpid in its lair.' In the short-legged, fitful advance, the gurgling and all the minutiae—we have the
classic

multitude of feet. To what purpose! Truth is no Apollo
Belvedere, no formal thing. The wave may go over it if it
30 likes.
Know that it will be there when it says,
'I shall be there when the wave has gone by.'

1919, 1935

POETRY

I, too, dislike it: there are things that are important beyond all this
fiddle.
Reading it, however, with a perfect contempt for it, one discovers in it after all, a place for the genuine.[1]
5   Hands that can grasp, eyes
that can dilate, hair that can rise
if it must, these things are important not because a

high-sounding interpretation can be put upon them but because they
are

[1]In Moore's final revision of the poem, she deleted all but these first three
lines.

useful. When they become so derivative as to become unintel-
10   ligible, the same thing may be said for all of us, that we
                do not admire what
                we cannot understand: the bat
                    holding on upside down or in quest of something to

eat, elephants pushing, a wild horse taking a roll, a tireless wolf
15   under a tree, the immovable critic twitching his skin like a
        horse that feels a
                            flea, the base-
                ball fan, the statistician—
                nor is it valid
20   to discriminate against 'business documents and

school-books'; all these phenomena are important. One must
        make a
                            distinction
                however: when dragged into prominence by half poets, the
25   result is
                            not poetry,
                nor till the poets among us can be
                'literalists of
                the imagination'—above
30   insolence and triviality and can present
for inspection, 'imaginary gardens with real toads in them', shall
        we
                have
        it. In the meantime, if you demand on the one hand,
35   the raw material of poetry in
                all its rawness and
                that which is on the other hand
                            genuine, you are interested in poetry.
                                                    1919, 1951

A GRAVE

Man looking into the sea,
taking the view from those who have as much right to it as
            you have to yourself,
it is human nature to stand in the middle of a thing,
5   but you cannot stand in the middle of this;
        the sea has nothing to give but a well excavated grave.
        The firs stand in a procession, each with an emerald turkey-

foot at the top,
    reserved as their contours, saying nothing;
10   repression, however, is not the most obvious characteristic of
        the sea;
    the sea is a collector, quick to return a rapacious look.
    There are others besides you who have worn that look—
    whose expression is no longer a protest; the fish no longer
15   investigate them
    for their bones have not lasted:
    men lower nets, unconscious of the fact that they are desecrat-
        ing a grave,
    and row quickly away—the blades of the oars
20   moving together like the feet of water-spiders as if there were
        no such thing as death.
    The wrinkles progress among themselves in a phalanx—beau-
        tiful under networks of foam,
    and fade breathlessly while the sea rustles in and out of the
25   seaweed;
    the birds swim through the air at top speed, emitting cat-calls
        as heretofore—
    the tortoise-shell scourges about the feet of the cliffs, in
        motion beneath them;
30   and the ocean, under the pulsation of lighthouses and noise of
        bell-buoys,
    advances as usual, looking as if it were not that ocean in
        which dropped things are bound to sink—
    in which if they turn and twist, it is neither with volition nor
35   consciousness.

                                   1921, 1935

THE STEEPLE-JACK

Dürer[1] would have seen a reason for living
    in a town like this, with eight stranded whales
to look at; with the sweet sea air coming into your house
    on a fine day, from water etched
5   with waves as formal as the scales
on a fish.

One by one in two's and three's, the seagulls keep
    flying back and forth over the town clock,

---

[1]Albrecht Dürer, German artist (1471–1528), known, among other things, for
his lifelike paintings of animals and landscapes.

or sailing around the lighthouse without moving their wings—
10   rising steadily with a slight
      quiver of the body—or flock
   mewing where
   a sea the purple of the peacock's neck is
      paled to greenish azure as Dürer changed
15   the pine green of the Tyrol to peacock blue and guinea
   gray. You can see a twenty-five-
      pound lobster; and fish nets arranged
   to dry. The

   whirlwind fife-and-drum of the storm bends the salt
20   marsh grass, disturbs stars in the sky and the
   star on the steeple; it is a privilege to see so
   much confusion. Disguised by what
      might seem the opposite, the sea-
   side flowers and

25   trees are favored by the fog so that you have
      the tropics at first hand: the trumpet vine,
   foxglove, giant snapdragon, a salpiglossis that has
   spots and stripes; morning-glories, gourds,
      or moon-vines trained on fishing twine
30   at the back door:

   cattails, flags, blueberries and spiderwort,
      striped grass, lichens, sunflowers, asters, daisies—
   yellow and crab-claw ragged sailors with green bracts—toad-plant,
   petunias, ferns; pink lilies, blue
35   ones, tigers; poppies; black sweet-peas.
   The climate

   is not right for the banyan, frangipani, or
      jack-fruit trees; or for exotic serpent
   life. Ring lizard and snakeskin for the foot, if you see fit;
40   but here they've cats, not cobras, to
      keep down the rats. The diffident
   little newt

   with white pin-dots on black horizontal spaced-
      out bands lives here; yet there is nothing that
45   ambition can buy or take away. The college student
   named Ambrose sits on the hillside
      with his not-native books and hat
   and sees boats

at sea progress white and rigid as if in
50   a groove. Liking an elegance of which
the source is not bravado, he knows by heart the antique
sugar-bowl shaped summerhouse of
      interlacing slats, and the pitch
of the church

55 spire, not true, from which a man in scarlet lets
      down a rope as a spider spins a thread;
he might be part of a novel, but on the sidewalk a
sign says C. J. Poole, Steeple Jack[10]
      in black and white; and one in red
60 and white says

Danger. The church portico has four fluted
      columns, each a single piece of stone, made
modester by whitewash. This would be a fit haven for
waifs, children, animals, prisoners,
65   and presidents who have repaid
sin-driven

senators by not thinking about them. The
      place has a schoolhouse, a post-office in a
store, fish-houses, hen-houses, a three-masted schooner on
70 the stocks. The hero, the student,
      the steeple jack, each in his way,
is at home.

It could not be dangerous to be living
      in a town like this, of simple people,
75 who have a steeple-jack placing danger signs by the church
while he is gilding the solid-
      pointed star, which on a steeple
stands for hope.

                                        1932, 1961

8. ERNEST HEMINGWAY

Hemingway (1899–1961) served in the Red Cross with the Italian Army during World War I and was badly wounded. As a young writer in Paris in the 1920s he became the voice of "the Lost Generation" of those wounded—physically or psychologically—by the war. His stories convey a distrust of "rhetoric"—the bombast of propaganda used to sustain morale during the war years. They strive to be "objective" with very little use of authorial voice—dramatic rather than narrative—and consequently make great demands on the reader.

A CLEAN, WELL-LIGHTED PLACE

(1933)

It was late and every one had left the cafe except an old man who sat in the shadow the leaves of the tree made, against the electric light. In the day time the street was dusty, but at night the dew settled the dust and the old man liked to sit late because he was deaf
5 and now at night it was quiet and he felt the difference. The two waiters inside the cafe knew that the old man was a little drunk, and while he was a good client they knew that if he became too drunk he would leave without paying, so they kept watch on him.

"Last week he tried to commit suicide," one waiter said.
10 "Why?"
"He was in despair."
"What about?"
"Nothing."
"How do you know it was nothing?"
15 "He had plenty of money."

They sat together at a table that was close against the wall near the door of the café and looked at the terrace where the tables were all empty except where the old man sat in the shadow of the leaves of the tree that moved slightly in the wind. A girl and a soldier went
20 by in the street. The street light shone on the brass number on his collar. The girl wore no head covering and hurried beside him.

"The guard will pick him up," one waiter said.
"What does it matter if he gets what he's after?"
"He had better get off the street now. The guard will get him.
25 They went by five minutes ago."

The old man sitting in the shadow rapped on his saucer with his glass. The younger waiter went over to him.

"What do you want?"

The old man looked at him. "Another brandy," he said.

5 "You'll be drunk," the waiter said. The old man looked at him. The waiter went away.

"He'll stay all night," he said to his colleague. "I'm sleepy now. I never get into bed before three o'clock. He should have killed himself last week."

10 The waiter took the brandy bottle and another saucer from the counter inside the cafe and marched out to the old man's table. He put down the saucer and poured the glass full of brandy.

"You should have killed yourself last week," he said to the deaf man. The old man motioned with his finger. "A little more," he said.

15 The waiter poured on into the glass so that the brandy slopped over and ran down the stem into the top saucer of the pile. "Thank you," the old man said. The waiter took the bottle back inside the cafe. He sat down at the table with his colleague again.

"He's drunk now," he said.

20 "He's drunk every night."

"What did he want to kill himself for?"

"How should I know."

"How did he do it?"

"He hung himself with a rope."

25 "Who cut him down?"

"His niece."

"Why did they do it?"

"Fear for his soul."

"How much money has he got?"

30 "He's got plenty."

"He must be eighty years old."

"Anyway I should say he was eighty."

"I wish he would go home. I never get to bed before three o'clock. What kind of hour is that to go to bed?"

35 "He stays up because he likes it."

"He's lonely. I'm not lonely. I have a wife waiting in bed for me."

"He had a wife once too."

"A wife would be no good to him now."

40 "You can't tell. He might be better with a wife."

"His niece looks after him. You said she cut him down."

"I know."

"I wouldn't want to be that old. An old man is a nasty thing."

"Not always. This old man is clean. He drinks without spilling.

45 Even now, drunk. Look at him."

"I don't want to look at him. I wish he would go home. He has no regard for those who must work."

The old man looked from his glass across the square, then over at the waiters.

5   "Another brandy," he said, pointing to his glass. The waiter who was in a hurry came over.

"Finished," he said, speaking with that omission of syntax stupid people employ when talking to drunken people or foreigners. "No more tonight. Close now."

10   "Another," said the old man.

"No. Finished." The waiter wiped the edge of the table with a towel and shook his head.

The old man stood up, slowly counted the saucers, took a leather coin purse from his pocket and paid for the drinks, leaving

15 half a peseta tip.

The waiter watched him go down the street, a very old man walking unsteadily but with dignity.

"Why didn't you let him stay and drink?" the unhurried waiter asked. They were putting up the shutters. "It is not half-past

20 two."

"I want to go home to bed."

"What is an hour?"

"More to me than to him."

"An hour is the same."

25   "You talk like an old man yourself. He can buy a bottle and drink at home."

"It's not the same."

"No, it is not," agreed the waiter with a wife. He did not wish to be unjust. He was only in a hurry.

30   "And you? You have no fear of going home before your usual hour?"

"Are you trying to insult me?"

"No, hombre, only to make a joke."

"No," the waiter who was in a hurry said, rising from pulling

35 down the metal shutters. "I have confidence. I am all confidence."

"You have youth, confidence, and a job," the older waiter said. "You have everything."

"And what do you lack?"

"Everything but work."

40   "You have everything I have."

"No. I have never had confidence and I am not young."

"Come on. Stop talking nonsense and lock up."

"I am of those who like to stay late at the café," the older waiter said. "With all those who do not want to go to bed. With all those

45 who need a light for the night."

"I want to go home and into bed."

"We are of two different kinds," the older waiter said. He was now dressed to go home. "It is not only a question of youth and confidence although those things are very beautiful. Each night I am reluctant to close up because there may be some one who needs the café."

"Hombre, there are bodegas open all night long."

"You do not understand. This is a clean and pleasant café. It is well lighted. The light is very good and also, now, there are shadows of the leaves."

"Good night," said the younger waiter.

"Good night," the other said. Turning off the electric light he continued the conversation with himself. It is the light of course but it is necessary that the place be clean and pleasant. You do not want music. Certainly you do not want music. Nor can you stand before a bar with dignity although that is all that is provided for these hours. What did he fear? It was not fear or dread. It was a nothing that he knew too well. It was all a nothing and a man was nothing too. It was only that and light was all it needed and a certain cleanness and order. Some lived in it and never felt it but he knew it all was nada y pues nada y nada y pues nada. Our nada who art in nada, nada be thy name thy kingdom nada thy will be nada in nada as it is in nada. Give us this nada our daily nada and nada us our nada as we nada our nadas and nada us not into nada but deliver us from nada; pues nada. Hail nothing full of nothing, nothing is with thee. He smiled and stood before a bar with a shining steam pressure coffee machine.

"What's yours?" asked the barman.

"Nada."

"Otro loco mas," said the barman and turned away.

"A little cup," said the waiter.

The barman poured it for him.

"The light is very bright and pleasant but the bar is unpolished," the waiter said.

The barman looked at him but did not answer. It was too late at night for conversation.

"You want another copita?" the barman asked.

"No, thank you," said the waiter and went out. He disliked bars and bodegas. A clean, well-lighted café was a very different thing. Now, without thinking further, he would go home to his room. He would lie in the bed and finally, with daylight, he would go to sleep. After all, he said to himself, it is probably only insomnia. Many must have it.

9. ANNA AKHMATOVA

Akhmatova (1889–1966) was one of three great Russian poets writing at the time of the Revolution. All were silenced, but each suffered a different fate when Socialist Realism became established doctrine and Stalin demanded of writers that they be "engineers of human souls." Osip Mandelstam was secretly murdered during the Stalinist purges of the 1930s; Boris Pasternak was silenced and spent the Stalinist years working quietly as a journalist and translator. Akhmatova, whom Stalin hated personally, was toyed with and humiliated. Her work was silenced, of course, but her son was arrested and placed inside the notorious Gulag Archipelago of the Soviet prison camp system. Although guilty of nothing whatever, he remained inside for most of eighteen years while his mother's pleas went unheeded.

REQUIEM[1]

No, not far beneath some foreign sky then,
Not with foreign wings to shelter me,—
I was with my people then, close by them
Where my luckless people chanced to be.

1961

BY WAY OF A PREFACE

In the terrible years of the Yezhovshchina[2], I spent seventeen months in the prison queues in Leningrad. Somehow, one day, someone "identified" me. Then a woman standing behind me, whose lips were blue with cold, and who, naturally enough, had
5   never even heard of my name, emerged from that state of torpor common to us all and, putting her lips close to my ear (there, everyone spoke in whispers), asked me:

---

[1]The Mass for the dead.

[2]Nikolai Yezhov was head of the KGB, the secret police, during Stalin's purges of the late 1930s when thousands of Russians were executed and many thousands more were imprisoned—all for political reasons.

—And could you describe this?
And I answered her:
10   —I can.
       Then something vaguely like a smile flashed across what once
had been her face.

1 April 1957

DEDICATION

       Mountains bow beneath that boundless sorrow,
5   And the mighty river stops its flow.
       But those prison bolts are tried and thorough,
       And beyond them, every "convict's burrow"
       Tells a tale of mortal woe.
       Someone, somewhere, feels the cool wind, bracing,
10   Sees the sun go nestling down to rest—
       We know nothing, we together facing
       Still the sickening clank of keys, the pacing
       Of the sentries with their heavy steps.
       We'd rise, as for early Mass, each morning,
15   Cross the callous city, wend our way,
       Meet, more lifeless than the dead, half mourning,
       Watch the sun sink, the Neva[3] mist forming,
       But with hope still singing far away.
       Sentenced . . . And at once the tears come rolling,
20   Cut off from the world, quite on her own,
       Heart reduced to shreds, and almost falling,
       Just as if some lout had sent her sprawling,
       Still . . . She staggers on her way . . . Alone . . .
       Where are now the friends of my misfortune,
25   Those that shared my own two years of hell?
       What do the Siberian snow-winds caution,
       What bodes the moon circle for their fortunes?
       Theirs be this, my greeting and farewell.

March 1940

---

[3]The river on which St. Petersburg (then called Leningrad) is built.

-68-

9. *Anna Akhmatova*

PRELUDE

It was when no one smiled any longer
Save the dead, who were glad of release.
And when Leningrad dangled, incongruous,
By its prisons—a needless caprice.
30   And when, out of their minds with sheer suffering,
The long lines of the newly condemned
Heard the engines' shrill whistles go sputtering
A brief song of farewell to their friends.
Stars of death stood above us, and Russia,
35   In her innocence, twisted in pain
Under blood-spattered boots, and the shudder
Of the Black Marias in their train.

I

It was dawn when they took you.[4] I followed,
As a widow walks after her bier.
40   By the icons—a candle, burnt hollow;
In the bed-room—the children, in tears.
Your lips—cool from the kiss of the icon,
Still to think—the cold sweat on your brow . . .
Like the wives of the Streltsy[5], now I come
45   To wait under the Kremlin's gaunt towers.   1935

II

Silent flows the silent Don[6],
Yellow moon looks quietly on,
Cap askew, looks in the room,
Sees a shadow in the gloom.

50   Sees this woman, sick, at home,
Sees this woman, all alone,

---

[4]This refers to Akhmatova's husband who was arrested in the usual fashion
at dawn.

[5]Russian soldiers executed by Peter the Great in view of their wives and
mothers.

[6]The major river of European Russia.

Husband buried[7], then to see
Son arrested[8] . . . Pray for me.

III

No, this is not me, this is somebody else that suffers.
55   I could never face that, and all that has happened:
Let sackcloth and ashes enshroud it,
And see all the lamps are removed . . .
    Night.

IV

You, my mocking one, pet of society,
60   And gay sinner of Tsarskoe Selo[9]:
Had you dreamt, in your sweet notoriety,
Of the future that lay in store—
How you'd stand at the Crosses, three-hundredth
In the queue, each bleak New Year,
65   Hug your precious parcel of comforts,
Melt the ice with your hot bright tears.
There the poplar, used to imprisonment,
Sways aloft. Not a sound. But think
Of the numbers rotting there, innocent . . .

V

70   For seventeen long months my pleas,
My cries have called you home.
I've begged the hangman[10] on my knees,
My son, my dread, my own.
My mind's mixed up for good, and I'm
75   No longer even clear

---

[7] Akhmatova's first husband had been executed back in 1921.

[8] Stalin had a vicious personal hatred for Akhmatova, and he chose to indulge it by arresting her son and keeping him imprisoned in the Gulag Archipelago—the Soviet prison camp system. Akhmatova was forced to beg Stalin for her son's life and even to write flattering verses about him—all to no avail. Stalin's sadism was having free play.

[9] Village where Akhmatova grew up; the Summer Palace of the Tsars was there. In this lyric she mocks her carefree early life and early fame.

[10] i.e., Stalin.

Who's man, who's beast, nor how much time
Before the end draws near.
And only flowers decked with dust,
And censers ringing, footprints thrust
80   Somewhere-nowhere, afar.
And, staring me straight in the eye
And warning me that death is nigh—
One monumental star.   1939

VI

Weeks fly past in light profusion,
85   How to fathom what's been done;
How those long white nights[11], dear son,
Watched you in your cell's seclusion.
How once more they watch you there,
Eyes like hawks' that burn right through you,
90   Speak to you of death, speak to you
Of the lofty cross you bear.   1939

VII

SENTENCE

And the word in stone has fallen heavy
On my breast, which was alive till now.
Never mind—for, mark you, I was ready.
95   I shall get along somehow.
So much to be done before tomorrow:
Crush the memory till no thoughts remain,
Carve a heart in stone, immune to sorrow,
Teach myself to face life once again,—

100   And if not . . . The rustling heat of summer
Fills my window with its festive tone.
I long since foresensed that there would come a
Sunny day like this—and empty home.   Summer, 1939

---

[11]Because it is so far north, Leningrad's summer days are extremely long.

VIII

TO DEATH

You'll come in any case—then why not right away?
105   I'm waiting—life has dragged me under.
I've put the lamp out, left the door to show the way
When you come in your simple wonder.
For that, choose any guise you like: Burst in on me,
A shell with poison-gas container,
110   Or bandit with a heavy weight, creep up on me,
Or poison me with typhus vapor,
Or be a fable, known *ad nauseam*
To everyone denounced in error,
So I may see the top of that blue cap[12], and scan
115   The face of the house-porter, white with terror.
But nothing matters now. The Yenisey[13] swirls by,
The Pole star shines above the torrent.
And the glint of those beloved eyes
Conceals the last, the final horror.   19 August 1939

IX

120   So madness now has wrapped its wings
Round half my soul and plies me, heartless,
With drafts of fiery wine, begins
To lure me toward the vale of darkness.

And I can see that I must now
125   Concede the victory—as I listen,
The dream that dogged my fevered brow
Already seems an outside vision.

---

[12]Worn by the secret police.

[13]A river in Siberia upon which a number of prison camps were located.

And though I go on bended knee
To plead, implore its intercession,
130   There's nothing I may take with me,
It countenances no concession:

Nor yet my son's distracted eyes—
The rock-like suffering rooted in them,
The day the storm broke from clear skies,
135   The hour spent visiting the prison,

Nor yet the kind, cool clasp of hands,
The lime-tree shadows' fitful darting,
The far light call across the land—
The soothing words exchanged on parting.   4 May 1940

X
[CRUCIFIXION]

140   *Weep not for Me, Mother,*
    that I am in the grave

I

The angels hailed that solemn hour and stately,
the heavens dissolved in tongues of fire. And He

Said to the Father; "Why didst Thou forsake Me!"[14]
145   And to His Mother: "Weep thou not for me . . ."

II

Magdalena sobbed, and the disciple
He whom Jesus loved, stood petrified.
But there, where His Mother stood in silence,
No one durst so much as lift their eyes.   1940–1943

---

[14]Matthew 27:46. Christ's moment of abandonment, kenosis, on the Cross.

EPILOGUE

I

150 I've learned how faces droop and then grow hollow,
How fear looks out from underneath the lids,
How cheeks, carved out of suffering and of sorrow,
Take on the lines of rough cuneiform scripts.
How heads of curls, but lately black or ashen,
155 Turn suddenly to silver overnight,
Smiles fade on lips reduced to dread submission,
A hoarse dry laugh stands in for trembling fright.
I pray, not for myself alone, my cry
Goes up for all those with me there—for all,
160 In heart of winter, heat-wave of July,
Who stood beneath that blind, deep-crimson wall.

II

The hour of remembrance is with us again.
I see you, I hear you, I feel you as then:

There's one they scarce dragged to the window, and one
165 Whose days in the land of her forebears are done,

And one tossed her beautiful head back when shown
Her corner, and said; "It's like being back home!"
I'd like to remember each one by her name,
But they took the list, and there's no more remain.

170 I've worked them a funeral shroud from each word
Of pain that escaped them, and I overheard.

I'll think of them everywhere, always, each one.
I shall not forget them in dark days to come.

9. Anna Akhmatova

And should they once silence my mortified lips,
175   Let one hundred millions for whom my voice speaks—

Let *them* take my place, and remember each year
Whenever my day of remembrance draws near.
And should they one day, in this country, agree
To raise a memorial somewhere to me,

180   I'd willingly give my consent to their plan,
But on one condition, which is—that it stand,

Not down by the sea, where I entered this world
(I've cut the last links that once bound us of old),

Not yet by the tree-stump in old Tsarsky Sad,[15]
185   Whose shade seeks me still with disconsolate love,

But here, where they let me stand three hundred hours,
And never so much as unbolted the doors.

For even in death I still fear to forget
The grim Black Marias, their thundering tread,   *cars, secret police*

190   The sickening slam of that loathsome cell-door,
The old woman's howl, like a wounded beast's roar.

And may the snow, melting, well forth clear and strong,
Like tears from my eyelids, unmoving, like bronze,

And may the lone prison-dove coo from afar,
195   And boats travel silently down the Neva.   March 1940

---

[15]The park around the Summer Palace.

10. GEORGE ORWELL

George Orwell, the pen name for Eric Blair (1903–1950), was born in Motihari, Bengal, where his father was employed with the Bengal Civil Service. He was brought to England at an early age for schooling (Eton), but rather than completing his education at the university he served with the Indian imperial police in Burma (1922–1927). He wrote about these experiences in his first novel, Burmese Days. Later he returned to Europe and worked at various jobs (described in Down and Out in Paris and London, 1933) before fighting on the Republican side in the Spanish civil war (see Homage to Catalonia, 1938). Orwell's attitudes toward war and government are reflected in his most famous books: Animal Farm (1945), 1984 (1949), and Shooting an Elephant and Other Essays (1950). In this title essay from the last volume, Orwell reports a "tiny incident" that gave him deeper insight into his own fears and "the real motives for which despotic governments act."

SHOOTING AN ELEPHANT
(1936)

In Moulmein, in lower Burma, I was hated by large numbers of people—the only time in my life that I have been important enough for this to happen to me. I was sub-divisional police officer of the town, and in an aimless, petty kind of way anti-European feeling
5   was very bitter. No one had the guts to raise a riot, but if a European woman went through the bazaars alone somebody would probably spit betel juice over her dress. As a police officer I was an obvious target and was baited whenever it seemed safe to do so. When a nimble Burman tripped me up on the football field and the referee
10 (another Burman) looked the other way, the crowd yelled with hideous laughter. This happened more than once. In the end the sneering yellow faces of young men that met me everywhere, the insults hooted after me when I was at a safe distance, got badly on my nerves. The young Buddhist priests were the worst of all. There
15 were several thousands of them in the town and none of them seemed to have anything to do except stand on street corners and jeer at Europeans.

All this was perplexing and upsetting. For at that time I had

already made up my mind that imperialism was an evil thing and the sooner I chucked up my job and got out of it the better. Theoretically—and secretly, of course—I was all for the Burmese and all against their oppressors, the British. As for the job I was
5   doing, I hated it more bitterly than I can perhaps make clear. In a job like that you see the dirty work of Empire at close quarters. The wretched prisoners huddling in the stinking cages of the lock-ups, the gray, cowed faces of the long-term convicts, the scarred buttocks of the men who had been flogged with bamboos—all these
10   oppressed me with an intolerable sense of guilt. But I could get nothing into perspective. I was young and ill-educated and I had had to think out my problems in the utter silence that is imposed on every Englishman in the East. I did not even know that the British Empire is dying, still less did I know that it is a great deal better
15   than the younger empires that are going to supplant it. All I knew was that I was stuck between my hatred of the empire I served and my rage against the evil-spirited little beasts who tried to make my job impossible. With one part of my mind I thought of the British Raj as an unbreakable tyranny, as something clamped down, *in saec-*
20   *ula saeculorum,* upon the will of prostrate peoples; with another part I thought that the greatest joy in the world would be to drive a bay-onet into a Buddhist priest's guts. Feelings like these are the normal by-products of imperialism; ask any Anglo-Indian official, if you can catch him off duty.
25   One day something happened which in a roundabout way was enlightening. It was a tiny incident in itself, but it gave me a better glimpse than I had had before of the real nature of imperialism—the real motives for which despotic governments act. Early one morn-ing the sub-inspector at a police station the other end of town rang
30   me up on the phone and said that an elephant was ravaging the bazaar. Would I please come and do something about it? I did not know what I could do, but I wanted to see what was happening and I got on to a pony and started out. I took my rifle, an old .44 Winchester and much too small to kill an elephant, but I thought the
35   noise might be useful *in terrorem.* Various Burmans stopped me on the way and told me about the elephant's doings. It was not, of course, a wild elephant, but a tame one which had gone "must." It had been chained up, as tame elephants always are when their attack of "must" is due, but on the previous night it had broken its
40   chain and escaped. Its mahout, the only person who could manage it when it was in that state, had set out in pursuit, but had taken the wrong direction and was now twelve hours' journey away, and in the morning the elephant had suddenly reappeared in the town. The Burmese population had no weapons and were quite helpless
45   against it. It had already destroyed somebody's bamboo hut, killed

a cow and raided some fruit-stalls and devoured the stock; also it had met the municipal rubbish van and, when the driver jumped out and took to his heels, had turned the van over and inflicted violence upon it.

5   The Burmese sub-inspector and some Indian constables were waiting for me in the quarter where the elephant had been seen. It was a very poor quarter, a labyrinth of squalid bamboo huts, thatched with palm-leaf, winding all over a steep hillside. I remember that it was a cloudy, stuffy morning at the beginning of the rains.

10 We began questioning the people as to where the elephant had gone and, as usual, failed to get any definite information. That is invariably the case in the East; a story always sounds clear enough at a distance, but the nearer you get to the scene of events the vaguer it becomes. Some of the people said that the elephant had gone in one

15 direction, some said that he had gone in another, some professed not even to have heard of any elephant. I had almost made up my mind that the whole story was a pack of lies, when we heard yells a little distance away. There was a loud, scandalized cry of "Go away, child! Go away this instant!" and an old woman with a switch in her

20 hand came round the corner of a hut, violently shooing away a crowd of naked children. Some more women followed, clicking their tongues and exclaiming; evidently there was something that the children ought not to have seen. I rounded the hut and saw a man's dead body sprawling in the mud. He was an Indian, a black

25 Dravidian coolie, almost naked, and he could not have been dead many minutes. The people said that the elephant had come suddenly upon him round the corner of the hut, caught him with its trunk, put its foot on his back and ground him into the earth. This was the rainy season and the ground was soft, and his face had

30 scored a trench a foot deep and a couple of yards long. He was lying on his belly with arms crucified and head sharply twisted to one side. His face was coated with mud, the eyes wide open, the teeth bared and grinning with an expression of unendurable agony. (Never tell me, by the way, that the dead look peaceful. Most of the

35 corpses I have seen looked devilish.) The friction of the great beast's foot had stripped the skin from his back as neatly as one skins a rabbit. As soon as I saw the dead man I sent an orderly to a friend's house nearby to borrow an elephant rifle. I had already sent back the pony, not wanting it to go mad with fright and throw me if it

40 smelled the elephant.

    The orderly came back in a few minutes with a rifle and five cartridges, and meanwhile some Burmans had arrived and told us that the elephant was in the paddy fields below, only a few hundred yards away. As I started forward practically the whole population

45 of the quarter flocked out of the houses and followed me. They had

seen the rifle and were all shouting excitedly that I was going to shoot the elephant. They had not shown much interest in the elephant when he was merely ravaging their homes, but it was different now that he was going to be shot. It was a bit of fun to them, as
5 it would be to an English crowd; besides they wanted the meat. It made me vaguely uneasy. I had no intention of shooting the elephant—I had merely sent for the rifle to defend myself if necessary—and it is always unnerving to have a crowd following you. I marched down the hill, looking and feeling a fool, with the rifle
10 over my shoulder and an ever-growing army of people jostling at my heels. At the bottom, when you got away from the huts, there was a metalled road and beyond that a miry waste of paddy fields a thousand yards across, not yet ploughed but soggy from the first rains and dotted with coarse grass. The elephant was standing
15 eighty yards from the road, his left side toward us. He took not the slightest notice of the crowd's approach. He was tearing up bunches of grass, beating them against his knees to clean them, and stuffing them into his mouth.

I had halted on the road. As soon as I saw the elephant I knew
20 with perfect certainty that I ought not to shoot him. It is a serious matter to shoot a working elephant—it is comparable to destroying a huge and costly piece of machinery—and obviously one ought not to do it if it can possibly be avoided. And at that distance, peacefully eating, the elephant looked no more dangerous than a cow. I
25 thought then and I think now that his attack of "must" was already passing off; in which case he would merely wander harmlessly about until the mahout came back and caught him. Moreover, I did not in the least want to shoot him. I decided that I would watch him for a little while to make sure that he did not turn savage again, and
30 then go home.

But at that moment I glanced round at the crowd that had followed me. It was an immense crowd, two thousand at the least and growing every minute. It blocked the road for a long distance on either side. I looked at the sea of yellow faces above the garish
35 clothes—faces all happy and excited over this bit of fun, all certain that the elephant was going to be shot. They were watching me as they would watch a conjurer about to perform a trick. They did not like me, but with the magical rifle in my hands I was momentarily worth watching. And suddenly I realized that I should have to
40 shoot the elephant after all. The people expected it of me and I had got to do it; I could feel their two thousand wills pressing me forward, irresistibly. And it was at this moment, as I stood there with the rifle in my hands, that I first grasped the hollowness, the futility of the white man's dominion in the East. Here was I, the white
45 man with his gun, standing in front of the unarmed native crowd—

seemingly the leading actor of the piece; but in reality I was only an
absurd puppet pushed to and fro by the will of those yellow faces
behind. I perceived in this moment that when the white man turns
tyrant it is his own freedom that he destroys. He becomes a sort of
5   hollow, posing dummy, the conventionalized figure of a sahib. For
it is the condition of his rule that he shall spend his life in trying to
impress the "natives," and so in every crisis he has got to do what
the "natives" expect of him. He wears a mask, and his face grows to
fit it. I had got to shoot the elephant. I had committed myself to
10 doing it when I sent for the rifle. A sahib has got to act like a sahib;
he has got to appear resolute, to know his own mind and do definite things. To come all that way, rifle in hand, with two thousand
people marching at my heels, and then to trail feebly away, having
done nothing—no, that was impossible. The crowd would laugh at
15 me. And my whole life, every white man's life in the East, was one
long struggle not to be laughed at.

But I did not want to shoot the elephant. I watched him beating
his bunch of grass against his knees with that preoccupied grand-
motherly air that elephants have. It seemed to me that it would be
20 murder to shoot him. At that age I was not squeamish about killing
animals, but I had never shot an elephant and never wanted to.
(Somehow it always seems worse to kill a *large* animal.) Besides,
there was the beast's owner to be considered. Alive, the elephant
was worth at least a hundred pounds; dead, he would only be
25 worth the value of his tusks, five pounds, possibly. But I had got to
act quickly. I turned to some experienced-looking Burmans who
had been there when we arrived, and asked them how the elephant
had been behaving. They all said the same thing: he took no notice
of you if you left him alone, but he might charge if you went too
30 close to him.

It was perfectly clear to me what I ought to do. I ought to walk
up to within, say twenty-five yards of the elephant and test his
behavior. If he charged, I could shoot; if he took no notice of me, it
would be safe to leave him until the mahout came back. But also I
35 knew that I was going to do no such thing. I was a poor shot with a
rifle and the ground was soft mud into which one would sink at
every step. If the elephant charged and I missed him, I should have
about as much chance as a toad under a steam-roller. But even then
I was not thinking particularly of my own skin, only of the watch-
40 ful yellow faces behind. For at that moment, with the crowd watching me, I was not afraid in the ordinary sense, as I would have been
if I had been alone. A white man mustn't be frightened in front of
"natives"; and so, in general, he isn't frightened. The sole thought
in my mind was that if anything went wrong those two thousand
45 Burmans would see me pursued, caught, trampled on, and reduced

to a grinning corpse like that Indian up the hill. And if that happened it was quite probable that some of them would laugh. That would never do. There was only one alternative. I shoved the cartridges into the magazine and lay down on the road to get a better
5   aim.

The crowd grew very still, and a deep, low, happy sigh, as of people who see the theater curtain go up at last, breathed from innumerable throats. They were going to have their bit of fun after all. The rifle was a beautiful German thing with cross-hair sights. I
10   did not then know that in shooting an elephant one should shoot to cut an imaginary bar running from ear-hole to ear-hole. I ought, therefore, as the elephant was sideways on, to have aimed straight at his ear-hole; actually I aimed several inches in front of this, thinking the brain would be further forward.
15   When I pulled the trigger I did not hear the bang or feel the kick—one never does when a shot goes home—but I heard the devilish roar of glee that went up from the crowd. In that instant, in too short a time, one would have thought, even for the bullet to get there, a mysterious, terrible change had come over the elephant. He
20   neither stirred, nor fell, but every line of his body had altered. He looked suddenly stricken, shrunken, immensely old, as though the frightful impact of the bullet had paralyzed him without knocking him down. At last, after what seemed a long time—it might have been five seconds, I dare say—he sagged flabbily to his knees. His
25   mouth slobbered. An enormous senility seemed to have settled upon him. One could have imagined him thousands of years old. I fired again into the same spot. At the second shot he did not collapse but climbed with desperate slowness to his feet and stood weakly upright, with legs sagging and head drooping. I fired a third
30   time. That was the shot that did for him. You could see the agony of it jolt his whole body and knock the last remnant of strength from his legs. But in falling he seemed for a moment to rise, for as his hind legs collapsed beneath him he seemed to tower upward like a huge rock toppling, his trunk reaching skyward like a tree. He
35   trumpeted, for the first and only time. And then down he came, his belly toward me, with a crash that seemed to shake the ground even where I lay.

I got up. The Burmans were already racing past me across the mud. It was obvious that the elephant would never rise again, but
40   he was not dead. He was breathing very rhythmically with long rattling gasps, his great mound of a side painfully rising and falling. His mouth was wide open—I could see far down into caverns of pale pink throat. I waited a long time for him to die, but his breathing did not weaken. Finally I fired my two remaining shots into the
45   spot where I thought his heart must be. The thick blood welled out

of him like red velvet, but still he did not die. His body did not even
jerk when the shots hit him, the tortured breathing continued without a pause. He was dying, very slowly and in great agony, but in
some world remote from me where not even a bullet could damage
5 him further. I felt that I had got to put an end to that dreadful noise.
It seemed dreadful to see the great beast lying there, powerless to
move and yet powerless to die, and not even to be able to finish
him. I sent back for my small rifle and poured shot after shot into
his heart and down his throat. They seemed to make no impression.
10 The tortured gasps continued as steadily as the ticking of a clock.

In the end I could not stand it any longer and went away. I
heard later that it took him half an hour to die. Burmans were bringing dahs and baskets even before I left, and I was told they had
stripped his body almost to the bones by the afternoon.
15 Afterward, of course, there were endless discussions about the
shooting of the elephant. The owner was furious, but he was only
an Indian and could no nothing. Besides, legally I had done the
right thing, for a mad elephant has to be killed, like a mad dog, if its
owner fails to control it. Among the Europeans opinion was divid-
20 ed. The older men said I was right, the younger men said it was a
damn shame to shoot an elephant for killing a coolie, because an
elephant was worth more than any damn Coringhee coolie. And
afterward I was very glad that the coolie had been killed; it put me
legally in the right and it gave me a sufficient pretext for shooting
25 the elephant. I often wondered whether any of the others grasped
that I had done it solely to avoid looking a fool.

POLITICS AND THE ENGLISH LANGUAGE

Most people who bother with the matter at all would admit that the English language is in a bad way, but it is generally assumed that we cannot by conscious action do anything about it. Our civilization is decadent and our language—so the argument
5   runs—must inevitably share in the general collapse. It follows that any struggle against the abuse of language is a sentimental archaism, like preferring candles to electric light or hansom cabs to aeroplanes. Underneath this lies the half-conscious belief that language is a natural growth and not an instrument which we shape
10   for our own purposes.

Now, it is clear that the decline of a language must ultimately have political and economic causes: it is not due simply to the bad influence of this or that individual writer. But an effect can become a cause, reinforcing the original cause and producing the same
15   effect in an intensified form, and so on indefinitely. A man may take to drink because he feels himself to be a failure, and then fail all the more completely because he drinks. It is rather the same thing that is happening to the English language. It becomes ugly and inaccurate because our thoughts are foolish, but the slovenliness of our
20   language makes it easier for us to have foolish thoughts. The point is that the process is reversible. Modern English, especially written English, is full of bad habits which spread by imitation and which can be avoided if one is willing to take the necessary trouble. If one gets rid of these habits one can think more clearly, and to think
25   clearly is a necessary first step towards political regeneration: so that the fight against bad English is not frivolous and is not the exclusive concern of professional writers. I will come back to this presently, and I hope that by that time the meaning of what I have said here will have become clearer. Meanwhile, here are five speci-
30   mens of the English language as it is now habitually written.

These five passages have not been picked out because they are especially bad—I could have quoted far worse if I had chosen—but because they illustrate various of the mental vices from which we now suffer. They are a little below the average, but are fairly repre-
35   sentative samples. I number them so that I can refer back to them when necessary:

(1) I am not, indeed, sure whether it is not true to say that the Milton who once seemed not unlike a seventeenth-century Shelley had not become, out of an experience ever more bitter in each year,

more alien [*sic*] to the founder of that Jesuit sect which nothing
could induce him to tolerate.

Professor Harold Laski
(Essay in *Freedom of Expression*).

5   (2) Above all, we cannot play ducks and drakes with a native battery of idioms which prescribes such egregious collocations of voca-
bles as the Basic *put up with* for *tolerate* or put *at a* loss for *bewilder*.

Professor Lancelot Hogben *(Interglossa)*.

(3) On the one side we have the free personality: by definition
10   it is not neurotic, for it has neither conflict nor dream. Its desires,
such as they are, are transparent, for they are just what institution-
al approval keeps in the forefront of consciousness; another institu-
tional pattern would alter their number and intensity; there is little
in them that is natural, irreducible, or culturally dangerous. But on
15   *the other side*, the social bond itself is nothing but the mutual reflection of these self-secure integrities. Recall the definition of love. Is
not this the very picture of a small academic? Where is there a place
in this hall of mirrors for either personality or fraternity?

Essay on psychology in *Politics* (New York).

20   (4) All the "best people" from the gentlemen's clubs, and all the
frantic fascist captains, united in common hatred of Socialism and
bestial horror of the rising tide of the mass revolutionary movement, have turned to acts of provocation, to foul incendiarism, to
medieval legends of poisoned wells, to legalize their own destruc-
25   tion of proletarian organizations, and rouse the agitated petty-bour-
geoisie to chauvinistic fervor on behalf of the fight against the revolutionary way out of the crisis.

Communist pamphlet.

(5) If a new spirit is to be Infused into this old country, there is
30   one thorny and contentious reform which must be tackled, and that
is the humanization and galvanization of the B.B.C. Timidity here
will bespeak canker and atrophy of the soul. The heart of Britain
may be sound and of strong beat, for instance, but the British lion's
roar at present is like that of Bottom in Shakespeare's *Midsummer
35   Night's Dream*—as gentle as any sucking dove. A virile new Britain
cannot continue indefinitely to be traduced in the eyes, or rather
ears, of the world by the effete languors of Langharn Place, brazen-
ly masquerading as "standard English:" When the Voice of Britain
is heard at nine o'clock, better far and infinitely less ludicrous to
40   hear aitches honestly dropped than the present priggish, inflated,

inhibited, school-ma'amish arch braying of blameless bashful mewing maidens!

Letter in Tribune

5   Each of these passages has faults of its own, but, quite apart from avoidable ugliness, two qualities are common to all of them. The first is staleness, of imagery; the other is lack of precision. The writer either has a meaning and cannot express it, or he inadvertently says something else, or he is almost indifferent as to whether his words mean anything or not. This mixture of vagueness and

10 sheer incompetence is the most marked characteristic of modern English prose, and especially of any kind of political writing. As soon as certain topics are raised, the concrete melts into the abstract and no one seems able to think of turns of speech that are not hackneyed: prose consists less and less of *words* chosen for the sake of

15 their meaning, and more and more of *phrases* tacked together like the sections of a prefabricated hen-house. I list below, with notes and examples, various of the tricks by means of which the work of prose-construction is habitually dodged:

DYING METAPHORS. A newly invented metaphor assists

20 thought by evoking a visual image, while on the other hand a metaphor which is technically "dead" (e.g. *iron resolution)* has in effect reverted to being an ordinary word and can generally be used without loss of vividness. But in between these two classes there is a huge dump of worn-out metaphors which have lost all evocative

25 power and are merely used because they save people the trouble of inventing phrases for themselves. Examples are: *Ring the changes on, take up the cudgels for, toe the line, ride roughshod over, stand shoulder to shoulder with, play into the hands of, no axe to grind, grist to the mill, fishing in troubled waters, on the order of the day, Achilles' heel, swan*

30 *song, hotbed.* Many of these are used without knowledge of their meaning (what is a "rift," for instance?), and incompatible metaphors are frequently mixed, a sure sign that the writer is not interested in what he is saying. Some metaphors now current have been twisted out of their original meaning without those who use

35 them even being aware of the fact. For example, *toe the line* is sometimes written *tow the line.* Another example is *the hammer and the anvil,* now always used with the implication that the anvil gets the worst of it. In real life it is always the anvil that breaks the hammer, never the other way about: a writer who stopped to think what he

40 was saying would be aware of this, and would avoid perverting the original phrase.

OPERATORS or VERBAL FALSE LIMBS. These save the trouble of picking out appropriate verbs and nouns, and at the same time pad each sentence with extra syllables which give it an appear-

ance of symmetry. Characteristic phrases are *render inoperative, mili-*
tate against, make contact with, be subjected to, give rise to, give grounds
for, have the effect of, play a leading part (role) in, make itself felt, take
effect, exhibit a tendency to, serve the purpose of, etc., etc. The keynote is
5   the elimination of simple verbs. Instead of being a single word, such
as *break, stop, spoil, mend, kill,* a verb becomes a *phrase,* made up of a
noun or adjective tacked on to some general-purposes verb such as
prove, serve, form, play, render. In addition, the passive voice is wherever possible used in preference to the active, and noun construc-
10   tions are used instead of gerunds *(by examination of* instead of *by*
examining). The range of verbs is further cut down by means of the
-ize and *de-* formations, and the banal statements are given an
appearance of profundity by means of the *not un-* formation. Simple
conjunctions and prepositions are replaced by such phrases as *with*
15   *respect to, having regard to, the fact that, by dint of, in view* of, *in the*
interests of, on the hypothesis that, and the ends of sentences are saved
from anticlimax by such resounding commonplaces as *greatly to be*
desired, cannot be left out of account, a development to be expected in the
near future, deserving of serious consideration, brought to a satisfactory
20   *conclusion,* and so on and so forth.
      PRETENTIOUS DICTION. Words like *phenomenon, element,*
individual (as noun), *objective, categorical, effective, virtual, basic, pri-*
mary, promote, constitute, exhibit, exploit, utilize, eliminate, liquidate are
used to dress up simple statement and give an air of scientific
25   impartiality to biased judgments. Adjectives like *epochmaking, epic,*
historic, unforgettable, triumphant, age-old, inevitable, inexorable, verita-
ble, are used *to* dignify the sordid processes of international politics,
while writing that aims at glorifying war usually takes on an archa-
ic color, its characteristic words being: *realm, throne, chariot, mailed*
30   *fist, trident, sword, shield, buckler, banner, jackboot, clarion.* Foreign
words and expressions such as *cul de sac, ancien régime, deus ex*
machina, mutatis mutandis, status quo, gleichschaltung, weltanschauung,
are used to give an air of culture and elegance. Except for the useful
abbreviations *i.e., e.g.,* and *etc.,* there is no real need for any of the
35   hundreds of foreign phrases now current in English. Bad writers,
and especially scientific, political and sociological writers, are nearly always haunted by the notion that Latin or Greek words are
grander than Saxon ones, and unnecessary words like *expedite, ame-*
liorate, predict, extraneous, deracinated, clandestine, subaqueous and
hundreds of others constantly gain ground from their Anglo-Saxon
opposite numbers.[1] The jargon peculiar to Marxist writing *(hyena,*

---

[1]An interesting illustration of this is the way in which the English flower
names which were in use till very recently are being ousted by Greek ones,
snapdragon becoming *antirrhinum, forget-me-not* becoming *myosotis,* etc. It is

hangman, cannibal, petty bourgeois, these gentry, lacquey, flunkey, mad dog, White Guard, etc.) consists largely of words and phrases translated from Russian, German or French; but the normal way of coining a new word is to use a Latin or Greek root with the appropriate
5   affix and, where necessary, the *-ize* formation. It is often easier to make up words of this kind *(deregionalize, impermissible, extramarital, non-fragmentary* and so forth) than to think up the English words that will cover one's meaning. The result, in general, is an increase in slovenliness and vagueness.
10   MEANINGLESS WORDS. In certain kinds of writing, particularly in art criticism and literary criticism, it is normal to come across long passages which are almost completely lacking in meaning.[2] Words like *romantic, plastic, values, human, dead, sentimental, natural, vitality,* as used in art criticism, are strictly meaningless, in
15 the sense that they not only do not point to any discoverable object, but are hardly ever expected to do so by the reader. When one critic writes, "The outstanding feature of Mr. X's work is its living quality," while another writes, "The immediately striking thing about Mr. Vs work is its peculiar deadness," the reader accepts this as a
20 simple difference of opinion. If words like *black* and *white* were involved, instead of the jargon words *dead* and *living,* he would see at once that language was being used in an improper way. Many political words are similarly abused. The word *Fascism* has now no meaning except in so far as it signifies "something not desirable."
25 The words *democracy, socialism, freedom, patriotic, realistic, justice,* have each of them several different meanings which cannot be reconciled with one another. In the case of a word like *democracy,* not only is there no agreed definition, but the attempt to make one is resisted from all sides. It is almost universally felt that when we call
30 a country democratic we are praising it: consequently the defenders of every kind of régime claim that it is a democracy, and fear that they might have to stop using the word if it were tied down to any one meaning. Words of this kind are often used in a consciously dishonest way. That is, the person who uses them has his own private
35 definition, but allows his hearer to think he means something quite

---

hard to see any practical reason for this change of fashion: it is probably due to an instinctive turning-away from the more homely word and a vague feeling that the Greek word is scientific.

[2]Example: "Comfort's catholicity of perception and image, strangely Whitmanesque in range, almost the exact opposite in aesthetic compulsion, continues to evoke that trembling atmospheric accumulative hinting at a cruel, an inexorably serene timelessness. . . . Wrey Gardiner scores by aiming at simple bull's-eyes with precision. Only they are not so simple, and through this contented sadness runs more than the surface bitter-sweet of resignation." *(Poetry Quarterly.)*

different. Statements like *Marshal Pétain was a true patriot, The Soviet Press is the freest in the world, The Catholic Church is opposed to persecution,* are almost always made with intent to deceive. Other words used in variable meanings, in most cases more or less dishonestly, are:
5   *class, totalitarian, science, progressive, reactionary, bourgeois, equality.*

Now that I have made this catalogue of swindles and perversions, let me give another example of the kind of writing that they lead to. This time it must of its nature be an imaginary one. I am going to translate a passage of good English into modern English of
10   the worst sort. Here is a well-known verse from *Ecclesiastes:*

> I returned and saw under the sun, that the race is not to the swift, nor the battle to the strong, neither yet bread to the wise, nor yet riches to men of understanding, nor yet favour to men of skill; but time and chance happeneth to them all.

15   Here it is in modern English:

> Objective consideration of contemporary phenomena compels the conclusion that success or failure in competitive activities exhibits no tendency to be commensurate with innate capacity, but that a considerable element of the unpredicable must
20   invariably be taken into account.

This is a parody, but not a very gross one. Exhibit (3), above, for instance, contains several patches of the same kind of English. It will be seen that I have not made a full translation. The beginning and ending of the sentence follow the original meaning fairly close-
25   ly, but in the middle the concrete illustrations—race, battle, bread— dissolve into the vague phrase "success or failure in competitive activities." This had to be so, because no modern writer of the kind I am discussing—no one capable of using phrases like "objective consideration of contemporary phenomena"—would ever tabulate
30   his thoughts in that precise and detailed way. The whole tendency of modern prose is away from concreteness. Now analyse these two sentences a little more closely. The first contains forty-nine words but only sixty syllables, and all its words are those of everyday life. The second contains thirty-eight words of ninety syllables: eighteen
35   of its words are from Latin roots, and one from Greek. The first sentence contains six vivid images, and only one phrase ("time and chance") that could be called vague. The second contains not a single fresh, arresting phrase, and in spite of its ninety syllables it gives only a shortened version of the meaning contained in the first. Yet
40   without a doubt it is the second kind of sentence that is gaining ground in modern English. I do not want to exaggerate. This kind

of writing is not yet universal, and outcrops of simplicity will occur here and there in the worst-written page. Still, if you or I were told to write a few lines on the uncertainty of human fortunes, we should probably come much nearer to my imaginary sentence than
5 to the one from *Ecclesiastes.*

As I have tried to show, modern writing at its worst does not consist in picking out words for the sake of their meaning and inventing images in order to make the meaning clearer. It consists in gumming together long strips of words which have already been set
10 in order by someone else, and making the results presentable by sheer humbug. The attraction of this way of writing is that it is easy. It is easier—even quicker, once you have the habit—to say *In my opinion it is not an unjustifiable assumption that* than to say I *think.* If you use readymade phrases, you not only don't have to hunt about
15 for words; you also don't have to bother with the rhythms of your sentences, since these phrases are generally so arranged as to be more or less euphonious. When you are composing in a hurry— when you are dictating to a stenographer, for instance, or making a public speech—it is natural to fall into a pretentious, Latinized style.
20 Tags like a *consideration which we should do well to bear in mind* or *a conclusion to which all of us would readily assent* will save many a sentence from coming down with a bump. By using stale metaphors, similes and idioms, you save much mental effort, at the cost of leaving your meaning vague, not only for your reader but for yourself.
25 This is the significance of mixed metaphors. The sole aim of a metaphor is to call up a visual image. When these images clash—as in *The Fascist octopus has sung its swan song, the jackboot is thrown into the melting* pot—it can be taken as certain that the writer is not seeing a mental image of the objects he is naming; in other words he is
30 not really thinking. Look again at the examples I gave at the beginning of this essay. Professor Laski (1) uses five negatives in fifty-three words. One of these is superfluous, making nonsense of the whole passage, and in addition there is the slip *alien* for akin, making further nonsense, and several avoidable pieces of clumsiness
35 which increase the general vagueness. Professor Hogben (2) plays ducks and drakes with a battery which is able to write prescriptions, and, while disapproving of the everyday phrase *put up with,* is unwilling to look *egregious* up in the dictionary and see what it means; (3), if one takes an uncharitable attitude towards it, is sim-
40 ply meaningless: probably one could work out its intended meaning by reading the whole of the article in which it occurs. In (4), the writer knows more or less what he wants to say, but an accumulation of stale phrases chokes him like tea leaves blocking a sink. In (5), words and meaning have almost parted company. People who
45 write in this manner usually have a general emotional meaning—

they dislike one thing and want to express solidarity with another—
but they are not interested in the detail of what they are saying. A
scrupulous writer, in every sentence that he writes, will ask himself
at least four questions, thus: What am I trying to say? What words
5 will express it? What image or idiom will make it clearer? Is this
image fresh enough to have an effect? And he will probably ask
himself two more: Could I put it more shortly? Have I said anything
that is avoidably ugly? But you are not obliged to go to all this trouble. You can shirk it by simply throwing your mind open and letting
10 the ready-made phrases come crowding in. They will construct
your sentences for you—even think your thoughts for you, to a certain extent—and at need they will perform the important service of
partially concealing your meaning even from yourself. It is at this
point that the special connection between politics and the debase-
15 ment of language becomes clear.

In our time it is broadly true that political writing is bad writing. Where it is not true, it will generally be found that the writer is
some kind of rebel, expressing his private opinions and not a "party
line." Orthodoxy, of whatever color, seems to demand a lifeless, imi-
20 tative style. The political dialects to be found in pamphlets, leading
articles, manifestos, White Papers and the speeches of under-secre-
taries do, of course, vary from party to party, but they are all alike
in that one almost never finds in them a fresh, vivid, home-made
turn of speech. When one watches some tired hack on the platform
25 mechanically repeating the familiar phrases—*bestial atrocities, iron
heel, bloodstained tyranny, free peoples of the world, stand shoulder to
shoulder*—one often has a curious feeling that one is not watching a
live human being but some kind of dummy: a feeling which suddenly becomes stronger at moments when the light catches the
30 speakers spectacles and turns them into blank discs which seem to
have no eyes behind them. And this is not altogether fanciful. A
speaker who uses that kind of phraseology has gone some distance
towards turning himself into a machine. The appropriate noises are
coming out of his larynx, but his brain is not involved as it would
35 be if he were choosing his words for himself. If the speech he is
making is one that he is accustomed to make over and over again,
he may be almost unconscious of what he is saying, as one is when
one utters the responses in church. And this reduced state of consciousness, if not indispensable, is at any rate favorable to political
40 conformity.

In our time, political speech and writing are largely the defence
of the indefensible. Things like the continuance of British rule in
India, the Russian purges and deportations, the dropping of the
atom bombs on Japan, can indeed be defended, but only by argu-
45 ments which are too brutal for most people to face, and which do

not square with the professed aims of political parties. Thus political language has to consist largely of euphemism, question-begging and sheer cloudy vagueness. Defenceless villages are bombarded from the air, the inhabitants driven out into the countryside, the cat
5 tle machine-gunned, the huts set on fire with incendiary bullets: this is called *pacification*. Millions of peasants are robbed of their farms and sent trudging along the roads with no more than they can carry: this is called *transfer of population* or *rectification of frontiers*. People are imprisoned for years without trial, or shot in the back of the
10 neck or sent to die of scurvy in Arctic lumber camps: this is called *elimination of unreliable elements*. Such phraseology is needed if one wants to name things without calling up mental pictures of them. Consider for instance some comfortable English professor defending Russian totalitarianism. He cannot say outright, "I believe in killing off your opponents when you can get good results by doing
15 so." Probably, therefore, he will say something like this:

> While freely conceding that the Soviet régime exhibits certain features which the humanitarian may be inclined to deplore, we must, I think, agree that a certain curtailment of the right to political opposition is an unavoidable concomitant of transitional periods, and that the rigors which the Russian people
> 20 have been called upon to undergo have been amply justified in the sphere of concrete achievement.

The inflated style is itself a kind of euphemism. A mass of Latin words falls upon the facts like soft snow, blurring the outlines and covering up all the details. The great enemy of clear language is
25 insincerity. When there is a gap between one's real and one's declared aims, one turns as it were instinctively to long words and exhausted idioms, like a cuttlefish squirting out ink. In our age there is no such thing as "keeping out of politics." All issues are political issues, and politics itself is a mass of lies, evasions, folly,
30 hatred and schizophrenia. When the general atmosphere is bad, language must suffer. I should expect to find—this is a guess which I have not sufficient knowledge to verify—that the German, Russian and Italian languages have all deteriorated in the last ten or fifteen years, as a result of dictatorship.
35 But if thought corrupts language, language can also corrupt thought. A bad usage can spread by tradition and imitation, even among people who should and do know better. The debased language that I have been discussing is in some ways very convenient. Phrases like *a not unjustifiable assumption, leaves much to be desired,*
40 *would serve no good purpose, a consideration which we should do well to bear in mind,* are a continuous temptation, a packet of aspirins

always at one's elbow. Look back through this essay, and for certain you will find that I have again and again committed the very faults I am protesting against. By this morning's post I have received a pamphlet dealing with conditions in Germany. The author tells me
5 that he "felt impelled" to write it. I open it at random, and here is almost the first sentence that I see: "[The Allies] have an opportunity not only of achieving a radical transformation of Germany's social and political structure in such a way as to avoid a nationalistic reaction in Germany itself, but at the same time of laying the
10 foundations of a cooperative and unified Europe." You see, he "feels impelled" to write—feels, presumably, that he has something new to say—and yet his words, like cavalry horses answering the bugle, group themselves automatically into the familiar dreary pattern. This invasion of one's mind by ready-made phrases *(lay the founda-*
15 *tions, achieve a radical transformation)* can only be prevented if one is constantly on guard against them, and every such phrase anaesthetizes a portion of one's brain.

I said earlier that the decadence of our language is probably curable. Those who deny this would argue, if they produced an
20 argument at all, that language merely reflects existing social conditions, and that we cannot influence its development by any direct tinkering with words and constructions. So far as the general tone or spirit of a language goes, this may be true, but it is not true in detail. Silly words and expressions have often disappeared, not
25 through any evolutionary process but owing to the conscious action of a minority. Two recent examples were *explore every avenue* and *leave no stone unturned*, which were killed by the jeers of a few journalists. There is a long list of flyblown metaphors which could similarly be got rid of if enough people would interest themselves in
30 the job; and it should also be possible to laugh the *not un-*formation out of existence,[3] to reduce the amount of Latin and Greek in the average sentence, to drive out foreign phrases and strayed scientific words, and, in general, to make pretentiousness unfashionable. But all these are minor points. The defence of the English language
35 implies more than this, and perhaps it is best to start by saying what it does *not* imply.

To begin with it has nothing to do with archaism, with the salvaging of obsolete words and turns of speech, or with the setting up of a "standard English!" which must never be departed from. On
40 the contrary, it is especially concerned with the scrapping of every

---

[3]One can cure oneself of the not un- formation by memorizing this sentence: *A not unblack dog was chasing a not unsmall rabbit across a not ungreen field.*

word or idiom which has outworn its usefulness. It has nothing to
do with correct grammar and syntax, which are of no importance so
long as one makes one's meaning clear, or with the avoidance of
Americanisms, or with having what is called a "good prose style."
On the other hand it is not concerned with fake simplicity and the
attempt to make written English colloquial. Nor does it even imply
in every case preferring the Saxon word to the Latin one, though it
does imply using the fewest and shortest words that will cover ones
meaning. What is above all needed is to let the meaning choose the
word, and not the other way about. In prose, the worst thing one
can do with words is to surrender to them. When you think of a concrete object, you think wordlessly, and then, if you want to describe
the thing you have been visualizing you probably hunt about till
you find the exact words that seem to fit it. When you think of
something abstract you are more inclined to use words from the
start, and unless you make a conscious effort to prevent it, the existing dialect will come rushing in and do the job for you, at the
expense of blurring or even changing your meaning. Probably it is
better to put off using words as long as possible and get one's meaning as clear as one can through pictures or sensations. Afterwards
one can choose—not simply *accept*—the phrases that will best cover
the meaning, and then switch round and decide what impression
one's words are likely to make on another person. This last effort of
the mind cuts out all stale or mixed images, all prefabricated phrases, needless repetitions, and humbug and vagueness generally. But
one can often be in doubt about the effect of a word or a phrase, and
one needs rules that one can rely on when instinct fails. I think, the
following rules will cover most cases:

> (i) Never use a metaphor, simile or other figure of speech
> which you are used to seeing in print.
> (ii) Never use a long word where a short one will do.
> (iii) If it is possible to cut a word out, always cut it out.
> (iv) Never use the passive where you can use the active.
> (v) Never use a foreign phrase, a scientific word or a jargon
> word if you can think of an everyday English equivalent.
> (vi) Break any of these rules sooner than say anything outright
> barbarous.

These rules sound elementary, and so they are, but they
demand a deep change in attitude in anyone who has grown used
to writing in the style now fashionable. One could keep all of them
and still write bad English, but one could not write the kind of stuff
that I quoted in those five specimens at the beginning of this article.
I have not here been considering the literary use of language,

but merely language as an instrument for expressing and not for concealing or preventing thought. Stuart Chase and others have come near to claiming that all abstract words are meaningless, and have used this as a pretext for advocating a kind of political qui-

5   etism. Since you don't know what Fascism is, how can you struggle against Fascism? One need not swallow such absurdities as this, but one ought to recognize that the present political chaos is connected with the decay of language, and that one can probably bring about some improvement by starting at the verbal end. If you simplify

10 your English, you are freed from the worst follies of orthodoxy. You cannot speak any of the necessary dialects, and when you make a stupid remark its stupidity will be obvious, even to yourself. Political language—and with variations this is true of all political parties, from Conservatives to Anarchists—is designed to make lies

15 sound truthful and murder respectable, and to give an appearance of solidity to pure wind. One cannot change this all in a moment, but one can at least change one's own habits, and from time to time one can even, if one jeers loudly enough, send some worn-out and useless phrase—some *jackboot, Achilles' heel, hotbed, melting pot, acid*

20 *test, veritable inferno* or other lump of verbal refuse—into the dustbin where it belongs.

(1946)

11. JEAN-PAUL SARTRE

Sartre (1905–1980) was the chief voice of existentialist philosophy in its atheistic mode, and from the end of World War II until his death he was probably the most famous philosopher in the world. His central concern was with human freedom, expressed most powerfully in choice. We are the choices we have made, Sartre said: "existence precedes essence." And it is no good deciding not to choose: such a decision is itself a choice and one made in "bad faith." Sartre was influential, in part, because he complemented his formal philosophical work with novels and plays, thereby reaching a wide audience. Sartre's existentialism became confused with Cold War Marxism. During the student riots of 1968, Sartre was left undisturbed by the police even though he was publicly distributing incendiary Maoist material because, as French President Charles de Gaulle explained, "One does not arrest Voltaire."

NO EXIT

A Play in One Act
(1945)

CHARACTERS IN THE PLAY
VALET
ESTELLE
GARCIN
INEZ

Huis Clos (No Exit) was presented for the first time at the Théâtre du Vieux-Colombier, Paris, in May 1944.
SCENE—*A drawing-room in Second Empire style. A massive bronze ornament stands on the mantelpiece.*

GARCIN. [*Enters accompanied by the* ROOM-VALET, *and glances around him*] Hm! So here we are?
VALET. Yes, Mr. Garcin.
GARCIN. And this is what it looks like?
5   VALET. Yes.
GARCIN. Second Empire furniture, I observe. . . . Well, well, I dare

say one gets used to it in time.

VALET. Some do. Some don't.

GARCIN. Are all the other rooms like this one?

5 VALET. How could they be? We cater for all sorts: Chinamen and Indians, for instance. What use would they have for a Second Empire chair?

GARCIN. And what use do you suppose *I* have for one? Do you know who I was? . . . Oh, well, it's no great matter. And, to tell the truth, I had quite a habit of living among furniture that I

10 didn't relish, and in false positions. I'd even come to like it. A false position in a Louis-Philippe dining-room—you know the style?—well, that had its points, you know. Bogus in bogus, so to speak.

VALET. And you'll find that living in a Second Empire drawing-

15 room has its points.

GARCIN. Really? . . . Yes, yes, I dare say. . . . [*He takes another look around.*] Still, I certainly didn't expect—this! You know what they tell us down there?

VALET. What about?

20 GARCIN. About [*Makes a sweeping gesture*] this—er—residence.

VALET. Really, sir, how could you believe such cock-and-bull stories? Told by people who'd never set foot here. For, of course, if they had—

GARCIN. Quite so. [*Both laugh. Abruptly the laugh dies from*

25 GARCIN'S *face.*] But, I say, where are the instruments of torture?

VALET. The what?

GARCIN. The racks and red-hot pincers and all the other paraphernalia?

30 VALET. Ah, you must have your little joke, sir!

GARCIN. My little joke? Oh, I see. No, I wasn't joking. [*A short silence. He strolls around the room.*] No mirrors, I notice. No windows. Only to be expected. And nothing breakable. [*Bursts out angrily.*] But, damn it all, they might have left me my tooth-

35 brush!

VALET. That's good! So you haven't yet got over your—what-do-you-call-it?—sense of human dignity? Excuse me smiling.

GARCIN. [*Thumping ragefully the arm of an armchair*] I'll ask you to be more polite. I quite realize the position I'm in, but I won't

40 tolerate . . .

VALET. Sorry, sir. No offense meant. But all our guests ask me the same questions. Silly questions, if you'll pardon me saying so. Where's the torture-chamber? That's the first thing they ask, all of them. They don't bother their heads about the bathroom req-

45 uisites, that I can assure you. But after a bit, when they've got

their nerve back, they start in about their toothbrushes and what-not. Good heavens Mr. Garcin, can't you use your brains? What, I ask you, would be the point of brushing your teeth?

GARCIN. [*More calmly*] Yes, of course you're right. [*He looks around*
5   *again.*] And why should one want to see oneself in a looking-glass? But that bronze contraption on the mantelpiece, that's another story. I suppose there will be times when I stare my eyes out at it. Stare my eyes out—see what I mean? . . . All right, let's put our cards on the table. I assure you I'm quite conscious
10   of my position. Shall I tell you what it feels like? A man's drowning, choking, sinking by inches, till only his eyes are just above water. And what does he see? A bronze atrocity by— what's the fellow's name?—Barbedienne. A collector's piece. As in a nightmare. That's their idea, isn't it? . . . No, I suppose
15   you're under orders not to answer questions; and I won't insist. But don't forget, my man, I've a good notion of what's coming to me, so don't you boast you've caught me off my guard. I'm facing the situation, facing it. [*He starts pacing the room again.*] So that's that; no toothbrush. And no bed, either. One never sleeps,
20   I take it?

VALET. That's so.

GARCIN. Just as I expected. *Why* should one sleep? A sort of drowsiness steals on you, tickles you behind the ears, and you feel your eyes closing—but why sleep? You lie down on the
25   sofa and—in a flash, sleep flies away. Miles and miles away. So you rub your eyes, get up, and it starts all over again.

VALET. Romantic, that's what you are.

GARCIN. Will you keep quiet, please! . . . I won't make a scene, I shan't be sorry for myself, I'll face the situation, as I said just
30   now. Face it fairly and squarely. I won't have it springing at me from behind, before I've time to size it up. And you call that being "romantic"! . . . So it comes to this; one doesn't need rest. Why bother about sleep if one isn't sleepy? That stands to reason, doesn't it? Wait a minute, there's a snag somewhere; some-
35   thing   disagreeable.   Why,   now,   should   it   be disagreeable? . . . Ah, I see; it's life without a break.

VALET. What do you mean by that?

GARCIN. What do I mean? [*Eyes the* VALET *suspiciously.*] I thought as much. That's why there's something so beastly, so damn
40   bad-mannered, in the way you stare at me. They're paralyzed.

VALET. What are you talking about?

GARCIN. Your eyelids. We move ours up and down. Blinking, we call it. It's like a small black shutter that clicks down and makes a break. Everything goes black; one's eyes are moistened. You
45   can't imagine how restful, refreshing, it is. Four thousand little

rests per hour. Four thousand little respites—just think! . . . So that's the idea. I'm to live without eyelids. Don't act the fool, you know what I mean. No eyelids, no sleep; it follows, doesn't it? I shall never sleep again. But then—how shall I endure
5 my own company? Try to understand. You see, I'm fond of teasing, it's a second nature with me—and I'm used to teasing myself. Plaguing myself, if you prefer; I don't tease nicely. But I can't go on doing that without a break. Down there I had my nights. I slept. I always had good nights. By way of compensa-
10 tion, I suppose. And happy little dreams. There was a green field. Just an ordinary field. I used to stroll in it . . . Is it daytime now?

VALET. Can't you see? The lights are on.

GARCIN. Ah yes, I've got it. It's your daytime. And outside?

15 VALET. Outside?

GARCIN. Damn it, you know what I mean. Beyond that wall.

VALET. There's a passage.

GARCIN. And at the end of the passage?

VALET. There's more rooms, more passages, and stairs.

20 GARCIN. And what lies beyond them?

VALET. That's all.

GARCIN. But surely you have a day off sometimes. Where do you
go?

VALET. To my uncle's place. he's the head valet here. He has a room
25 on the third floor.

GARCIN. I should have guessed as much. Where's the light-switch?

VALET. There isn't any.

GARCIN. What? Can't one turn off the light?

VALET. Oh, the management can cut off the current if they want to.
30 But I can't remember their having done so on this floor. We have all the electricity we want.

GARCIN. So one has to live with one's eyes open all the time?

VALET. To *live*, did you say?

GARCIN. Don't let's quibble over words. With one's eyes open.
35 Forever. Always broad daylight in my eyes—and in my head. [*Short silence.*] And suppose I took that contraption on the mantelpiece and dropped it on the lamp—wouldn't it go out?

VALET. You can't move it. It's too heavy.

GARCIN. [*Seizing the bronze ornament and trying to lift it*] You're
40 right. It's too heavy.

[*A short silence follows.*]

VALET. Very well, sir, if you don't need me any more, I'll be off.

GARCIN. What? You're going? [*The VALET goes up to the door.*] Wait. [*VALET looks round.*] That's a bell, isn't it? [*VALET nods.*] And if
45 I ring, you're bound to come?

VALET. Well, yes, that's so—in a way. But you can never be sure
about that bell. There's something wrong with the wiring, and
it doesn't always work. [GARCIN *goes to the bell-push and presses the button. A bell purrs outside.*]

5   GARCIN. It's working all right.

VALET. [*Looking surprised*] So it is. [*He, too, presses the button.*] But I
shouldn't count on it too much if I were you. It's—capricious.
Well, I really must go now. [GARCIN *makes a gesture to detain
him.*] Yes, sir?

10   GARCIN. No, never mind. [*He goes to the mantelpiece and picks up a
paper-knife.*] What's this?

VALET. Can't you see? An ordinary paper-knife.

GARCIN. Are there books here?

VALET. No.

15   GARCIN. Then what's the use of this? [VALET *shrugs his shoulders.*]
Very well. You can go. [VALET *goes out.*]

[GARCIN *is by himself. He goes to the bronze ornament and strokes
it reflectively. He sits down; then gets up, goes to the bell-push, and
presses the button. The bell remains silent. He tries two or three*

20   *times, without success. Then he tries to open the door, also without
success. He calls the* VALET *several times, but gets no result. He
beats the door with his fists, still calling. Suddenly he grows calm and
sits down again. At the moment the door opens and* INEZ *enters, followed by the* VALET.]

25   VALET. Did you call sir?

GARCIN. [*On the point of answering "Yes"—but then his eyes fall on
INEZ.*] No.

VALET. [*Turning to* INEZ] This is your room, madam. [INEZ *says
nothing.*] If there's any information you require—? INEZ *still*

30   *keeps silent, and the* VALET *looks slightly huffed.*] Most of our
guests have quite a lot to ask me. But I won't insist. Anyhow, as
regards the toothbrush, and the electric bell, and that thing on
the mantelshelf, this gentleman can tell you anything you want
to know as well as I could. We've had a little chat, him and me.

35   [VALET *goes out.*]

[GARCIN *refrains from looking at* INEZ, *who is inspecting the
room. Abruptly she turns to* GARCIN.]

INEZ. Where's Florence? [GARCIN *does not reply.*] Didn't you hear?
I asked you about Florence. Where is she?

40   GARCIN. I haven't an idea.

INEZ. Ah, that's the way it works, is it? Torture by separation. Well,
as far as I'm concerned, you won't get anywhere. Florence was
a tiresome little fool, and I shan't miss her in the least.

GARCIN. I beg your pardon. Who do you suppose I am?

45   INEZ. You? Why, the torturer, of course.

GARCIN. [*Looks startled, then bursts out laughing*] Well, that's a good
one! Too comic for words. I the torturer! So you came in, had a
look at me, and thought I was—er—one of the staff. Of course,
it's that silly fellow's fault; he should have introduced us. A tor-
5 turer indeed! I'm Joseph Garcin, journalist and man of letters
by profession. And as we're both in the same boat, so to speak,
might I ask you, Mrs.—?
INEZ. [*Testily*] Not "Mrs." I'm unmarried.
GARCIN. Right. That's a start, anyway. Well, now that we've bro-
10 ken the ice, do you *really* think I look like a torturer? And, by
the way, how does one recognize torturers when one sees
them? Evidently you've ideas on the subject.
INEZ. They look frightened.
GARCIN. Frightened! But how ridiculous! Of whom should they be
15 frightened? Of their victims?
INEZ. Laugh away, but I know what I'm talking about. I've often
watched my face in the glass.
GARCIN. In the glass? [*He looks around him.*] How beastly of them!
They've removed everything in the least resembling a glass.
20 [*Short silence*] Anyhow, I can assure you I'm not frightened. Not
that I take my position lightly; I realize its gravity only too well.
But I'm not afraid.
INEZ. [*Shrugging her shoulders*] That's your affair. [*Silence*] Must you
be here all the time, or do you take a stroll outside, now and
25 then?
GARCIN. The door's locked.
INEZ. Oh! . . . That's too bad.
GARCIN. I can quite understand that it bores you having me here.
And I, too—well, quite frankly, I'd rather be alone. I want to
30 think things out, you know; to set my life in order, and one
does that better by oneself. But I'm sure we'll manage to pull
along together somehow. I'm no talker, I don't move much; in
fact I'm a peaceful sort of fellow. Only, if I may venture on a
suggestion, we should make a point of being extremely courte-
35 ous to each other. That will ease the situation for us both.
INEZ. I'm not polite.
GARCIN. Then I must be polite for two.
[*A longish silence. GARCIN is sitting on a sofa, while INEZ paces
up and down the room.*]
40 INEZ. [*Fixing her eyes on him*] Your mouth!
GARCIN. [*As if waking from a dream*] I beg your pardon.
INEZ. Can't you keep your mouth still? You keep twisting it about
all the time. It's grotesque.
GARCIN. So sorry. I wasn't aware of it.
45 INEZ. That's just what I reproach you with. [GARCIN'S *mouth*

twitches.] There you are! You talk about politeness, and you don't even try to control your face. Remember you're not alone; you've no right to inflict the sight of your fear on me.

GARCIN. [*Getting up and going towards her*] How about you? Aren't
5   you afraid?

INEZ. What would be the use? There was some point in being afraid *before*; while one still had hope.

GARCIN. [*In a low voice*] There's no more hope—but it's still "before." We haven't yet begun to suffer.

10 INEZ. That's so. [*A short silence*] Well? What's going to happen?

GARCIN. I don't know. I'm waiting.

[*Silence again.* GARCIN *sits down and* INEZ *resumes her pacing up and down the room.* GARCIN'S *mouth twitches; after a glance at* INEZ *he buries his face in his hands. Enter* ESTELLE *with the*
15   VALET. ESTELLE *looks at* GARCIN, *whose face is still hidden by his hands.*]

ESTELLE. [*To* GARCIN] No! Don't look up. I know what you're hiding with your hands. I know you've no face left. [GARCIN *removes his hands.*] What! [*A short pause. Then, in a tone of sur-*
20   *prise*] But I don't know you!

GARCIN. I'm not the torturer, madam.

ESTELLE. I never thought you were. I—I thought someone was trying to play a rather nasty trick on me. [*To the* VALET] Is anyone else coming?

25 VALET. No, madam. No one else is coming.

ESTELLE. Oh! Then we're to stay by ourselves, the three of us, this gentleman, this lady, and myself. [*She starts laughing.*]

GARCIN. [*Angrily*] There's nothing to laugh about.

ESTELLE. [*Still laughing*] It's those sofas. They're so hideous. And
30   just look how they've been arranged. It makes me think of New Year's Day—when I used to visit that boring old aunt of mine, Aunt Mary. Her house is full of horrors like that. . . . I suppose each of us has a sofa of his own. Is that one mine? [*To the* VALET] But you can't expect me to sit on that one. It would be
35   too horrible for words. I'm in pale blue and it's vivid green.

INEZ. Would you prefer mine?

ESTELLE. That claret-colored one, you mean? That's very sweet of you, but really—no, I don't think it'd be so much better. What's the good of worrying, anyhow? We've got to take what comes
40   to us, and I'll stick to the green one. [*Pause*] The only one which might do, at a pinch, is that gentleman's. [*Another pause*]

INEZ. Did you hear, Mr. Garcin?

GARCIN. [*With a slight start*] Oh—the sofa, you mean. So sorry. [*He rises.*] Pleases take it, madam.

45 ESTELLE. Thanks. [*She takes off her coat and drops it on the sofa. A short*

silence.] Well, as we're to live together, I suppose we'd better introduce ourselves. My name's Rigault. Estelle Rigault. [GARCIN *bows and is going to announce his name, but* INEZ *steps in front of him.*]

5   INEZ. And I'm Inez Serrano. Very pleased to meet you.

GARCIN. [*Bowing again*] Joseph Garcin.

VALET. Do you require me any longer?

ESTELLE. No, you can go. I'll ring when I want you.

   [*Exit* VALET, *with polite bows to everyone.*]

10 INEZ. You're very pretty. I wish we'd had some flowers to welcome you with.

ESTELLE. Flowers? Yes, I loved flowers. Only they'd fade so quickly here, wouldn't they? It's so stuffy. Oh, well, the great thing is to keep as cheerful as we can, don't you agree? Of course, you,

15   too, are—

INEZ. Yes. Last week. What about you?

ESTELLE. I'm—quite recent. Yesterday. As a matter of fact, the ceremony's not quite over. [*Her tone is natural enough, but she seems to be seeing what she describes.*] The wind's blowing my sister's

20   veil all over the place. She's trying her best to cry. Come, dear! Make another effort. That's better. Two tears, two little tears are twinkling under the black veil. Oh dear! What a sight Olga looks this morning! She's holding my sister's arm, helping her along. She's not crying, and I don't blame her; tears always

25   mess one's face up, don't they? Olga was my bosom friend, you know.

INEZ. Did you suffer much?

ESTELLE. No. I was half conscious, mostly.

INEZ. What was it?

30 ESTELLE. Pneumonia. [*In the same tone as before*] It's over now, they're leaving the cemetery. Good-by. Good-by. Quite a crowd they are. My husband stayed at home. Prostrated with grief, poor man. [*To* INEZ] How about you?

INEZ. The gas stove.

35 ESTELLE. And you, Mr. Garcin?

GARCIN. Twelve bullets through my chest. [ESTELLE *makes a horrified gesture.*] Sorry! I fear I'm not good company among the dead.

ESTELLE. Please, please don't use that word. It's so—so crude. In

40   terribly bad taste, really. It doesn't mean much anyhow. Somehow I feel we've never been so much alive as now. If we've absolutely got to mention this—this state of things, I suggest we call ourselves—wait!—absentees. Have you been—been absent for long?

45 GARCIN. About a month.

ESTELLE. Where do you come from?

GARCIN. From Rio.

ESTELLE. I'm from Paris. Have you anyone left down there?

GARCIN. Yes, my wife. [*In the same tone* ESTELLE *has been using*]
5   She's waiting at the entrance of the barracks. She comes there
       every day. But they won't let her in. Now she's trying to peep
       between the bars. She doesn't yet know I'm—absent, but she
       suspects it. Now she's going away. She's wearing her black
       dress. So much the better, she won't need to change. She isn't
10   crying, but she never did cry, anyhow. It's a bright sunny day
       and she's like a black shadow creeping down the empty street.
       Those big tragic eyes of hers—with that martyred look they
       always had. Oh, how she got on my nerves!
       [*A short silence.* GARCIN *sits on the central sofa and buries his head*
15   *in his hands*]

INEZ. Estelle!

ESTELLE. Please, Mr. Garcin!

GARCIN. What is it?

ESTELLE. You're sitting on my sofa.

20   GARCIN. I beg your pardon. [*He gets up.*]

ESTELLE. You looked so—so far away. Sorry I disturbed you.

GARCIN. I was setting my life in order. [INEZ *starts laughing.*] You
       may laugh, but you'd do better to follow my example.

INEZ. No need. My life's in perfect order. It tidied itself up nicely of
25   its own accord. So I needn't bother about it now.

GARCIN. Really? You imagine it's so simple as that. [*He runs his*
       hand over his forehead.] Whew! How hot it is here! Do you mind
       if—? [*He begins taking off his coat.*]

ESTELLE. How dare you! [*More gently*] No, please don't. I loathe
30   men in their shirt sleeves.

GARCIN. [*Putting on his coat again*] All right. [*A short pause*] Of
       course, I used to spend my nights in the newspaper office, and
       it was a regular Black Hole, so we never kept our coats on.
       Stiflingly hot it could be. [*Short pause. In the same tone as previ-*
35   *ously*] Stifling, that it *is*. It's night now.

ESTELLE. That's so. Olga's undressing; it must be after midnight.
       How quickly the time passes, on earth!

INEZ. Yes, after midnight. They've sealed up my room. It's dark,
       pitch-dark, and empty.

40   GARCIN. They've slung their coats on the backs of the chairs and
       rolled up their shirt-sleeves above the elbow. The air stinks of
       men and cigar-smoke. [*A short silence*] I used to like living
       among men in their shirt-sleeves.

ESTELLE. [*Aggressively*] Well, in that case our tastes differ. That's all
45   it proves. [*Turning to* INEZ] What about you? Do you like men

in their shirt-sleeves?

INEZ. Oh, I don't care much for men any way.

ESTELLE. [*Looking at the other two with a puzzled air*] Really I can't imagine why they put us three together. It doesn't make sense.

5 INEZ. [*Stifling a laugh*] What's that you said?

ESTELLE. I'm looking at you two and thinking that we're going to live together. . . . It's so absurd. I expected to meet old friends, or relatives.

INEZ. Yes, a charming old friend—with a hole in the middle of his
10   face.

ESTELLE. Yes, him too. He danced the tango so divinely. Like a professional. . . . Buy why, why should we of all people be put together?

GARCIN. A pure fluke, I should say. They lodge folks as they can,
15   in the order of their coming. [*To* INEZ] Why are you laughing?

INEZ. Because you amuse me, with your "flukes." As if they left anything to chance! But I suppose you've got to reassure yourself somehow.

ESTELLE. [*Hesitantly*] I wonder, now. Don't you think we may have
20   met each other at some time in our lives?

INEZ. Never. I shouldn't have forgotten you.

ESTELLE. Or perhaps we have friends in common. I wonder if you know the Dubois-Seymours?

INEZ. Not likely.

25 ESTELLE. But *everyone* went to their parties.

INEZ. What's their job?

ESTELLE. Oh, they don't do anything. But they have a lovely house in the country, and hosts of people visit them.

INEZ. I didn't. I was a post-office clerk.

30 ESTELLE. [*Recoiling a little*] Ah, yes. . . . Of course, in that case—[*A pause*] And you, Mr. Garcin?

GARCIN. We've never met. I always lived in Rio.

ESTELLE. Then you must be right. It's mere chance that has brought us together.

35 INEZ. Mere chance? Then it's by chance this room is furnished as we see it. It's an accident that the sofa on the right is a livid green, and that the one on the left's wine-red. Mere chance? Well, just try to shift the sofas and you'll see the difference quick enough. And that statue on the mantelpiece, do you
40   think it's there by accident? And what about the heat here? How about that? [*A short silence*] I tell you they've thought it all out. Down to the last detail. Nothing was left to chance. This room was all set for us.

ESTELLE. But really! Everything here's so hideous; all in angles, so
45   uncomfortable. I always loathed angles.

INEZ. [*Shrugging her shoulders*] And do you think I lived in a Second
   Empire drawing-room?

ESTELLE. So it was all fixed up beforehand?

INEZ. Yes. And they've put us together deliberately.

5   ESTELLE. Then it's not mere chance that *you* precisely are sitting
   opposite *me*? But what can be the idea behind it?

INEZ. Ask me another! I only know they're waiting.

ESTELLE. I never could bear the idea of anyone's expecting something from me. It always made me want to do just the opposite.

10   INEZ. Well, do it. Do it if you can. You don't even know what they
   expect.

ESTELLE. [*Stamping her foot*] It's outrageous! So something's coming to me from you two? [*She eyes each in turn.*] Something
   nasty, I suppose. There are some faces that tell me everything at

15   once. Yours don't convey anything.

GARCIN. [*Turning abruptly towards* INEZ] Look here! Why are we
   together? You've given us quite enough hints, you may as well
   come out with it.

INEZ. [*In a surprised tone*] But I know nothing, absolutely nothing

20   about it. I'm as much in the dark as you are.

GARCIN. We've got to know. [*Ponders for a while*]

INEZ. If only each of us had the guts to tell—

GARCIN. Tell what?

INEZ. Estelle!

25   ESTELLE. Yes?

INEZ. What have you done? I mean, why have they sent you here?

ESTELLE. [*Quickly*] That's just it. I haven't a notion, not the foggi-
   est. In fact, I'm wondering if there hasn't been some ghastly
   mistake. [*To* INEZ] Don't smile. Just think of the number of

30   people who—who become absentees every day. There must be
   thousands and thousands, and probably they're sorted out
   by—by understrappers, you know what I mean. Stupid
   employees who don't know their job. So they're bound to make
   mistakes sometimes. . . . Do stop smiling. [*To* GARCIN] Why

35   don't you speak? If they made a mistake in my case, they may
   have done the same about you. [*To* INEZ] And you, too.
   Anyhow, isn't it better to think we've got here by mistake?

INEZ. Is that all you have to tell us?

ESTELLE. What else should I tell? I've nothing to hide. I lost my

40   parents when I was a kid, and I had my young brother to bring
   up. We were terribly poor and when an old friend of my people asked me to marry him I said yes. He was very well off, and
   quite nice. My brother was a very delicate child and needed all
   sorts of attention, so really that was the right thing for me to do,

45   don't you agree? My husband was old enough to be my father,

but for six years we had a happy married life. Then two years ago I met the man I was fated to love. We knew it the moment we set eyes on each other. He asked me to run away with him, and I refused. Then I got pneumonia and it finished me. That's

5 the whole story. No doubt, by certain standards, I did wrong to sacrifice my youth to a man nearly three times my age. [*To GARCIN*] Do *you* think that could be called a sin?

GARCIN. Certainly not. [*A short silence*] And now, tell me, do you think it's a crime to stand by one's principles?

10 ESTELLE. Of course not. Surely no one could blame a man for that!

GARCIN. Wait a bit! I ran a pacifist newspaper. Then war broke out. What was I to do? Everyone was watching me, wondering: "Will he dare?" Well, I dared. I folded my arms and they shot me. Had I done anything wrong?

15 ESTELLE. [*Laying her hand on his arm*] Wrong? On the contrary. You were—

INEZ. [*Breaks in ironically*]—a hero! And how about your wife, Mr. Garcin?

GARCIN. That's simple. I'd rescued her from—from the gutter.

20 ESTELLE. [*To INEZ*] You see! You see!

INEZ. Yes, I see. [*A pause*] Look here! What's the point of play-acting, trying to throw dust in each other's eyes? We're all tarred with the same brush.

ESTELLE. [*Indignantly*] How dare you!

25 INEZ. Yes, we are criminals—murderers—all three of us. We're in hell, my pets; they never make mistakes, and people aren't damned for nothing.

ESTELLE. Stop! For heaven's sake—

INEZ. In hell! Damned souls—that's us, all three!

30 ESTELLE. Keep quiet! I forbid you to use such disgusting words.

INEZ. A damned soul—that's you, my little plaster saint. And ditto our friend there, the noble pacifist. We've had our hour of pleasure, haven't we? There have been people who burned their lives out for our sakes—and we chuckled over it. So now

35 we have to pay the reckoning.

GARCIN. [*Raising his fist*] Will you keep your mouth shut, damn it!

INEZ. [*Confronting him fearlessly, but with a look of vast surprise*] Well, well! [*A pause*] Ah, I understand now. I know why they've put us three together.

40 GARCIN. I advise you to—to think twice before you say anymore.

INEZ. Wait! You'll see how simple it is. Childishly simple. Obviously there aren't any physical torments—you agree, don't you? And yet we're in hell. And no one else will come here. We'll stay in this room together, the three of us, for ever

45 and ever. . . . In short, there's someone absent here, the official

torturer.

GARCIN. [*Sotto voce*] I'd noticed that.

INEZ. It's obvious what they're after—an economy of man-
power—or devil-power, if you prefer. The same idea as in the
5   cafeteria, where customers serve themselves.

ESTELLE. What ever do you mean?

INEZ. I mean that each of us will act as torturer of the two others.

[*There is a short silence while they digest this information.*]

GARCIN. [*Gently*] No, I shall never be your torturer. I wish neither
10   of you any harm, and I've no concern with you. None at all. So
the solution's easy enough, each of us stays put in his or her
corner and takes no notice of the others. You here, you here,
and I there. Like soldiers at our posts. Also, we mustn't speak.
Not one word. That won't be difficult; each of us has plenty of
15   material for self-communings. I think I could stay ten thousand
years with only my thoughts for company.

ESTELLE. Have *I* got to keep silent, too?

GARCIN. Yes. And that way we—we'll work out our salvation.
Looking into ourselves, never raising our heads. Agreed?

20 INEZ. Agreed.

ESTELLE. [*After some hesitation*] I agree.

GARCIN. Then—good-by.

[*He goes to his sofa and buries his head in his hands. There is a long
silence; then INEZ begins singing to herself.*]

25 INEZ. [*Singing*]

    What a crowd in Whitefriars Lane!
    They've set trestles in a row,
    With a scaffold and the knife,
    And a pail of bran below.
30   Come, good folks, to Whitefriars Lane.
    Come to see the merry show!
    The headsman rose at crack of dawn,
    He'd a long day's work in hand,
    Chopping heads off generals,
35   Priests and peers and admirals,
    All the highest in the land.
    What a crowd in Whitefriars Lane!

    See them standing in a line,
    Ladies all dressed up so fine.
40   But their heads have got to go,
    Heads and hats roll down below.
    Come, good folks, to Whitefriars Lane,
    Come to see the merry show!

[*Meanwhile* ESTELLE *has been plying her powder-puff and lipstick. She looks round for a mirror, fumbles in her bag, then turns towards* GARCIN.]

ESTELLE. Excuse me, have you a glass? [GARCIN *does not answer.*]
5   Any sort of glass, a pocket-mirror will do. [GARCIN *remains silent.*] Even if you won't speak to me, you might lend me a glass.

[*His head still buried in his hands,* GARCIN *ignores her.*]

INEZ. [*Eagerly*] Don't worry. I've a glass in my bag. [*She opens her*
10   *bag. Angrily*] It's gone! They must have taken it from me at the entrance.

ESTELLE. How tiresome!

[*A short silence.* ESTELLE *shuts her eyes and sways, as if about to faint.* INEZ *turns forward and holds her up.*]

15   INEZ. What's the matter?

ESTELLE. [*Opens her eyes and smiles*] I feel so queer. [*She pats herself.*] Don't you ever get taken that way? When I can't see myself I begin to wonder if I really and truly exist. I pat myself just to make sure, but it doesn't help much.

20   INEZ. You're lucky. I'm always conscious of myself—in my mind. Painfully conscious.

ESTELLE. Ah yes, in your mind. But everything that goes on in one's head is so vague, isn't it? It makes one want to sleep. [*She is silent for a while.*] I've six big mirrors in my bedroom. There
25   they are. I can see them. But they don't see me. They're reflecting the carpet, the settee, the window—but how empty it is, a glass in which I'm absent! When I talked to people I always made sure there was one near by in which I could see myself. I watched myself talking. And somehow, it kept me alert, seeing
30   myself as the others saw me. . . . Oh dear! My lipstick! I'm sure I've put it on all crooked. No, I can't do without a looking-glass for ever and ever, I simply can't.

INEZ. Suppose I try to be your glass? Come and pay me a visit, dear. Here's a place for you on my sofa.

35   ESTELLE. But— [*Points to* GARCIN]

INEZ. Oh, he doesn't count.

ESTELLE. But we're going to—to hurt each other. You said it yourself.

INEZ. Do I look as if I wanted to hurt you?

40   ESTELLE. One never can tell.

INEZ. Much more likely *you'll* hurt *me*. Still, what does it matter? If I've got to suffer, it may as well be at your hands, your pretty hands. Sit down. Come closer. Closer. Look into my eyes. What do you see?

45   ESTELLE. Oh, I'm there! But so tiny I can't see myself properly.

INEZ. But *I* can. Every inch of you. Now ask me questions. I'll be as candid as any looking-glass.

[ESTELLE *seems rather embarrassed and turns to* GARCIN, *as if appealing to him for help.*]

5 ESTELLE. Please, Mr. Garcin. Sure our chatter isn't boring you?

[GARCIN *makes no reply.*]

INEZ. Don't worry about him. As I said, he doesn't count. We're by ourselves. . . . Ask away.

ESTELLE. Are my lips all right?

10 INEZ. Show! No, they're a bit smudgy.

ESTELLE. I thought as much. Luckily [*Throws a quick glance at* GARCIN] no one's seen me. I'll try again.

INEZ. That's better. No. Follow the line of your lips. Wait! I'll guide your hand. There. That's quite good.

15 ESTELLE. As good as when I came in?

INEZ. Far better. Crueler. Your mouth looks quite diabolical that way.

ESTELLE. Good gracious! And you say you like it! How maddening, not being able to see for myself! You're quite sure, Miss

20 Serrano, that it's all right now?

INEZ. Won't you call me Inez?

ESTELLE. Are you sure it looks all right?

INEZ. You're lovely, Estelle.

ESTELLE. But how can I rely upon your taste? Is it the same as *my*

25 taste? Oh, how sickening it all is, enough to drive one crazy!

INEZ. I *have* your taste, my dear, because I like you so much. Look at me. No, straight. Now smile. I'm not so ugly, either. Am I not nicer than your glass?

ESTELLE. Oh, I don't know. You scare me rather. My reflection in

30 the glass never did that; of course, I knew it so well. Like something I had tamed. . . . I'm going to smile, and my smile will sink down into your pupils, and heaven knows what it will become.

INEZ. And why shouldn't you "tame" *me*? [*The women gaze at each*

35 *other,* ESTELLE *with a sort of fearful fascination.*] Listen! I want you to call me Inez. We must be great friends.

ESTELLE. I don't make friends with women very easily.

INEZ. Not with postal clerks, you mean? Hullo, what's that—that nasty red spot at the bottom of your cheek? A pimple?

40 ESTELLE. A pimple? Oh, how simply foul! Where?

INEZ. There. . . . You know the way they catch larks—with a mirror? I'm your lark-mirror, my dear, and you can't escape me. . . . There isn't any pimple, not a trace of one. So what about it? Suppose the mirror started telling lies? Or suppose I covered

45 my eyes—as he is doing—and refused to look at you, all that

loveliness of yours would be wasted on the desert air. No, don't
be afraid, I can't help looking at you, I shan't turn my eyes
away. And I'll be nice to you, ever so nice. Only you must be
nice to me, too.

5   [*A short silence*]

ESTELLE. Are you really—attracted by me?

INEZ. Very much indeed.

       [*Another short silence*]

ESTELLE. [*Indicating* GARCIN *by a slight movement of her head*] But I
10   wish he'd notice me, too.

INEZ. Of course! Because he's a Man! [*To* GARCIN] You've won.
       [GARCIN *says nothing.*] But look at her, damn it! [*Still no reply
       from* GARCIN] Don't pretend. You haven't missed a word of
       what we've said.

15 GARCIN. Quite so; not a word. I stuck my fingers in my ears, but
       your voices thudded in my brain. Silly chatter. Now will you
       leave me in peace, you two? I'm not interested in you.

INEZ. Not in me, perhaps—but how about this child? Aren't you
       interested in her? Oh, I saw through your game; you got on
20   your high horse just to impress her.

GARCIN. I asked you to leave me in peace. There's someone talk-
       ing about me in the newspaper office and I want to listen. And,
       if it'll make you any happier, let me tell you that I've no use for
       the "child," as you call her.

25 ESTELLE. Thanks.

GARCIN. Oh, I didn't mean it rudely.

ESTELLE. You cad!

       [*They confront each other in silence for some moments.*]

GARCIN. So that's that. [*Pause*] You know I begged you not to
30   speak.

ESTELLE. It's *her* fault; she started. I didn't ask anything of her and
       she came and offered me her—her glass.

INEZ. So you say. But all the time you were making up to him, try-
       ing every trick to catch his attention.

35 ESTELLE. Well, why shouldn't I?

GARCIN. You're crazy, both of you. Don't you see where this is
       leading us? For pity's sake, keep your mouths shut. [*Pause*]
       Now let's all sit down again quite quietly; we'll look at the floor
       and each must try to forget the others are there.

40   [*A longish silence.* GARCIN *sits down. The women return hesitant-
       ly to their places. Suddenly,* INEZ *swings round on him.*]

INEZ. To forget about the others? How utterly absurd! I *feel* you
       there, in every pore. Your silence clamors in my ears. You can
       nail up your mouth, cut your tongue out—but you can't pre-
45   vent your *being there*. Can you stop your thoughts? I hear them

ticking away like a clock, tick-tock, tick-tock, and I'm certain you hear mine. It's all very well skulking on your sofa, but you're everywhere, and every sound comes to me soiled, because you've intercepted it on its way. Why, you've even
5   stolen my face; you know it and I don't! And what about her, about Estelle? You've stolen her from me, too; if she and I were alone do you suppose she'd treat me as she does? No, take your hands from your face, I won't leave you in peace—that would suit your book too well. You'd go on sitting there, in a sort of
10   trance, like a yogi, and even if I didn't see her I'd feel it in my bones—that she was making every sound, even the rustle of her dress, for your benefit, throwing you smiles you didn't see. . . . Well, I won't stand for that, I prefer to choose my hell; I prefer to look you in the eyes and fight it out face to face.

15   GARCIN. Have it your own way. I suppose we were bound to come to this; they knew what they were about, and we're easy game. If they'd put me in a room with men—men can keep their mouths shut. But it's no use wanting the impossible. [*He goes to* ESTELLE *and lightly fondles her neck.*] So I attract you, little girl?
20   It seems you were making eyes at me?

ESTELLE. Don't touch me.

GARCIN. Why not? We might, anyhow, be natural. . . . Do you know, I used to be mad about women? And some were fond of me. So we may as well stop posing, we've nothing to lose. Why
25   trouble about politeness, and decorum, and the rest of it? We're between ourselves. And presently we shall be naked as—as new-born babes.

ESTELLE. Oh, let me be!

GARCIN. As new-born babes. Well, I'd warned you, anyhow. I
30   asked so little of you, nothing but peace and a little silence. I'd put my fingers in my ears. Gomez was spouting away as usual, standing in the center of the room, with all the pressmen listening. In their shirtsleeves. I tried to hear, but it wasn't too easy. Things on earth move so quickly, you know. Couldn't you
35   have held your tongues? Now it's over, he's stopped talking, and what he thinks of me has gone back into his head. Well, we've got to see it through somehow. . . . Naked as we were born. So much the better; I want to know whom I have to deal with.

40   INEZ. You know already. There's nothing more to learn.

GARCIN. You're wrong. So long as each of us hasn't made a clean breast of it—why they've damned him or her—we know nothing. Nothing that counts. You, young lady, you shall begin. Why? Tell us why. If you are frank, if we bring our specters into
45   the open, it may save us from disaster. So—out with it! Why?

ESTELLE. I tell you I haven't a notion. They wouldn't tell me why.

GARCIN. That's so. They wouldn't tell me, either. But I've a pretty good idea. . . . Perhaps you're shy of speaking first? Right. I'll lead off. [*A short silence*] I'm not a very estimable person.

5 INEZ. No need to tell us that. We know you were a deserter.

GARCIN. Let that be. It's only a side-issue. I'm here because I treated my wife abominably. That's all. For five years. Naturally, she's suffering still. There she is: the moment I mention her, I see her. It's Gomez who interests me, and it's she I see. Where's

10 Gomez got to? For five years. There! They've given her back my things; she sitting by the window, with my coat on her knees. The coat with the twelve bullet-holes. The blood's like rust; a brown ring round each hole. It's quite a museum-piece, that coat; scarred with history. And I used to wear it,

15 fancy! . . . Now, can't you shed a tear, my love? Surely you'll squeeze one out—at last? No? You can't manage it? . . . Night after night I came home blind drunk, stinking of wine and women. She'd sat up for me, of course. But she never cried, never uttered a word of reproach. Only her eyes spoke. Big,

20 tragic eyes. I don't regret anything. I must pay the price, but I shan't whine. . . . It's snowing in the street. Won't you cry, confound you? That woman was a born martyr, you know, a victim by vocation.

INEZ. [*Almost tenderly*] Why did you hurt her like that?

25 GARCIN. It was so easy. A word was enough to make her flinch. Like a sensitive-plant. But never, never a reproach. I'm fond of teasing. I watched and waited. But no, not a tear, not a protest. I'd picked her up out of the gutter, you understand. . . . Now she's stroking the coat. Her eyes are shut and she's feeling with

30 her fingers for the bullet-holes. What are you after? What do you expect? I tell you I regret nothing. The truth is, she admired me too much. Does that mean anything to you?

INEZ. No. Nobody admired *me*.

GARCIN. So much the better. So much the better for you. I suppose

35 all this strikes you as very vague. Well, here's something you can get your teeth into. I brought a half-caste girl to stay in our house. My wife slept upstairs; she must have heard—everything. She was an early riser and, as I and the girl stayed in bed late, she served us our morning coffee.

40 INEZ. You brute!

GARCIN. Yes, a brute, if you like. But a well-beloved brute. [*A faraway look comes to his eyes*] No, it's nothing. Only Gomez, and he's not talking about *me*. . . . What were you saying? Yes, a brute. Certainly. Else why should I be here? [*To* INEZ] Your

45 turn.

INEZ. Well, I was what some people down there called "a damned
bitch." Damned already. So it's no surprise, being here.

GARCIN. Is that all you have to say?

INEZ. No. There was that affair with Florence. A dead men's tale.
5   With three corpses to it. He to start with; then she and I. So
there's no one left, I've nothing to worry about; it was a clean
sweep. Only that room. I see it now and then. Empty, with the
doors locked. . . . No, they've just unlocked them. "To Let." It's
to let; there's a notice on the door. That's—too ridiculous.

10 GARCIN. Three. Three deaths, you said?

INEZ. Three.

GARCIN. One man and two women?

INEZ. Yes.

GARCIN. Well, well. [*A pause*] Did he kill himself?

15 INEZ. He? No, he hadn't the guts for that. Still, he'd every reason;
we led him a dog's life. As a matter of fact, he was run over by
a tram. A silly sort of end. . . . I was living with them; he was
my cousin.

GARCIN. Was Florence fair?

20 INEZ. Fair? [*Glances at* ESTELLE] You know, I don't regret a thing;
still, I'm not so very keen on telling you the story.

GARCIN. That's all right. . . . So you got sick of him?

INEZ. Quite gradually. All sorts of little things got on my nerves.
For instance, he made a noise when he was drinking—a sort of
25   gurgle. Trifles like that. He was rather pathetic really.
Vulnerable. Why are you smiling?

GARCIN. Because I, anyhow, am *not* vulnerable.

INEZ. Don't be too sure. . . . I crept inside her skin, she saw the
world through my eyes. When she left him, I had her on my
30   hands. We shared a bed-sitting-room at the other end of the
town.

GARCIN. And then?

INEZ. Then the tram did its job. I used to remind her every day:
"Yes, my pet, we killed him between us." [*A pause*] I'm rather
35   cruel, really.

GARCIN. So am I.

INEZ. No, you're not cruel. It's something else.

GARCIN. What?

INEZ. I'll tell you later. When I say I'm cruel, I mean I can't get on
40   without making people suffer. Like a live coal. A live coal in
others' hearts. When I'm alone I flicker out. For six months I
flamed away in her heart, till there was nothing but a cinder.
One night she got up and turned on the gas while I was asleep.
Then she crept back into bed. So now you know.

45 GARCIN. Well! Well!

INEZ. Yes? What's in your mind?

GARCIN. Nothing. Only that it's not a pretty story.

INEZ. Obviously. But what matter?

GARCIN. As you say, what matter? [*To* ESTELLE] Your turn. What
5   have you done?

ESTELLE. As I told you, I haven't a notion. I rack my brain, but it's
no use.

GARCIN. Right. Then we'll give you a hand. That fellow with the
smashed face, who was he?

10 ESTELLE. Who—who do you mean?

INEZ. You know quite well. The man you were so scared of seeing
when you came in.

ESTELLE. Oh him! A friend of mine.

GARCIN. Why were you afraid of him?

15 ESTELLE. That's my business, Mr. Garcin.

INEZ. Did he shoot himself on you account?

ESTELLE. Of course not. How absurd you are!

GARCIN. Then why should you have been so scared? He blew his
brains out, didn't he? That's how his face got smashed.

20 ESTELLE. Don't! Please don't go on.

GARCIN. Because of you. Because of you.

INEZ. He shot himself because of you.

ESTELLE. Leave me alone! It's—it's not fair, bullying me like that. I
want to go! I want to go!

25 [*She runs to the door and shakes it.*]

GARCIN. Go if you can. Personally, I ask for nothing better.
Unfortunately, the door's locked.

[ESTELLE *presses the bell-push, but the bell does not ring.* INEZ
and GARCIN *laugh.* ESTELLE *swings round on them, her back to*
30 *the door.*]

ESTELLE. [*In a muffled voice*] You're hateful, both of you.

INEZ. Hateful? Yes, that's the word. Now get on with it. That fellow
who killed himself on your account—you were his mistress,
eh?

35 GARCIN. Of course she was. And he wanted her to have her to
himself alone. That's so, isn't it?

INEZ. He danced the tango like a professional, but he was poor as
a church mouse—that's right, isn't it?

[*A short silence*]

40 GARCIN. Was he poor or not? Give a straight answer.

ESTELLE. Yes, he was poor.

GARCIN. And then you had your reputation to keep up. One day
he came and implored you to run away with him, and you
laughed in his face.

45 INEZ. That's it. You laughed at him. And so he killed himself.

ESTELLE. Did you use to look at Florence in that way?

INEZ. Yes.

[*A short pause, then* ESTELLE *bursts out laughing.*]

ESTELLE. You've got it all wrong, you two. [*She stiffens her shoulders,*
5   *still leaning against the door, and faces them. He voice grows shrill,*
    truculent.] He wanted me to have a baby. So there!

GARCIN. And you didn't want one?

ESTELLE. I certainly didn't. But the baby came, worse luck. I went
    to Switzerland for five months. No one knew anything. It was
10   a girl. Roger was with me when she was born. It pleased him
    no end, having a daughter. It didn't please *me*!

GARCIN. And then?

ESTELLE. There was a balcony overlooking the lake. I brought a big
    stone. He could see what I was up to and he kept on shouting:
15   "Estelle, for God's sake, don't!" I hated him then. He saw it all.
    He was leaning over the balcony and he saw the rings spread-
    ing on the water—

GARCIN. Yes? And then?

ESTELLE. That's all. I came back to Paris—and he did as he wished.
20 GARCIN. You mean he blew his brains out?

ESTELLE. It was absurd of him, really, my husband never suspected
    anything. [*A pause*] Oh, how I loathe you! [*She sobs tearlessly.*]

GARCIN. Nothing doing. Tears don't flow in this place.

ESTELLE. I'm a coward. A coward! [*Pause*] If you knew how I hate
25   you!

INEZ. [*Taking her in her arms*] Poor child! [*To* GARCIN] So the hear-
    ing's over. But there's no need to look like a hanging judge.

GARCIN. A hanging judge? [*He glances around him.*] I'd give a lot to
    be able to see myself in a glass. [*Pause*] How hot it is!
30   [*Unthinkingly he takes off his coat.*] Oh, sorry! [*He starts putting it*
    on again.]

ESTELLE. Don't bother. You can stay in your shirt-sleeves. As
    things are—

GARCIN. Just so. [*He drops his coat on the sofa.*] You mustn't be angry
35   with me, Estelle.

ESTELLE. I'm not angry with you.

INEZ. And what about me? Are you angry with me?

ESTELLE. Yes.

[*A short silence*]
40 INEZ. Well, Mr. Garcin, now you have us in the nude all right. Do
    you understand things any better for that?

GARCIN. I wonder. Yes, perhaps a trifle better. [*Timidly*] And now
    suppose we start trying to help each other.

INEZ. I don't need help.
45 GARCIN. Inez, they've laid their snare damned cunningly—like a

cobweb. If you make any movement, if you raise your hand to fan yourself, Estelle and I feel a little tug. Alone, none of us can save himself or herself; we're linked together inextricably. So you can take your choice. [*A pause*] Hullo? What's happening?

5   INEZ. They've let it. The windows are wide open, a man is sitting on my bed. *My* bed, if you please! They've let it, let it! Step in, step in, make yourself at home, you brute! Ah, there's a woman, too. She's going up to him, putting her hands on his shoulders. . . . Damn it, why don't they turn the lights on? It's

10   getting dark. Now he's going to kiss her. But that's my room, *my* room. Pitch-dark now. I can't see anything, but I hear them whispering, whispering. Is he going to make love to her on *my* bed? What's that she said? That it's noon and the sun is shining? I must be going blind. [*A pause*] Blacked out. I can't see or

15   hear a thing. So I'm done with the earth, it seems. No more alibis for me! [*She shudders*] I feel so empty, desiccated—really dead at last. All of me's here in this room. [*A pause*] What were you saying? Something about helping me, wasn't it?

GARCIN. Yes.

20   INEZ. Helping me to do what?

GARCIN. To defeat their devilish tricks.

INEZ. And what do you expect me to do, in return?

GARCIN. To help *me*. It only needs a little effort, Inez; just a spark of human feeling.

25   INEZ. Human feeling. That's beyond my range. I'm rotten to the core.

GARCIN. And how about me? [*A pause*] All the same, suppose we try?

INEZ. It's no use. I'm all dried up. I can't give and I can't receive.

30   How could *I* help you? A dead twig, ready for the burning. [*She falls silent, gazing at* ESTELLE, *who has buried her head in her hands.*] Florence was fair, a natural blonde.

GARCIN. Do you realize that this young woman's fated to be your torturer?

35   INEZ. Perhaps I've guessed it.

GARCIN. It's through her they'll get you. I, of course, I'm different—aloof. I take no notice of her. Suppose you had a try—

INEZ. Yes?

GARCIN. It's a trap. They're watching you, to see if you'll fall into

40   it.

INEZ. I know. And you're another trap. Do you think they haven't foreknown every word you say? And of course there's a whole nest of pitfalls that we can't see. Everything here's a booby-trap. But what do I care? I'm a pitfall, too. For her, obviously.

45   And perhaps I'll catch her.

GARCIN. You won't catch anything. We're chasing after each other,
round and round in a vicious circle, like the horses on a roundabout. That's part of their plan, of course. . . . Drop it, Inez.
Open your hands and let go of everything. Or else you'll bring
5   disaster on all three of us.

INEZ. Do I look the sort of person who lets go? I know what's coming to me. I'm going to burn, and it's to last forever. Yes, I *know*
everything. But do you think I'll let go? I'll catch her, she'll see
you through my eyes, as Florence saw that other man. What's
10   the good of trying to enlist my sympathy? I assure you I know
everything, and I can't feel sorry even for myself. A trap! Don't
I know it, and that I'm in a trap myself, up to the neck, and
there's nothing to be done about it? And if it suits their book,
so much the better!

15 GARCIN. [*Gripping her shoulders*] Well, I, anyhow, can feel sorry for
you, too. Look at me, we're naked, naked right through, and I
can see into your heart. That's one link between us. Do you
think I'd want to hurt you? I don't regret anything, I'm dried
up, too. But for you I can still feel pity.

20 INEZ. [*Who has let him keep his hands on her shoulders until now, shakes
herself loose*] Don't. I hate being pawed about. And keep your
pity for yourself. Don't forget, Garcin, that there are traps for
you, too, in this room. All nicely set for you. You'd do better to
watch your own interests. [*A pause.*] But, if you will leave us in
25   peace, this child and me, I'll see I don't do you any harm.

GARCIN. [*Gazes at her for a moment, then shrugs his shoulders*] Very
well.

ESTELLE. [*Raising her head*] Please, Garcin.

GARCIN. What do you want of me?

30 ESTELLE. [*Rises and goes up to him*] You can help *me*, anyhow.

GARCIN. If you want help, apply to her.

[INEZ *has come up and is standing behind* ESTELLE, *but without
touching her. During the dialogue that follows she speaks almost in
her ear. But* ESTELLE *keeps her eyes on* GARCIN, *who observes her*
35   *without speaking, and she addresses her answers to him, as if it were
he who is questioning her.*]

ESTELLE. I implore you, Garcin—you gave me your promise, did-
n't you? Help me quick. I don't want to be left alone. Olga's
taken him to a cabaret.

40 INEZ. Taken whom?

ESTELLE. Peter. . . . Oh, now they're dancing together.

INEZ. Who's Peter?

ESTELLE. Such a silly boy. He called me his glancing stream—just
fancy! He was terribly in love with me. . . . She's persuaded him
45   to come out with her tonight.

INEZ. Do you love him?

ESTELLE. They're sitting down now. She's puffing like a grampus. What a fool the girl is to insist on dancing! I dare say she does it to reduce. . . . No, of course I don't love him; he's only eight-
5   een, and I'm not a baby-snatcher.

INEZ. They why bother about them? What difference can it make?

ESTELLE. He belonged to me.

INEZ. Nothing on earth belongs to you any more.

ESTELLE. I tell you he was mine. All mine.

10 INEZ. Yes, he was yours—once. But now—Try to make him hear, try to touch him. Olga can touch him, talk to him as much as she likes. That's so, isn't it? She can squeeze his hands, rub her-self against him—

ESTELLE. Yes, look! She's pressing her great fat chest against him,
15   puffing and blowing in his face. But, my poor little lamb, can't you see how ridiculous she is? Why don't you laugh at her? Oh, once I'd have only had to glance at them and she'd have slunk away. Is there really nothing, nothing left of me?

INEZ. Nothing whatever. Nothing of you's left on earth—not even
20   a shadow. All you own is here. Would you like that paper-knife? Or that ornament on the mantelpiece? That blue sofa's yours. And I, my dear, am yours forever.

ESTELLE. You mine! That's good! Well, which of you two would dare to call me his glancing stream, his crystal girl? You know
25   too much about me, you know I'm rotten through and through. . . . Peter dear, think of me, fix your thoughts on me, and save me. All the time you're thinking "my glancing stream, my crystal girl," I'm only half here, I'm only half wicked, and half of me is down there with you, clean and bright and crys-
30   tal-clear as running water. . . . Oh, just look at her face, all scar-let, like a tomato. No, it's absurd, we've laughed at her togeth-er, you and I, often and often. . . . What's that tune?—I always loved it. Yes, the *St. Louis Blues* . . . All right, dance away, dance away. Garcin, I wish you could see her, you'd die of laughing.
35   Only—she'll never know I see her. Yes, I see you Olga, with your hair all anyhow and you do look a dope, my dear. Oh, now you're treading on his toes. It's a scream! Hurry up! Quicker! Quicker! He's dragging her along, bundling her round and round—it's too ghastly! He always said I was so
40   light, he loved to dance with me. [*She is dancing as she speaks.*] I tell you, Olga, I can see you. No, she doesn't care, she's danc-ing through my gaze. What's that? What's that you said? "Our poor dear Estelle"? Oh, don't be such a humbug! You didn't even shed a tear at the funeral. . . . And she has the nerve to talk
45   to him about her poor dear friend Estelle! How dare she discuss

me with Peter? Now then, keep time. She never could dance and talk at once. Oh, what's that? No, no. Don't tell him. Please, please don't tell him. You can keep him, do what you like with him, but please don't tell him about—that! [*She has stopped dancing.*] All right. You can have him now. Isn't it *foul*, Garcin? She's told him everything about Roger, my trip to Switzerland, the baby. "Poor Estelle wasn't exactly—" No, I wasn't exactly—True enough. He's looking grave, shaking his head, but he doesn't seem so very much surprised, not what one would expect. Keep him, then—I won't haggle with you over his long eyelashes, his pretty girlish face. They're yours for the asking. His glancing stream, his crystal. Well, the crystal's shattered into bits. "Poor Estelle!" Dance, dance, dance. On with it. But do keep time. One, two. One, two. How I'd love to go down to earth for just a moment and dance with him again. [*She dances again for some moments.*] The music's growing fainter. They've turned down the lights, as they do for a tango. Why are they playing so softly? Louder, please. I can't hear. It's so far away, so far away. I—I can't hear a sound. [*She stops dancing.*] All over. It's the end. The earth has left me. [*To* GARCIN] Don't turn from me—please. Take me in your arms. [*Behind* ESTELLE'S *back,* INEZ *signs to* GARCIN *to move away.*]

INEZ. [*Commandingly*] Now then, Garcin!

[GARCIN *moves back a step, and, glancing at* ESTELLE, *points to* INEZ.]

GARCIN. It's to her you should say that.

ESTELLE. [*Clinging to him*] Don't turn away. You're a man, aren't you, and surely I'm not such a fright as all that! Everyone says I've lovely hair and, after all, a man killed himself on my account. You have to look at something, and there's nothing here to see except the sofas and that awful ornament and the table. Surely I'm better to look at than a lot of stupid furniture. Listen! I've dropped out of their hearts like a little sparrow fallen from its nest. So gather me up, dear, fold me to your heart—and you'll see how nice I can be.

GARCIN. [*Freeing himself from her, after a short struggle*] I tell you it's to that lady you should speak.

ESTELLE. To her? But she doesn't count, she's a woman.

INEZ. Oh, I don't count? Is that what you think? But, my poor little fallen nestling, you've been sheltering in my heart for ages, though you didn't realize it. Don't be afraid; I'll keep looking at you for ever and ever, without a flutter of my eyelids, and you'll live in my gaze like a mote in a sunbeam.

ESTELLE. A sunbeam indeed! Don't talk such rubbish! You've tried that trick already, and you should know it doesn't work.

INEZ. Estelle! My glancing stream! My crystal!

ESTELLE. *Your* crystal? It's grotesque. Do you think you can fool me with that sort of talk? Everyone knows by now what I did to my baby. The crystal's shattered, but I don't care. I'm just a hol-

5 low dummy, all that's left of me is the outside—but it's not for you.

INEZ. Come to me, Estelle. You shall be whatever you like: a glanc-ing stream, a muddy stream. And deep down in my eyes you'll see yourself just as you want to be.

10 ESTELLE. Oh, leave me in peace. You haven't any eyes. Oh, damn it, isn't there anything I can do to get rid of you? I've an idea. [*She spits in* INEZ's *face.*] There!

INEZ. Garcin, you shall pay for this.

[*A pause,* GARCIN *shrugs his shoulders and goes to* ESTELLE.]

15 GARCIN. So it's a man you need?

ESTELLE. Not *any* man. You.

GARCIN. No humbug now. Any man would do your business. As I happen to be here, you want me. Right!—[*He grips her shoul-ders.*] Mind, I'm not your sort at all, really; I'm not a young nin-

20 compoop and I don't dance the tango.

ESTELLE. I'll take you as you are. And perhaps I shall change you.

GARCIN. I doubt it. I shan't pay much attention; I've other things to think about.

ESTELLE. What things?

25 GARCIN. They wouldn't interest you.

ESTELLE. I'll sit on your sofa and wait for you to take some notice of me. I promise not to bother you at all.

INEZ. [*With a shrill laugh*] That's right, fawn on him, like the silly bitch you are. Grovel and cringe! And he hasn't even good

30 looks to commend him.

ESTELLE. [*To* GARCIN] Don't listen to her. She has no eyes, no ears. She's—nothing.

GARCIN. I'll give you what I can. It doesn't amount to much. I shan't love you; I know you too well.

35 ESTELLE. Do you want me, anyhow?

GARCIN. Yes.

ESTELLE. I ask no more.

GARCIN. In that case—[*He bends over her.*]

INEZ. Estelle! Garcin! You must be going crazy. You're not alone.

40 I'm here too.

GARCIN. Of course—but what does it matter?

INEZ. Under my eyes? You couldn't—couldn't do it.

ESTELLE. Why not? I often undressed with my maid looking on.

INEZ. [*Gripping* GARCIN'S *arm*] Let her alone. Don't paw her with

45 your dirty man's hands.

GARCIN. [*Thrusting her away roughly*] Take care. I'm no gentleman, and I'd have no compunction about striking a woman.

INEZ. But you promised me; you promised. I'm only asking you to keep your word.

5 GARCIN. Why should I, considering you were the first to break our agreement?

[INEZ *turns her back on him and retreats to the far end of the room.*]

INEZ. Very well, have it you own way. I'm the weaker party, one against two. But don't forget I'm here, and watching. I shan't

10 take my eyes off you, Garcin; when you're kissing her, you'll feel them boring into you. Yes, have it your own way, make love and get it over. We're in hell; my turn will come.

[*During the following scene she watches them without speaking.*]

GARCIN. [*Coming back to* ESTELLE *and grasping her shoulders*] Now

15 then. Your lips. Give me your lips.

[*A pause. He bends to kiss her, then abruptly straightens up.*]

ESTELLE. [*Indignantly*] Really! [*A pause*] Didn't I tell you not to pay any attention to her?

GARCIN. You've got it wrong. [*Short silence*] It's Gomez; he's back

20 in the press-room. They've shut the windows; it must be winter down there. Six months since I—Well, I warned you I'd be absent-minded sometimes, didn't I? They're shivering, they've kept their coats on. Funny they should feel the cold like that, when I'm feeling so hot. Ah, this time he's talking about me.

25 ESTELLE. Is it going to last long? [*Short silence*] You might at least tell me what he's saying.

GARCIN. Nothing. Nothing worth repeating. He's a swine, that's all. [*He listens attentively.*] A god-damned bloody swine. [*He turns to* ESTELLE.] Let's come back to—to ourselves. Are you

30 going to love me?

ESTELLE. [*Smiling*] I wonder now!

GARCIN. Will you trust me?

ESTELLE. What a quaint thing to ask! Considering you'll be under my eyes all the time, and I don't think I've much to fear from

35 Inez, so far as you're concerned.

GARCIN. Obviously. [*A pause. He takes his hands off* ESTELLE'S *shoulders.*] I was thinking of another kind of trust. [*Listens*] Talk away, talk away, you swine. I'm not there to defend myself. [*To* ESTELLE] Estelle, you must give me your trust.

40 ESTELLE. Oh, what a nuisance you are! I'm giving you my mouth, my arms, my whole body—and everything could be so simple. . . . My trust! I haven't any to give, I'm afraid, and you're making me terribly embarrassed. You must have something pretty ghastly on your conscience to make such a fuss about my

45 trusting you.

GARCIN. They shot me.

ESTELLE. I know. Because you refused to fight. Well, why should-n't you?

GARCIN. I—I didn't exactly refuse. [*In a far-away voice*] I must say
5   he talks well, he makes out a good case against me, but he never says what I should have done instead. Should I have gone to the general and said: "General, I decline to fight"? A mug's game; they'd have promptly locked me up. But I want-ed to show my colors, my true colors, do you understand? I
10   wasn't going to be silenced. [*To* ESTELLE] So I—I took the train. . . . They caught me at the frontier.

ESTELLE. Where were you trying to go?

GARCIN. To Mexico. I meant to launch a pacifist newspaper down there. [*A short silence*] Well, why don't you speak?

15 ESTELLE. What could I say? You acted quite rightly, as you didn't want to fight. [GARCIN *makes a fretful gesture*.] But, darling, how on earth can I guess what you want me to answer?

INEZ. Can't you guess? Well, *I* can. He wants you to tell him that he bolted like a lion. For "bolt" he did, and that's what's biting
20   him.

GARCIN. "Bolted," "went away"—we won't quarrel over words.

ESTELLE. But you *had* to run away. If you'd stayed they'd have sent you to jail, wouldn't they?

GARCIN. Of course. [*A pause*] Well, Estelle, am I a coward?

25 ESTELLE. How can I say? Don't be so unreasonable, darling. I can't put myself in your skin. You must decide that for yourself.

GARCIN. [*Wearily*] I can't decide.

ESTELLE. Anyhow, you must remember. You must have had rea-sons for acting as you did.

30 GARCIN. I had.

ESTELLE. Well?

GARCIN. But were they the real reasons?

ESTELLE. You've a twisted mind, that's your trouble. Plaguing yourself over such trifles!

35 GARCIN. I'd thought it all out, and I wanted to make a stand. But was that my real motive?

INEZ. Exactly. That's the question. Was that your real motive? No doubt you argued it out with yourself, you weighed the pros and cons, you found good reasons for what you did. But fear
40   and hatred and all the dirty little instincts one keeps dark—they're motives too. So carry on, Mr. Garcin, and try to be hon-est with yourself—for once.

GARCIN. Do I need you to tell me that? Day and night I paced my cell, from the window to the door, from the door to the win-
45   dow. I pried into my heart, I sleuthed myself like a detective. By

the end of it I felt as if I'd given my whole life to introspection. But always I harked back to the one thing certain—that I had acted as I did, I'd taken that train to the frontier. But why? Why? Finally I thought: My death will settle it. If I face death

5   courageously, I'll prove I am no coward.

INEZ. And how did you face death?

GARCIN. Miserably. Rottenly. [INEZ *laughs*.] Oh, it was only a physical lapse—that might happen to anyone; I'm not ashamed of it. Only everything's been left in suspense, forever. [*To*

10   ESTELLE] Come here, Estelle. Look at me. I want to feel someone looking at me while they're talking about me on earth. . . . I like green eyes.

INEZ. Green eyes! Just hark to him! And you, Estelle, do you like cowards?

15 ESTELLE. If you knew how little I care! Coward or hero, it's all one—provided he kisses well.

GARCIN. There they are, slumped in their chairs, sucking at their cigars. Bored they look. Half-asleep. They're thinking: "Garcin's a coward." But only vaguely, dreamily. One's got to

20   think of something. "That chap Garcin was a coward." That's what they've decided, those dear friends of mine. In six months' time they'll be saying: "Cowardly as that skunk Garcin." You're lucky, you two; no one on earth is giving you another thought. But I—I'm long in dying.

25 INEZ. What about your wife, Garcin?

GARCIN. Oh, didn't I tell you? She's dead.

INEZ. Dead?

GARCIN. Yes, she died just now. About two months ago.

INEZ. Of grief?

30 GARCIN. What else should she die of? So all is for the best, you see; the war's over, my wife's dead, and I've carved out my place in history.

[*He gives a choking sob and passes his hand over his face.* ESTELLE *catches his arm.*]

35 ESTELLE. My poor darling! Look at me. Please look. Touch me. Touch me. [*She takes his hand and puts it on her neck.*] There! Keep your hand there. [GARCIN *makes a fretful movement.*] No, don't move. Why trouble what those men are thinking? They'll die off one by one. Forget them. There's only me, now.

40 GARCIN. But *they* won't forget *me*, not they! They'll die, but others will come after them to carry on the legend. I've left my fate in their hands.

ESTELLE. You think too much, that's your trouble.

GARCIN. What else is there to do now? I was a man of action

45   once. . . . Oh, if only I could be with them again, for just one

day—I'd fling their lie in their teeth. But I'm locked out; they're passing judgment on my life without troubling about me, and they're right, because I'm dead. Dead and done with. [*Laughs*] A back number.

5   [*A short pause*]

ESTELLE. [*Gently*] Garcin.

GARCIN. Still there? Now listen! I want you to do me a service. No, don't shrink away. I know it must seem strange to you, having someone asking you for help; you're not used to that. But if
10   you'll make the effort, if you'll only *will* it hard enough, I dare say we can really love each other. Look at it this way. A thousand of them are proclaiming I'm a coward; but what do numbers matter? If there's someone, just one person, to say quite positively I did not run away, that I'm not the sort who runs
15   away, that I'm brave and decent and the rest of it—well, that one person's faith would save me. Will you have that faith in me? Then I shall love you and cherish you for ever. Estelle—will you?

ESTELLE. [*Laughing*] Oh, you dear silly man, do you think I could
20   love a coward?

GARCIN. But just now you said—

ESTELLE. I was only teasing you. I like men, my dear, who're real men, with tough skin and strong hands. You haven't a coward's chin, or a coward's mouth, or a coward's voice, or a cow-
25   ard's hair. And it's for your mouth, your hair, your voice, I love you.

GARCIN. Do you really mean this? *Really* mean it?

ESTELLE. Shall I swear it?

GARCIN. Then I snap my fingers at them all, those below and those
30   in here. Estelle, we shall climb out of hell. [INEZ *gives a shrill laugh. He breaks off and stares at her.*] What's that?

INEZ. [*Still laughing*] But she doesn't mean a word of what she says. How can you be such a simpleton? "Estelle, am I a coward?" As if she cared a damn either way.

35 ESTELLE. Inez, how dare you? [*To* GARCIN] Don't listen to her. If you want me to have faith in you, you must begin by trusting me.

INEZ. That's right! That's right! Trust away! She wants a man—that far you can trust her—she wants a man's arm around her waist,
40   a man's smell, a man's eyes glowing with desire. And that's all she wants. She'd assure you you were God Almighty if she thought it would give you pleasure.

GARCIN. Estelle, is this true? Answer me. Is it true?

ESTELLE. What do you expect me to say? Don't you realize how
45   maddening it is to have to answer questions one can't make

head or tail of? [*She stamps her foot.*] You do make things difficult. . . . Anyhow, I'd love you just the same, even if you were
a coward. Isn't that enough?

[*A short pause*]

5 GARCIN. [*To the two women*] You disgust me, both of you. [*He goes towards the door.*]

ESTELLE. What are you up to?

GARCIN. I'm going.

INEZ. [*Quickly*] You won't get far. The door is locked.

10 GARCIN. I'll make them open it. [*He presses the bell-push. The bell does not ring.*]

ESTELLE. Please! Please!

INEZ. [*To ESTELLE*] Don't worry, my pet. The bell doesn't work.

GARCIN. I tell you they shall open. [*Drums on the door*] I can't
15 endure it any longer, I'm through with you both. [ESTELLE
runs to him; he pushes her away.] Go away. You're even fouler
than she. I won't let myself get bogged in your eyes. You're soft
and slimy. Ugh! [*Bangs on the door again*] Like an octopus. Like
a quagmire.

20 ESTELLE. I beg you, oh, I beg you not to leave me. I'll promise not
to speak again, I won't trouble you in any way—but don't go.
I daren't be left alone with Inez, now she's shown her claws.

GARCIN. Look after yourself. I never asked you to come here.

ESTELLE. Oh, how mean you are! Yes, it's quite true you're a cow-
25 ard.

INEZ. [*Going up to ESTELLE*] Well, my little sparrow fallen from the
nest, I hope you're satisfied now. You spat in my face—playing
up to him, of course—and we had a tiff on his account. But he's
going, and a good riddance it will be. We two women will have
30 the place to ourselves.

ESTELLE. You won't gain anything. If that door opens, I'm going,
too.

INEZ. Where?

ESTELLE. I don't care where. As far from you as I can.

35 [GARCIN *has been drumming on the door while they talk.*]

GARCIN. Open the door! Open, blast you! I'll endure anything,
your red-hot tongs and molten lead, your racks and prongs and
garrotes—all your fiendish gadgets, everything that burns and
flays and tears—I'll put up with any torture you impose.
40 Anything, anything would be better than this agony of mind,
this creeping pain that gnaws and fumbles and caresses one
and never hurts quite enough. [*He grips the door-knob and rattles
it.*] Now will you open? [*The door flies open with a jerk, and he just
avoids falling.*] Ah! [*A long silence*]

45 INEZ. Well, Garcin? You're free to go.

GARCIN. [*Meditatively*] Now I wonder why that door opened.

INEZ. What are you waiting for? Hurry up and go.

GARCIN. I shall not go.

5 INEZ. And you, Estelle? [ESTELLE *does not move.* INEZ *bursts out laughing.*] So what? Which shall it be? Which of the three of us will leave? The barrier's down, why are we waiting? . . . But what a situation! It's a scream! We're—inseparables!

[ESTELLE *springs at her from behind.*]

ESTELLE. Inseparables? Garcin, come and lend a hand. Quickly.
10 We'll push her out and slam the door on her. That'll teach her a lesson.

INEZ. [*Struggling with* ESTELLE] Estelle! I beg you, let me stay. I won't go, I won't go! Not into the passage.

GARCIN. Let go of her.

15 ESTELLE. You're crazy. She hates you.

GARCIN. It's because of her I'm staying here.

[ESTELLE *releases* INEZ *and stares dumbfoundedly at* GARCIN.]

INEZ. Because of me? [*Pause*] All right, shut the door. It's ten times hotter here since it opened. [GARCIN *goes to the door and shuts*
20 *it.*] Because of me, you said?

GARCIN. Yes. *You*, anyhow, know what it means to be a coward.

INEZ. Yes, I know.

GARCIN. And you know what wickedness is, and shame, and fear. There were days when you peered into yourself, into the secret
25 places of your heart, and what you saw there made you faint with horror. And then, next day, you didn't know what to make of it, you couldn't interpret the horror you had glimpsed the day before. Yes, you know what evil *costs*. And when you say I'm a coward, you know from experience what that means. Is
30 that so?

INEZ. Yes.

GARCIN. So it's you whom I have to convince; you are of my kind. Did you suppose I meant to go? No, I couldn't leave you here, gloating over my defeat, with all those thoughts about me run-
35 ning in your head.

INEZ. Do you really wish to convince me?

GARCIN. That's the one and only thing I wish for now. I can't hear them any longer, you know. Probably that means they're through with me. For good and all. The curtain's down, noth-
40 ing of me is left on earth—not even the name of coward. So, Inez, we're alone. Only you two remain to give a thought to me. She—she doesn't count. It's you who matter; you who hate me. If you'll have faith in me I'm saved.

INEZ. It won't be easy. Have a look at me. I'm a hard-headed
45 woman.

GARCIN. I'll give you all the time that's needed.

INEZ. Yes, we've lots of time in hand. *All* time.

GARCIN. [*Putting his hands on her shoulders*] Listen! Each man has
an aim in life, a leading motive; that's so, isn't it? Well, I didn't
5 give a damn for wealth, or for love. I aimed at being a real man.
A tough, as they say. I staked everything on the same
horse. . . . Can one possibly be a coward when one's deliberately courted danger at every turn? And can one judge a life by
a single action?

10 INEZ. Why not? For thirty years you dreamt you were a hero, and
condoned a thousand petty lapses—because a hero, of course,
can do no wrong. An easy method, obviously. Then a day came
when you were up against it, the red light of real danger—and
you took the train to Mexico.

15 GARCIN. I "dreamt," you say. It was no dream. When I chose the
hardest path, I made my choice deliberately. A man is what he
wills himself to be.

INEZ. Prove it. Prove it was no dream. It's what one does, and nothing else, that shows the stuff one's made of.

20 GARCIN. I died too soon. I wasn't allowed time to—to do my
deeds.

INEZ. One always dies too soon—or too late. And yet one's whole
life is complete at that moment, with a line drawn neatly under
it, ready for the summing up. You are—your life, and nothing
25 else.

GARCIN. What a poisonous woman you are! With an answer for
everything.

INEZ. Now then! Don't lose heart. It shouldn't be so hard, convinc-
ing me. Pull yourself together, man, rake up some arguments.
30 [GARCIN *shrugs his shoulders.*] Ah, wasn't I right when I said
you were vulnerable? Now you're going to pay the price, and
what a price! You're a coward, Garcin, because I wish it. I wish
it—do you hear?—I wish it. And yet, just look at me, see how
weak I am, a mere breath on the air, a gaze observing you, a
35 formless thought that thinks you. [*He walks towards her, opening
his hands.*] Ah, they're open now, those big hands, those coarse,
man's hands! But what do you hope to do! You can't throttle
thoughts with hands. So you've no choice, you must convince
me, and you're at my mercy.

40 ESTELLE. Garcin!

GARCIN. What?

ESTELLE. Revenge yourself.

GARCIN. How?

ESTELLE. Kiss me, darling—then you'll hear her squeal.

45 GARCIN. That's true, Inez. I'm at your mercy, but you're at mine as

well. [*He bends over* ESTELLE. INEZ *gives a little cry.*]

INEZ. Oh, you coward, you weakling, running to women to console you!

ESTELLE. That's right, Inez. Squeal away.

5   INEZ. What a lovely pair you make! If you could see his big paw splayed out on your back, rucking up your skin and creasing the silk. Be careful, though! He's perspiring, his hand will leave a blue stain on your dress.

ESTELLE. Squeal away, Inez, squeal away! . . . Hug me tight, dar-

10   ling; tighter still—that'll finish her off, and a good thing too!

INEZ. Yes, Garcin, she's right. Carry on with it, press her to you till you feel your bodies melting into each other; a lump of warm, throbbing flesh. . . . Love's a grand solace, isn't it, my friend? Deep and dark as sleep. But I'll see you don't sleep.

15   [GARCIN *makes a slight movement.*]

ESTELLE. Don't listen to her. Press your lips to my mouth. Oh, I'm yours, yours, yours.

INEZ. Well, what are you waiting for? Do as you're told. What a lovely scene: coward Garcin holding baby-killer Estelle in his

20   manly arms! Make your stakes, everyone. Will coward Garcin kiss the lady, or won't he dare? What's the betting? I'm watching you, everybody's watching, I'm a crowd all by myself. Do you hear the crowd? Do you hear them muttering, Garcin? Mumbling and muttering. "Coward! Coward! Coward!

25   Coward!"—that's what they're saying. . . . It's no use trying to escape, I'll never let you go. What do you hope to get from her silly lips? Forgetfulness? But I shan't forget you, not I! "It's I you must convince." So come to me. I'm waiting. Come along, now. . . . Look how obedient he is, like a well-trained dog who

30   comes when his mistress calls. You can't hold him, and you never will.

GARCIN. Will night never come?

INEZ. Never.

GARCIN. You will always see me?

35   INEZ. Always.

[*Garcin moves away from* ESTELLE *and takes some steps across the room. He goes to the bronze ornament.*]

GARCIN. This bronze. [*Strokes it thoughtfully*] Yes, now's the moment; I'm looking at this thing on the mantelpiece, and I

40   understand that I'm in hell. I tell you, everything's been thought out beforehand. They knew I'd stand at the fireplace stroking this thing of bronze, with all those eyes intent on me. Devouring me. [*He swings round abruptly.*] What? Only two of you? I thought there were more; many more. [*Laughs*] So this is

45   hell. I'd never have believed it. You remember all we were told

about the torture-chambers, the fire and brimstone, the "burning marl." Old wives' tales! There's no need for red-hot pokers.
Hell is—other people!

ESTELLE. My darling! Please—

5 GARCIN. [*Thrusting her away*] No, let me be. She is between us. I
cannot love you when she's watching.

ESTELLE. Right! In that case, I'll stop her watching. [*She picks up the
paper-knife from the table, rushes at INEZ, and stabs her several
times.*]

10 INEZ. [*Struggling and laughing*] But, you crazy creature, what do
you think you're doing? You know quite well I'm dead.

ESTELLE. Dead?

[*She drops the knife. A pause. INEZ picks up the knife and jabs herself with it regretfully.*]

15 INEZ. Dead! Dead! Dead! Knives, poison, ropes—all useless. It has
happened already, do you understand? Once and for all. So
here we are, forever. [*Laughs*]

ESTELLE. [*With a peal of laughter*] Forever. My God, how funny!
Forever.

20 GARCIN. [*Looks at the two women, and joins in the laughter*] For ever,
and ever, and ever.

[*They slump onto their respective sofas. A long silence. Their laughter dies away and they gaze at each other.*]

GARCIN. Well, well, let's get on with it. . . .

CURTAIN

12. Naguib Mahfouz

Naguib Mahfouz was born in Cairo, Egypt, in 1911, and was educated at the University of Cairo where he earned a degree in philosophy. He is one of the most famous contemporary Arab writers, although his books have been banned in many Islamic countries. In his stories and novels, Mahfouz is often concerned with spiritual sterility and the loss of genuine Islamic values in the modern world. He was awarded the Nobel Prize for Literature in 1988.

ZAABALAWI

(1963)

Finally I became convinced that I had to find Sheikh[1] Zaabalawi.

The first time I had heard of his name had been in a song:

Oh what's become of the world, Zaabalawi?
5   They've turned it upside down and taken away its taste.

It had been a popular song in my childhood, and one day it had occurred to me to demand of my father, in the way children have of asking endless questions:

"Who is Zaabalawi?"

10   He had looked at me hesitantly as though doubting my ability to understand the answer. However, he had replied, "May his blessing descend upon you, he's a true saint of God, a remover of worries and troubles. Were it not for him I would have died miserably—"

In the years that followed, I heard my father many a time sing
15   the praises of this good saint and speak of the miracles he performed. The days passed and brought with them many illnesses, for each one of which I was able, without too much trouble and at a cost I could afford, to find a cure, until I became afflicted with that illness for which no one possesses a remedy. When I had tried every-
20   thing in vain and was overcome by despair, I remembered by

---

[1]A title of respect (originally "old man"), often indicating rulership.

chance what I had heard in my childhood: Why, I asked myself, should I not seek out Sheikh Zaabalawi? I recollected my father saying that he had made his acquaintance in Khan Gaafar[2] at the house of Sheikh Qamar, one of those sheikhs who practiced law in the religious courts, and so I took myself off to his house. Wishing to make sure that he was still living there, I made inquiries of a vendor of beans whom I found in the lower part of the house.

"Sheikh Qamar!" he said, looking at me in amazement. "He left the quarter ages ago. They say he's now living in Garden City and has his office in al-Azhar Square."[3]

I looked up the office address in the telephone book and immediately set off to the Chamber of Commerce Building, where it was located. On asking to see Sheikh Qamar, I was ushered into a room just as a beautiful woman with a most intoxicating perfume was leaving it. The man received me with a smile and motioned me toward a fine leather-upholstered chair. Despite the thick soles of my shoes, my feet were conscious of the lushness of the costly carpet. The man wore a lounge suit and was smoking a cigar; his manner of sitting was that of someone well satisfied both with himself and with his worldly possessions. The look of warm welcome he gave me left no doubt in my mind that he thought me a prospective client, and I felt acutely embarrassed at encroaching upon his valuable time.

"Welcome!" he said, prompting me to speak.

"I am the son of your old friend Sheikh Ali al-Tatawi," I answered so as to put an end to my equivocal position.

A certain languor was apparent in the glance he cast at me; the languor was not total in that he had not as yet lost all hope in me.

"God rest his soul," he said. "He was a fine man."

The very pain that had driven me to go there now prevailed upon me to stay.

"He told me," I continued, "of a devout saint named Zaabalawi whom he met at Your Honor's. I am in need of him, sir, if he be still in the land of the living."

The languor became firmly entrenched in his eyes, and it would have come as no surprise if he had shown the door to both me and my father's memory.

"That," he said in the tone of one who has made up his mind to terminate the conversation, "was a very long time ago and I scarcely recall him now."

Rising to my feet so as to put his mind at rest regarding my intention of going, I asked, "Was he really a saint?"

---

[2]Gaafar Market, an area of shops.

[3]An area of Cairo close to the famous mosque and university of al-Azhar.

"We used to regard him as a man of miracles."

"And where could I find him today?" I asked, making another move toward the door.

5 "To the best of my knowledge he was living in the Birgawi Residence in al-Azhar," and he applied himself to some papers on his desk with a resolute movement that indicated he would not open his mouth again. I bowed my head in thanks, apologized several times for disturbing him, and left the office, my head so buzzing with embarrassment that I was oblivious to all sounds
10 around me.

I went to the Birgawi Residence, which was situated in a thickly populated quarter. I found that time had so eaten at the building that nothing was left of it save an antiquated façade and a courtyard that, despite being supposedly in the charge of a caretaker, was
15 being used as a rubbish dump. A small, insignificant fellow, a mere prologue to a man, was using the covered entrance as a place for the sale of old books on theology and mysticism.

When I asked him about Zaabalawi, he peered at me through narrow, inflamed eyes and said in amazement, "Zaabalawi! Good
20 heavens, what a time ago that was! Certainly he used to live in this house when it was habitable. Many were the times he would sit with me talking of bygone days, and I would be blessed by his holy presence. Where, though, is Zaabalawi today?"

He shrugged his shoulders sorrowfully and soon left me, to
25 attend to an approaching customer. I proceeded to make inquiries of many shopkeepers in the district. While I found that a large number of them had never even heard of Zaabalawi, some, though recalling nostalgically the pleasant times they had spent with him, were ignorant of his present whereabouts, while others openly
30 made fun of him, labeled him a charlatan, and advised me to put myself in the hands of a doctor—as though I had not already done so. I therefore had no alternative but to return disconsolately home.

With the passing of days like motes in the air, my pains grew so severe that I was sure I would not be able to hold out much longer.
35 Once again I fell to wondering about Zaabalawi and clutching at the hope his venerable name stirred within me. Then it occurred to me to seek the help of the local sheikh of the district; in fact, I was surprised I had not thought of this to begin with. His office was in the nature of a small shop, except that it contained a desk and a tele-
40 phone, and I found him sitting at his desk, wearing a jacket over his striped galabeya.[4] As he did not interrupt his conversation with a man sitting beside him, I stood waiting till the man had gone. The

---

[4]The traditional Arab robe, over which this modernized district officer wears a European jacket.

sheikh then looked up at me coldly. I told myself that I should win him over by the usual methods, and it was not long before I had him cheerfully inviting me to sit down.

"I'm in need of Sheikh Zaabalawi," I answered his inquiry as to the purpose of my visit.

He gazed at me with the same astonishment as that shown by those I had previously encountered.

"At least," he said, giving me a smile that revealed his gold teeth, "he is still alive. The devil of it is, though, he has no fixed abode. You might well bump into him as you go out of here, on the other hand you might spend days and months in fruitless searching."

"Even you can't find him!"

"Even I! He's a baffling man, but I thank the Lord that he's still alive!"

He gazed at me intently, and murmured, "It seems your condition is serious. "

"Very.

"May God come to your aid! But why don't you go about it systematically?" He spread out a sheet of paper on the desk and drew on it with unexpected speed and skill until he had made a full plan of the district, showing all the various quarters, lanes, alleyways, and squares. He looked at it admiringly and said, "These are dwelling-houses, here is the Quarter of the Perfumers, here the Quarter of the Coppersmiths, the Mouski,[5] the police and fire stations. The drawing is your best guide. Look carefully in the cafés, the places where the dervishes perform their rites, the mosques and prayer-rooms, and the Green Gate, for he may well be concealed among the beggars and be indistinguishable from them. Actually, I myself haven't seen him for years, having been somewhat preoccupied with the cares of the world, and was only brought back by your inquiry to those most exquisite times of my youth."

I gazed at the map in bewilderment. The telephone rang, and he took up the receiver.

"Take it," he told me, generously. "We're at your service."

Folding up the map, I left and wandered off through the quarter, from square to street to alleyway, making inquiries of everyone I felt was familiar with the place. At last the owner of a small establishment for ironing clothes told me, "Go to the calligrapher Hassanein in Umm al-Ghulam—they were friends."

I went to Umm al-Ghulam,[6] where I found old Hassanein working in a deep, narrow shop full of signboards and jars of color.

---

[5]The central bazaar.

[6]A street in Cairo.

A strange smell, a mixture of glue and perfume, permeated its every corner. Old Hassanein was squatting on a sheepskin rug in front of a board propped against the wall; in the middle of it he had inscribed the word "Allah" in silver lettering. He was engrossed in
5   embellishing the letters with prodigious care. I stood behind him, fearful of disturbing him or breaking the inspiration that flowed to his masterly hand. When my concern at not interrupting him had lasted some time, he suddenly inquired with unaffected gentleness, "Yes?"

10   Realizing that he was aware of my presence, I introduced myself. "I've been told that Sheikh Zaabalawi is your friend; I'm looking for him," I said.

His hand came to a stop. He scrutinized me in astonishment. "Zaabalawi! God be praised!" he said with a sigh.

15   "He *is* a friend of yours, isn't he?" I asked eagerly.

"He was, once upon a time. A real man of mystery: he'd visit you so often that people would imagine he was your nearest and dearest, then would disappear as though he'd never existed. Yet saints are not to be blamed. "

20   The spark of hope went out with the suddenness of a lamp snuffed by a power-cut.

"He was so constantly with me," said the man, "that I felt him to be a part of everything I drew. But where is he today?"

"Perhaps he is still alive?"

25   "He's alive, without a doubt. . . . He had impeccable taste, and it was due to him that I made my most beautiful drawings."

"God knows," I said, in a voice almost stifled by the dead ashes of hope, "how dire my need for him is, and no one knows better than you[7] of the ailments in respect of which he is sought."

30   "Yes, yes. May God restore you to health. He is, in truth, as is said of him, a man, and more. . . .

Smiling broadly, he added, "And his face possesses an unforgettable beauty. But where is he?"

Reluctantly I rose to my feet, shook hands, and left. I continued
35 wandering eastward and westward through the quarter, inquiring about Zaabalawi from everyone who, by reason of age or experience, I felt might be likely to help me. Eventually I was informed by a vendor of lupine that he had met him a short while ago at the house of Sheikh Gad, the well-known composer. I went to the musi-
40 cian's house in Tabakshiyya,[8] where I found him in a room tastefully furnished in the old style, its walls redolent with history. He

---

[7]One of the calligrapher's major tasks is to write religious documents and prayers to Allah.

[8]A quarter named for the straw trays made and sold there.

was seated on a divan, his famous lute beside him, concealing within itself the most beautiful melodies of our age, while somewhere
from within the house came the sound of pestle and mortar and the
clamor of children. I immediately greeted him and introduced
5   myself, and was put at my ease by the unaffected way in which he
received me. He did not ask, either in words or gesture, what had
brought me, and I did not feel that he even harbored any such
curiosity. Amazed at his understanding and kindness, which boded
well, I said, "O Sheikh Gad, I am an admirer of yours, having long
10   been enchanted by the renderings of your songs."
      "Thank you," he said with a smile.
      "Please excuse my disturbing you," I continued timidly, "but I
was told that Zaabalawi was your friend, and I am in urgent need
of him."
15   "Zaabalawi!" he said, frowning in concentration. "You need
him? God be with you, for who knows, O Zaabalawi, where you are."
      "Doesn't he visit you?" I asked eagerly.
      "He visited me some time ago. He might well come right now;
on the other hand I mightn't see him till death!"
20   I gave an audible sigh and asked, "What made him like that?"
      The musician took up his lute. "Such are saints or they would
not be saints," he said, laughing.
      "Do those who need him suffer as I do?"
      "Such suffering is part of the cure!"
25   He took up the plectrum and began plucking soft strains from
the strings. Lost in thought, I followed his movements. Then, as
though addressing myself, I said, "So my visit has been in vain."
      He smiled, laying his cheek against the side of the lute. "God
forgive you," he said, "for saying such a thing of a visit that has
caused me to know you and you me!"
      I was much embarrassed and said apologetically, "Please for-
30   give me; my feelings of defeat made me forget my manners."
      "Do not give in to defeat. This extraordinary man brings
fatigue to all who seek him. It was easy enough with him in the old
days when his place of abode was known. Today, though, the world
has changed, and after having enjoyed a position attained only by
35   potentates, he is now pursued by the police on a charge of false pre-
tenses. It is therefore no longer an easy matter to reach him, but
have patience and be sure that you will do so."
      He raised his head from the lute and skillfully fingered the
opening bars of a melody. Then he sang:

I make lavish mention, even though I blame myself, of those I
love,
For the stories of the beloved are my wine.[9]

5   With a heart that was weary and listless, I followed the beauty
of the melody and the singing.
    "I composed the music to this poem in a single night," he told
me when he had finished. I remember that it was the eve of the
Lesser Bairam.[10] Zaabalawi was my guest for the whole of that
night, and the poem was of his choosing. He would sit for a while
10 just where you are, then would get up and play with my children as
though he were one of them. Whenever I was overcome by weariness or my inspiration failed me, he would punch me playfully in
the chest and joke with me, and I would bubble over with melodies,
and thus I continued working till I finished the most beautiful piece
15 I have ever composed."
    "Does he know anything about music?"
    "He is the epitome of things musical. He has an extremely
beautiful speaking voice, and you have only to hear him to want to
burst into song and to be inspired to creativity. . . ."
20   "How was it that he cured those diseases before which men are
powerless?"
    "That is his secret. Maybe you will learn it when you meet
him."
    But when would that meeting occur? We relapsed into silence,
25 and the hubbub of children once more filled the room.
    Again the sheikh began to sing. He went on repeating the
words "and I have a memory of her" in different and beautiful variations until the very walls danced in ecstasy. I expressed my whole-
hearted admiration, and he gave me a smile of thanks. I then got up
30 and asked permission to leave, and he accompanied me to the front
door. As I shook him by the hand, he said, "I hear that nowadays he
frequents the house of Hagg Wanas al-Damanhouri. Do you know
him?"
    I shook my head, though a modicum of renewed hope crept
35 into my heart.
    "He is a man of private means," the sheikh told me, "who from
time to time visits Cairo, putting up at some hotel or other. Every
evening, though, he spends at the Negma Bar in Alfi Street."
    I waited for nightfall and went to the Negma Bar. I asked a
40 waiter about Hagg Wanas, and he pointed to a corner that was

[9]Words from a poem by the medieval mystic poet, Ibn al-Farid.
[10]A major holiday, celebrated for three days to end the month's fasting during Ramadan.

semisecluded because of its position behind a large pillar with mirrors on all four sides. There I saw a man seated alone at a table with two bottles in front of him, one empty, the other two-thirds empty. There were no snacks or food to be seen, and I was sure that I was
5   in the presence of a hardened drinker. He was wearing a loosely flowing silk galabeya and a carefully wound turban; his legs were stretched out toward the base of the pillar, and as he gazed into the mirror in rapt contentment, the sides of his face, rounded and handsome despite the fact that he was approaching old age, were flushed
10 with wine. I approached quietly till I stood but a few feet away from him. He did not turn toward me or give any indication that he was aware of my presence.

     "Good evening, Mr. Wanas," I greeted him cordially.

     He turned toward me abruptly, as though my voice had roused
15 him from slumber, and glared at me in disapproval. I was about to explain what had brought me to him when he interrupted in an almost imperative tone of voice that was none the less not devoid of an extraordinary gentleness, "First, please sit down, and, second, please get drunk!"
20   I opened my mouth to make my excuses but, stopping up his ears with his fingers, he said, "Not a word till you do what I say."

     I realized I was in the presence of a capricious drunkard and told myself that I should at least humor him a bit. "Would you permit me to ask one question?" I said with a smile, sitting down.
25   Without removing his hands from his ears he indicated the bottle. "When engaged in a drinking bout like this, I do not allow any conversation between myself and another unless, like me, he is drunk, otherwise all propriety is lost and mutual comprehension is rendered impossible."
30   I made a sign indicating that I did not drink.

     "That's your lookout," he said offhandedly. "And that's my condition!"

     He filled me a glass, which I meekly took and drank. No sooner had the wine settled in my stomach than it seemed to ignite. I
35 waited patiently till I had grown used to its ferocity, and said, "It's very strong, and I think the time has come for me to ask you about—"

     Once again, however, he put his fingers in his ears. "I shan't listen to you until you're drunk!"
40   He filled up my glass for the second time. I glanced at it in trepidation; then, overcoming my inherent objection, I drank it down at a gulp. No sooner had the wine come to rest inside me than I lost all willpower. With the third glass, I lost my memory, and with the fourth the future vanished. The world turned round about me and
45 I forgot why I had gone there. The man leaned toward me atten-

tively, but I saw him—saw everything—as a mere meaningless
series of colored planes. I don't know how long it was before my
head sank down onto the arm of the chair and I plunged into deep
sleep. During it, I had a beautiful dream the like of which I had
5   never experienced. I dreamed that I was in an immense garden surrounded on all sides by luxuriant trees, and the sky was nothing but
stars seen between the entwined branches, all enfolded in an atmosphere like that of sunset or a sky overcast with cloud. I was lying on
a small hummock of jasmine petals, more of which fell upon me like
10 rain, while the lucent spray of a fountain unceasingly sprinkled the
crown of my head and my temples. I was in a state of deep con-
tentedness, of ecstatic serenity. An orchestra of warbling and cooing
played in my ear. There was an extraordinary sense of harmony
between me and my inner self, and between the two of us and the
15 world, everything being in its rightful place, without discord or distortion. In the whole world there was no single reason for speech or
movement, for the universe moved in a rapture of ecstasy. This lasted but a short while. When I opened my eyes, consciousness struck
at me like a policeman's fist and I saw Wanas al-Damanhouri
20 regarding me with concern. Only a few drowsy customers were left
in the bar.

    "You have slept deeply," said my companion. "You were obvi-
ously hungry for sleep."

    I rested my heavy head in the palms of my hands. When I took
25 them away in astonishment and looked down at them, I found that
they glistened with drops of water.

    "My head's wet," I protested.

    "Yes, my friend tried to rouse you," he answered quietly.

    "Somebody saw me in this state?"

30   "Don't worry, he is a good man. Have you not heard of Sheikh
Zaabalawi?"

    "Zaabalawi!" I exclaimed, jumping to my feet.

    "Yes," he answered in surprise. "What's wrong?"

    "Where is he?"

35   "I don't know where he is now. He was here and then he left."

    I was about to run off in pursuit but found I was more exhaust-
ed than I had imagined. Collapsed over the table, I cried out in
despair, "My sole reason for coming to you was to meet him! Help
me to catch up with him or send someone after him."

40   The man called a vendor of prawns and asked him to seek out
the sheikh and bring him back. Then he turned to me. "I didn't realize you were afflicted. I'm very sorry. . . ."

    "You wouldn't let me speak, " I said irritably.

    "What a pity! He was sitting on this chair beside you the whole
45 time. He was playing with a string of jasmine petals he had around

his neck, a gift from one of his admirers, then, taking pity on you, he began to sprinkle some water on your head to bring you around."

"Does he meet you here every night?" I asked, my eyes not
5 leaving the doorway through which the vendor of prawns had left.

"He was with me tonight, last night and the night before that, but before that I hadn't seen him for a month."

"Perhaps he will come tomorrow," I answered with a sigh.

"Perhaps."
10 "I am willing to give him any money he wants."

Wanas answered sympathetically, "The strange thing is that he is not open to such temptations, yet he will cure you if you meet him."

"Without charge?"
15 "Merely on sensing that you love him."

The vendor of prawns returned, having failed in his mission.

I recovered some of my energy and left the bar, albeit unsteadily. At every street corner I called out "Zaabalawi!" in the vague hope that I would be rewarded with an answering shout. The street
20 boys turned contemptuous eyes on me till I sought refuge in the first available taxi.

The following evening I stayed up with Wanas al-Damanhouri till dawn, but the sheikh did not put in an appearance. Wanas informed me that he would be going away to the country and
25 would not be returning to Cairo until he had sold the cotton crop.

I must wait, I told myself; I must train myself to be patient. Let me content myself with having made certain of the existence of Zaabalawi, and even of his affection for me, which encourages me to think that he will be prepared to cure me if a meeting takes place
30 between us.

Sometimes, however, the long delay wearied me. I would become beset by despair and would try to persuade myself to dismiss him from my mind completely. How many weary people in this life know him not or regard him as a mere myth! Why, then,
35 should I torture myself about him in this way?

No sooner, however, did my pains force themselves upon me than I would again begin to think about him, asking myself when I would be fortunate enough to meet him. The fact that I ceased to have any news of Wanas and was told he had gone to live abroad
40 did not deflect me from my purpose; the truth of the matter was that I had become fully convinced that I had to find Zaabalawi.

Yes, I have to find Zaabalawi.

13. RALPH ELLISON

Ralph Ellison (1914–1994) is widely regarded as one of the finest twentieth-century American novelists. Invisible Man (1952), from which the following selection has been taken, is an extraordinarily powerful account of a young black man, coming to consciousness both of his own identity and of the expectations of his society, in the American south at mid-century. The novel is a searing indictment of racism in all of its forms, from the most brutal abuses to the more subtle slights and stereotypes.

FROM INVISIBLE MAN

(1952)

PROLOGUE

I am an invisible man. No, I am not a spook like those who haunted Edgar Allan Poe; nor am I one of your Hollywood-movie ectoplasms. I am a man of substance, of flesh and bone, fiber and liquids—and I might even be said to possess a mind. I am invisible,
5 understand, simply because people refuse to see me. Like the bodiless heads you see sometimes in circus sideshows, it is as though I have been surrounded by mirrors of hard, distorting glass. When they approach me they see only my surroundings, themselves, or figments of their imagination—indeed, everything and anything
10 except me.

Nor is my invisibility exactly a matter of a biochemical accident to my epidermis. That invisibility to which I refer occurs because of a peculiar disposition of the eyes of those with whom I come in contact. A matter of the construction of their *inner* eyes, those eyes with
15 which they look through their physical eyes upon reality. I am not complaining, nor am I protesting either. It is sometimes advantageous to be unseen, although it is most often rather wearing on the nerves. Then too, you are constantly being bumped against by those of poor vision. Or again, you often doubt if you really exist. You
20 wonder whether you aren't simply a phantom in other people's minds. Say, a figure in a nightmare which the sleeper tries with all his strength to destroy. It's when you feel like this that, out of resent-

ment, you begin to bump people back. And, let me confess, you feel that way most of the time. You ache with the need to convince yourself that you do exist in the real world, that you're a part of all the sound and anguish, and you strike out with your fists, you curse
5   and you swear to make them recognize you. And, alas, it's seldom successful.

One night I accidentally bumped into a man, and perhaps because of the near darkness he saw me and called me an insulting name. I sprang at him, seized his coat lapels and demanded that he
10 apologize. He was a tall blond man, and as my face came close to his he looked insolently out of his blue eyes and cursed me, his breath hot in my face as he struggled. I pulled his chin down sharp upon the crown of my head, butting him as I had seen the West Indians do, and I felt his flesh tear and the blood gush out, and I
15 yelled, "Apologize! Apologize!" But he continued to curse and struggle, and I butted him again and again until he went down heavily, on his knees, profusely bleeding. I kicked him repeatedly, in a frenzy because he still uttered insults though his lips were frothy with blood. Oh yes, I kicked him! And in my outrage I got
20 out my knife and prepared to slit his throat, right there beneath the lamplight in the deserted street, holding him in the collar with one hand, and opening the knife with my teeth—when it occurred to me that the man had not *seen* me, actually; that he, as far as he knew, was in the midst of a walking nightmare! And I stopped the blade,
25 slicing the air as I pushed him away, letting him fall back to the street. I stared at him hard as the lights of a car stabbed through the darkness. He lay there, moaning on the asphalt; a man almost killed by a phantom. It unnerved me. I was both disgusted and ashamed. I was like a drunken man myself, wavering about on weakened
30 legs. Then I was amused: Something in this man's thick head had sprung out and beaten him within an inch of his life. I began to laugh at this crazy discovery. Would he have awakened at the point of death? Would Death himself have freed him for wakeful living? But I didn't linger. I ran away into the dark, laughing so hard I
35 feared I might rupture myself. The next day I saw his picture in the *Daily News*, beneath a caption stating that he had been "mugged." Poor fool, poor blind fool, I thought with sincere compassion, mugged by an invisible man!

Most of the time (although I do not choose as I once did to deny
40 the violence of my days by ignoring it) I am not so overtly violent. I remember that I am invisible and walk softly so as not to awaken the sleeping ones. Sometimes it is best not to awaken them; there are few things in the world as dangerous as sleepwalkers. I learned in time though that it is possible to carry on a fight against them with-
45 out their realizing it. For instance, I have been carrying on a fight

with Monopolated Light & Power for some time now. I use their
service and pay them nothing at all, and they don't know it. Oh,
they suspect that power is being drained off, but they don't know
where. All they know is that according to the master meter back
5   there in their power station a hell of a lot of free current is disap-
pearing somewhere into the jungle of Harlem. The joke, of course,
is that I don't live in Harlem but in a border area. Several years ago
(before I discovered the advantages of being invisible) I went
through the routine process of buying service and paying their out-
10 rageous rates. But no more. I gave up all that, along with my apart-
ment, and my old way of life: That way based upon the fallacious
assumption that I, like other men, was visible. Now, aware of my
invisibility, I live rent-free in a building rented strictly to whites, in
a section of the basement that was shut off and forgotten during the
15 nineteenth century, which I discovered when I was trying to escape
in the night from Ras the Destroyer. But that's getting too far ahead
of the story, almost to the end, although the end is in the beginning,
and lies far ahead.
       The point now is that I found a home—or a hole in the ground,
20 as you will. Now don't jump to the conclusion that because I call my
home a "hole" it is damp and cold like a grave; there are cold holes
and warm holes. Mine is a warm hole. And remember, a bear retires
to his hole for the winter and lives until spring; then he comes
strolling out like the Easter chick breaking from its shell. I say all
25 this to assure you that it is incorrect to assume that, because I'm
invisible and live in a hole, I am dead. I am neither dead nor in a
state of suspended animation. Call me Jack-the-Bear, for I am in a
state of hibernation.
       My hole is warm and full of light. Yes, *full* of light. I doubt if
30 there is a brighter spot in all New York than this hole of mine, and
I do not exclude Broadway. Or the Empire State Building on a pho-
tographer's dream night. But that is taking advantage of you. Those
two spots are among the darkest of our whole civilization—pardon
me, our whole *culture* (an important distinction, I've heard)—which
35 might sound like a hoax, or a contradiction, but that (by contradiction, I mean) is how the world moves: Not like an arrow, but a
boomerang. (Beware of those who speak of the *spiral* of history; they
are preparing a boomerang. Keep a steel helmet handy.) I know; I
have been boomeranged across my head so much that I now can see
40 the darkness of lightness. And I love light. Perhaps you'll think it
strange that an invisible man should need light, desire light, love
light. But maybe it is exactly because I *am* invisible. Light confirms
my reality, gives birth to my form. A beautiful girl once told me of
a recurring nightmare in which she lay in the center of a large dark
45 room and felt her face expand until it filled the whole room, becom-

[handwritten margin notes: "ironic" and "A light hole"]

ing a formless mass while her eyes ran in bilious jelly up the chimney. And so it is with me. Without light I am not only invisible, but formless as well; and to be unaware of one's form is to live a death. I myself, after existing some twenty years, did not become alive
5 until I discovered my invisibility.

That is why I fight my battle with Monopolated Light & Power. The deeper reason, I mean: It allows me to feel my vital aliveness. I also fight them for taking so much of my money before I learned to protect myself. In my hole in the basement there are exactly 1,369
10 lights. I've wired the entire ceiling, every inch of it. And not with fluorescent bulbs, but with the older, more-expensive-to-operate kind, the filament type. An act of sabotage, you know. I've already begun to wire the wall. A junk man I know, a man of vision, has supplied me with wire and sockets. Nothing, storm or flood, must get
15 in the way of our need for light and ever more and brighter light. The truth is the light and light is the truth. When I finish all four walls, then I'll start on the floor. Just how that will go, I don't know. Yet when you have lived invisible as long as I have you develop a certain ingenuity. I'll solve the problem. And maybe I'll invent a
20 gadget to place my coffee pot on the fire while I lie in bed, and even invent a gadget to warm my bed—like the fellow I saw in one of the picture magazines who made himself a gadget to warm his shoes! Though invisible, I am in the great American tradition of tinkers. That makes me kin to Ford, Edison and Franklin. Call me, since I
25 have a theory and a concept, a "thinker-tinker." Yes, I'll warm my shoes; they need it, they're usually full of holes. I'll do that and more.

Now I have one radio-phonograph; I plan to have five. There is a certain acoustical deadness in my hole, and when I have music I
30 want to *feel* its vibration, not only with my ear but with my whole body. I'd like to hear five recordings of Louis Armstrong playing and singing "What Did I Do to Be so Black and Blue"—all at the same time. Sometimes now I listen to Louis while I have my favorite dessert of vanilla ice cream and sloe gin. I pour the red liquid over
35 the white mound, watching it glisten and the vapor rising as Louis bends that military instrument into a beam of lyrical sound. Perhaps I like Louis Armstrong because he's made poetry out of being invisible. I think it must be because he's unaware that he *is* invisible. And my own grasp of invisibility aids me to understand
40 his music. Once when I asked for a cigarette, some jokers gave me a reefer, which I lighted when I got home and sat listening to my phonograph. It was a strange evening. Invisibility, let me explain, gives one a slightly different sense of time, you're never quite on the beat. Sometimes you're ahead and sometimes behind. Instead of the
45 swift and imperceptible flowing of time, you are aware of its nodes,

those points where time stands still or from which it leaps ahead. And you slip into the breaks and look around. That's what you hear vaguely in Louis' music.

5 Once I saw a prizefighter boxing a yokel. The fighter was swift and amazingly scientific. His body was one violent flow of rapid rhythmic action. He hit the yokel a hundred times while the yokel held up his arms in stunned surprise. But suddenly the yokel, rolling about in the gale of boxing gloves, struck one blow and knocked science, speed and footwork as cold as a well-digger's pos-
10 terior. The smart money hit the canvas. The long shot got the nod. The yokel had simply stepped inside of his opponent's sense of time. So under the spell of the reefer I discovered a new analytical way of listening to music. The unheard sounds came through, and each melodic line existed of itself, stood out clearly from all the rest,
15 said its piece, and waited patiently for the other voices to speak. That night I found myself hearing not only in time, but in space as well. I not only entered the music but descended, like Dante, into its depths. *And beneath the swiftness of the hot tempo there was a slower tempo and a cave and I entered it and looked around and heard an old*
20 *woman singing a spiritual as full of Weltschmerz as flamenco, and beneath that lay a still lower level on which I saw a beautiful girl the color of ivory pleading in a voice like my mother's as she stood before a group of slaveowners who bid for her naked body, and below that I found a lower level and a more rapid tempo and I heard someone shout:*
25 *"Brothers and sisters, my text this morning is the 'Blackness of Blackness.'"*

And a congregation of voices answered. "That blackness is most black, brother, most black . . ."
"In the beginning . . ."
30 *"At the very start, " they cried.*
". . . there was blackness . . ."
"Preach it . . ."
". . . and the sun . . ."
"The sun, Lawd . . ."
35 *". . . was bloody red . . ."*
"Red . . ."
"Now black is . . ." the preacher shouted.
"Bloody . . ."
"I said black is . . ."
40 *"Preach it, brother . . ."*
". . . an' black ain't . . ."
"Red, Lawd, red. He said it's red!"
"Amen, brother. . ."
"Black will git you . . ."
45 *"Yes, it will . . ."*

13. Ralph Ellison

"Yes, it will . . ."

". . . an' black won't . . ."

"Naw, it won't!"

"It do, Lawd . . ."

5   "It do, Lawd. . .

". . . an' it don't."

'Halleluiah . . ."

". . . It'll put you, glory, glory, Oh my Lawd, in the WHALE'S BELLY."

"Preach it, dear brother . . ."

10   ". . . an' make you tempt . . ."

"Good God a-mighty!"

"Old Aunt Nelly!"

"Black will make you . . ."

"Black . . ."

15   ". . . or black will un-make you."

"Ain't it the truth, Lawd?"

And at that point a voice of trombone timbre screamed at me, "Git out of here, you fool! Is you ready to commit treason?"

And I tore myself away, hearing the old singer of spirituals moaning,

20 "Go curse your God, boy, and die."

I stopped and questioned her, asked her what was wrong.

"I dearly loved my master, son," she said.

"You should have hated him," I said.

"He gave me several sons," she said, "and because I loved my sons I

25 learned to love their father though I hated him too."

"I too have become acquainted with ambivalence, " I said. "That's why I'm here."

"What's that?"

"Nothing, a word that doesn't explain it. Why do you moan?"

30   "I moan this way 'cause he's dead," she said.

"Then tell me, who is that laughing upstairs?"

"Them's my sons. They glad."

"Yes, I can understand that too," I said.

"I laughs too, but I moans too. He promised to set us free but he never

35 could bring hisself to do it. Still I loved him . . ."

"Loved him? You mean . . ."

"Oh yes, but I loved something else even more."

"What more?"

"Freedom."

40   "Freedom," I said. "Maybe freedom lies in hating."

"Naw, son, it's in loving. I loved him and give him the poison and he withered away like a frost-bit apple. Them boys woulda tore him to pieces with they homemade knives."

"A mistake was made somewhere," I said, "I'm confused." And I

45 wished to say other things, but the laughter upstairs became too loud and

moan-like for me and I tried to break out of it, but I couldn't. Just as I was leaving I felt an urgent desire to ask her what freedom was and went back. She sat with her head in her hands, moaning softly; her leather-brown face was filled with sadness.

5   "Old woman, what is this freedom you love so well?" I asked around a corner of my mind.

     She looked surprised, then thoughtful, then baffled. "I done forgot, son. It's all mixed up. First I think it's one thing, then I think it's another. It gits my head to spinning. I guess now it ain't nothin but knowing how
10 to say what I got up in my head. But it's a hard job, son. Too much is done happen to me in too short a time. Hit's like I have a fever. Ever' time I starts to walk my head gits to swirling and I falls down. Or if it ain't that, it's the boys; they gits to laughing and wants to kill up the white folks. They's bitter, that's what they is . . .

15   "But what about freedom?"

     "Leave me 'lone, boy; my head aches!"

     I left her, feeling dizzy myself. I didn't get far.

     Suddenly one of the sons, a big fellow six feet tall, appeared out of nowhere and struck me with his fist.

20   "What's the matter, man?" I cried.

     "You made Ma cry!"

     "But how?" I said, dodging a blow.

     "Askin' her them questions, that's how. Git outa here and stay, and next time you got questions like that, ask yourself!"

25   He held me in a grip like cold stone, his fingers fastening upon my windpipe until I thought I would suffocate before he finally allowed me to go. I stumbled about dazed, the music beating hysterically in my ears. It was dark. My head cleared and I wandered down a dark narrow passage, thinking I heard his footsteps hurrying behind me. I was sore, and into my
30 being had come a profound craving for tranquillity, for peace and quiet, a state I felt I could never achieve. For one thing, the trumpet was blaring and the rhythm was too hectic. A tom-tom beating like heart-thuds began drowning out the trumpet, filling my ears. I longed for water and I heard it rushing through the cold mains my fingers touched as I felt my way, but
35 I couldn't stop to search because of the footsteps behind me.

     "Hey, Ras," I called. "Is it you, Destroyer? Rinehart?"

     No answer, only the rhythmic footsteps behind me. Once I tried crossing the road, but a speeding machine struck me, scraping the skin from my leg as it roared past.

40   Then somehow I came out of it, ascending hastily from this underworld of sound to hear Louis Armstrong innocently asking,

> What did I do
> To be so black
> And blue?

45   At first I was afraid; this familiar music had demanded action,

the kind of which I was incapable, and yet had I lingered there beneath the surface I might have attempted to act. Nevertheless, I know now that few really listen to this music.

5 I sat on the chair's edge in a soaking sweat, as though each of my 1,369 bulbs had every one become a klieg light in an individual setting for a third degree with Ras and Rinehart in charge. It was exhausting—as though I had held my breath continuously for an hour under the terrifying serenity that comes from days of intense hunger. And yet, it was a strangely satisfying experience for an
10 invisible man to hear the silence of sound. I had discovered unrecognized compulsions of my being—even though I could not answer "yes" to their promptings. I haven't smoked a reefer since, however; not because they're illegal, but because to *see* around corners is enough (that is not unusual when you are invisible). But to hear
15 around them is too much; it inhibits action. And despite Brother Jack and all that sad, lost period of the Brotherhood, I believe in nothing if not in action.

Please, a definition. A hibernation is a covert preparation for a more overt action.

20 Besides, the drug destroys one's sense of time completely. If that happened, I might forget to dodge some bright morning and some cluck would run me down with an orange and yellow street car, or a bilious bus! Or I might forget to leave my hole when the moment for action presents itself.

25 Meanwhile I enjoy my life with the compliments of Monopolated Light & Power. Since you never recognize me even when in closest contact with me, and since, no doubt, you'll hardly believe that I exist, it won't matter if you know that I tapped a power line leading into the building and ran it into my hole in the
30 ground. Before that I lived in the darkness into which I was chased, but now I see. I've illuminated the blackness of my invisibility—and vice versa. And so I play the invisible music of my isolation. The last statement doesn't seem just right, does it? But it is; you hear this music simply because music is heard and seldom seen, except by
35 musicians. Could this compulsion to put invisibility down in black and white be thus an urge to make music of invisibility? But I am an orator, a rabble rouser—Am? I *was*, and perhaps shall be again. Who knows? All sickness is not unto death, neither is invisibility.

I can hear you say, "What a horrible, irresponsible bastard!"
40 And you're right. I leap to agree with you. I am one of the most irresponsible beings that ever lived. Irresponsibility is part of my invisibility; any way you face it, it is a denial. But to whom can I be responsible, and why should I be, when you refuse to see me? And wait until I reveal how truly irresponsible I am. Responsibility rests
45 upon recognition, and recognition is a form of agreement. Take the

man whom I almost killed: Who was responsible for that near murder—I? I don't think so, and I refuse it. I won't buy it. You can't give
it to me. *He* bumped *me*, he insulted *me*. Shouldn't he, for his own
personal safety, have recognized my hysteria, my "danger poten-
5   tial"? He, let us say, was lost in a dream world. But didn't *he* control
that dream world—which, alas, is only too real!—and didn't *he* rule
me out of it? And if he had yelled for a policeman, wouldn't *I* have
been taken for the offending one? Yes, yes, yes! Let me agree with
you, I was the irresponsible one; for I should have used my knife to
10 protect the higher interests of society. Some day that kind of foolishness will cause us tragic trouble. All dreamers and sleepwalkers
must pay the price, and even the invisible victim is responsible for
the fate of all. But I shirked that responsibility; I became too snarled
in the incompatible notions that buzzed within my brain. I was a
15 coward . . .
     But what did *I* do to be so blue? Bear with me.

CHAPTER ONE

     It goes a long way back, some twenty years. All my life I had
been looking for something, and everywhere I turned someone
tried to tell me what it was. I accepted their answers too, though
they were often in contradiction and even self-contradictory. I was
5   naïve. I was looking for myself and asking everyone except myself
questions which I, and only I, could answer. It took me a long time
and much painful boomeranging of my expectations to achieve a
realization everyone else appears to have been born with: That I am
nobody but myself. But first I had to discover that I am an invisible
10 man!
     And yet I am no freak of nature, nor of history. I was in the
cards, other things having been equal (or unequal) eighty-five years
ago. I am not ashamed of my grandparents for having been slaves.
I am only ashamed of myself for having at one time been ashamed.
15 About eighty-five years ago they were told that they were free, united with others of our country in everything pertaining to the common good, and, in everything social, separate like the fingers of the
hand. And they believed it. They exulted in it. They stayed in their
place, worked hard, and brought up my father to do the same. But
20 my grandfather is the one. He was an odd old guy, my grandfather,
and I am told I take after him. It was he who caused the trouble. On
his deathbed he called my father to him and said, "Son, after I'm
gone I want you to keep up the good fight, I never told you, but our
life. is a war and I have been a traitor all my born days, a spy in the
25 enemy's country ever since I give up my gun back in the
Reconstruction. Live with your head in the lion's mouth. I want you

to overcome 'em with yeses, undermine 'em with grins, agree 'em to death and destruction, let 'em swoller you till they vomit or bust wide open." They thought the old man had gone out of his mind. He had been the meekest of men. The younger children were
5 rushed from the room, the shades drawn and the flame of the lamp turned so low that it sputtered on the wick like the old man's breathing. "Learn it to the younguns," he whispered fiercely; then he died.

But my folks were more alarmed over his last words than over
10 his dying. It was as though he had not died at all, his words caused so much anxiety. I was warned emphatically to forget what he had said and, indeed, this is the first time it has been mentioned outside the family circle. It had a tremendous effect upon me, however. I could never be sure of what he meant. Grandfather had been a quiet
15 old man who never made any trouble, yet on his deathbed he had called himself a traitor and a spy, and he had spoken of his meekness as a dangerous activity. It became a constant puzzle which lay unanswered in the back of my mind. And whenever things went well for me I remembered my grandfather and felt guilty and
20 uncomfortable. It was as though I was carrying out his advice in spite of myself. And to make it worse, everyone loved me for it. I was praised by the most lily-white men of the town. I was considered an example of desirable conduct—just as my grandfather had been. And what puzzled me was that the old man had defined it as
25 *treachery*. When I was praised for my conduct I felt a guilt that in some way I was doing something that was really against the wishes of the white folks, that if they had understood they would have desired me to act just the opposite, that I should have been sulky and mean, and that that really would have been what they wanted,
30 even though they were fooled and thought they wanted me to act as I did. It made me afraid that some day they would look upon me as a traitor and I would be lost. Still I was more afraid to act any other way because they didn't like that at all. The old man's words were like a curse. On my graduation day I delivered an oration in
35 which I showed that humility was the secret, indeed, the very essence of progress. (Not that I believed this—how could I, remembering my grandfather?—I only believed that it worked.) It was a great success. Everyone praised me and I was invited to give the speech at a gathering of the town's leading white citizens. It was a
40 triumph for our whole community.

It was in the main ballroom of the leading hotel. When I got there I discovered that it was on the occasion of a smoker, and I was told that since I was to be there anyway I might as well take part in the battle royal to be fought by some of my schoolmates as part of
45 the entertainment. The battle royal came first.

All of the town's big shots were there in their tuxedoes, wolf-
ing down the buffet foods, drinking beer and whiskey and smoking
black cigars. It was a large room with a high ceiling. Chairs were
arranged in neat rows around three sides of a portable boxing ring.
5   The fourth side was clear, revealing a gleaming space of polished
floor. I had some misgivings over the battle royal, by the way. Not
from a distaste for fighting, but because I didn't care too much for
the other fellows who were to take part. They were tough guys who
seemed to have no grandfather's curse worrying their minds. No
10   one could mistake their toughness. And besides, I suspected that
fighting a battle royal might detract from the dignity of my speech.
In those pre-invisible days I visualized myself as a potential Booker
T. Washington. But the other fellows didn't care too much for me
either, and there were nine of them. I felt superior to them in my
15   way, and I didn't like the manner in which we were all crowded
together into the servants' elevator. Nor did they like my being
there. In fact, as the warmly lighted floors flashed past the elevator
we had words over the fact that I, by taking part in the fight, had
knocked one of their friends out of a night's work.
20   We were led out of the elevator through a rococo hall into an
anteroom and told to get into our fighting togs. Each of us was
issued a pair of boxing gloves and ushered out into the big mirrored
hall, which we entered looking cautiously about us and whispering,
lest we might accidentally be heard above the noise of the room. It
25   was foggy with cigar smoke. And already the whiskey was taking
effect. I was shocked to see some of the most important men of the
town quite tipsy. They were all there—bankers, lawyers, judges,
doctors, fire chiefs, teachers, merchants. Even one of the more fashionable pastors. Something we could not see was going on up front.
30   A clarinet was vibrating sensuously and the men were standing up
and moving eagerly forward. We were a small tight group, clus-
tered together, our bare upper bodies touching and shining with
anticipatory sweat; while up front the big shots were becoming
increasingly excited over something we still could not see.
35   Suddenly I heard the school superintendent, who had told me to
come, yell, "Bring up the shines, gentlemen! Bring up the little
shines!"
        We were rushed up to the front of the ballroom, where it
smelled even more strongly of tobacco and whiskey. Then we were
40   pushed into place. I almost wet my pants. A sea of faces, some hostile, some amused, ringed around us, and in the center, facing us,
stood a magnificent blonde—stark naked. There was dead silence. I
felt a blast of cold air chill me. I tried to back away, but they were
behind me and around me. Some of the boys stood with lowered
45   heads, trembling. I felt a wave of irrational guilt and fear. My teeth

chattered, my skin turned to goose flesh, my knees knocked. Yet I
was strongly attracted and looked in spite of myself. Had the price
of looking been blindness, I would have looked. The hair was yellow like that of a circus kewpie doll, the face heavily powdered and
5   rouged, as though to form an abstract mask, the eyes hollow and
smeared a cool blue, the color of a baboon's butt. I felt a desire to
spit upon her as my eyes brushed slowly over her body. Her breasts
were firm and round as the domes of East Indian temples, and I
stood so close as to see the fine skin texture and beads of pearly per-
10 spiration glistening like dew around the pink and erected buds of
her nipples. I wanted at one and the same time to run from the
room, to sink through the floor, or go to her and cover her from my
eyes and the eyes of the others with my body; to feel the soft thighs,
to caress her and destroy her, to love her and murder her, to hide
15 from her, and yet to stroke where below the small American flag tat-
tooed upon her belly her thighs formed a capital V. I had a notion
that of all in the room she saw only me with her impersonal eyes.

 And then she began to dance, a slow sensuous movement; the
smoke of a hundred cigars clinging to her like the thinnest of veils.
20 She seemed like a fair bird-girl girdled in veils calling to me from
the angry surface of some gray and threatening sea. I was trans-
ported. Then I became aware of the clarinet playing and the big
shots yelling at us. Some threatened us if we looked and others if we
did not. On my right I saw one boy faint. And now a man grabbed
25 a silver pitcher from a table and stepped close as he dashed ice
water upon him and stood him up and forced two of us to support
him as his head hung and moans issued from his thick bluish lips.
Another boy began to plead to go home. He was the largest of the
group, wearing dark red fighting trunks much too small to conceal
30 the erection which projected from him as though in answer to the
insinuating low-registered moaning of the clarinet. He tried to hide
himself with his boxing gloves.

 And all the while the blonde continued dancing, smiling faintly at the big shots who watched her with fascination, and faintly
35 smiling at our fear. I noticed a certain merchant who followed her
hungrily, his lips loose and drooling. He was a large man who wore
diamond studs in a shirtfront which swelled with the ample paunch
underneath, and each time the blonde swayed her undulating hips
he ran his hand through the thin hair of his bald head and, with his
40 arms upheld, his posture clumsy like that of an intoxicated panda,
wound his belly in a slow and obscene grind. This creature was
completely hypnotized. The music had quickened. As the dancer
flung herself about with a detached expression on her face, the men
began reaching out to touch her. I could see their beefy fingers sink
45 into the soft flesh. Some of the others tried to stop them and she

began to move around the floor in graceful circles, as they gave chase, slipping and sliding over the polished floor. It was mad. Chairs went crashing, drinks were spilt, as they ran laughing and howling after her. They caught her just as she reached a door, raised

5   her from the floor, and tossed her as college boys are tossed at a hazing, and above her red, fixed-smiling lips I saw the terror and disgust in her eyes, almost like my own terror and that which I saw in some of the other boys. As I watched, they tossed her twice and her soft breasts seemed to flatten against the air and her legs flung wild-

10 ly as she spun. Some of the sober ones helped her to escape. And I started off the floor, heading for the anteroom with the rest of the boys.

Some were still crying and in hysteria. But as we tried to leave we were stopped and ordered to get into the ring. There was noth-

15 ing to do but what we were told. All ten of us climbed under the ropes and allowed ourselves to be blindfolded with broad bands of white cloth. One of the men seemed to feel a bit sympathetic and tried to cheer us up as we stood with our backs against the ropes. Some of us tried to grin. "See that boy over there?" one of the men

20 said. "I want you to run across at the bell and give it to him right in the belly. If you don't get him, I'm going to get you. I don't like his looks."

Each of us was told the same. The blindfolds were put on. Yet even then I had been going over my speech. In my mind each word

25 was as bright as flame. I felt the cloth pressed into place, and frowned so that it would be loosened when I relaxed.

But now I felt a sudden fit of blind terror. I was unused to darkness. It was as though I had suddenly found myself in a dark room filled with poisonous cottonmouths. I could hear the bleary voices

30 yelling insistently for the battle royal to begin.

"Get going in there!"

"Let me at that big nigger!"

I strained to pick up the school superintendent's voice, as though to squeeze some security out of that slightly more familiar

35 sound.

"Let me at those black sonsabitches!" someone yelled.

"No, Jackson, no!" another voice yelled. "Here, somebody, help me hold Jack."

"I want to get at that ginger-colored nigger. Tear him limb from

40 limb," the first voice yelled.

I stood against the ropes trembling. For in those days I was what they called ginger-colored, and he sounded as though he might crunch me between his teeth like a crisp ginger cookie.

Quite a struggle was going on. Chairs were being kicked about

45 and I could hear voices grunting as with a terrific effort. I wanted to

see, to see more desperately than ever before. But the blindfold was tight as a thick skin-puckering scab and when I raised my gloved hands to push the layers of white aside a voice yelled, "Oh, no you don't, black bastard! Leave that alone!"

5   "Ring the bell before Jackson kills him a coon!" someone boomed in the sudden silence. And I heard the bell clang and the sound of the feet scuffling forward.

A glove smacked against my head. I pivoted, striking out stiffly as someone went past, and felt the jar ripple along the length of my
10   arm to my shoulder. Then it seemed as though all nine boys had turned upon me at once. Blows pounded me from all sides while I struck out as best I could. So many blows landed upon me that I wondered if I were not the only blindfolded fighter in the ring, or if the man called Jackson hadn't succeeded in getting me after all.

15   Blindfolded, I could no longer control my motions. I had no dignity. I stumbled about like a baby or a drunken man. The smoke had become thicker and with each new blow it seemed to sear and further restrict my lungs. My saliva became like hot bitter glue. A glove connected with my head, filling my mouth with warm blood.
20   It was everywhere. I could not tell if the moisture I felt upon my body was sweat or blood. A blow landed hard against the nape of my neck. I felt myself going over, my head hitting the floor. Streaks of blue light filled the black world behind the blindfold. I lay prone, pretending that I was knocked out, but felt myself seized by hands
25   and yanked to my feet. "Get going, black boy! Mix it up!" My arms were like lead, my head smarting from blows. I managed to feel my way to the ropes and held on, trying to catch my breath. A glove landed in my mid-section and I went over again, feeling as though the smoke had become a knife jabbed into my guts. Pushed this way
30   and that by the legs milling around me, I finally pulled erect and discovered that I could see the black, sweat-washed forms weaving in the smoky-blue atmosphere like drunken dancers weaving to the rapid drum-like thuds of blows.

Everyone fought hysterically. It was complete anarchy.
35   Everybody fought everybody else. No group fought together for long. Two, three, four, fought one, then turned to fight each other, were themselves attacked. Blows landed below the belt and in the kidney, with the gloves open as well as closed, and with my eye partly opened now there was not so much terror. I moved carefully,
40   avoiding blows, although not too many to attract attention, fighting from group to group. The boys groped about like blind, cautious crabs crouching to protect their mid-sections, their heads pulled in short against their shoulders, their arms stretched nervously before them, with their fists testing the smoke-filled air like the knobbed
45   feelers of hypersensitive snails. In one corner I glimpsed a boy vio-

lently punching the air and heard him scream in pain as he smashed his hand against a ring post. For a second I saw him bent over holding his hand, then going down as a blow caught his unprotected head. I played one group against the other, slipping in and throwing a punch then stepping out of range while pushing the others into the melee to take the blows blindly aimed at me. The smoke was agonizing and there were no rounds, no bells at three minute intervals to relieve our exhaustion. The room spun round me, a swirl of lights, smoke, sweating bodies surrounded by tense white faces. I bled from both nose and mouth, the blood spattering upon my chest.

The men kept yelling, "Slug him, black boy! Knock his guts out!"

"Uppercut him! Kill him! Kill that big boy!"

Taking a fake fall, I saw a boy going down heavily beside me as though we were felled by a single blow, saw a sneaker-clad foot shoot into his groin as the two who had knocked him down stumbled upon him. I rolled out of range, feeling a twinge of nausea.

The harder we fought the more threatening the men became. And yet, I had begun to worry about my speech again. How would it go? Would they recognize my ability? What would they give me?

I was fighting automatically when suddenly I noticed that one after another of the boys was leaving the ring. I was surprised, filled with panic, as though I had been left alone with an unknown danger. Then I understood. The boys had arranged it among themselves. It was the custom for the two men left in the ring to slug it out for the winner's prize. I discovered this too late. When the bell sounded two men in tuxedoes leaped into the ring and removed the blindfold. I found myself facing Tatlock, the biggest of the gang. I felt sick at my stomach. Hardly had the bell stopped ringing in my ears than it clanged again and I saw him moving swiftly toward me. Thinking of nothing else to do I hit him smash on the nose. He kept coming, bringing the rank sharp violence of stale sweat. His face was a black blank of a face, only his eyes alive—with hate of me and aglow with a feverish terror from what had happened to us all. I became anxious. I wanted to deliver my speech and he came at me as though he meant to beat it out of me. I smashed him again and again, taking his blows as they came. Then on a sudden impulse I struck him lightly and as we clinched, I whispered, "Fake like I knocked you out, you can have the prize."

"I'll break your behind," he whispered hoarsely.

"For *them*?"

"For *me*, sonofabitch!"

They were yelling for us to break it up and Tatlock spun me half around with a blow, and as a joggled camera sweeps in a reel-ing scene, I saw the howling red faces crouching tense beneath the cloud of blue-gray smoke. For a moment the world wavered, unraveled, flowed, then my head cleared and Tatlock bounced before me. The fluttering shadow before my eyes was his jabbing left hand.

5 Then falling forward, my head against his damp shoulder, I whispered,

"I'll make it five dollars more."

"Go to hell!"

But his muscles relaxed a trifle beneath my pressure and I
10 breathed, "Seven?"

"Give it to your ma," he said, ripping me beneath the heart.

And while I still held him I butted him and moved away. I felt myself bombarded with punches. I fought back with hopeless desperation. I wanted to deliver my speech more than anything else in
15 the world, because I felt that only these men could judge truly my ability, and now this stupid clown was ruining my chances. I began fighting carefully now, moving in to punch him and out again with my greater speed. A lucky blow to his chin and I had him going too—until I heard a loud voice yell, "I got my money on the big
20 boy."

Hearing this, I almost dropped my guard. I was confused: Should I try to win against the voice out there? Would not this go against my speech, and was not this a moment for humility, for nonresistance? A blow to my head as I danced about sent my right eye
25 popping like a jack-in-the-box and settled my dilemma. The room went red as I fell. It was a dream fall, my body languid and fastidious as to where to land, until the floor became impatient and smashed up to meet me, A moment later I came to. An hypnotic vice said FIVE emphatically. And I lay there, hazily watching a dark red
30 spot of my own blood shaping itself into a butterfly, glistening and soaking into the soiled gray world of the canvas.

When the voice drawled TEN I was lifted up and dragged to a chair. I sat dazed. My eye pained and swelled with each throb of my pounding heart and I wondered if now I would be allowed to
35 speak. I was wringing wet, my mouth still bleeding. We were grouped along the wall now. The other boys ignored me as they congratulated Tatlock and speculated as to how much they would be paid. One boy whimpered over his smashed hand. Looking up front, I saw attendants in white jackets rolling the portable ring
40 away and placing a small square rug in the vacant space surrounded by chairs. Perhaps, I thought, I will stand on the rug to deliver my speech.

Then the M.C. called to us, "Come on up here boys and get your money."

45 We ran forward to where the men laughed and talked in their

chairs, waiting. Everyone seemed friendly now.

"There it is on the rug," the man said. I saw the rug covered with coins of all dimensions and a few crumpled bills. But what excited me, scattered here and there, were the gold pieces.

5   "Boys, it's all yours," the man said. "You get all you grab."

"That's right, Sambo," a blond man said, winking at me confidentially.

I trembled with excitement, forgetting my pain. I would get the gold and the bills, I thought. I would use both hands. I would throw

10 my body against the boys nearest me to block them from the gold.

"Get down on the rug now," the man commanded, "and don't anyone touch it until I give the signal."

"This ought to be good," I heard.

As told, we got around the square rug on our knees. Slowly the

15 man raised his freckled hand as we followed it upward with our eyes.

I heard, "These niggers took like they're about to pray!"

Then, "Ready," the man said, "Go!"

I lunged for a yellow coin lying on the blue design of the car-

20 pet, touching it and sending a surprised shriek to join those rising around me. I tried frantically to remove my hand but could not let go. A hot, violent force tore through my body, shaking me like a wet rat. The rug was electrified. The hair bristled up on my head as I shook myself free. My muscles jumped, my nerves jangled,

25 writhed. But I saw that this was not stopping the other boys. Laughing in fear and embarrassment, some were holding back and scooping up the coins knocked off by the painful contortions of the others. The men roared above us as we struggled.

"Pick it up, goddammit, pick it up!" someone called like a bass-

30 voiced parrot. "Go on, get it!"

I crawled rapidly around the floor, picking up the coins, trying to avoid the coppers and to get greenbacks and the gold. Ignoring the shock by laughing, as I brushed the coins off quickly, I discovered that I could contain the electricity—a contradiction, but it

35 works. Then the men began to push us onto the rug. Laughing embarrassedly, we struggled out of their hands and kept after the coins. We were all wet and slippery and hard to hold. Suddenly I saw a boy lifted into the air, glistening with sweat like a circus seal, and dropped, his wet back landing flush upon the charged rug,

40 heard him yell and saw him literally dance upon his back, his elbows beating a frenzied tattoo upon the floor, his muscles twitching like the flesh of a horse stung by many flies. When he finally rolled off, his face was gray and no one stopped him when he ran from the floor amid booming laughter.

45   "Get the money, " the M.C. called. "That's good hard American

13. Ralph Ellison

cash!"

And we snatched and grabbed, snatched and grabbed. I was careful not to come too close to the rug now, and when I felt the hot whiskey breath descend upon me like a cloud of foul air I reached
5   out and grabbed the leg of a chair. It was occupied and I held on desperately.

"Leggo, nigger! Leggo!"

The huge face wavered down to mine as he tried to push me free. But my body was slippery and he was too drunk. It was Mr.
10   Colcord, who owned a chain of movie houses and "entertainment palaces." Each time he grabbed me I slipped out of his hands. It became a real struggle. I feared the rug more than I did the drunk, so I held on, surprising myself for a moment by trying to topple *him* upon the rug. It was such an enormous idea that I found myself
15   actually carrying it out. I tried not to be obvious, yet when I grabbed his leg, trying to tumble him out of the chair, he raised up roaring with laughter, and, looking at me with soberness dead in the eye, kicked me viciously in the chest. The chair leg flew out of my hand and I felt myself going and rolled. It was as though I had rolled
20   through a bed of hot coals. It seemed a whole century would pass before I would roll free, a century in which I was seared through the deepest levels of my body to the fearful breath within me and the breath seared and heated to the point of explosion. It'll all be over in a flash, I thought as I rolled clear. It'll all be over in a flash.
25   But not yet, the men on the other side were waiting, red faces swollen as though from apoplexy as they bent forward in their chairs. Seeing their fingers coming toward me, I rolled away as a fumbled football rolls off the receiver's fingertips, back into the coals. That time I luckily sent the rug sliding out of place and heard
30   the coins ringing against the floor and the boys scuffling to pick them up and the M.C. calling, "All right, boys that's all. Go get dressed and get your money. "

I was limp as a dish rag. My back felt as though it had been beaten with wires.
35   When we had dressed the M.C. came in and gave us each five dollars, except Tatlock, who got ten for being last in the ring. Then he told us to leave. I was not to get a chance to deliver my speech, I thought. I was going out into the dim alley in despair when I was stopped and told to go back. I returned to the ballroom, where the
40   men were pushing back their chairs and gathering in groups to talk.

The M.C. knocked on a table for quiet. "Gentlemen," he said, "we almost forgot about an important part of the program. A most serious part, gentlemen. This boy was brought here to deliver a speech which he made at his graduation yesterday. . . "
45   "Bravo!"

"I'm told that he is the smartest boy we've got out there in Greenwood. I'm told that he knows more big words than a pocket -sized dictionary."

Much applause and laughter.

5   "So now, gentlemen, I want you to give him your attention."

There was still laughter as I faced them, my mouth dry, my eye throbbing. I began slowly, but evidently my throat was tense, because they began shouting, "Louder! Louder!"

"We of the younger generation extol the wisdom of that great
10 leader and educator," I shouted, "who first spoke these flaming words of wisdom: 'A ship lost at sea for many days suddenly sight- ed a friendly vessel. From the mast of the unfortunate vessel was seen a signal: "Water, water; we die of thirst!" The answer from the friendly vessel came back: "Cast down your bucket where you are."
15 The captain of the distressed vessel, at last heeding the injunction, cast down his bucket, and it came up full of fresh sparkling water from the mouth of the Amazon River.' And like him I say, and in his words, 'To those of my race who depend upon bettering their con- dition in a foreign land, or who underestimate the importance of
20 cultivating friendly relations with the Southern white man, who is his next-door neighbor, I would say: "Cast down your bucket where you are"—cast it down in making friends in every manly way of the people of all races by whom we are surrounded. . .'"

I spoke automatically and with such fervor that I did not real-
25 ize that the men were still talking and laughing until my dry mouth, filling up with blood from the cut, almost strangled me. I coughed, wanting to stop and go to one of the tall brass, sand-filled spittoons to relieve myself, but a few of the men, especially the superintend- ent, were listening and I was afraid. So I gulped it down, blood, sali-
30 va and all, and continued. (What powers of endurance I had during those days! What enthusiasm! What a belief in the rightness of things!) I spoke even louder in spite of the pain. But still they talked and still they laughed, as though deaf with cotton in dirty ears. So I spoke with greater emotional emphasis. I closed my ears and swal-
35 lowed blood until I was nauseated. The speech seemed a hundred times as long as before, but I could not leave out a single word. All had to be said, each memorized nuance considered, rendered. Nor was that all. Whenever I uttered a word of three syllables a group of voices would yell for me to repeat it. I used the phrase "social
40 responsibility" and they yelled:

"What's that word you say, boy?"

"Social responsibility," I said.

"What?"

"Social. . . "

45   "Louder."

"... responsibility."

"More! "

"Respon—"

"Repeat!"

5   "—sibility."

The room filled with the uproar of laughter until, no doubt, distracted by having to gulp down my blood, I made a mistake and yelled a phrase I had often seen denounced in newspaper editorials, heard debated in private.

10   "Social. . . "

"What?" they yelled.

"... equality—"

The laughter hung smokelike in the sudden stillness. I opened my eyes, puzzled. Sounds of displeasure filled the room. The M.C.
15 rushed forward. They shouted hostile phrases at me. But I did not understand.

A small dry mustached man in the front row blared out, "Say that slowly, son!"

"What, sir?"

20   "What you just said!"

"Social responsibility, sir," I said.

"You weren't being smart, were you, boy?" he said, not unkindly.

"No, sir!"

25   "You sure that about 'equality' was a mistake?"

"Oh, yes, sir," I said. "I was swallowing blood."

"Well, you had better speak more slowly so we can understand. We mean to do right by you, but you've got to know your place at all times. All right, now, go on with your speech."

30   I was afraid. I wanted to leave but I wanted also to speak and I was afraid they'd snatch me down.

"Thank you, sir," I said, beginning where I had left off, and having them ignore me as before.

Yet when I finished there was a thunderous applause. I was
35 surprised to see the superintendent come forth with a package wrapped in white tissue paper, and, gesturing for quiet, address the men.

"Gentlemen, you see that I did not overpraise this boy. He makes a good speech and some day he'll lead his people in the
40 proper paths. And I don't have to tell you that that is important in these days and times. This is a good, smart boy, and so to encourage him in the right direction, in the name of the Board of Education I wish to present him a prize in the form of this . . . "

He paused, removing the tissue paper and revealing a gleam-
45 ing calfskin brief case.

". . . in the form of this first-class article from Shad Whitmore's shop."

"Boy," he said, addressing me, "take this prize and keep it well. Consider it a badge of office. Prize it. Keep developing as you are
5   and some day it will be filled with important papers that will help shape the destiny of your people."

I was so moved that I could hardly express my thanks. A rope of bloody saliva forming a shape like an undiscovered continent drooled upon the leather and I wiped it quickly away. I felt an
10 importance that I had never dreamed.

"Open it and see what's inside," I was told.

My fingers a-tremble, I complied, smelling the fresh leather and finding an official-looking document inside. It was a scholar- ship to the state college for Negroes. My eyes filled with tears and I
15 ran awkwardly off the floor.

I was overjoyed; I did not even mind when I discovered that the gold pieces I had scrambled for were brass pocket tokens adver- tising a certain make of automobile.

When I reached home everyone was excited. Next day the
20 neighbors came to congratulate me. I even felt safe from grandfa- ther, whose deathbed curse usually spoiled my triumphs. I stood beneath his photograph with my brief case in hand and smiled tri- umphantly into his stolid black peasant's face. It was a face that fas- cinated me. The eyes seemed to follow everywhere I went.

25   That night I dreamed I was at a circus with him and that he refused to laugh at the clowns no matter what they did. Then later he told me to open my brief case and read what was inside and I did, finding an official envelope stamped with the state seal; and inside the envelope, I found another and another, endlessly, and I
30 thought I would fall of weariness. "Them's years," he said. "Now open that one." And I did and in it I found an engraved document containing a short message in letters of gold. "Read it," my grand- father said. "Out loud!"

"To Whom It May Concern," I intoned. "Keep This Nigger-Boy
35 Running."

I awoke with the old man's laughter ringing in my ears.

(It was a dream I was to remember and dream again for many years after. But at that time I had no insight into its meaning. First I had to attend college.)

14. LANGSTON HUGHES

Hughes (1902–1967) was a black American who, like Ellison, was strongly influenced by jazz and by the Blues. His powerful lyrics express the rage of an oppressed minority and they reach back to a proud sense of the history and traditions of African Americans.

I, TOO

I, too, sing America.

I am the darker brother.
They send me to eat in the kitchen
When company comes,
5   But I laugh,
And eat well,
And grow strong.

Tomorrow,   *Optimism*
I'll be at the table
10 When company comes.
Nobody'll dare
Say to me,
"Eat in the kitchen,"
Then.

15 Besides,
They'll see how beautiful I am
And be ashamed—

I, too, am America.   1926

-161-

HARLEM

What happens to a dream deferred?

      Does it dry up
      like a raisin in the sun?
      Or fester like a sore—
5   And then run?
      Does it stink like rotten meat?
      Or crust and sugar over—
      like a syrupy sweet?

      Maybe it just sags
10   like a heavy load.   *hard masculine rhyme*

      Or does it explode?   *explosion of culture*
                               1951

THE NEGRO SPEAKS OF RIVERS
(TO W. E. B. DUBOIS)

I've known rivers:
I've known rivers ancient as the world and older than the
      flow of human blood in human veins.

My soul has grown deep like the rivers.

5   I bathed in the Euphrates when dawns were young.
      I built my hut near the Congo and it lulled me to sleep.

      I looked upon the Nile and raised the pyramids above it.
      I heard the singing of the Mississippi when Abe Lincoln
           went down to New Orleans, and I've seen its muddy
10   bosom turn all golden in the sunset.

I've known rivers:
Ancient, dusky rivers.

My soul has grown deep like the rivers.

THE WEARY BLUES

Droning a drowsy syncopated tune,
Rocking back and forth to a mellow croon,
    I heard a Negro play.
Down on Lenox Avenue the other night
5   By the pale dull pallor of an old gas light
        He did a lazy sway. . . .
        He did a lazy sway. . . .
To the tune o' those Weary Blues.
With his ebony hands on each ivory key
10   He made that poor piano moan with melody.
        O Blues!
Swaying to and fro on his rickety stool
He played that sad raggy tune like a musical fool.
        Sweet Blues!
15   Coming from a black man's soul.
        O Blues!
In a deep song voice with a melancholy tone
I heard that Negro sing, that old piano moan—
        "Ain't got nobody in all this world,
20   Ain't got nobody but ma self.
        I's gwine to quit ma frownin'
        And put ma troubles on the shelf."
Thump, thump, thump, went his foot on the floor.
He played a few chords then he sang some more—
25   "I got the Weary Blues
        And I can't be satisfied.
        Got the Weary Blues
        And can't be satisfied—
        I ain't happy no mo'
30   And I wish that I had died."
And far into the night he crooned that tune.
The stars went out and so did the moon.
The singer stopped playing and went to bed
While the Weary Blues echoed through his head.
35   He slept like a rock or a man that's dead.

[handwritten: Real Simple Ballad form (song)]

SONG FOR A DARK GIRL

[handwritten: young but this is serious]

Way Down South in Dixie
    ⚹ (Break the heart of me)
They hung my black young lover
    To a cross roads tree.

[handwritten: connection to Jesus (cross) → At a cross-road]

5   Way Down South in Dixie
    ⚹ (Bruised body high in air)
asked the white Lord Jesus
    What was the use of prayer.

Way Down South in Dixie
10   ⚹ (Break the heart of me)
Love is a naked shadow
    On a gnarled and naked tree.

THEME FOR ENGLISH B

The instructor said,

Go home and write
a page tonight.
And let that page come out of you—
5   *Then, it will be true.*

I wonder if it's that simple?
I am twenty-two, colored, born in Winston-Salem.
I went to school there, then Durham, then here
to this college on the hill above Harlem.
10   I am the only colored student in my class.
The steps from the hill lead down into Harlem,
through a park, then I cross St. Nicholas,
Eighth Avenue, Seventh, and I come to the Y,
the Harlem Branch Y, where I take the elevator
15   up to my room, sit down, and write this page:

It's not easy to know what is true for you or me
at twenty-two, my age. But I guess I'm what
I feel and see and hear, Harlem, I hear you:
hear you, hear me—we two—you, me, talk on this page.
20   (I hear New York, too.) Me—who?
Well, I like to eat, sleep, drink, and be in love.
I like to work, read, learn, and understand life.

I like a pipe for a Christmas present,
or records—Bessie, bop, or Bach.
25   I guess being colored doesn't make me *not* like
the same things other folks like who are other races.
So will my page be colored that I write?
Being me, it will not be white.
But it will be
30   a part of you, instructor.
You are white—
yet a part of me, as I am a part of you.
That's American.
Sometimes perhaps you don't want to be a part of me.
35   Nor do I often want to be a part of you.
But we are, that's true!
As I learn from you,
I guess you learn from me—
although you're older—and white—
40   and somewhat more free.
This is my page for English B.

ON THE ROAD

He was not interested in the snow. When he got off the freight, one early evening during the depression, Sargeant never even noticed the snow. But he must have felt it seeping down his neck, cold, wet, sopping in his shoes. But if you had asked him, he would-
5   n't have known it was snowing. Sargeant didn't see the snow, not even under the bright lights of the main street, falling white and flaky against the night. He was too hungry, too sleepy, too tired.

The Reverend Mr. Dorset, however, saw the snow when he switched on his porch light, opened the front door of his parsonage,
10   and found standing there before him a big black man with snow on his face, a human piece of night with snow on his face—obviously unemployed.

Said the Reverend Mr. Dorset before Sargeant even realized he'd opened his mouth: "I'm sorry. No! Go right on down this street
15   four blocks and turn to your left, walk up seven and you'll see the Relief Shelter. I'm sorry. No!" He shut the door.

Sargeant wanted to tell the holy man that he had already been to the Relief Shelter, been to hundreds of relief shelters during the depression years, the beds were always gone and supper was over,
20   the place was full, and they drew the color line anyhow. But the minister said, "No," and shut the door. Evidently he didn't want to hear about it. And he *had* a door to shut.

The big black man turned away. And even yet he didn't see the snow, walking right into it. Maybe he sensed it, cold, wet, sticking to his jaws, wet on his black hands, sopping in his shoes. He stopped and stood on the sidewalk hunched over—hungry, sleepy,
5 cold—looking up and down. Then he looked right where he was— in front of a church. Of course! A church! Sure, right next to a parsonage, certainly a church.

✱ It had *two* doors. *double the chances of getting into church*

Broad white steps in the night all snowy white. Two high
10 arched doors with slender stone pillars on either side. And way up, a round lacy window with a stone crucifix in the middle and Christ on the crucifix in stone. All this was pale in the street lights, solid and stony pale in the snow.

Sergeant blinked. When he looked up the snow fell into his
15 eyes. For the first time that night he *saw* the snow. He shook his head. He shook the snow from his coat sleeves, felt hungry, felt lost, felt not lost, felt cold. He walked up the steps of the church. He knocked at the door. No answer. He tried the handle. Locked. He put his shoulder against the door and his long black body slanted
20 like a ramrod. He pushed. With loud rhythmic grunts, like the grunts in a chain-gang song, he pushed against the door.

"I'm tired . . . Huh! . . . Hongry . . . Uh! . . . I'm sleepy . . . Huh! I'm cold . . . I got to sleep somewheres," Sergeant said. "This here is a church, ain't it? Well, uh! "
25 He pushed against the door.

Suddenly, with an undue cracking and screaking, the door began to give way to the tall black Negro who pushed ferociously against the door.

By now two or three white people had stopped in the street,
30 and Sergeant was vaguely aware of some of them yelling at him concerning the door. Three or four more came running, yelling at him.

"Hey!" they said. "Hey!"

"Un-huh," answered the big tall Negro, "I know it's a white
35 folks' church, but I got to sleep somewhere." He gave another lunge at the door. "Huh!"

✱ And the door broke open.

But just when the door gave way, two white cops arrived in a car, ran up the steps with their clubs and grabbed Sergeant. But
40 Sergeant for once had no intention of being pulled or pushed away from the door.

Sergeant grabbed, but not for anything so weak as a broken door. He grabbed for one of the tall stone pillars beside the door, grabbed at it and caught it. And held it. The cops pulled and
45 Sergeant pulled. Most of the people in the street got behind the cops

and helped them pull.

"A big black unemployed Negro holding onto our church!" *metaphor*
thought the people. "The idea!"

The cops began to beat Sargeant over the head, and nobody
5   protested. But he held on.

✗   And then the church fell down.

Gradually, the big stone front of the church fell down, the walls
and the rafters, the crucifix and the Christ. Then the whole thing fell
down, covering the cops and the people with bricks and stories and
10   debris. The whole church fell down in the snow.

Sargeant got out from under the church and went walking on
up the street with the stone pillar on his shoulder. He was under the
impression that he had buried the parsonage and the Reverend Mr.
Dorset who said, "No!" So he laughed, and threw the pillar six
15   blocks up the street and went on.

Sargeant thought he was alone, but listening to the crunch,
crunch, crunch on the snow of his own footsteps, he heard other
footsteps, too, doubling his own. He looked around and there was
Christ walking along beside him, the same Christ that had been on
20   the cross on the church still stone with a rough stone surface, walking along beside him just like he was broken off the cross when the
church fell down.

"Well, I'll be dogged," said Sargeant. "This here's the first time
I ever seed you off the cross."

25   "Yes," said Christ, crunching his feet in the snow. "You had to
pull the church down to get me off the cross."

"You glad?" said Sargeant.

"I sure am," said Christ.

They both laughed.

30   "I'm a hell of a fellow, ain't I?" said Sargeant. "Done pulled the   ✗
church down! "

✗   "You did a good job," said Christ. "They have kept me nailed
on a cross for nearly two thousand years."

"Whee-ee-e! " said Sargeant. "I know you are glad to get off."

35   "I sure am," said Christ.

They walked on in the snow. Sargeant looked at the man of
stone.

"And you been up there two thousand years?"

"I sure have," Christ said.

40   "Well, if I had a little cash," said Sergeant, "I'd show you
around a bit."

"I been around," said Christ.   *society has been*
like this

"Yeah, but that was a long time ago."

"All the same," said Christ, "I've been around."

45   They walked on in the snow until they came to the railroad

yards. Sargeant was tired, sweating and tired.

"Where you goin'?" Sargeant said, stopping by the tracks. He looked at Christ. Sargeant said, "I'm just a bum on the road. How about you? Where you goin'?"

5   "God knows," Christ said, "but I'm leavin' here."

ironic

They saw the red and green lights of the railroad yard half veiled by the snow that fell out of the night. Away down the track they saw in a hobo jungle.

"I can go there and sleep," Sargeant said.

10   "You can?"

"Sure," said Sargeant. "That place ain't got no doors."

Outside the town, along the tracks, there were barren trees and bushes below the embankment, snow-gray in the dark. And down among the trees and bushes there were makeshift houses made out

15   of boxes and tin and old pieces of wood and canvas. You couldn't see them in the dark, but you knew they were there if you'd ever been on the road, if you had ever lived with the homeless and hungry in a depression.

"I'm side-tracking," Sargeant said. "I'm tired."

20   "I'm gonna make it on to Kansas City," said Christ.

"O.K.," Sargeant said. "So long!"

He went down into the hobo jungle and found himself a place to sleep. He never did see Christ no more. About six A.M. a freight came by. Sargeant scrambled out of the jungle with a dozen or so

25   more hoboes and ran along the track, grabbing at the freight. It was dawn, early dawn, cold and gray.

"Wonder where Christ is by now?" Sargeant thought. "He must-a gone on way on down the road. He didn't sleep in this jungle."

30   Sargeant grabbed the train and started to pull himself up into a moving coal car, over the edge of a wheeling coal car. But strangely enough, the car was full of cops. The nearest cop rapped Sargeant soundly across the knuckles with his night stick. Wham! Rapped his big black hands for clinging to the top of the car. Wham! But

35   Sargeant did not turn loose. He clung on and tried to pull himself into the car. He hollered at the top of his voice, "Damn it, lemme in this car!"

"Shut up," barked the cop. "You crazy coon!" He rapped Sargeant across the knuckles and punched him in the stomach.

40   "You ain't out in no jungle now. This ain't no train. You in jail."

Wham! across his bare black fingers clinging to the bars of his cell. Wham! between the steel bars low down against his shins.

Suddenly Sargeant realized that he really was in jail. He wasn't on no train. The blood of the night before had dried on his face, his

45   head hurt terribly, and a cop outside in the corridor was hitting him

across the knuckles for holding onto the door, yelling and shaking the cell door.

"They must-a took me to jail for breaking down the door last night," Sargeant thought, "that church door."

5   Sargeant went over and sat on a wooden bench against the cold stone wall. He was emptier than ever. His clothes were wet, clammy cold wet, and shoes sloppy with snow water. It was just about dawn. There he was, locked up behind a cell door, nursing his bruised fingers.

10   The bruised fingers were his, but not the *door.*
Not the *club*, but the fingers.

"You wait," mumbled Sargeant, black against the jail wall. "I'm gonna break down this door, too."

"Shut up—or I'll paste you one," said the cop.

15   "I'm gonna break down this door," yelled Sargeant as he stood up in his cell.

Then he must have been talking to himself because he said, "I wonder where Christ's gone? I wonder if he's gone to Kansas City?"

MULATTO

I am your son, white man!

Georgia dusk
And the turpentine woods.
One of the pillars of the temple fell.

5   *You are my son!*
Like Hell!

The moon over the turpentine woods.
The Southern night
Full of stars,
10   Great big yellow stars.

        What's a body but a toy?
                Juicy bodies
                Of nigger wenches
                Blue black
15   Against black fences.
                O, you little bastard boy,
                What's a body but a toy?

The scent of pine wood stings the soft night air.

What's the body of your mother?

Silver moonlight everywhere.

What's the body of your mother?

Sharp pine scent in the evening air.

5
   A nigger night,
   A nigger joy,
   A little yellow
   Bastard boy.
   Naw, you ain't my brother.
10
   Niggers ain't my brother.
   Not ever.
   Niggers ain't my brother.

The Southern night is full of stars,
Great big yellow stars.

15
   O, sweet as earth,
   Dusk dark bodies
   Give sweet birth

To little yellow bastard boys.

   Git on back there in the night,
20
   You ain't white

The bright stars scatter everywhere.
Pine wood scent in the evening air.

   A nigger night,
   A nigger joy.
25
   I am your son, white man!
   A little yellow
   Bastard boy.

15. HELENE JOHNSON

In 1926, then unknown poet Helene Johnson (1905–95) achieved a literary coup when prominent poets Robert Frost and James Weldon Johnston judged three of her poems to be the winners of a literary contest. The next year, Johnson moved from her hometown of Boston to Harlem and attended classes at Columbia University. In Harlem, Johnson befriended fellow writer Zora Neale Hurston and continued developing her poetry, much of which blends an assertive eroticism with strong political conviction. Like that of many fellow Harlem Renaissance writers, Johnson's poetry blends themes of race and gender with innovations in poetic language and form. "Sonnet to a Negro in Harlem" is a love poem with an edge, a commentary on the limited options available to urban black Americans and a call for the oppressed to transcend these limitations.

SONNET TO A NEGRO IN HARLEM

You are disdainful and magnificent—
Your perfect body and your pompous gait,
Your dark eyes flashing solemnly with hate,
Small wonder that you are incompetent
5   To imitate those whom you so despise—
Your shoulders towering high above the throng,
Your head thrown back in rich, barbaric song,
Palm trees and mangoes stretched before your eyes.
Let others toil and sweat for labor's sake
10   And wring from grasping hands their meed[1] of gold.
Why urge ahead your supercilious feet?
Scorn will efface each footprint that you make.
I love your laughter arrogant and bold.
You are too splendid for this city street!

---

[1]Reward or recompense.

16. CLAUDE MCKAY

Jamaican-born Claude McKay (1889–1948) began writing dialect poetry about the difficult lives of ordinary Jamaican people while living in Kingston. After moving to Harlem, McKay, like fellow Jamaican Marcus Garvey, was a vocal advocate for civil rights, both for African Americans and for black Africans in colonized Africa. In 1922, McKay published Harlem Shadows, *focusing on contemporary black urban life. After this volume appeared in print, McKay traveled widely in Europe and the USSR, turning his literary attention to prose fiction and political essays. McKay's poetry, like that of contemporary Harlem Renaissance writers Langston Hughes and Helene Johnson, is known for its ingenious combination of traditional poetic forms (such as the sonnet) with incendiary political subject matter, which attacked and condemned segregation, racism, and oppression.*

THE TROPICS IN NEW YORK

Bananas ripe and green, and ginger-root,
    Cocoa in pods and alligator pears,
And tangerines and mangoes and grape fruit,
    Fit for the highest prize at parish fairs,

5   Set in the window, bringing memories
    Of fruit-trees laden by low-singing rills,
And dewy dawns, and mystical blue skies
    In benediction over nun-like hills.

My eyes grew dim, and I could no more gaze;
10   A wave of longing through my body swept,
And, hungry for the old, familiar ways,
    I turned aside and bowed my head and wept.   (1920)

THE HARLEM DANCER

Applauding youths laughed with young prostitutes
And watched her perfect, half-clothed body sway;
Her voice was like the sound of blended flutes
Blown by black players upon a picnic day.
5   She sang and danced on gracefully and calm,
The light gauze hanging loose about her form;
To me she seemed a proudly-swaying palm
Grown lovelier for passing through a storm.
Upon her swarthy neck black shiny curls
10   Profusely fell; and, tossing coins in praise,
The wine-flushed, bold-eyed boys, and even the girls,
Devoured her with their eager, passionate gaze;
But looking at her falsely-smiling face,
I knew her self was not in that strange place.   (1917)

IF WE MUST DIE

If we must die, let it not be like hogs
Hunted and penned in an inglorious spot,
While round us bark the mad and hungry dogs,
Making their mock at our accursed lot.
5   If we must die, O let us nobly die,
So that our precious blood may not be shed
In vain; then even the monsters we defy
Shall be constrained to honor us though dead!
O kinsmen! we must meet the common foe!
10   Though far outnumbered let us show us brave,
And for their thousand blows deal one deathblow!
What though before us lies the open grave?
Like men we'll face the murderous, cowardly pack,
Pressed to the wall, dying, but fighting back!   (1919)

17. COUNTEE CULLEN

Often considered the poet laureate of the Harlem Renaissance, Countee Cullen (1903–46) was born Countee Porter and adopted by the strictly religious Cullen family in his second decade of life. From his adopted parents, he internalized feelings of religious guilt, as well as a commitment to education. Twice married (once to the granddaughter of civil rights pioneer W. E. B. DuBois) and educated at New York University and Harvard, Cullen lived in the United States and in France; he was a French teacher in New York City as well as a poet for much of his adult life. Cullen wrote his greatest poetry in the 1920s; in 1925, his first volume of poetry, Color, was published. In this collection, Cullen examines themes of race, race relations, and religious doubt — personal and political issues that were to inform his poetry throughout his career.

YET DO I MARVEL

I doubt not God is good, well-meaning, kind,
And did He stoop to quibble could tell why
The little buried mole continues blind,
Why flesh that mirrors Him must some day die,
Make plain the reason tortured Tantalus[1]
5   Is baited by the fickle fruit, declare
If merely brute caprice dooms Sisyphus[2]
To struggle up a never-ending stair.
Inscrutable His ways are, and immune
To catechism by a mind too strewn
10   With petty cares to slightly understand
What awful brain compels His awful hand.
Yet do I marvel at this curious thing:
To make a poet black, and bid him sing!

---

[1]Tantalus was a king of Sispylus in Lydia, the father of Niobe and Pelops, and a friend of the gods, who was punished for the crime of either: (1) killing his son Pelops and serving him to the gods; (2) stealing nectar and ambrosia, the gods' food; or (3) revealing the secrets he learned from the gods. He was dispatched to Hades, where he stood up to his neck in water which would recede whenever he tried to drink. The fruit just above his head would ascend whenever he tried to reach for it.

[2]Sisyphus was a king of Corinth who was punished in Hades by having to roll a huge stone up a hill, only to have the stone roll down again as soon as be brought it to the top.

HERITAGE

(FOR HAROLD JACKMAN)[3]

What is Africa to me:
Copper sun or scarlet sea,
Jungle star or jungle track,
Strong bronzed men, or regal black
5   Women from whose loins I sprang
When the birds of Eden sang?
One three centuries removed
From the scenes his fathers loved,
Spicy grove, cinnamon tree,
10   *What is Africa to me?*
So I lie, who all day long
Want no sound except the song
Sung by wild barbaric birds
Goading massive jungle herds,
15   Juggernauts[4] of flesh that pass
Trampling tall defiant grass
Where young forest lovers lie,
Plighting troth beneath the sky.
So I lie, who always hear,
20   Though I cram against my ear
Both my thumbs, and keep them there,
Great drums throbbing through the air.
So I lie, whose fount of pride,
Dear distress, and joy allied,
25   Is my somber flesh and skin,
With the dark blood dammed within
Like great pulsing tides of wine
That, I fear, must burst the fine
Channels of the chafing net
30   Where they surge and foam and fret.

---

[3]Harold Jackman (1900–1960) was Cullen's best friend. Of West Indian descent, Jackman was quite handsome, and his portrait by Winold Reiss became a noted icon of the Harlem Renaissance. He was largely a fringe player, but his journals and letters contain a great deal of gossipy information about Harlem happenings. He was the recipient of most of Cullen's papers when Cullen died.

[4]Among the Hindus in India, the juggernaut is a sacred idol conveyed on a huge cart in the path of which believers often throw themselves.

Africa? A book one thumbs
Listlessly, till slumber comes.
Unremembered are her bats
Circling through the night, her cats

35   Crouching in the river reeds,
Stalking gentle flesh that feeds
By the river brink; no more
Does the bugle-throated roar
Cry that monarch claws have leapt

40   From the scabbards where they slept.
Silver snakes that once a year
Doff the lovely coats you wear,
Seek no covert in your fear
Lest a mortal eye should see;

45   What's your nakedness to me?
Here no leprous flowers rear
Fierce corollas[5] in the air;
Here no bodies sleek and wet,
Dripping mingled rain and sweat,

50   Tread the savage measures of
Jungle boys and girls in love.
What is last year's snow to me,
Last year's anything? The tree
Budding yearly must forget

55   How its past arose or set—
Bough and blossom, flower, fruit,
Even what shy bird with mute
Wonder at her travail there,
Meekly labored in its hair.

60   *One three centuries removed*
From the scenes his fathers loved,
Spice grove, cinnamon tree,
What is Africa to me?

So I lie, who find no peace

65   Night or day, no slight release
From the unremittent beat
Made by cruel padded feet
Walking through my body's street.
Up and down they go, and back,

70   Treading out a jungle track.

---

[5]Corollas are the petals that form the inner envelope of a flower.

So I lie, who never quite
Safely sleep from rain at night—
I can never rest at all
When the rain begins to fall;
75 Like a soul gone mad with pain
I must match its weird refrain;
Ever must I twist and squirm,
Writhing like a baited worm,
While its primal measures drip
80 Through my body, crying, "Strip!
Doff this new exuberance.
Come and dance the Lover's Dance!"
In an old remembered way
Rain works on me night and day.

85 Quaint, outlandish heathen gods
Black men fashion out of rods,
Clay, and brittle bits of stone,
In a likeness like their own,
My conversion came high-priced;
90 I belong to Jesus Christ,
Preacher of humility;
Heathen gods are naught to me.

Father, Son, and Holy Ghost,
So I make an idle boast;
95 Jesus of the twice-turned cheek,
Lamb of God, although I speak
With my mouth thus, in my heart
Do I play a double part.
Ever at Thy glowing altar
100 Must my heart grow sick and falter,
Wishing He I served were black,
Thinking then it would not lack
Precedent of pain to guide it,
Let who would or might deride it,
105 Surely then this flesh would know
Yours had borne a kindred woe.
Lord, I fashion dark gods, too,
Daring even to give You
Dark despairing features where,

110   Crowned with dark rebellious hair,
Patience wavers just so much as
Mortal grief compels, while touches
Quick and hot, of anger, rise
To smitten cheek and weary eyes.
115   Lord, forgive me if my need
Sometimes shapes a human creed.

All day long and all night through,
One thing only must I do:
Quench my pride and cool my blood,
120   *Lest I perish in the flood.*

Lest a hidden ember set
Timber that I thought was wet
Burning like the dryest flax,
Melting like the merest wax,
125   *Lest the grave restore its dead.*
Not yet has my heart or head
In the least way realized
They and I are civilized.

INCIDENT

(FOR ERIC WALROND)[6]

Once riding in old Baltimore,
   Heart-filled, head-filled with glee,
I saw a Baltimorean
   Keep looking straight at me.

5   Now I was eight and very small,
   And he was no whit bigger,
And so I smiled, but he poked out
   His tongue, and called me, "Nigger."

I saw the whole of Baltimore
10   From May until December;
Of all the things that happened there
   That's all that I remember.

simple, like a nusery rhyme

that's the way his whole experience was

---

[6]Eric Walrond (1898–1966) was one of the touted young West Indian writers of the Harlem Renaissance. His collection of stories *Tropic Death* is uneven but contains good work. He worked for Marcus Garvey's publications on and off in the twenties and the thirties. He was impressed with Cullen's *Color* and gave it a very favorable review in *The New Republic*. Walrond won a Guggenheim in the same year as Cullen (1928).

18. Zora Neale Hurston

self-taught

Zora Neale Hurston (1891?–1960) is one of the foremost writers of the Harlem Renaissance, though many of her works are set not in the urban environment of New York, but in rural southern African American communities, some of which closely resemble the all-black town of Eatonville, Florida, where Hurston was born and raised. Hurston wrote novels, stories, folklore, anthropology, and memoirs, and in the 1930s became a leading voice of the Harlem Renaissance. Many of Hurston's works espouse a feminist perspective and profess a commitment to defining a strong and independent role for women within African-American culture. They are also renowned for presenting this culture in an authentic way, and Hurston's use of dialect is a distinctive quality in her writing. This use of language has thematic and political as well as stylistic implications: Henry Louis Gates, Jr. has pointed out the importance, in Hurston's work, of "finding a voice, with language as an instrument of injury and salvation, of selfhood and empowerment."

SPUNK

A giant of a brown skinned man sauntered up the one street of the Village and out into the palmetto thickets with a small pretty woman clinging lovingly to his arm.

"Looka theah, folkses!" cried Elijah Mosley, slapping his leg
5 gleefully. "Theah they go, big as life an' brassy as tacks."

All the loungers in the store tried to walk to the door with an air of nonchalance but with small success.

"Now pee-eople!" Walter Thomas gasped. "Will you look at 'em!"

"But that's one thing Ah likes about Spunk Banks—he ain't
10 skeered of nothin' on God's green foot-stool—*nothin'!* He rides that log down at saw-mill jus' like he struts round wid another man's wife—jus' don't give a kitty. When Tes' Miller got cut to giblets on that circle-saw, Spunk steps right up and starts ridin'. The rest of us was skeered to go near it."

15 A round-shouldered figure in overalls much too large, came nervously in the door and the talking ceased. The men looked at each other and winked.

"Gimme some soda-water. Sass'prilla Ah reckon," the new-comer ordered, and stood far down the counter near the open pick-
20 led pig-feet tub to drink it.

18. Zora Neale Hurston

Elijah nudged Walter and turned with mock gravity to the newcomer.

"Say Joe, how's everything up yo' way? How's yo' wife?"

Joe started and all but dropped the bottle he held in his hands.
5 He swallowed several times painfully and his lips trembled.

"Aw 'Lige, you oughtn't to do nothin' like that," Walter grumbled. Elijah ignored him.

"She jus'passed heah a few minutes ago goin' thata way," with a wave of his hand in the direction of the woods.

10 Now Joe knew his wife had passed that way. He knew that the men lounging in the general store had seen her, moreover, he knew that the men knew *he* knew. He stood there silent for a long moment staring blankly, with his Adam's apple twitching nervously up and down his throat. One could actually *see* the pain he was suffering,
15 his eyes, his face, his hands and even the dejected slump of his shoulders. He set the bottle down upon the counter. He didn't bang it, just eased it out of his hand silently and fiddled with his suspender buckle.

"Well, Ah'm goin'. after her today. Ah'm goin' an' fetch her
20 back. Spunk's done gone too fur."

He reached deep down into his trouser pocket and drew out a hollow ground razor, large and shiny, and passed his moistened thumb back and forth over the edge.

"Talkin' like a man, Joe. Course that's *yo'* fambly affairs, but Ah
25 like to see grit in anybody."

Joe Kanty laid down a nickel and stumbled out into the street.

Dusk crept in from the woods. Ike Clarke lit the swinging oil lamp that was almost immediately surrounded by candle-flies. The men laughed boisterously behind Joe's back as they watched him
30 shamble woodward.

"You oughtn't to said whut you did to him, 'Lige,—look how it worked him up," Walter chided.

"And Ah hope it did work him up. Tain't even decent for a man to take and take like he do."

35 "Spunk will sho' kill him."

"Aw, Ah doan' know. You never kin tell. He might turn him up an' spank him fur gettin' in the way, but Spunk wouldn't shoot no unarmed man. Dat razor he carried outa heah ain't gonna run Spunk down an' cut him, an' Joe ain't got the nerve to go up to
40 Spunk with it knowing he totes that Army 45. He makes that break outa heah to bluff us. He's gonna hide that razor behind the first likely palmetto root an' sneak back home to bed. Don't tell me nothin' 'bout that rabbit-foot colored man. Didn't he meet Spunk an' Lena face to face one day las' week an' mumble sumthin' to Spunk
45 'bout lettin' his wife alone?"

"What did Spunk say?" Walter broke in—"Ah like him fine but tain't right the way he carries on wid Lena Kanty, jus' cause Joe's timid 'bout fightin.'"

"You wrong theah, Walter. 'Tain't cause Joe's timid at all, it's
5 cause Spunk wants Lena. If Joe was a passel of wile cats Spunk would tackle the job just the same. He'd go after *anything* he wanted the same way. As Ah wuz sayin' a minute ago, he tole Joe right to his face that Lena was his. 'Call her,' he says to Joe. 'Call her and see if she'll come. A woman knows her boss an' she answers when
10 he calls.' 'Lena, ain't I yo' husband?' Joe sorter whines out. Lena looked at him real disgusted but she don't answer and she don't move outa her tracks. Then Spunk reaches out an' takes hold of her arm an' says: 'Lena, youse mine. From now on Ah works for you an' fights for you an' Ah never wants you to look to nobody for a crumb
15 of bread, a stitch of close or a shingle to go over yo' head, but *me* long as Ah live. Ah'll git the lumber foh owah house tomorrow. Go home an' git yo' things together!' 'Thass mah house,' Lena speaks up. 'Papa gimme that.' 'Well,' says Spunk, 'doan give up whut's yours, but when youse inside don't forgit youse mine, an' let no
20 other man git outa his place wid you!' Lena looked up at him with her eyes so full of love that they wuz runnin' over an' Spunk seen it an' Joe seen it too, and his lips started to tremblin' and his Adam's apple was galloping up and down his neck like a race horse. Ah bet he's wore out half a dozen Adam's apples since Spunk's been on the
25 job with Lena. That's all he'll do. He'll be back heah after while swallowin' an' workin' his lips like he wants to say somethin' an' can't."

"But didn't he do *nothin'* to stop 'em?"

"Nope, not a frazzlin' thing—jus' stood there. Spunk took Lena's arm and walked off jus' like nothin' ain't happened and he
30 stood there gazin' after them till they was outa sight. Now you know a woman don't want no man like that. I'm jus' waitin' to see whut he's goin' to say when he gits back."

II

But Joe Kanty never came back, never. The men in the store heard the sharp report of a pistol somewhere distant in the palmet-
35 to thicket and soon Spunk came walking leisurely, with his big black Stetson set at the same rakish angle and Lena clinging to his arm, came walking right into the general store. Lena wept in a frightened manner.

"Well," Spunk announced calmly, "Joe come out there wid a
40 meatax an' made me kill him."

He sent Lena home and led the men back to Joe—Joe crumple and limp with his right hand still clutching his razor.

"See mah back? Mah close cut clear through. He sneaked up

an' tried to kill me from the back, but Ah got him, an' got him good, first shot," Spunk said.

The men glared at Elijah, accusingly.

"Take him up an' plant him in 'Stoney lonesome,'" Spunk said
5   in a careless voice. "Ah didn't wanna shoot him but he made me do it. He's a dirty coward, jumpin' on a man from behind."

Spunk turned on his heel and sauntered away to where he knew his love wept in fear for him and no man stopped him. At the general store later on, they all talked of locking him up until the
10   sheriff should come from Orlando, but no one did anything but talk.

A clear case of self-defense, the trial was a short one, and Spunk walked out of the court house to freedom again. He could work again, ride the dangerous log-carriage that fed the singing, snarling, biting, circle-saw; he could stroll the soft dark lanes with his guitar.
15   He was free to roam the woods again; he was free to return to Lena. He did all of these things.

III

"Whut you reckon, Walt?" Elijah asked one night later. "Spunk's gittin' ready to marry Lena!"

"Naw! Why Joe ain't had time to git cold yit. Nohow Ah didn't
20   figger Spunk was the marryin' kind."

"Well, he is," rejoined Elijah. "He done moved most of Lena's things—and her along wid 'em—over to the Bradley house. He's buying it. Jus' like Ah told yo' all right in heah the night Joe wuz kilt. Spunk's crazy 'bout Lena. He don't want folks to keep on
25   talkin' 'bout her—thass reason he's rushin' so. Funny thing 'bout that bob-cat, wan't it?"

"Whut bob-cat, 'Lige? Ah ain't heered 'bout none."

"Ain't cher? Well, night befo' las' was the fust night Spunk an Lena moved together an' jus' as they was goin' to bed, a big black
30   bob-cat, black all over, you hear me, *black*, walked round and round that house and howled like forty, an' when Spunk got his gun an' went to the winder to shoot it, he says it stood right still an' looked him in the eye, an' howled right at him. The thing got Spunk so nervoused up he couldn't shoot. But Spunk says twan't no bob-cat
35   nohow. He says it was Joe done sneaked back from Hell!"

"Humph!" sniffed Walter, "he oughter be nervous after what he done. Ah reckon Joe come back to dare him to marry Lena, or to come out an' fight. Ah bet he'll be back time and agin, too. Know what Ah think? Joe wuz a braver man than Spunk."

40   There was a general shout of derision from the group.

"Thass a fact," went on Walter. "Lookit whut he done; took a razor an' went out to fight a man he knowed toted a gun an' wuz a crack shot, too; 'nother thing Joe wuz skeered of Spunk, skeered

plumb stiff! But he went jes' the same. It took him a long time to get his nerve up. 'Tain't nothin' for Spunk to fight when he ain't skeered of nothin'. Now, Joe's done come back to have it out wid the man that's got all he ever had. Y'all know Joe ain't never had nothin' nor
5 wanted nothin' besides Lena. It musta been a h'ant cause ain' nobody never seen no black bob-cat."

"Nother thing," cut in one of the men, "Spunk wuz cussin' a blue streak today 'cause he 'lowed dat saw wuz wobblin'—almos' got 'im once. The machinist come, looked it over an' said it wuz
10 alright. Spunk musta been leanin' t'wards it some. Den he claimed somebody pushed 'im but 'twant nobody close to 'im. Ah wuz glad when knockin' off time come. I'm skeered of dat man when he gits hot. He'd beat you full of button holes as quick as he's look atcher."

IV

The men gathered the next evening in a different mood, no
15 laughter. No badinage this time.

"Look 'Lige, you goin' to set up wid Spunk?"

"Naw, Ah reckon not, Walter. Tell yuh the truth, Ah'm a lil bit skittish. Spunk died too wicket—died cussin' he did. You know he thought he wuz done outa life."

20 "Good Lawd, who'd he think done it?"

"Joe."

"Joe Kanty? How come?"

"Walter, Ah b'leeve Ah will walk up thata way an' set. Lena would like it Ah reckon."

25 "But whut did he say, 'Lige?"

Elijah did not answer until they had left the lighted store and were strolling down the dark street.

"Ah wuz loadin' a wagon wid scantlin' right near the saw when Spunk fell on the carriage but 'fore Ah could git to him the
30 saw got him in the body—awful sight. Me an' Skint Miller got him off but it was too late. Anybody could see that. The fust thing he said wuz: 'He pushed me, 'Lige—the dirty hound pushed me in the back!' He was spittin' blood at ev'ry breath. We laid him on the saw-dust pile with his face to the East so's he could die easy. He helt mah
35 han' till the last, Walter, and said: 'It was Joe, 'Lige—the dirty sneak shoved me . . . he didn't dare come to mah face . . . but Ah'll git the son-of-a-wood louse soon's Ah get there an' make hell too hot for him . . . . Ah felt him shove me. . . !' Thass how he died."

"If spirits kin fight, there's a powerful tussle goin' on some-
40 where ovah Jordan 'cause Ah b'leeve Joe's ready for Spunk an' ain't skeered anymore—yas, Ah b'leeve Joe pushed 'im mahself. "

They had arrived at the house. Lena's lamentations were deep and loud. She had filled the room with magnolia blossoms that gave

off a heavy sweet odor. The keepers of the wake tipped about whispering in frightened tones. Everyone in the Village was there, even old Jeff Kanty, Joe's father, who a few hours before would have been afraid to come within ten feet of him, stood leering triumphantly
5   down upon the fallen giant as if his fingers had been the teeth of steel that laid him low.

The cooling board consisted of three sixteen-inch boards on saw horses, a dingy sheet was his shroud.

The women ate heartily of the funeral baked meats and won-
10   dered who would be Lena's next. The men whispered coarse conjectures between guzzles of whiskey.

SWEAT

It was eleven o'clock of a Spring night in Florida. It was Sunday. Any other night, Delia Jones would have been in bed for two hours by this time. But she was a washwoman, and Monday morning meant a great deal to her. So she collected the soiled
5   clothes on Saturday when she returned the clean things. Sunday night after church, she sorted them and put the white things to soak. It saved her almost a half day's start. A great hamper in the bedroom held the clothes that she brought home. It was so much neater than a number of bundles lying around.
10   She squatted in the kitchen floor beside the great pile of clothes, sorting them into small heaps according to color, and humming a song in a mournful key, but wondering through it all where Sykes, her husband, had gone with her horse and buckboard.

Just then something long, round, limp and black fell upon her
15   shoulders and slithered to the floor beside her. A great terror took hold of her. It softened her knees and dried her mouth so that it was a full minute before she could cry out or move. Then she saw that it was the big bull whip her husband liked to carry when he drove.

She lifted her eyes to the door and saw him standing there bent
20   over with laughter at her fright. She screamed at him.

"Sykes, what you throw dat whip on me like dat? You know it would skeer me—looks just like a snake, an' you knows how skeered Ah is of snakes."

"Course Ah knowed it! That's how come Ah done it." He
25   slapped his leg with his hand and almost rolled on the ground in his mirth. "If you such a big fool dat you got to have a fit over a earth worm or a string, Ah don't keer how bad Ah skeer you."

"You aint got no business doing it. Gawd knows it's a sin. Some, day Ah'm gointuh drop dead from some of yo' foolishness.
30   'Nother thing, where you been wid mah rig? Ah feeds dat pony. He

aint fuh you to be drivin' wid no bull whip."

"You sho is one aggravatin' nigger woman!" he declared and stepped into the room. She resumed her work and did not answer him at once. "Ah done tole you time and again to keep them white
5   folks' clothes outa dis house."

He picked up the whip and glared down at her. Delia went on with her work. She went out into the yard and returned with a galvanized tub and sat it on the washbench. She saw that Sykes had kicked all of the clothes together again, and now stood in way truc-
10 ulently, his whole manner hoping, praying, for an argument. But she walked calmly around him and commenced to re-sort the things.

"Next time, Ah'm gointer kick 'em outdoors," he threatened as he struck a match along the leg of his corduroy breeches.

Delia never looked up from her work, and her thin, stooped
15 shoulders sagged further.

"Ah aint for no fuss t'night, Sykes. Ah just come from taking sacrament at the church house."

He snorted scornfully. "Yeah, you just come from de church house on a Sunday night, but heah you is gone to work on them
20 clothes. You ain't nothing but a hypocrite. One of them amen-corner Christians—sing, whoop, and shout, then come home and wash white folks clothes on the Sabbath."

He stepped roughly upon the whitest pile of things, kicking them helter-skelter as he crossed the room. His wife gave a little
25 scream of dismay, and quickly gathered them together again.

"Sykes, you quit grindin' dirt into these clothes! How can Ah git through by Sat'day if Ah don't start on Sunday?"

"Ah don't keer if you never git through. Anyhow, Ah done promised Gawd and a couple of other men, Ah aint gointer have it
30 in mah house. Don't gimme no lip neither, else Ah'll throw 'em out and put mah fist up side yo' head to boot."

Delia's habitual meekness seemed to slip from her shoulders like a blown scarf. She was on her feet; her poor little body, her bare knuckly hands bravely defying the strapping hulk before her.
35 "Looka heah, Sykes, you done gone too fur. Ah been married to you fur fifteen years, and Ah been takin' in washin' fur fifteen years. Sweat, sweat, sweat! Work and sweat, cry and sweat, pray and sweat!"

"What's that got to do with me?" he asked brutally.

"What's it got to do with you, Sykes? Mah tub of suds is filled
40 yo' belly with vittles more times than yo' hands is filled it. Mah sweat is done paid for this house and Ah reckon Ah kin keep on sweatin' in it."

She seized the iron skillet from the stove and struck a defensive pose, which act surprised him greatly, coming from her. It cowed
45 him and he did not strike her as he usually did.

"Naw you won't," she panted, "that ole snaggle-toothed black woman you runnin' with aint comin' heah to pile up on *mah* sweat and blood. You aint paid for nothin' on this place, and Ah'm gointer stay right heah till Ah'm toted out foot foremost."

5   "Well, you better quit gittin' me riled up, else they'll be totin' you out sooner than you expect. Ah'm so tired of you Ah don't know whut to do. Gawd! how Ah hates skinny wimmen!"

A little awed by this new Delia, he sidled out of the door and slammed the back gate after him. He did not say where he had

10 gone, but she knew too well. She knew very well that he would not return until nearly daybreak also. Her work over, she went on to bed but not to sleep at once. Things had come to a pretty pass!

She lay awake, gazing upon the debris that cluttered their matrimonial trail. Not an image left standing along the way. Anything

15 like flowers had long ago been drowned in the salty stream that had been pressed from her heart. Her tears, her sweat, her blood. She had brought love to the union and he had brought a longing after the flesh. Two months after the wedding, he had given her the first brutal beating. She had the memory of his numerous trips to

20 Orlando with all of his wages when he had returned to her penniless, even before the first year had passed. She was young and soft then, but now she thought of her knotty, muscled limbs, her harsh knuckly hands, and drew herself up into an unhappy little ball in the middle of the big feather bed. Too late now to hope for love,

25 even if it were not Bertha it would be someone else. This case differed from the others only in that she was bolder than the others. Too late for everything except her little home. She had built it for her old days, and planted one by one the trees and flowers there. It was lovely to her, lovely.

30 Somehow, before sleep came, she found herself saying aloud: "Oh well, whatever goes over the Devil's back, is got to come under his belly. Sometime or ruther, Sykes, like everybody else, is gointer reap his sowing." After that she was able to build a spiritual earthworks against her husband. His shells could no longer reach her.

35 *Amen.* She went to sleep and slept until he announced his presence in bed by kicking her feet and rudely snatching the cover away.

"Gimme some kivah heah, an' git yo' damn foots over on yo' own side! Ah oughter mash you in yo' mouf fuh drawing dat skillet on me."

40 Delia went clear to the rail without answering him. A triumphant indifference to all that he was or did.

The week was as full of work for Delia as all other weeks, and Saturday found her behind her little pony, collecting and delivering clothes.

It was a hot, hot day near the end of July. The village men on
Joe Clarke's porch even chewed cane listlessly. They did not hurl
the cane-knots as usual. They let them dribble over the edge of the
porch. Even conversation had collapsed under the heat.

5   "Heah come Delia Jones," Jim Merchant said, as the shaggy
pony came 'round the bend of the road toward them. The rusty
buckboard was heaped with baskets of crisp, clean laundry.

    "Yep," Joe Lindsay agreed. "Hot or col', rain or shine, jes ez
reg'lar ez de weeks roll roun' Delia carries 'em an' fetches 'em on
10 Sat'day. "

    "She better if she wanter eat," said Moss. "Sykes Jones aint wuth
de shot an' powder hit would tek tuh kill 'em. Not to *huh* he aint. "

    "He sho' aint," Walter Thomas chimed in. "It's too bad, too,
cause she wuz a right pritty li'l trick when he got huh. Ah'd uh
15 mah'ied huh mahseff if he hadnter beat me to it."

    Delia nodded briefly at the men as she drove past.

    "Too much knockin' will ruin *any* 'oman. He done beat huh
'nough tuh kill three women, let 'lone change they looks," said
Elijah Moseley. "How Sykes kin stommuck dat big black greasy
20 Mogul he's layin' roun' wid, gits me. Ah swear dat eight-rock
couldn't kiss a sardine can Ah done thowed out de back do' 'way
las' yeah."

    "Aw, she's fat, thass how come. He's allus been crazy 'bout fat
women," put in Merchant. "He'd a' been tied up wid one long time
25 ago if he could a' found one tuh have him. Did Ah tell yuh 'bout
him come sidlin' roun' *mah* wife—bringin' her a basket uh pee-cans
outa his yard fuh a present? Yessir, mah wife! She tol' him tuh take
'em right straight back home, cause Delia works so hard ovah dat
washtub she reckon everything on de place taste lak sweat an' soap-
30 suds. Ah jus' wisht Ah'd a' caught 'im 'roun' dere! Ah'd a' made his
hips ketch on fiah down dat shell road."

    "Ah know he done it, too. Ah sees 'im grinnin' at every 'oman
dat passes," Walter Thomas said. "But even so, he useter eat some
mighty big hunks uh humble pie tuh git dat lil' 'oman he got. She
35 wuz ez pritty ez a speckled pup! Dat wuz fifteen yeahs ago. He
useter be so skeered uh losin' huh, she could make him do some
parts of a husband's duty. Dey never wuz de same in de mind."

    "There oughter be a law about him," said Lindsay. "He aint fit
tuh carry guts tuh a bear."

40   Clarke spoke for the first time. "Taint no law on earth dat kin
make a man be decent if it aint in 'im. There's plenty men dat takes
a wife lak dey do a joint uh sugar-cane. It's round, juicy an' sweet
when dey gits it. But dey squeeze an' grind, squeeze an' grind an'
wring tell dey wring every drop uh pleasure dat's in 'em out. When
45 dey's satisfied dat dey is wrung dry, dey treats 'em jes lak dey do a

cane-chew. Dey thows 'em away. Dey knows whut dey is doin' while dey is at it, an' hates theirselves fuh it but they keeps on hangin' after huh tell she's empty. Den dey hates huh fuh bein' a cane-chew an' in de way."

5   "We oughter take Sykes an' dat stray 'oman uh his'n down in Lake Howell swamp an' lay on de rawhide till they cain't say 'Lawd a' mussy.' He allus wuz uh ovahbearin' niggah, but since dat white 'oman from up north done teached 'im how to run a automobile, he done got too biggety to live—an' we oughter kill 'im," Old Man
10 Anderson advised.

A grunt of approval went around the porch. But the heat was melting their civic virtue and Elijah Moseley began to bait Joe Clarke.

"Come on, Joe, git a melon outa dere an' slice it up for yo' customers. We'se all sufferin' wid de heat. De bear's done got *me!*"

15 "Thass right, Joe, a watermelon is jes' whut Ah needs tuh cure de eppizudicks." Walter Thomas joined forces with Moseley. "Come on dere, Joe. We all is steady customers an' you aint set us up in a long time. Ah chooses dat long, bowlegged Floridy favorite."

"A god, an' be dough. You all gimme twenty cents and slice
20 away," Clarke retorted. "Ah needs a col' slice m'self. Heah, everybody chip in. Ah'll lend y'all mah meat knife."

The money was quickly subscribed and the huge melon brought forth. At that moment, Sykes and Bertha arrived. A determined silence fell on the porch and the melon was put away again.

25 Merchant snapped down the blade of his jack-knife and moved toward the store door.

Come on in, Joe, an' gimme a slab uh sow belly an' uh pound uh coffee—almost fuhgot 'twas Sat'day. Got to git on home." Most of the men left also.

30 Just then Delia drove past on her way home, as Sykes was ordering magnificently for Bertha. It pleased him for Delia to see.

"Git whutsoever yo' heart desires, Honey. Wait a minute, Joe. Give huh two botles uh strawberry soda-water, uh quart uh parched ground-peas, an a block uh chewin' gum."

35 With all this they left the store, with Sykes reminding Bertha that this was his town and she could have it if she wanted it.

The men returned soon after they left, and held their watermelon feast.

"Where did Sykes Jones git dat 'oman from nohow?" Lindsay
40 asked.

"Ovah Apopka. Guess dey musta been cleanin' out de town when she lef'. She don't look lak a thing but a hunk uh liver wid hair on it."

"Well, she sho' kin squall," Dave Car-ter contributed. "When
45 she gits ready tuh laff, she jes' opens huh mouf an' latches it back

tuh de las' notch. No ole grandpa alligator down in Lake Bell aint got nothin' on huh."

5　Bertha had been in town three months now. Sykes was still paying her room rent at Della Lewis'—the only house in town that would have taken her in. Sykes took her frequently to Winter Park to "stomps." He still assured her that he was the swellest man in the state.

"Sho' you kin have dat lil' ole house soon's Ah kin git dat
10　'oman outa dere. Everything b'longs tuh me an' you sho' kin have it. Ah sho' 'bominates uh skinny 'oman. Lawdy, you sho' is got one portly shape on you! You kin git *anything* you wants. Dis is *mah* town an' you sho' kin have it."

Delia's work-worn knees crawled over the earth in
15　Gethsemane and up the rocks of Calvary many, many times during these months. She avoided the villagers and meeting places in her efforts to be blind and deaf. But Bertha nullified this to a degree, by coming to Delia's house to call Sykes out to her at the gate.

Delia and Sykes fought all the time now with no peaceful inter-
20　ludes. They slept and ate in silence. Two or three times Delia had attempted a timid friendliness, but she was repulsed each time. It was plain that the breaches must remain agape.

* * * * *

The sun had burned July to August. The heat streamed down like a million hot arrows, smiting all things living upon the earth.
25　Grass withered, leaves browned, snakes went blind in shedding and men and dogs went mad. Dog days!

Delia came home one day and found Sykes there before her. She wondered, but started to go on into the house without speaking, even though he was standing in the kitchen door and she must
30　either stoop under his arm or ask him to move. He made no room for her. She noticed a soap box beside the steps, but paid no particular attention to it, knowing that he must have brought it there. As she was stooping to pass under his outstretched arm, he suddenly pushed her backward, laughingly.

35　"Look in de box dere Delia, Ah done brung yuh somethin'!"

She nearly fell upon the box in her stumbling, and when she saw what it held, she all but fainted outright.

"Sykes! Sykes, mah Gawd! You take dat rattlesnake 'way from heah! You *gottuh*. Oh, Jesus, have mussy!"
40　"Ah aint gut tuh do nuthin' uh de kin'—fact is Ah aint got tuh do nothin' but die. Taint no use uh you puttin' on airs makin' out lak you skeered uh dat snake—he's gointer stay right heah tell he die. He wouldn't bite me cause Ah knows how tuh handle 'im. Nohow he wouldn't risk breakin' out his fangs 'gin *yo'* skinny laigs."

"Naw, now Sykes, don't keep dat thing 'roun' heah tuh skeer
me tuh death. You knows Ah'm even feared uh earth worms. Thass
de biggest snake Ah evah did see. Kill 'im Sykes, please."

" Doan ast me tuh do nothin' fuh yuh. Goin' 'roun' tryin' tuh
5   be so damn astorperious. Naw, Ah aint gonna kill it. Ah think uh
damn sight mo' uh him dan you! Dat's a nice snake an' anybody
doan lak 'im kin jes' hit de grit."

The village soon heard that Sykes had the snake, and came to
see and ask questions.

10   "How de hen-fire did you ketch dat six-foot rattler, Sykes?"
Thomas asked.

"He's full uh frogs so he caint hardly move, thass how Ah
eased up on 'm. But Ah'm a snake charmer an' knows how tuh handle em. Shux, dat aint nothin'. Ah could ketch one eve'y day if Ah
15   so wanted tuh."

"Whut he needs is a heavy hick'ry club leaned real heavy on his
head. Dat's de bes' way tuh charm a rattlesnake."

"Naw, Walt, y'all jes' don't understand dese diamon' backs lak
Ah do," said Sykes in a superior tone of voice.

20   The village agreed with Walter, but the snake stayed on. His
box remained by the kitchen door with its screen wire covering.
Two or three days later it had digested its meal of frogs and literally came to life. It rattled at every movement in the kitchen or the
yard. One day as Delia came down the kitchen steps she saw his
25   chalky-white fangs curved like scimitars hung in the wire meshes.
This time she did not run away with averted eyes as usual. She
stood for a long time in the doorway in a red fury that grew blood-
ier for every second that she regarded the creature that was her tor-
ment.

30   That night she broached the subject as soon as Sykes sat down
to the table.

"Sykes, Ah wants you tuh take dat snake 'way fum heah. You
done starved me an' Ah put up widcher, you done beat me an Ah
took dat, but you done kilt all mah insides bringin' dat varmint
35   heah."

Sykes poured out a saucer full of coffee and drank it deliberately before he answered her.

"A whole lot Ah keer 'bout how you feels inside uh out. Dat
snake aint goin' no damn wheah till Ah gits ready fuh 'im tuh go.
40   So fur as beatin' is concerned, yuh aint took near all dat you gointer take ef yuh stay 'roun' *me*."

Delia pushed back her plate and got up from the table. "Ah
hates you, Sykes," she said calmly. "Ah hates you tuh de same
degree dat Ah useter love yuh. Ah done took an' took till mah belly
45   is full up tuh mah neck. Dat's de reason Ah got mah letter fum de

church an' moved mah membership tuh Woodbridge—so Ah don't
haftuh take no sacrament wid yuh. Ah don't wantuh see yuh roun'
me a-tall. Lay 'roun' wid dat 'oman all yuh wants tuh, but gwan
'way fum me an' mah house. Ah hates yuh lak uh suck-egg dog."

5   Sykes almost let the huge wad of com bread and collard he was
chewing fall out of his mouth in amazement. He had a hard time
whipping himself up to the proper fury to try to answer Delia.

    "Well, Ah'm glad you does hate me. Ah'm sho' tiahed uh you
hangin' ontuh me. Ah don't want yuh. Look at yuh stringey ole
10 neck! Yo' rawbony laigs an' arms is enough tuh cut uh man tuh
death. You looks jes' lak de devvul's doll-baby tuh *me*. You cain't
hate me no worse dan Ah hates you. Ah been hatin *you* fuh years."

    "Yo' ole black hide don't look lak nothin' tuh me, but uh passel
uh wrinkled up rubber, wid yo' big ole yeahs flappin' on each side
15 lak uh paih uh buzzard wings. Don't think Ah'm gointuh be run
'way fum mah house neither. Ah'm goin' tuh de white folks bout
you, mah young man, de very nex' time you lay yo' han's on me.
Mah cup is done run ovah," Delia said this with no signs of fear and
Sykes departed from the house, threatening her, but made not the
20 slightest move to carry out any of them.

    That night he did not return at all, and the next day being
Sunday, Delia was glad that she did not have to quarrel before she
hitched up her pony and drove the four miles to Woodridge.

    She stayed to the night service—"love feast"—which was very
25 warm and full of spirit. In the emotional winds her domestic trials
were borne far and wide so that she sang as she drove homeward

    Jurden water, black an'col'
    Chills de body, not de soul
    An'Ah wantah cross Jurden in uh calm time.

30   She came from the barn to the kitchen door and stopped.

    "Whut's de mattah, ol' satan, you aint kickin' up yo' racket?"
She addressed the snake's box. Complete silence. She went on into
the house with a new hope in its birth struggles. Perhaps her threat
to go to the white folks had frightened Sykes! Perhaps he was sorry!
Fifteen years of misery and suppression had brought Delia to the
35 place where she would hope *anything* that looked towards a way
over or through her wall of inhibitions.

    She felt in the match safe behind the stove at once for a match.
There was only one there.

    "Dat niggah wouldn't fetch nothin' heah tuh save his rotten
neck, but he kin run thew whut Ah brings quick enough. Now he
40 done toted off nigh on tuh haff uh box uh matches. He done had dat
'oman heah in mah house, too."

18. Zora Neale Hurston

Nobody but a woman could tell how she knew this even before she struck the match. But she did and it put her into a new fury.

Presently she brought in the tubs to put the white things to soak. This time she decided she need not bring the hamper out of the bedroom; she would go in there and do the sorting. She picked up the pot-bellied lamp and went in. The room was small and the hamper stood hard by the foot of the white iron bed. She could sit and reach through the bedposts—resting as she worked.

"Ah wantah cross Jurden in uh calm time." She was singing again. The mood of the "love feast" had returned. She threw back the lid of the basket almost gaily. Then, moved by both horror and terror, she sprung back toward the door. *There lay the snake in the basket!* He moved sluggishly at first, but even as she turned round and round, jumped up and down in an insanity of fear, he began to stir vigorously. She saw him pouring his awful beauty from the basket upon the bed, then she seized the lamp and ran as fast as she could to the kitchen. The wind from the open door blew out the light and the darkness added to her terror. She sped to the darkness of the yard, slamming the door after her before she thought to set down the lamp. She did not feel safe even on the ground, so she climbed up in the hay barn.

There for an hour or more she lay sprawled upon the hay a gibbering wreck.

Finally she grew quiet, and after that, coherent thought. With this, stalked through her a cold, bloody rage. Hours of this. A period of introspection, a space of retrospection, then a mixture of both. Out of this an awful calm.

"Well, Ah done de bes' Ah could. If things aint right, Gawd knows taint mah fault."

She went to sleep—a twitchy sleep—and woke up to a faint gray sky. There was a loud hollow sound below. She peered out. Sykes was at the wood-pile, demolishing a wire-covered box.

He hurried to the kitchen door, but hung outside there some minutes before he entered, and stood some minutes more inside before he closed it after him.

The gray in the sky was spreading. Delia descended without fear now, and crouched beneath the low bedroom window. The drawn shade shut out the dawn, shut in the night. But the thin walls held back no sound.

"Dat ol' scratch is woke up now!" She mused at the tremendous whirr inside, which every woodsman knows, is one of the sound illusions. The rattler is a ventriloquist. His whirr sounds to the right, to the left, straight ahead, behind, close under foot—everywhere but where it is. Woe to him who guesses wrong unless he is prepared to hold up his end of the argument! Sometimes he strikes without rattling at all.

Inside, Sykes heard nothing until he knocked a pot lid off the stove while trying to reach the match safe in the dark. He had emptied his pockets at Bertha's.

5 The snake seemed to wake up under the stove and Sykes made a quick leap into the bedroom. In spite of the gin he had had, his head was clearing now.

"Mah Gawd! " he chattered, "ef Ah could on'y strack uh light!"

The rattling ceased for a moment as he stood paralyzed. He 10 waited. It seemed that the snake waited also.

"Oh fuh de light! Ah thought he'd be too sick"—Sykes was muttering to himself when the whirr began again, closer, right underfoot this time. Long before this, Sykes' ability to think had been flattened down to primitive instinct and he leaped—onto the 15 bed.

Outside Delia heard a cry that might have come from a maddened chimpanzee, a stricken gorilla. All the terror, all the horror, all the rage that man possibly could express, without a recognizable human sound.

20 A tremendous stir inside there, another series of animal screams, the intermittent whirr of the reptile. The shade torn violently down from the window, letting in the red dawn, a huge brown hand seizing the window stick, great dull blows upon the wooden floor punctuating the gibberish of sound long after the rat- 25 tle of the snake had abruptly subsided. All this Delia could see and hear from her place beneath the window, and it made her ill. She crept over to the four-o'clocks and stretched herself on the cool earth to recover.

She lay there. "Delia, Delia!" She could hear Sykes calling in a 30 most despairing tone as one who expected no answer. The sun crept on up, and he called. Delia could not move—her legs were gone flabby. She never moved, he called, and the sun kept rising.

"Mah Gawd! " she heard him moan. " Mah Gawd fum Heben!" She heard him stumbling about and got up from her flower-bed. 35 The sun was growing warm. As she approached the door she heard him call out hopefully, "Delia, is dat you Ah heah?"

She saw him on his hands and knees as soon as she reached the door. He crept an inch or two toward her—all that he was able, and she saw his horribly swollen neck and his one open eye shining 40 with hope. A surge of pity too strong to support bore her away from that eye that must, could not, fail to see the tubs. He would see the lamp. Orlando with its doctors was too far. She could scarcely reach the Chinaberry tree, where she waited in the growing heat while inside she knew the cold river was creeping up and up to extinguish 45 that eye which must know by now that she knew.

19. JEAN TOOMER

Born Nathan Eugene Toomer, Jean Toomer (1894–1967) experienced life in diverse areas of America. As a light-skinned African-American child, he lived in white neighborhoods of Brooklyn and New Rochelle, New York, and in affluent neighborhoods of Washington, D.C. In pursuit of higher education, Toomer attended the University of Wisconsin at Madison, the Massachusetts College of Agriculture, the University of Chicago, New York University, and the City College of New York. While he found focusing on formal academic studies to be a struggle, Toomer wrote in his spare time, and in 1919, he settled in New York to become a full-time writer. He taught himself about Buddhism, Eastern philosophy, and other non-western forms of spirituality while cultivating friendships with prominent American writers. "Bona and Paul" is excerpted from his first published book, Cane (1923), an experimental and highly imaginative work that defies generic categorization; scholars debate whether to call Cane a novel, a collection of short stories, or a series of prose poems. Although Toomer preferred to be considered an "American writer" rather than an "African-American writer," his writings demonstrate a serious and nuanced exploration of race relations in the American past and present while participating in the literary movements of Modernism and the Harlem Renaissance.

BONA AND PAUL

1

On the school gymnasium floor, young men and women are drilling. They are going to be teachers, and go out into the world . . . thud, thud . . . and give precision to the movements of sick
5   people who all their lives have been drilling. One man is out of step. In step. The teacher glares at him. A girl in bloomers, seated on a mat in the corner because she has told the director that she is sick, sees that the footfalls of the men are rhythmical and syncopated. The dance of his blue-trousered limbs thrills her.
10   Bona: He is a candle that dances in a grove swung with pale balloons.

Columns of the drillers thud towards her. He is in the front row.

He is in no row at all. Bona can look close at him. His red-brown face—

Bona: He is a harvest moon. He is an autumn leaf. He is a nigger. Bona! But dont all the dorm girls say so? And dont you, when
5   you are sane, say so? Thats why I love—Oh, nonsense. You have never loved a man who didnt first love you. Besides—

Columns thud away from her. Come to a halt in line formation. Rigid. The period bell rings, and the teacher dismisses them.

A group collects around Paul. They are choosing sides for basket-
10   ball. Girls against boys. Paul has his. He is limbering up beneath the basket. Bona runs to the girl captain and asks to be chosen. The girls fuss. The director comes to quiet them. He hears what Bona wants.

"But, Miss Hale, you were excused—"

"So I was, Mr. Boynton, but—"
15   "—you can play basket-ball, but you are too sick to drill."

"If you wish to put it that way."

She swings away from him to the girl captain.

"Helen, I want to play, and you must let me. This is the first time I've asked and I dont see why—"
20   "Thats just it, Bona. We have our team."

"Well, team or no team, I want to play and thats all there is to it."

She snatches the ball from Helen's hands, and charges down the floor.

Helen shrugs. One of the weaker girls says that she'll drop out.
25   Helen accepts this. The team is formed. The whistle blows. The game starts. Bona, in center, is jumping against Paul. He plays with her. Out-jumps her, makes a quick pass, gets a quick return, and shoots a goal from the middle of the floor. Bona burns crimson. She fights, and tries to guard him. One of her team-mates advises her
30   not to play so hard. Paul shoots his second goal.

Bona begins to feel a little dizzy and all in. She drives on. Almost hugs Paul to guard him. Near the basket, he attempts to shoot, and Bona lunges into his body and tries to beat his arms. His elbow, going up, gives her a sharp crack on the jaw. She whirls. He
35   catches her. Her body stiffens. Then becomes strangely vibrant, and bursts to a swift life within her anger. He is about to give way before her hatred when a new passion flares at him and makes his stomach fall. Bona squeezes him. He suddenly feels stifled, and wonders why in hell the ring of silly gaping faces that's caked about him
40   doesnt make way and give him air. He has a swift illusion that it is himself who has been struck. He looks at Bona. Whir. Whir. They seem to be human distortions spinning tensely in a fog. Spinning ... dizzy ... spinning ... Bona jerks herself free, flushes a startling crimson, breaks through the bewildered teams, and rushes
45   from the hall.

2

Paul is in his room of two windows.

Outside, the South-Side L track cuts them in two.

Bona is one window. One window, Paul.

Hurtling Loop-jammed L trains throw them in swift shadow.

5   Paul goes to his. Gray slanting roofs of houses are tinted lavender in the setting sun. Paul follows the sun, over the stock-yards
where a fresh stench is just arising, across wheat lands that are still
waving above their stubble, into the sun. Paul follows the sun to a
pine-matted hillock in Georgia. He sees the slanting roofs of gray
unpainted cabins tinted lavender. A Negress chants a lullaby
10 beneath the mate-eyes of a southern planter. Her breasts are ample
for the suckling of a song. She weans it, and sends it, curiously
weaving, among lush melodies of cane and corn. Paul follows the
sun into himself in Chicago.

He is at Bona's window.

15 With his own glow he looks through a dark pane.

Paul's room-mate comes in.

"Say, Paul, I've got a date for you. Come on. Shake a leg, will
you?"

His blonde hair is combed slick. His vest is snug about him.
20 He is like the electric light which he snaps on.

"Whatdoysay, Paul? Get a wiggle on. Come on. We havent got
much time by the time we eat and dress and everything."

His bustling concentrates on the brushing of his hair.

Art: What in hell's getting into Paul of late, anyway? Christ, but
25 he's getting moony. Its his blood. Dark blood: moony. Doesnt get
anywhere unless you boost it. You've got to keep it going—

"Say, Paul!"

—or it'll go to sleep on you. Dark blood; nigger? Thats what
those jealous she-hens say. Not Bona though, or she . . . from the
30 South . . . wouldnt want me to fix a date for him and her. Hell of a
thing, that Paul's dark: you've got to always be answering questions.

"Say, Paul, for Christ's sake leave that window, cant you?"

"Whats it, Art?"

35 "Hell, I've told you about fifty times. Got a date for you. Come
on."

"With who?"

Art: He didnt use to ask; now he does. Getting up in the air.
Getting funny.
40 "Heres your hat. Want a smoke? Paul! Here. I've got a match.
Now come on and I'll tell you all about it on the way to supper."

Paul: He's going to Life this time. No doubt of that. Quit your

kidding. Some day, dear Art, I'm going to kick the living slats out of
you, and you wont know what I've done it for. And your slats will
bring forth Life . . . beautiful woman . . .

Pure Food Restaurant.

5   "Bring me some soup with a lot of crackers, understand? And
then a roast-beef dinner. Same for you, eh, Paul? Now as I was saying, you've got a swell chance with her. And she's game. Best proof:
she dont give a damn what the dorm girls say about you and her in
the gym, or about the funny looks that Boynton gives her, or about
10   what they say about, well, hell, you know, Paul. And say, Paul, she's
a sweetheart. Tall, not puffy and pretty, more serious and deep—the
kind you like these days. And they say she's got a car. And say, she's
on fire. But you know all about that. She got Helen to fix it up with
me. The four of us—remember the last party? Crimson Gardens!
15   Boy!"
        Paul's eyes take on a light that Art can settle in.

3

        Art has on his patent-leather pumps and fancy vest. A loose fall
coat is swung across his arm. His face has been massaged, and over
a close shave, powdered. It is a healthy pink the blue of evening
20   tints a purple pallor. Art is happy and confident in the good looks
that his mirror gave him. Bubbling over with a joy he must spend
now if the night is to contain it all. His bubbles, too, are curiously
tinted purple as Paul watches them. Paul, contrary to what he had
thought he would be like, is cool like the dusk, and like the dusk,
25   detached. His dark face is a floating shade in evening's shadow. He
sees Art, curiously. Art is a purple fluid, carbon-charged, that effer-
vesces besides him. He loves Art. But is it not queer, this pale purple facsimile of a red-blooded Norwegian friend of his? Perhaps for
some reason, white skins are not supposed to live at night. Surely,
30   enough nights would transform them fantastically, or kill them.
And their red passion? Night paled that too, and made it moony.
Moony. Thats what Art thought of him. Bona didnt, even in the daytime. Bona, would she be pale? Impossible. Not that red glow. But
the conviction did not set his emotion flowing.
35   "Come right in, wont you? The young ladies will be right
down. Oh, Mr. Carlstrom, do play something for us while you are
waiting. We just love to listen to your music. You play so well."
        Houses, and dorm sitting-rooms are places where white faces
seclude themselves at night. There is a reason . . .
40   Art sat on the piano and simply tore it down. Jazz. The picture

of Our Poets hung perilously.

Paul: I've got to get the kid to play that stuff for me in the day-time. Might be different. More himself. More nigger. Different? There is. Curious, though.

5 The girls come in. Art stops playing, and almost immediately takes up a petty quarrel, where he had last left it, with Helen.

Bona, black-hair curled staccato, sharply contrasting with Helen's puffy yellow, holds Paul's hand. She squeezes it. Her own emotion supplements the return pressure. And then, for no tangible
10 reason, her spirits drop. Without them, she is nervous, and slightly afraid. She resents this. Paul's eyes are critical. She resents Paul. She flares at him. She flares to poise and security.

"Shall we be on our way?"

"Yes, Bona, certainly."

15 The Boulevard is sleek in asphalt, and, with arc-lights and lim-ousines, aglow. Dry leaves scamper behind the whir of cars. The scent of exploded gasoline that mingles with them is faintly sweet. Mellow stone mansions overshadow clapboard homes which now resemble Negro shanties in some southern alley. Bona and Paul, and
20 Art and Helen, move along an island-like, far-stretching strip of leaf-soft ground. Above them, worlds of shadow-planes and solids, silently moving. As if on one of these, Paul looks down on Bona. No doubt of it: her face is pale. She is talking. Her words have no feel to them. One sees them. They are pink petals that fall upon velvet
25 cloth. Bona is soft, and pale, and beautiful.

"Paul, tell me something about yourself—or would you rather wait?"

"I'll tell you anything you'd like to know."

"Not what I want to know, Paul; what you want to tell me."

30 "You have the beauty of a gem fathoms under sea."

"I feel that, but I dont want to be. I want to be near you. Perhaps I will be if I tell you something. Paul, I love you."

The sea casts up its jewel into his hands, and burns them furi-ously. To tuck her arm under his and hold her hand will ease the
35 burn.

"What can I say to you, brave dear woman—I cant talk love. Love is a dry grain in my mouth unless it is wet with kisses."

"You would dare? right here on the Boulevard? before Arthur and Helen?"

40 "Before myself? I dare."

"Here then."

Bona, in the slim shadow of a tree trunk, pulls Paul to her. Suddenly she stiffens. Stops.

"But you have not said you love me."

"I cant—yet—Bona."

"Ach, you never will. Youre cold. Cold."

Bona: Colored; cold. Wrong somewhere.

She hurries and catches up with Art and Helen.

4

5   Crimson Gardens. Hurrah! So one feels. People . . . University
of Chicago students, members of the stock exchange, a large Negro
in crimson uniform who guards the door. . . had watched them
enter. Had leaned towards each other over ash-smeared tablecloths
and highballs and whispered: What is he, a Spaniard, an Indian, an
10   Italian, a Mexican, a Hindu, or a Japanese? Art had at first fidgeted
under their stares . . . what are you looking at, you godam pack of
owl-eyed hyenas? . . . but soon settled into his fuss with Helen, and
forgot them. A strange thing happened to Paul. Suddenly he knew
that he was apart from the people around him. Apart from the pain
15   which they had unconsciously caused. Suddenly he knew that people saw, not attractiveness in his dark skin, but difference. Their
stares, giving him to himself, filled something long empty within
him, and were like green blades sprouting in his consciousness.
There was fullness, and strength and peace about it all. He saw him-
20   self, cloudy, but real. He saw the faces of the people at the tables
round him. White lights, or as now, the pink lights of the Crimson
Gardens gave a glow and immediacy to white faces. The pleasure of
it, equal to that of love or dream, of seeing this. Art and Bona and
Helen? He'd look. They were wonderfully flushed and beautiful.
25   Not for himself ; because they were. Distantly. Who were they, anyway? God, if he knew them. He'd come in with them. Of that he was
sure. Come where? Into life? Yes. No. Into the Crimson Gardens. A
part of life. A carbon bubble. Would it look purple if he went out
into the night and looked at it? His sudden starting to rise almost
30   upset the table.

"What in hell—pardon—whats the matter, Paul?"

"I forgot my cigarettes—"

"Youre smoking one."

"So I am. Pardon me."

35   The waiter straightens them out. Takes their order.

Art: What in hell's eating Paul? Moony aint the word for it.
From bad to worse. And those godam people staring so. Paul's a
queer fish. Doesnt seem to mind . . . He's my pal, let me tell you, you
horn-rimmed owl-eyed hyena at that table, and a lot better than you
40   whoever you are . . . Queer about him. I could stick up for him if
he'd only come out, one way or the other, and tell a feller. Besides,

a room-mate has a right to know. Thinks I wont understand. Said
so. He's got a swell head when it comes to brains, all right. God, he's
a good straight feller, though. Only, moony. Nut. Nuttish. Nuttery.
Nutmeg . . . "What'd you say, Helen?"

5   "I was talking to Bona, thank you."
       "Well, its nothing to get spiffy about."
       "What? Oh, of course not. Please lets dont start some silly argu-
ment all over again."
       "Well."

10   "Well."
       "Now thats enough. Say, waiter, whats the matter with our
order? Make it snappy, will you?"
       Crimson Gardens. Hurrah! So one feels. The drinks come. Four
highballs. Art passes cigarettes. A girl dressed like a bare-back rider

15   in flaming pink, makes her way through tables to the dance floor.
All lights are dimmed till they seem a lush afterglow of crimson.
Spotlights the girl. She sings. "Liza, Little Liza Jane."
       Paul is rosy before his window.
       He moves, slightly, towards Bona.

20   With his own glow, he seeks to penetrate a dark pane.
       Paul: From the South. What does that mean, precisely, except
that you'll love or hate a nigger? Thats a lot. What does it mean
except that in Chicago you'll have the courage to neither love or
hate. A priori. But it would seem that you have. Queer words, arent

25   these, for a man who wears blue pants on a gym floor in the daytime. Well, never matter. You matter. I'd like to know you whom I
look at. Know, not love. Not that knowing is a greater pleasure; but
that I have just found the joy of it. You came just a month too late.
Even this afternoon I dreamed. To-night, along the Boulevard, you

30   found me cold. Paul Johnson, cold! Thats a good one, eh, Art, you
fine old stupid fellow, you! But I feel good! The color and the music
and the song . . . A Negress chants a lullaby beneath the mate-eyes
of a southern planter. O song! . . . And those flushed faces. Eager
brilliant eyes. Hard to imagine them as unawakened. Your own. Oh,

35   they're awake all right. "And you know it too, dont you Bona?"
       "What, Paul?"
       "The truth of what I was thinking."
       "I'd like to know I know—something of you."
       "You will—before the evening's over. I promise it."

40   Crimson Gardens. Hurrah! So one feels. The bare-back rider
balances agilely on the applause which is the tail of her song.
Orchestral instruments warm up for jazz. The flute is a cat that rip-
ples its fur against the deep-purring saxophone. The drum throws
sticks. The cat jumps on the piano keyboard. Hi diddle, hi diddle,

45   the cat and the fiddle. Crimson Gardens . . . hurrah! . . . jumps over

the moon. Crimson Gardens! Helen . . . O Eliza . . . rabbit-eyes sparkling, plays up to, and tries to placate what she considers to be Paul's contempt. She always does that. . . Little Liza Jane. . . Once home, she burns with the thought of what she's done. She says all
5   manner of snidy things about him, and swears that she'll never go out again when he is along. She tries to get Art to break with him, saying, that if Paul, whom the whole dormitory calls a nigger, is more to him than she is, well, she's through. She does not break with Art. She goes out as often as she can with Art and Paul. She
10 explains this to herself by a piece of information which a friend of hers had given her: men like him (Paul) can fascinate. One is not responsible for fascination. Not one girl had really loved Paul; he fascinated them. Bona didnt; only thought she did. Time would tell. And of course, *she* didnt. Liza . . . She plays up to, and tries to pla-
15 cate, Paul.

"Paul is so deep these days, and I'm so glad he's found some one to interest him."

"I dont believe I do."

The thought escapes from Bona just a moment before her anger
20 at having said it.

Bona: You little puffy cat, I do. I do!

Dont I, Paul? her eyes ask.

Her answer is a crash of jazz from the palm-hidden orchestra. Crimson Gardens is a body whose blood flows to a clot upon the
25 dance floor. Art and Helen clot. Soon, Bona and Paul. Paul finds her a little stiff, and his mind, wandering to Helen (silly little kid who wants every highball spoon her hands touch, for a souvenir), sup-ple, perfect little dancer, wishes for the next dance when he and Art will exchange.
30 Bona knows that she must win him to herself.

"Since when have men like you grown cold?"

"The first philosopher."

"I thought you were a poet—or a gym director."

"Hence, your failure to make love."
35 Bona's eyes flare. Water. Grow red about the rims. She would like to tear away from him and dash across the clotted floor.

"What do you mean?"

"Mental concepts rule you. If they were flush with mine—good. I dont believe they are."
40 "How do you know, Mr. Philosopher?"

"Mostly a priori."

"You talk well for a gym director."

"And you—"

"I hate you. Ou!"
45 She presses away. Paul, conscious of the convention in it, pulls

her to him. Her body close. Her head still strains away. He nearly crushes her. She tries to pinch him. Then sees people staring, and lets her arms fall. Their eyes meet. Both, contemptuous. The dance takes blood from their minds and packs it, tingling, in the torsos of
5   their swaying bodies. Passionate blood leaps back into their eyes. They are a dizzy blood clot on a gyrating floor. They know that the pink-faced people have no part in what they feel. Their instinct leads them away from Art and Helen, and towards the big uniformed black man who opens and closes the gilded exit door. The
10 cloak-room girl is tolerant of their impatience over such trivial things as wraps. And slightly superior. As the black man swings the door for them, his eyes are knowing. Too many couples have passed out, flushed and fidgety, for him not to know. The chill air is a shock to Paul. A strange thing happens. He sees the Gardens purple, as if
15 he were way off. And a spot is in the purple. The spot comes furiously towards him. Face of the black man. It leers. It smiles sweetly like a child's. Paul leaves Bona and darts back so quickly that he doesn't give the door-man a chance to open. He swings in. Stops. Before the huge bulk of the Negro.
20   "Youre wrong."
        "Yassur."
        "Brother, youre wrong."
        "I came back to tell you, to shake your hand, and tell you that you are wrong. That something beautiful is going to happen. That
25 the Gardens are purple like a bed of roses would be at dusk. That I came into the Gardens, into life in the Gardens with one whom I did not know. That I danced with her, and did not know her. That I felt passion, contempt and passion for her whom I did not know. That I thought of her. That my thoughts were matches thrown into a dark
30 window. And all the while the Gardens were purple like a bed of roses would be at dusk. I came back to tell you, brother, that white faces are petals of roses. That dark faces are petals of dusk. That I am going out and gather petals. That I am going out and know her whom I brought here with me to these Gardens which are purple
35 like a bed of roses would be at dusk."
        Paul and the black man shook hands.
        When he reached the spot where they had been standing, Bona was gone.

20. ROBERT HAYDEN

Robert Hayden (1913–1980) taught at Fisk University and the University of Michigan. His poetry could speak movingly of black oppression, and it could also range into universal themes.

THOSE WINTER SUNDAYS

Sundays too my father got up early
and put his clothes on in the blueblack cold,
then with cracked hands that ached
from labor in the weekday weather made
5   banked fires blaze. No one ever thanked him.

I'd wake and hear the cold splintering, breaking.
When the rooms were warm, he'd call
and slowly I would rise and dress,
fearing the chronic angers of that house,
             →illness

10   Speaking indifferently to him,
who had driven out the cold
and polished my good shoes as well.
What did I know, what did I know,
of love's austere and lonely offices?

                                             1962

MIDDLE PASSAGE

I

Jesus, Estrella, Esperanza, Mercy:

    Sails flashing to the wind like weapons,
        sharks following the moans the fever and the dying;
    horror the corposant and compass rose.

5   Middle Passage:

voyage through death
      to life upon these shores.
"10 April 1800—
    Blacks rebellious. Crew uneasy. Our linguist says
10   their moaning is a prayer for death,
    ours and their own. Some try to starve themselves.
    Lost three this morning leaped with crazy laughter
    to the waiting sharks, sang as they went under."

Desire, Adventure, Tartar, Ann:

15   Standing to America, bringing home
    black gold, black ivory, black seed.

        Deep in the festering hold thy father lies,
        of his bones New England pews are made,
        those are altar lights that were his eyes.

20   Jesus   Saviour   Pilot   Me
    Over   Life's   Tempestuous   Sea

We pray that Thou will grant, O Lord,
safe passage to our vessels bringing
heathen souls unto Thy chastening.

25   Jesus   Saviour

    "8 bells. I cannot sleep. for I am sick
    with fear, but writing eases fear a little
    since still my eyes can see these words take shape
    upon the page & so I write, as one
30   would turn to exorcism. 4 days scudding,
    but now the sea is calm again. Misfortune
    follows in our wake like sharks (our grinning
    tutelary gods). Which one of us
    has killed an albatross? A plague among
35   our blacks—Ophthalmia: blindness—& we
    have jettisoned the blind to no avail.
    It spreads, the terrifying sickness spreads.
    Its claws have scratched sight from the Capt.'s eyes
    & there is blindness in the fo'c'sle
40   & we must sail 3 weeks before we come
    to port."

> *What port awaits us, Davy Jones'*
> *or home? I've heard of slavers drifting, drifting,*
> *playthings of wind and storm and chance, their crews*
45   *gone blind, the jungle hatred*
> *crawling up on deck.*

Thou   Who   Walked   On   Galilee

"Deponent further sayeth *The Bella J*
left the Guinea Coast
50   with cargo of five hundred blacks and odd
for the barracoons of Florida.

"That there was hardly room 'tween-decks for half
the sweltering cattle stowed spoon-fashion there;
that some went mad of thirst and tore their flesh
55   and sucked the blood:

"That Crew and Captain lusted with the comeliest
of the savage girls kept naked in the cabins;
that there was one they called The Guinea Rose
and they cast lots and fought to lie with her:

60   "That when the Bo's'n piped all hands, the flames
spreading from starboard already were beyond
control, the negroes howling and their chains
entangled with the flames:

"That the burning blacks could not be reached,
65   that the Crew abandoned ship,
leaving their shrieking negresses behind,
that the Captain perished drunken with the wenches:

"Further Deponent sayeth not."

Pilot   Oh   Pilot   Me

II

70   Aye, lad, and I have seen those factories,
Gambia, Rio Pongo, Calabar;
have watched the artful mongos baiting traps
of war wherein the victor and the vanquished

Were caught as prizes for our barracoons.
75   Have seen the nigger kings whose vanity
and greed turned wild black hides of Fellatah,
Mandingo, Ibo, Kru to gold for us,

20. Robert Hayden

And there was one—King Anthracite we named him—
fetish face beneath French parasols
80   of brass and orange velvet, impudent mouth
whose cups were carven skulls of enemies:

He'd honor us with drum and feast and conjo
and palm-oil-glistening wenches deft in love,
and for tin crowns that shone with paste,
85   red calico and German-silver trinkets

Would have the drums talk war and send
his warriors to burn the sleeping villages
and kill the sick and old and lead the young
in coffles to our factories.

90   Twenty years a trader, twenty years,
for there was wealth aplenty to be harvested
from those black fields, and I'd be trading still
but for the fevers melting down my bones.

III

Shuttles in the rocking loom of history,
95   the dark ships move, the dark ships move.
their bright ironical names
like jests of kindness on a murderer's mouth;
plough through thrashing glister toward
fata morgana's lucent melting shore,
100   weave toward New World littorals that are
mirage and myth and actual shore.

Voyage through death,
                    voyage whose chartings are unlove.

A charnel stench, effluvium of living death
105   spreads outward from the hold,
where the living and the dead, the horribly dying,
lie interlocked, lie foul with blood and excrement.

Deep in the festering hold thy father lies,
the corpse of mercy rots with him,
110   *rats eat love's rotten gelid eyes*

But, oh, the living look at you
with human eyes whose suffering accuses you,
whose hatred reaches through the swill of dark
to strike you like a leper's claw.

115   You cannot stare that hatred down
or chain the fear that stalks the watches
and breathes on you its fetid scorching breath;
cannot kill the deep immortal human wish,
the timeless will.

120   "But for the storm that flung up barriers
of wind and wave, *The Amistad*, señores,
would have reached the port of Príncipe in two,
three days at most; but for the storm we should
have been prepared for what befell.

125   Swift as the puma's leap it came. There was
that interval of moonless calm filled only
with the water's and the rigging's usual sounds,
then sudden movement, blows and snarling cries
and they had fallen on us with machete

130   and marlinspike. It was as though the very
air, the night itself were striking us.
Exhausted by the rigors of the storm,
we were no match for them. Our men went down
before the murderous Africans. Our loyal

135   Celestino ran from below with gun
and lantern and I saw, before the cane-
knife's wounding flash, Cinquez,
that surly brute who calls himself a prince,
directing, urging on the ghastly work.

140   He hacked the poor mulatto down, and then
he turned on me. The decks were slippery
when daylight finally came. It sickens me
to think of what I saw, of how these apes
threw overboard the butchered bodies of

145   our men, true Christians all, like so much jetsam.
Enough, enough. The rest is quickly told:
Cinquez was forced to spare the two of us
you see to steer the ship to Africa,
and we like phantoms doomed to rove the sea

150   voyaged east by day and west by night,
deceiving them, hoping for rescue,
prisoners on our own vessel, till
at length we drifted to the shores of this

155

your land, America, where we were freed
from our unspeakable misery. Now we
demand, good sirs, the extradition of
Cinquez and his accomplices to La
Havana. And it distresses us to know
there are so many here who seem inclined

160

to justify the mutiny of these blacks.
We find it paradoxical indeed
that you whose wealth, whose tree of liberty
are rooted in the labor of your slaves
should suffer the August John Quincy Adams

165

to speak with so much passion of the right
of chattel slaves to kill their lawful masters
and with his Roman rhetoric weave a hero's
garland for Cinquez. I tell you that
we are determined to return to Cuba

170

with our slaves and there see justice done. Cinquez—
or let us say 'the Prince'—Cinquez shall die."

The deep immortal human wish,
the timeless will:

Cinquez its deathless primaveral image,

175

life that transfigures many lives.

Voyage through death

to life upon these shores.

21. EUDORA WELTY

Welty (1909–) was a leading figure of the Southern Renaissance in American literature. Her brilliant short stories express a vision that is essentially comic, but one with a profound sense of the suffering of the human condition. The email server Eudora is named in honor of her for her famous story, "Why I Live at the P.O."

A WORN PATH
(1940)

It was December—a bright frozen day in the early morning. Far out in the country there was an old Negro woman with her head tied in a red rag, coming along a path through the pinewoods. Her name was Phoenix Jackson. She was very old and small and she
5 walked slowly in the dark pine shadows, moving a little from side to side in her steps, with the balanced heaviness and lightness of a pendulum in a grandfather clock. She carried a thin, small cane made from an umbrella, and with this she kept tapping the frozen earth in front of her. This made a grave and persistent noise in the
10 still air, that seemed meditative like the chirping of a solitary little bird.

She wore a dark striped dress reaching down to her shoe tops, and an equally long apron of bleached sugar sacks, with a full pocket: all neat and tidy, but every time she took a step she might have
15 fallen over her shoelaces, which dragged from her unlaced shoes. She looked straight ahead. Her eyes were blue with age. Her skin had a pattern all its own of numberless branching wrinkles and as though a whole little tree stood in the middle of her forehead, but a golden color ran underneath, and the two knobs of her cheeks were
20 illumined by a yellow burning under the dark. Under the red rag her hair came down on her neck in the frailest of ringlets, still black, and with an odor like copper.

Now and then there was a quivering in the thicket. Old Phoenix said, "Out of my way, all you foxes, owls, beetles, jack rab-
25 bits, coons and wild animals! . . . Keep out from under these feet, little bob-whites. . . . Keep the big wild hogs out of my path. Don't let

none of those come running my direction. I got a long way." Under her small black-freckled hand her cane, limber as a buggy whip, would switch at the brush as if to rouse up any hiding things.

5 On she went. The woods were deep and still. The sun made the pine needles almost too bright to look at, up where the wind rocked. The cones dropped as light as feather. Down in the hollow was the mourning dove—it was not too late for him.

The path ran up a hill. "Seem like there is chains about my feet, time I get this far," she said, in the voice of argument old people 10 keep to use with themselves. "Something always take a hold of me on this hill—pleads I should stay."

After she got to the top she turned and gave a full, severe look behind her where she had come. "Up through pines," she said at length. "Now down through oaks."

15 Her eyes opened their widest, and she started down gently. But before she got to the bottom of the hill a bush caught her dress.

Her fingers were busy and intent, but her skirts were full and long, so that before she could pull them free in one place they were caught in another. It was not possible to allow the dress to tear. "I in 20 the thorny bush," she said. "Thorns, you doing your appointed work. Never want to let folks pass, no sir. Old eyes thought you was a pretty little *green* bush."

Finally, trembling all over, she stood free, and after a moment dared to stoop for her cane.

25 "Sun so high!" she cried, leaning back and looking, while the thick tears went over her eyes. "The time getting all gone here."

At the foot of this hill was a place where a log was laid across the creek.

"Now comes the trial," said Phoenix.

30 Putting her right foot out, she mounted the log and shut her eyes. Lifting her skirt, leveling her cane fiercely before her, like a festival figure in some parade, she began to march across. Then she opened her eyes and she was safe on the other side.

"I wasn't as old as I thought," she said.

35 But she sat down to rest. She spread her skirts on the bank around her and folded her hands over her knees. Up above her was a tree in a pearly cloud of mistletoe. She did not dare to close her eyes, and when a little boy brought her a plate with a slice of marble-cake on it she spoke to him. "That would be acceptable," she 40 said. But when she went to take it there was just her own hand in the air.

So she left that tree, and had to go through a barbed-wire fence. There she had to creep and crawl, spreading her knees and stretching her fingers like a baby trying to climb the steps. But she talked 45 loudly to herself: she could not let her dress be torn now, so late in the day, and she could not pay for having her arm or her leg sawed off if she got caught fast where she was.

At last she was safe through the fence and risen up out in the clearing. Big dead trees, like black men with one arm, were stand-
5 ing in the purple stalks of the withered cotton field. There sat a buz-zard.

"Who you watching?"

In the furrow she made her way along.

"Glad this not the season for bulls," she said, looking sideways,
10 "and the good Lord made his snakes to curl up and sleep in the win-ter. A pleasure I don't see no two-headed snake coming around that tree, where it come once. It took a while to get by him, back in the summer."

She passed through the old cotton and went into a field of dead
15 corn. It whispered and shook and was taller than her head. "Through the maze now," she said, for there was no path.

Then there was something tall, black, and skinny there, moving before her.

At first she took it for a man. It could have been a man dancing
20 in the field. But she stood still and listened, and it did not make a sound. It was as silent as a ghost.

"Ghost," she said sharply, "who be you the ghost of? For I have heard of nary death close by."

But there was no answer—only the ragged dancing in the
25 wind.

She shut her eyes, reached out her hand, and touched a sleeve. She found a coat and inside that an emptiness, cold as ice.

"You scarecrow," she said. Her face lighted. "I ought to be shut up for good," she said with laughter. "My senses is gone. I too old.
30 I the oldest people I ever know. Dance, old scarecrow," she said, "while I dancing with you."

She kicked her foot over the furrow, and with mouth drawn down, shook her head once or twice in a little strutting way. Some husks blew down and whirled in streamers about her skirts.
35 Then she went on, parting her way from side to side with the cane, through the whispering field. At last she came to the end, to a wagon track where the silver grass blew between the red ruts. The quail were walking around like pullets, seeming all dainty and unseen.
40 "Walk pretty," she said. "This the easy place. This the easy going."

She followed the track, swaying through the quiet bare fields, through the little strings of trees silver in their dead leaves, past cab-ins silver from weather, with the doors and windows boarded shut,
45 all like old women under a spell sitting there. "I walking in their

sleep," she said, nodding her head vigorously.

In a ravine she went where a spring was silently flowing through a hollow log. Old Phoenix bent and drank. "Sweet-gum makes the water sweet," she said, and drank more. "Nobody know
5 who made this well, for it was here when I was born."

The track crossed a swampy part where the moss hung as white as lace from every limb. "Sleep on, alligators, and blow your bubbles." Then the track went into the road.

Deep, deep the road went down between the high green-col-
10 ored banks. Overhead the live-oaks met, and it was as dark as a cave.

A black dog with a lolling tongue came up out of the weeds by the ditch. She was meditating, and not ready, and when he came at her she only hit him a little with her cane. Over she went in the
15 ditch, like a little puff of milkweed.

Down there, her senses drifted away. A dream visited her, and she reached her hand up, but nothing reached down and gave her a pull. So she lay there and presently went to talking. "Old woman," she said to herself, "that black dog come up out of the weeds to stall
20 you off, and now there he sitting on his fine tail, smiling at you."

A white man finally came along and found her—a hunter, a young man, with his dog on a chain.

"Well, Granny!" he laughed. "What are you doing there?"

"Lying on my back like a June-bug waiting to be turned over,
25 mister," she said, reaching up her hand.

He lifted her up, gave her a swing in the air, and set her down. "Anything broken, Granny?"

"No sir, them old dead weeds is springy enough," said Phoenix, when she had got her breath. "I thank you for your trou-
30 ble."

"Where do you live, Granny?" he asked, while the two dogs were growling at each other.

"Away back yonder, sir, behind the ridge. You can't even see it from here."
35 "On your way home?"

"No sir, I going to town."

"Why, that's too far! That's as far as I walk when I come out myself, and I get something for my trouble." He patted the stuffed bag he carried, and there hung down a little closed claw. It was one
40 of the bob-whites, with its beak hooked bitterly to show it was dead. "Now you go on home, Granny!"

"I bound to go to town, mister," said Phoenix. "The time come around."

He gave another laugh, filling the whole landscape. "I know
45 you old colored people! Wouldn't miss going to town to see Santa

Claus!"

But something held old Phoenix very still. The deep lines in her face went into a fierce and different radiation. Without warning, she had seen with her own eyes a flashing nickel fall out of the man's
5   pocket onto the ground.

"How old are you, Granny?" he was saying.

"There is no telling, mister," she said, "no telling."

Then she gave a little cry and clapped her hands and said, "Git on away from her, dog! Look! Look at that dog!" She laughed as if
10   in admiration. "He ain't scared of nobody. He is a big black dog." She whispered, "Sic him!"

"Watch me get rid of that cur," said the man.

"Sic him, Pete! Sic him!"

Phoenix heard the dogs fighting, and heard the man running
15   and throwing sticks. She even heard a gunshot. But she was slowly bending forward by that time, further and further forward, the lids stretched down over her eyes, as if she were doing this in her sleep. Her chin was lowered almost to her knees. The yellow palm of her hand came out from the fold of her apron. Her fingers slid down
20   and along the ground under the piece of money with the grace and care they would have in lifting an egg from under a setting hen. Then she slowly straightened up, she stood erect, and the nickel was in her apron pocket. A bird flew by. Her lips moved. "God watching me the whole time. I come to stealing."

25   The man came back, and his own dog panted about them. "Well, I scared him off that time," he said, and then he laughed and lifted his gun and pointed it at Phoenix.

She stood straight and faced him.

"Doesn't the gun scare you?' he said, still pointing it.
30   "No, sir, I seen plenty go off closer by, in my day, and for less than what I done," she said, holding utterly still.

He smiled, and shouldered the gun. "Well, Granny," he said, "you must be a hundred years old, and scared of nothing. I'd give you a dime if I had any money with me. But you take my advice and
35   stay home, and nothing will happen to you."

"I bound to go on my way, mister," said Phoenix. She inclined her head in the red rag. Then they went in different directions, but she could hear the gun shooting again and again over the hill.

She walked on. The shadows hung from the oak trees to the
40   road like curtains. Then she smelled wood-smoke, and smelled the river, and she saw a steeple and the cabins on their steep steps. Dozens of little black children whirled around her. There ahead was Natchez shining. Bells were ringing. She walked on.

In the paved city it was Christmas time. There were red and
45   green electric lights strung and crisscrossed everywhere, and all

turned on in the daytime. Old Phoenix would have been lost if she had not distrusted her eyesight and depended on her feet to know where to take her.

5 She paused quietly on the sidewalk where people were passing by. A lady came along in the crowd, carrying an armful of red, green and silver-wrapped presents; she gave off perfume like the red roses in hot summer, and Phoenix stopped her.

"Please, missy, will you lace up my shoe?" She held up her foot.

"What do you want, Grandma?"

10 "See my shoe," said Phoenix. "Do all right for out in the country, but wouldn't look right to go in a big building."

"Stand still then, Grandma," said the lady. She put her packages down on the sidewalk beside her and laced and tied both shoes tightly.

15 "Can't lace 'em with a cane," said Phoenix. "Thank you, missy. I doesn't mind asking a nice lady to tie up my shoe, when I gets out on the street."

Moving slowly and from side to side, she went into the big building, and into a tower of steps, where she walked up and 20 around and around until her feet knew to stop.

She entered a door, and there she saw nailed up on the wall the document that had been stamped with the gold seal and framed in the gold frame, which matched the dream that was hung up in her head.

25 "Here I be," she said. There was a fixed and ceremonial stiffness over her body.

"A charity case, I suppose," said an attendant who sat at the desk before her.

But Phoenix only looked above her head. There was sweat on 30 her face, the wrinkles in her skin shone like a bright net.

"Speak up, Grandma," the woman said. "What's your name? We must have your history, you know. Have you been here before? What seems to be the trouble with you?"

Old Phoenix only gave a twitch to her face as if a fly were both-35 ering her.

"Are you deaf?" cried the attendant.

But then the nurse came in.

"Oh, that's just old Aunt Phoenix," she said. "She doesn't come for herself—she has a little grandson. She makes these trips just as 40 regular as clockwork. She lives away back off the Old Natchez Trace." She bent down. "Well, Aunt Phoenix, why don't you just take a seat? We won't keep you standing after your long trip." She pointed.

The old woman sat down, bolt upright in the chair.

45 "Now, how is the boy?" asked the nurse.

Old Phoenix did not speak.

"I said, how is the boy?"

But Phoenix only waited and stared straight ahead, her face very solemn and withdrawn into rigidity.

5   "Is his throat any better?" asked the nurse. "Aunt Phoenix, don't you hear me? Is your grandson's throat any better since the last time you came for the medicine?"

With her hands on her knees, the old woman waited, silent, erect and motionless, just as if she were in armor.

10   "You mustn't take up our time this way, Aunt Phoenix," the nurse said. "Tell us quickly about your grandson, and get it over. He isn't dead, is he?"

At last there came a flicker and then a flame of comprehension across her face, and she spoke.

15   "My grandson. It was my memory had left me. There I sat and forgot why I made my long trip."

"Forgot?" The nurse frowned. "After you came so far?"

Then Phoenix was like an old woman begging a dignified forgiveness for waking up frightened in the night. "I never did go to 20 school, I was too old at the Surrender," she said in a soft voice. "I'm an old woman without an education. It was my memory fail me. My little grandson, he is just the same, and I forgot it in the coming."

"Throat never heals, does it?" said the nurse, speaking in a loud, sure voice to old Phoenix. By now she had a card with some-25 thing written on it, a little list. "Yes. Swallowed lye. When was it?— January—two, three years ago—"

Phoenix spoke unasked now. "No, missy, he not dead, he just the same. Every little while his throat begin to close up again, and he not able to swallow. He not get his breath. He not able to help 30 himself. So the time come around, and I go on another trip for the soothing medicine."

"All right. The doctor said as long as you came to get it, you could have it," said the nurse. "But it's an obstinate case."

"My little grandson, he sit up there in the house all wrapped 35 up, waiting by himself," Phoenix went on. "We is the only two left in the world. He suffer and it don't seem to put him back at all. He got a sweet look. He going to last. He wear a little patch quilt and peep out holding his mouth open like a little bird. I remembers so plain now. I not going to forget him again, no, the whole enduring 40 time. I could tell him from all the others in creation."

"All right." The nurse was trying to hush her now. She brought her a bottle of medicine. "Charity," she said, making a check mark in a book.

Old Phoenix held the bottle close to her eyes, and then careful-45 ly put it into her pocket.

"I thank you," she said.

"It's Christmas time, Grandma," said the attendant. "Could I give you a few pennies out of my purse?"

"Five pennies is a nickel," said Phoenix stiffly.

5   "Here's a nickel," said the attendant.

Phoenix rose carefully and held out her hand. She received the nickel and then fished the other nickel out of her pocket and laid it beside the new one. She stared at her palm closely with her head on one side.

10   Then she gave a tap with her cane on the floor.

"This is what come to me to do," she said. "I going to the store and buy my child a little windmill they sells, made out of paper. He going to find it hard to believe there such a thing in the world. I'll march myself back where he waiting, holding it straight up in this

15 hand."

She lifted her free hand, gave a little nod, turned around, and walked out of the doctor's office. Then her slow step began on the stairs, going down.

22. FLANNERY O'CONNOR

O'Connor (1925–1964) was the greatest short-story writer of her generation in America. Her stories are set in the Bible-belt South of fundamentalist Protestantism, but they express an essentially Catholic vision rooted in O'Connor's profound reading in philosophy and theology. Her comic stories convey a vision of "fallen man perverted by false philosophies" and though evil often seems to triumph, it does so only to prepare the way for the mysterious actions of God's grace.

A GOOD MAN IS HARD TO FIND
(1953)

The Grandmother didn't want to go to Florida. She wanted to visit some of her connections in east Tennessee and she was seizing at every chance to change Bailey's mind. Bailey was the son she lived with, her only boy. He was sitting on the edge of his chair at

5   the table, bent over the orange sports section of the *Journal*. "Now look here, Bailey," she said, "see here, read this," and she stood with one hand on her head. "Here this fellow that calls himself The Misfit is aloose from the Federal Pen and headed toward Florida and you read here what it says he did to these people. Just you read it. I

10   wouldn't take my children in any direction with a criminal like that aloose in it. I couldn't answer to my conscience if I did."

Bailey didn't look up from his reading so she wheeled around then and faced the children's mother, a young woman in slacks, whose face was as broad and innocent as a cabbage and was tied

15   around with a green head-kerchief that had two points on the top like rabbit's ears. She was sitting on the sofa, feeding the baby his apricots out of a jar. "The children have been to Florida before," the old lady said. "You all ought to take them somewhere else for a change so they would see different parts of the world and be broad.

20   They never have been to east Tennessee."

The children's mother didn't seem to hear her but the eight-year-old boy, John Wesley, a stocky child with glasses, said, "If you don't want to go to Florida, why dontcha stay at home?" He and the little girl, June Star, were reading the funny papers on the floor.

"She wouldn't stay at home to be queen for a day," June Star said without raising her yellow head.

"Yes and what would you do if this fellow, The Misfit, caught you?" the grandmother asked.

5   "I'd smack his face," John Wesley said.

"She wouldn't stay at home for a million bucks," June Star said. "Afraid she'd miss something. She has to go everywhere we go."

"All right, Miss," the grandmother said. "Just remember that the next time you want me to curl your hair."

10   June Star said her hair was naturally curly.

The next morning the grandmother was the first one in the car, ready to go. She had her big black valise that looked like the head of a hippopotamus in one corner, and underneath it she was hiding a basket with Pitty Sing, the cat, in it. She didn't intend for the cat

15   to be left alone in the house for three days because he would miss her too much and she was afraid he might brush against one of the gas burners and accidentally asphyxiate himself. Her son, Bailey, didn't like to arrive at a motel with a cat.

She sat in the middle of the back seat with John Wesley and

20   June Star on either side of her. Bailey and the children's mother and the baby sat in front and they left Atlanta at eight forty-five with the mileage on the car at 55890. The grandmother wrote this down because she thought it would be interesting to say how many miles they had been when they got back. It took them twenty minutes to

25   reach the outskirts of the city.

The old lady settled herself comfortably, removing her white cotton gloves and putting them up with her purse on the shelf in front of the back window. The children's mother still had on slacks and still had her head tied up in a green kerchief, but the grand-

30   mother had on a navy blue straw sailor hat with a bunch of white violets on the brim and a navy blue dress with a small white dot in the print. Her collars and cuffs were white organdy trimmed with lace and at her neckline she had pinned a purple spray of cloth violets containing a sachet. In case of an accident, anyone seeing her

35   dead on the highway would know at once that she was a lady.

She said she thought it was going to be a good day for driving, neither too hot nor too cold, and she cautioned Bailey that the speed limit was fifty-five miles an hour and that the patrolmen hid themselves behind billboards and small clumps of trees and sped out

40   after you before you had a chance to slow down. She pointed out interesting details of the scenery: Stone Mountain; the blue-granite that in some places came up to both sides of the highway; the brilliant red clay banks slightly streaked with purple; and the various crops that made rows of green lace-work on the ground. The trees

45   were full of silver-white sunlight and the meanest of them sparkled.

The children were reading comic magazines and their mother had
gone back to sleep.

"Let's go through Georgia fast so we won't have to look at it
much," John Wesley said.

5   "If I were a little boy," said the grandmother, "I wouldn't talk
about my native state that way. Tennessee has the mountains and
Georgia has the hills."

"Tennessee is just a hillbilly dumping ground," John Wesley
said, "and Georgia is a lousy state too."

10   "You said it," June Star said.

"In my time," said the grandmother, folding her thin veined
fingers, "children were more respectful of their native states and
their parents and everything else. People did right then. Oh look at
the cute little pickaninny!" she said and pointed to a Negro child
15   standing in the door of a shack. "Wouldn't that make a picture
now?" she asked and they all turned and looked at the little Negro
out of the back window. He waved.

"He didn't have any britches on," June Star said.

"He probably didn't have any," the grandmother explained.
20   "Little niggers in the country don't have things like we do. If I
could paint, I'd paint that picture," she said.

The children exchanged comic books.

The grandmother offered to hold the baby and the children's
mother passed him over the front seat to her. She set him on her
25   knee and bounced him and told him about the things they were
passing. She rolled her eyes and screwed up her mouth and stuck
her leathery thin face into his smooth bland one. Occasionally he
gave her a faraway smile. They passed a large cotton field with five
or six graves fenced in the middle of it, like a small island. "Look at
30   the graveyard!" the grandmother said, pointing it out. "That was
the old family burying ground. That belonged to the plantation."

"Where's the plantation?" John Wesley asked.

"Gone With the Wind," said the grandmother. "Ha. Ha."

When the children finished all the comic books they had
35   brought, they opened the lunch and ate it. The grandmother ate a
peanut butter sandwich and an olive and would not let the children
throw the box and the paper napkins out the window. When there
was nothing else to do they played a game by choosing a cloud and
making the other two guess what shape it suggested. John Wesley
40   took one the shape of a cow and June Star guessed a cow and John
Wesley said, no, an automobile, and June Star said he didn't play
fair, and they began to slap each other over the grandmother.

The grandmother said she would tell them a story if they
would keep quiet. When she told a story, she rolled her eyes and
45   waved her head and was very dramatic. She said once when she

was a maiden lady she had been courted by a Mr. Edgar Atkins
Teagarden from Jasper, Georgia. She said he was a good-looking
man and a gentleman and that he brought her a watermelon every
Saturday afternoon with his initials cut in it, E. A. T. Well, one
5   Saturday, she said, Mr. Teagarden brought the watermelon and
there was nobody at home and he left it on the front porch and
returned in his buggy to Jasper, but she never got the watermelon,
she said, because a nigger boy ate it when he saw the initials, E. A.
T.! This story tickled John Wesley's funny bone and he giggled and
10   giggled but June Star didn't think it was any good. She said she
wouldn't marry a man that just brought her a watermelon on
Saturday. The grandmother said she would have done well to
marry Mr. Teagarden because he was a gentleman and had bought
Coca-Cola stock when it first came out and that he had died only a
15   few years ago, a very wealthy man.

They stopped at The Tower for barbecued sandwiches. The
Tower was a part stucco and part wood filling station and dance
hall set in a clearing outside of Timothy. A fat man named Red
Sammy Butts ran it and there were signs stuck here and there on the
20   building and for miles up and down the highway saying, TRY RED
SAMMY'S FAMOUS BARBECUE. NONE LIKE FAMOUS RED
SAMMY'S! RED SAM! THE FAT BOY WITH THE HAPPY LAUGH.
A VETERAN! RED SAMMY'S YOUR MAN!

Red Sammy was lying on the bare ground outside The Tower
25   with his head under a truck while a gray monkey about a foot high,
chained to a small chinaberry tree, chattered nearby. The monkey
sprang back into the tree and got on the highest limb as soon as he
saw the children jump out of the car and run toward him.

Inside, The Tower was a long dark room with a counter at one
30   end and tables at the other and dancing space in the middle. They
all sat down at a board table next to the nickelodeon and Red Sam's
wife, a tall burnt-brown woman with hair and eyes lighter than her
skin, came and took their order. The children's mother put a dime
in the machine and played "The Tennessee Waltz," and the grand-
35   mother said that tune always made her want to dance. She asked
Bailey if he would like to dance but he only glared at her. He didn't
have a naturally sunny disposition like she did and trips made him
nervous. The grandmother's brown eyes were very bright. She
swayed her head from side to side and pretended she was dancing
40   in her chair. June Star said play something she could tap to so the
children's mother put in another dime and played a fast number
and June Star stepped out onto the dance floor and did her tap routine.

"Ain't she cute?" Red Sam's wife said, leaning over the count-
45   er. "Would you like to come be my little girl?"

"No I certainly wouldn't," June Star said. "I wouldn't live in a broken-down place like this for a million bucks!" and she ran back to the table.

"Ain't she cute?" the woman repeated, stretching her mouth politely.

"Aren't you ashamed?" hissed the grandmother.

Red Sam came in and told his wife to quit lounging on the counter and hurry up with these people's order. His khaki trousers reached just to his hip bones and his stomach hung over them like a sack of meal swaying under his shirt. He came over and sat down at a table nearby and let out a combination sigh and yodel. "You can't win," he said. "You can't win," and he wiped his sweating red face off with a gray handkerchief. "These days you don't know who to trust," he said. "Ain't that the truth?"

"People are certainly not nice like they used to be," said the grandmother.

"Two fellers come in here last week," Red Sammy said, "driving a Chrysler. It was a old beat-up car but it was a good one and these boys looked all right to me. Said they worked at the mill and you know I let them fellers charge the gas they bought? Now why did I do that?"

"Because you're a good man!" the grandmother said at once.

"Yes'm, I suppose so," Red Sam said as if he were struck with this answer.

His wife brought the orders, carrying the five plates all at once without a tray, two in each hand and one balanced on her arm. "It isn't a soul in this green world of God's that you can trust," she said. "And I don't count nobody out of that, not nobody," she repeated, looking at Red Sammy.

"Did you read about that criminal, The Misfit, that escaped?" asked the grandmother.

"I wouldn't be a bit surprised if he didn't attact this place right here," said the woman. "If he hears about it being here, I wouldn't be none surprised to see him. If he hears it's two cent in the cash register, I wouldn't be a tall surprised if he . . ."

"That'll do," Red Sam said, "Go bring these people their Co'-Colas," and the woman went off to get the rest of the order.

"A good man is hard to find," Red Sammy said. "Everything is getting terrible. I remember the day you could go off and leave your screen door unlatched. Not no more."

He and the grandmother discussed better times. The old lady said that in her opinion Europe was entirely to blame for the way things were now. She said the way Europe acted you would think we were made of money and Red Sam said it was no use talking about it, she was exactly right. The children ran outside into the white sunlight and looked at the monkey in the lacy chinaberry tree. He was busy catching fleas on himself and biting each one careful- ly between his teeth as if it were a delicacy.

They drove off again into the hot afternoon. The grandmother
5 took cat naps and woke up every few minutes with her own snor- ing. Outside of Toombsboro she woke up and recalled an old plan- tation that she had visited in the neighborhood once when she was a young lady. She said the house had six white columns across the front and that there was an avenue of oaks leading up to it and two
10 little wooden trellis arbors on either side in front where you sat down with your suitor after a stroll in the garden. She recalled exactly which road to turn off to get to it. She knew that Bailey would not be willing to lose any time looking at an old house, but the more she talked about it, the more she wanted to see it once
15 again and find out if the little twin arbors were still standing. "There was a secret panel in this house," she said craftily, not telling the truth but wishing that she were, "and the story went that all the family silver was hidden in it when Sherman came through but it was never found . . ."
20   "Hey!" John Wesley said. "Let's go see it! We'll find it! We'll poke all the woodwork and find it! Who lives there? Where do you turn off at? Hey Pop, can't we turn off there?"

"We never have seen a house with a secret panel!" June Star shrieked. "Let's go to the house with the secret panel! Hey Pop,
25 can't we go see the house with the secret panel!"

"It's not far from here, I know," the grandmother said. "It wouldn't take over twenty minutes."

Bailey was looking straight ahead. His jaw was as rigid as a horseshoe. "No," he said.
30   The children began to yell and scream that they wanted to see the house with the secret panel. John Wesley kicked the back of the front seat and June Star hung over her mother's shoulder and whined desperately into her ear that they never had any fun even on their vacation, that they could never do what THEY wanted to
35 do. The baby began to scream and John Wesley kicked the back of the seat so hard that his father could feel the blows in his kidney.

"All right!" he shouted and drew the car to a stop at the side of the road. "Will you shut up? Will you all just shut up for one sec- ond? If you don't shut up, we won't go anywhere."
40   "It would be very educational for them," the grandmother murmured.

"All right," Bailey said, "but get this: this is the only time we're going to stop for anything like this. This is the one and only time."

"The dirt road that you have to turn down is about a mile
45 back," the grandmother directed. "I marked it when we passed."

"A dirt road," Bailey groaned.

After they had turned around and were headed toward the dirt road, the grandmother recalled other points about the house, the beautiful glass over the front doorway and the candle-lamp in the
5 hall. John Wesley said that the secret panel was probably in the fireplace.

"You can't go inside this house," Bailey said. "You don't know who lives there."

"While you all talk to the people in front, I'll run around behind
10 and get in a window," John Wesley suggested.

"We'll all stay in the car," his mother said.

They turned onto the dirt road and the car raced roughly along in a swirl of pink dust. The grandmother recalled the times when there were no paved roads and thirty miles was a day's journey. The
15 dirt road was hilly and there were sudden washes in it and sharp curves on dangerous embankments. All at once they would be on a hill, looking down over the blue tops of trees for miles around, then the next minute, they would be in a red depression with the dust-coated trees looking down on them.

20 "This place had better turn up in a minute," Bailey said, "or I'm going to turn around."

The road looked as if no one had traveled on it in months.

"It's not much farther," the grandmother said and just as she said it, a horrible thought came to her. The thought was so embar-
25 rassing that she turned red in the face and her eyes dilated and her feet jumped up, upsetting her valise in the corner. The instant the valise moved, the newspaper top she had over the basket under it rose with a snarl and Pitty Sing, the cat, sprang onto Bailey's shoulder.

30 The children were thrown to the floor and their mother, clutch-ing the baby, was thrown out the door onto the ground; the old lady was thrown into the front seat. The car turned over once and land-ed right-side-up in a gulch off the side of the road. Bailey remained in the driver's seat with the cat—gray-striped with a broad white
35 face and an orange nose—clinging to his neck like a caterpillar.

As soon as the children saw they could move their arms and legs, they scrambled out of the car, shouting, "We've had an ACCI-DENT!" The grandmother was curled up under the dashboard, hoping she was injured so that Bailey's wrath would not come
40 down on her all at once. The horrible thought she had had before the accident was that the house she had remembered so vividly was not in Georgia but in Tennessee.

Bailey removed the cat from his neck with both hands and flung it out the window against the side of a pine tree. Then he got
45 out of the car and started looking for the children's mother. She was

sitting against the side of the red gutted ditch, holding the screaming baby, but she only had a cut down her face and a broken shoulder. "We've had an ACCIDENT!" the children screamed in a frenzy
of delight.

5   "But nobody's killed," June Star said with disappointment as
the grandmother limped out of the car, her hat still pinned to her
head but the broken front brim standing up at a jaunty angle and
the violet spray hanging off the side. They all sat down in the ditch,
except the children, to recover from the shock. They were all shak-
10   ing.

"Maybe a car will come along," said the children's mother
hoarsely.

"I believe I have injured an organ," said the grandmother,
pressing her side, but no one answered her. Bailey's teeth were clat-
15   tering. He had on a yellow sport shirt with bright blue parrots
designed in it and his face was as yellow as the shirt. The grandmother decided that she would not mention that the house was in
Tennessee.

The road was about ten feet above and they could see only the
20   tops of the trees on the other side of it. Behind the ditch they were
sitting in there were more woods, tall and dark and deep. In a few
minutes they saw a car some distance away on top of a hill, coming
slowly as if the occupants were watching them. The grandmother
stood up and waved both arms dramatically to attract their atten-
25   tion. The car continued to come on slowly, disappeared around a
bend and appeared again, moving even slower, on top of the hill
they had gone over. It was a big black battered hearse-like automobile. There were three men in it.

It came to a stop just over them and for some minutes, the driv-
30   er looked down with a steady expressionless gaze to where they
were sitting, and didn't speak. Then he turned his head and mut-
tered something to the other two and they got out. One was a fat
boy in black trousers and a red sweat shirt with a silver stallion
embossed on the front of it. He moved around on the right side of
35   them and stood staring, his mouth partly open in a kind of loose
grin. The other had on khaki pants and a blue striped coat and a
gray hat pulled down very low, hiding most of his face. He came
around slowly on the left side. Neither spoke.

The driver got out of the car and stood by the side of it, looking
40   down at them. He was an older man than the other two. His hair
was just beginning to gray and he wore silver-rimmed spectacles
that gave him a scholarly look. He had a long creased face and did-
n't have on any shirt or undershirt. He had on blue jeans that were
too tight for him and was holding a black hat and a gun. The two
45   boys also had guns.

"We've had an ACCIDENT!" the children screamed.

The grandmother had the peculiar feeling that the bespectacled man was someone she knew. His face was as familiar to her as if she had known him all her life but she could not recall who he was. He
5   moved away from the car and began to come down the embankment, placing his feet carefully so that he wouldn't slip. He had on tan and white shoes and no socks, and his ankles were red and thin. "Good afternoon," he said. "I see you all had you a little spill."

"We turned over twice!" said the grandmother.
10   "Oncet," he corrected. "We seen it happen. Try their car and see will it run, Hiram," he said quietly to the boy with the gray hat.

"What you got that gun for?" John Wesley asked. "Whatcha gonna do with that gun?"

"Lady," the man said to the children's mother, "would you
15   mind calling them children to sit down by you? Children make me nervous. I want all you all to sit down right together there where you're at."

"What are you telling US what to do for?" June Star asked.

Behind them the line of woods gaped like a dark open mouth.
20   "Come here," said their mother.

"Look here now," Bailey began suddenly, "we're in a predicament! We're in . . ."

The grandmother shrieked. She scrambled to her feet and stood staring. "You're The Misfit!" she said. "I recognized you at once!"
25   "Yes'm," the man said, smiling slightly as if he were pleased in spite of himself to be known, "but it would have been better for all of you lady, if you hadn't of reckernized me."

Bailey turned his head sharply and said something to his mother that shocked even the children. The old lady began to cry and
30   The Misfit reddened.

"Lady," he said, "don't you get upset. Sometimes a man says things he don't mean. I don't reckon he meant to talk to you thataway."

"You wouldn't shoot a lady, would you?" the grandmother
35   said and removed a clean handkerchief from her cuff and began to slap at her eyes with it.

The Misfit pointed the toe of his shoe into the ground and made a little hole and then covered it up again. "I would hate to have to," he said.
40   "Listen," the grandmother almost screamed. "I know you're a good man. You don't look a bit like you have common blood. I know you must come from nice people!"

"Yes mam," he said, "finest people in the world." When he smiled he showed a row of strong white teeth. "God never made a
45   finer woman than my mother and my daddy's heart was pure

gold," he said. The boy with the red sweat shirt had come around behind them and was standing with his gun at his hip. The Misfit squatted down on the ground. "Watch them children, Bobby Lee," he said. "You know they make me nervous." He looked at the six of
5 them huddled together in front of him and he seemed to be embarrassed as if he couldn't think of anything to say. "Ain't a cloud in the sky," he remarked, looking up at it. "Don't see no sun but don't see no cloud neither."

"Yes, it's a beautiful day," said the grandmother. "Listen," she
10 said, "you shouldn't call yourself The Misfit because I know you're a good man at heart. I can just look at you and tell."

"Hush!" Bailey yelled. "Hush! Everybody shut up and let me handle this!" He was squatting in the position of a runner about to sprint forward but he didn't move.

15 "I pre-chate that, lady," The Misfit said and drew a little circle in the ground with the butt of his gun.

"It'll take a half a hour to fix this here car," Hiram called, looking over the raised hood of it.

"Well, first you and Bobby Lee get him and that little boy to
20 step over yonder with you," The Misfit said, pointing to Bailey and John Wesley. "The boys want to ast you something," he said to Bailey. "Would you mind stepping back in them woods there with them?"

"Listen," Bailey began, "we're in a terrible predicament!
25 Nobody realizes what this is," and his voice cracked. His eyes were as blue and intense as the parrots in his shirt and he remained perfectly still.

The grandmother reached up to adjust her hat brim as if she were going to the woods with him but it came off in her hand. She
30 stood staring at it and after a second she let it fall on the ground. Hiram pulled Bailey up by the arm as if he were assisting an old man. John Wesley caught hold of his father's hand and Bobby Lee followed. They went off toward the woods and just as they reached the dark edge, Bailey turned and supporting himself against a gray
35 naked pine trunk, he shouted, "I'll be back in a minute, Mamma, wait on me!"

"Come back this instant!" his mother shrilled but they all disappeared into the woods.

"Bailey Boy!" the grandmother called in a tragic voice but she
40 found she was looking at The Misfit squatting on the ground in front of her. "I just know you're a good man," she said desperately. "You're not a bit common!"

"Nome, I ain't a good man," The Misfit said after a second as if he had considered her statement carefully, "but I ain't the worst in
45 the world neither. My daddy said I was a different breed of dog

from my brothers and sisters. 'You know,' Daddy said, 'it's some that can live their whole life out without asking about it and it's others has to know why it is, and this boy is one of the latters. He's going to be into everything!'" He put on his black hat and looked
5 up suddenly and then away deep into the woods as if he were embarrassed again. "I'm sorry I don't have on a shirt before you ladies," he said, hunching his shoulders slightly. "We buried our clothes that we had on when we escaped and we're just making do until we can get better. We borrowed these from some folks we
10 met," he explained.

"That's perfectly all right," the grandmother said. "Maybe Bailey has an extra shirt in his suitcase."

"I'll look and see terrectly," The Misfit said.

"Where are they taking him?" the children's mother screamed.
15 "Daddy was a card himself," The Misfit said. "You couldn't put anything over on him. He never got in trouble with the Authorities though. Just had the knack of handling them."

"You could be honest too if you'd only try," said the grandmother. "Think how wonderful it would be to settle down and live
20 a comfortable life and not have to think about somebody chasing you all the time."

The Misfit kept scratching in the ground with the butt of his gun as if he were thinking about it. "Yes'm, somebody is always after you," he murmured.
25 The grandmother noticed how thin his shoulder blades were just behind his hat because she was standing up looking down on him. "Do you ever pray?" she asked.

He shook his head. All she saw was the black hat wiggle between his shoulder blades. "Nome," he said.
30 There was a pistol shot from the woods, followed closely by another. Then silence. The old lady's head jerked around. She could hear the wind move through the tree tops like a long satisfied insuck of breath. "Bailey Boy!" she called.

"I was a gospel singer for a while," The Misfit said. "I been
35 most everything. Been in the arm service, both land and sea, at home and abroad, been twict married, been an undertaker, been with the railroads, plowed Mother Earth, been in a tornado, seen a man burnt alive oncet," and he looked up at the children's mother and the little girl who were sitting close together, their faces white
40 and their eyes glassy; "I even seen a woman flogged," he said.

"Pray, pray," the grandmother began, "pray, pray . . ."

"I never was a bad boy that I remember of," The Misfit said in an almost dreamy voice, "but somewheres along the line I done something wrong and got sent to the penitentiary. I was buried
45 alive," and he looked up and held her attention to him by a steady

stare.

"That's when you should have started to pray," she said. "What did you do to get sent to the penitentiary that first time?"

"Turn to the right, it was a wall," The Misfit said, looking up
5 again at the cloudless sky. "Turn to the left, it was a wall. Look up it was a ceiling, look down it was a floor. I forget what I done, lady. I set there and set there, trying to remember what it was I done and I ain't recalled it to this day. Oncet in a while, I would think it was coming to me, but it never come."

10 "Maybe they put you in by mistake," the old lady said vaguely.

"Nome," he said. "It wasn't no mistake. They had the papers on me."

"You must have stolen something," she said.

15 The Misfit sneered slightly. "Nobody had nothing I wanted," he said. "It was a head-doctor at the penitentiary said what I had done was kill my daddy but I known that for a lie. My daddy died in nineteen ought nineteen of the epidemic flu and I never had a thing to do with it. He was buried in the Mount Hopewell Baptist
20 churchyard and you can go there and see for yourself."

"If you would pray," the old lady said, "Jesus would help you."

"That's right," The Misfit said.

"Well then, why don't you pray?" she asked trembling with delight suddenly.

25 "I don't want no hep," he said. "I'm doing all right by myself."

Bobby Lee and Hiram came ambling back from the woods. Bobby Lee was dragging a yellow shirt with bright blue parrots in it.

"Throw me that shirt, Bobby Lee," The Misfit said. The shirt
30 came flying at him and landed on his shoulder and he put it on. The grandmother couldn't name what the shirt reminded her of. "No, lady," The Misfit said while he was buttoning it up, "I found out the crime don't matter. You can do one thing or you can do another, kill a man or take a tire off his car, because sooner or later you're going
35 to forget what it was you done and just be punished for it."

The children's mother had begun to make heaving noises as if she couldn't get her breath. "Lady," he asked, "would you and that little girl like to step off yonder with Bobby Lee and Hiram and join your husband?"

40 "Yes, thank you," the mother said faintly. Her left arm dangled helplessly and she was holding the baby, who had gone to sleep, in the other. "Hep that lady up, Hiram," The Misfit said as she struggled to climb out of the ditch, "and Bobby Lee, you hold onto that little girl's hand."

45 "I don't want to hold hands with him," June Star said. "He

reminds me of a pig."

The fat boy blushed and laughed and caught her by the arm and pulled her off into the woods after Hiram and her mother.

Alone with The Misfit, the grandmother found that she had lost
5 her voice. There was not a cloud in the sky nor any sun. There was nothing around her but woods. She wanted to tell him that he must pray. She opened and closed her mouth several times before anything came out. Finally she found herself saying, "Jesus, Jesus," meaning Jesus will help you, but the way she was saying it, it
10 sounded as if she might be cursing.

"Yes'm," The Misfit said as if he agreed. "Jesus thown everything off balance. It was the same case with Him as with me except He hadn't committed any crime and they could prove I had committed one because they had the papers on me. Of course," he said,
15 "they never shown me my papers. That's why I sign myself now. I said long ago, you get you a signature and sign everything you do and keep a copy of it. Then you'll know what you done and you can hold up the crime to the punishment and see do they match and in the end you'll have something to prove you ain't been treated right.
20 I call myself The Misfit," he said, "because I can't make what all I done wrong fit what all I gone through in punishment."

There was a piercing scream from the woods, followed closely by a pistol report. "Does it seem right to you, lady, that one is punished a heap and another ain't punished at all?"
25 "Jesus!" the old lady cried. "You've got good blood! I know you wouldn't shoot a lady! I know you come from nice people! Pray! Jesus, you ought not to shoot a lady. I'll give you all the money I've got!"

"Lady," The Misfit said, looking beyond her far into the woods,
30 "there never was a body that give the undertaker a tip."

There were two more pistol reports and the grandmother raised her head like a parched old turkey hen crying for water and called, "Bailey Boy, Bailey Boy!" as if her heart would break.

"Jesus was the only One that ever raised the dead," The Misfit
35 continued, "and He shouldn't have done it. He thown everything off balance. If He did what He said, then it's nothing for you to do but throw away everything and follow Him, and if He didn't, then it's nothing for you to do but enjoy the few minutes you got left the best way you can—by killing somebody or burning down his house
40 or doing some other meanness to him. No pleasure but meanness," he said and his voice had become almost a snarl.

"Maybe He didn't raise the dead" the old lady mumbled, not knowing what she was saying and feeling so dizzy that she sank down in the ditch with her legs twisted under her.
45 "I wasn't there so I can't say He didn't," The Misfit said. "I

wisht I had of been there," he said, hitting the ground with his fist. "It ain't right I wasn't there because if I had of been there I would of known. Listen lady," he said in a high voice, "if I had of been there I would of known and I wouldn't be like I am now." His voice

5   seemed about to crack and the grandmother's head cleared for an instant. She saw the man's face twisted close to her own as if he were going to cry and she murmured, "Why you're one of my babies. You're one of my own children!" She reached out and touched him on the shoulder. The Misfit sprang back as if a snake

10   had bitten him and shot her three times through the chest. Then he put his gun down on the ground and took of his glasses and began to clean them.

     Hiram and Bobby Lee returned from the woods and stood over the ditch, looking down at the grandmother who half sat and half

15   lay in a puddle of blood with her legs crossed under her like a child's and her face smiling up at the cloudless sky.

     Without his glasses, The Misfit's eyes were red-rimmed and pale and defenseless-looking. "Take her off and thow her where you thrown the others," he said, picking up the cat that was rubbing

20   itself against his leg.

     "She was a talker, wasn't she?" Bobby Lee said, sliding down the ditch with a yodel.

     "She would of been a good woman," The Misfit said, "if it had been somebody there to shoot her every minute of her life."

25   "Some fun!" Bobby Lee said.

     "Shut up, Bobby Lee," The Misfit said. "It's no real pleasure in life."

23. ALEXANDER SOLZHENITSYN

Solzhenitsyn (1918–) is the greatest Russian writer of the twentieth century, a fitting counterpart to Dostoevsky and Tolstoy. Arrested in 1945 for a slighting reference to Stalin in a private letter, he spent eight years inside the Soviet prison camp system. Released at Stalin's death in 1953, he was thought to be terminally ill with cancer. The cancer went into remission and Solzhenitsyn became a high school teacher of math and physics. His first novella, One Day in the Life of Ivan Denisovich, *was published with the approval of Nikita Khrushchev himself. In it, for the first time, the prison camp system was acknowledged to have existed. His later novels* Cancer Ward *and* The First Circle, *won him the Nobel Prize and the hatred of the Soviet authorities. The discovery by the secret police of his manuscript of* The Gulag *led to his forced exile in 1974. He spent twenty years in Vermont writing his magnum opus,* The Red Wheel, *a multi-volume historical novel on the Russian Revolution. Like Akhmatova, Solzhenitsyn sees the writer as a witness to Truth and his work has been an attempt to restore to the Russian people their history which the Soviet authorities had stolen.*

MATRYONA'S HOUSE
(1963)

A hundred and fifteen miles from Moscow trains were still slowing down to a crawl a good six months after it happened. Passengers stood glued to the windows or went out to stand by the doors. Was the line under repair, or what? Would the train be late?

5   It was all right. Past the crossing the train picked up speed again and the passengers went back to their seats.

Only the engine drivers knew what it was all about.

The engine drivers and I.

1

In the summer of 1953 I was coming back from the hot and
10   dusty desert, just following my nose—so long as it led me back to European Russia. Nobody waited or wanted me at my particular place, because I was a little matter of ten years overdue. I just want-

ed to get to the central belt, away from the great heats, close to the leafy muttering of forests. I wanted to efface myself, to lose myself in deepest Russia . . . if it was still anywhere to be found.

A year earlier I should have been lucky to get a job carrying a
5 hod this side of the Urals. They wouldn't have taken me as an electrician on a decent construction job. And I had an itch to teach. Those who knew told me that it was a waste of money buying a ticket, that I should have a journey for nothing.

But things were beginning to move. When I went up the stairs
10 of the N———Regional Education Department and asked for the Personnel Section, I was surprised to find Personnel sitting behind a glass partition, like in a chemist's shop, instead of the usual black leather-padded door. I went timidly up to the window, bowed, and asked, "Please, do you need any mathematicians somewhere where
15 the trains don't run? I should like to settle there for good."

They passed every dot and comma in my documents through a fine comb, went from one room to another, made telephone calls. It was something out of the ordinary for them too—people always wanted the towns, the bigger the better. And lo and behold, they
20 found just the place for me—Vysokoe Polye. The very sound of it gladdened my heart.

Vysokoe Polye did not belie its name. It stood on rising ground, with gentle hollows and other little hills around it. It was enclosed by an unbroken ring of forest. There was a pool behind a weir. Just
25 the place where I wouldn't mind living and dying. I spent a long time sitting on a stump in a coppice and wishing with all my heart that I didn't need breakfast and dinner every day but could just stay here and listen to the branches brushing against the roof in the night, with not a wireless anywhere to be heard and the whole
30 world silent.

Alas, nobody baked bread in Vysokoe Polye. There was nothing edible on sale. The whole village lugged its victuals in sacks from the big town.

I went back to the Personnel Section and raised my voice in
35 prayer at the little window. At first they wouldn't even talk to me. But then they started going from one room to another, made a telephone call, scratched with their pens, and stamped on my orders the word "Torfoprodukt."

Torfoprodukt? Turgenev never knew that you can put words
40 like that together in Russian.

On the station building at Torfoprodukt, an antiquated temporary hut of gray wood, hung a stern notice, BOARD TRAINS ONLY FROM THE PASSENGERS' HALL. A further message had been scratched on the boards with a nail, *And Without Tickets*. And by the
45 booking office, with the same melancholy wit, somebody had

carved for all time the words, *No Tickets*. It was only later that I fully appreciated the meaning of these addenda. Getting to Torfoprodukt was easy. But not getting away.

Here too, deep and trackless forests had once stood and were
5 still standing after the Revolution. Then they were chopped down by the peat cutters and the neighboring kolkhoz.[1] Its chairman, Shashkov, had razed quite a few hectares of timber and sold it at a good profit down in the Odessa region.

The workers' settlement sprawled untidily among the peat
10 bogs—monotonous shacks from the thirties, and little houses with carved façades and glass verandas, put up in the fifties. But inside these houses I could see no partitions reaching up to the ceilings, so there was no hope of renting a room with four real walls.

Over the settlement hung smoke from the factory chimney.
15 Little locomotives ran this way and that along narrow-gauge railway lines, giving out more thick smoke and piercing whistles, pulling loads of dirty brown peat in slabs and briquettes. I could safely assume that in the evening a loudspeaker would be crying its heart out over the door of the club and there would be drunks
20 roaming the streets and, sooner or later, sticking knives in each other.

This was what my dream about a quiet corner of Russia had brought me to—when I could have stayed where I was and lived in an adobe hut looking out on the desert, with a fresh breeze at night
25 and only the starry dome of the sky overhead.

I couldn't sleep on the station bench, and as soon as it started getting light I went for another stroll round the settlement. This time I saw a tiny marketplace. Only one woman stood there at that early hour, selling milk, and I took a bottle and started drinking it
30 on the spot.

I was struck by the way she talked. Instead of a normal speaking voice, she used an ingratiating singsong, and her words were the ones I was longing to hear when I left Asia for this place.

"Drink, and God bless you. You must be a stranger round
35 here?"

"And where are you from?" I asked, feeling more cheerful.

I learnt that the peat workings weren't the only thing, that over the railway lines there was a hill, and over the hill a village, that this village was Talnovo, and it had been there ages ago, when the
40 "gipsy woman" lived in the big house and the wild woods stood all round. And farther on there was a whole countryside full of villages—Chaslitsy, Ovintsy, Spudni, Shevertni, Shestimirovo, deeper and deeper into the woods, farther and farther away from the rail-

---

[1]Collective farm.

way, up towards the lakes.

The names were like a soothing breeze to me. They held a promise of backwoods Russia. I asked my new acquaintance to take me to Talnovo after the market was over and find a house for me to
5   lodge in.

It appeared that I was a lodger worth having: in addition to my rent, the school offered a truckload of peat for the winter to whoever took me. The woman's ingratiating smile gave way to a thoughtful frown. She had no room herself, because she and her husband
10   were "keeping" her aged mother, so she took me first to one lot of relatives then to another. But there wasn't a separate room to be had and both places were crowded and noisy.

We had come to a dammed-up stream that was short of water and had a little bridge over it. No other place in all the village took
15   my fancy as this did: there were two or three willows, a lopsided house, ducks swimming on the pond, geese shaking themselves as they stepped out of the water.

"Well, perhaps we might just call on Matryona," said my guide, who was getting tired of me by now. "Only it isn't so neat and cozy-
20   like in her house, neglects things she does. She's unwell."

Matryona's house stood quite near by. Its row of four windows looked out on the cold backs, the two slopes of the roof were covered with shingles, and a little attic window was decorated in the old Russian style. But the shingles were rotting, the beam ends of
25   the house and the once mighty gates had turned gray with age, and there were gaps in the little shelter over the gate.

The small gate was fastened, but instead of knocking my companion just put her hand under and turned the catch, a simple device to prevent animals from straying. The yard was not covered,
30   but there was a lot under the roof of the house. As you went through the outer door a short flight of steps rose to a roomy landing, which was open, to the roof high overhead. To the left, other steps led up to the top room, which was a separate structure with no stove, and yet another flight led down to the basement. To the
35   right lay the house proper, with its attic and its cellar.

It had been built a long time ago, built sturdily, to house a big family, and now one lonely woman of nearly sixty lived in it.

When I went into the cottage she was lying on the Russian stove[2] under a heap of those indeterminate dingy rags which are so
40   precious to a working man or woman.

The spacious room, and especially the big part near the windows, was full of rubber plants in pots and tubs standing on stools

---

[2]A large stove built of masonry, used both for heating and cooking.

and benches. They peopled the householder's loneliness like a
speechless but living crowd. They had been allowed to run wild,
and they took up all the scanty light on the north side. In what was
left of the light, and half-hidden by the stovepipe, the mistress of the
5   house looked yellow and weak. You could see from her clouded
eyes that illness had drained all the strength out of her.

While we talked she lay on the stove face downward, without
a pillow, her head toward the door, and I stood looking up at her.
She showed no pleasure at getting a lodger, just complained about
10   the wicked disease she had. She was just getting over an attack; it
didn't come upon her every month, but when it did, "It hangs on
two or three days so as I shan't manage to get up and wait on you.
I've room and to spare, you can live here if you like."

Then she went over the list of other housewives with whom I
15   should be quieter and cozier and wanted me to make the round of
them. But I had already seen that I was destined to settle in this
dimly lit house with the tarnished mirror, in which you couldn't see
yourself, and the two garish posters (one advertising books, the
other about the harvest), bought for a ruble each to brighten up the
20   walls.

Matryona Vasilyevna made me go off round the village again,
and when I called on her the second time she kept trying to put me
off, "We're not clever, we can't cook, I don't know how we shall
suit. . . ." But this time she was on her feet when I got there, and I
25   thought I saw a glimmer of pleasure in her eyes to see me back. We
reached an agreement about the rent and the load of peat which the
school would deliver.

Later on I found out that, year in year out, it was a long time since
Matryona Vasilyevna had earned a single ruble. She didn't get a
30   pension. Her relatives gave her very little help. In the kolkhoz she
had worked not for money but for credits; the marks recording her
labor days in her well-thumbed workbook.

So I moved in with Matryona Vasilyevna. We didn't divide the
room. Her bed was in the corner between the door and the stove,
35   and I unfolded my camp bed by one window and pushed
Matryona's beloved rubber plants out of the light to make room for
a little table by another. The village had electric light, laid on back
in the twenties, from Shatury. The newspapers were writing about
"Ilyich's little lamps," but the peasants talked wide-eyed about
40   "Tsar Light."[3]

---

[3]The newspapers reflect the new order, "Ilyich" standing for Vladimir Ilyich
Lenin (1870–1924), leader of the 1917 Russian Revolution and first head of the
new state; the peasants still think in terms of the emperor (Tsar).

23. Alexander Solzhenitsyn

Some of the better-off people in the village might not have thought Matryona's house much of a home, but it kept us snug enough that autumn and winter. The roof still held the rain out, and the freezing winds could not blow the warmth of the stove away all
5   at once, though it was cold by morning, especially when the wind blew on the shabby side.

In addition to Matryona and myself, a cat, some mice, and some cockroaches lived in the house.

The cat was no longer young, and was gammy-legged as well.
10   Matryona had taken her in out of pity, and she had stayed. She walked on all four feet but with a heavy limp: one of her feet was sore and she favored it. When she jumped from the stove she didn't land with the soft sound a cat usually makes, but with a heavy thud as three of her feet struck the floor at once—such a heavy thud that
15   until I got used to it, it gave me a start. This was because she stuck three feet out together to save the fourth.

It wasn't because the cat couldn't deal with them that there were mice in the cottage: she would pounce into the corner like lightning and come back with a mouse between her teeth. But the
20   mice were usually out of reach because somebody, back in the good old days, had stuck embossed wallpaper of a greenish color on Matryona's walls, and not just one layer of it but five. The layers held together all right, but in many places the whole lot had come away from the wall, giving the room a sort of inner skin. Between
25   the timber of the walls and the skin of wallpaper the mice had made themselves runs where they impudently scampered about, running at times right up to the ceiling. The cat followed their scamperings with angry eyes, but couldn't get at them.

Sometimes the cat ate cockroaches as well, but they made her
30   sick. The only thing the cockroaches respected was the partition which screened the mouth of the Russian stove and the kitchen from the best part of the room.

They did not creep into the best room. But the kitchen at night swarmed with them, and if I went in late in the evening for a drink
35   of water and switched on the light the whole floor, the big bench, and even the wall would be one rustling brown mass. From time to time I brought home some borax from the school laboratory and we mixed it with dough to poison them. There would be fewer cock-roaches for a while, but Matryona was afraid that we might poison
40   the cat as well. We stopped putting down poison and the cock-roaches multiplied anew.

At night, when Matryona was already asleep and I was work-ing at my table, the occasional rapid scamper of mice behind the wallpaper would be drowned in the sustained and ceaseless
45   rustling of cockroaches behind the screen, like the sound of the sea

-237-

in the distance. But I got used to it because there was nothing evil in
it, nothing dishonest. Rustling was life to them.

    I even got used to the crude beauty on the poster, forever reach-
ing out from the wall to offer me Belinsky, Panferov,[4] and a pile of
5   other books—but never saying a word. I got used to everything in
Matryona's cottage.

    Matryona got up at four or five o'clock in the morning. Her
wall clock was twenty-seven years old and had been bought in the
village shop. It was always fast, but Matryona didn't worry about
10   that—just as long as it didn't lose and make her late in the morning.
She switched on the light behind the kitchen screen and moving
quietly, considerately, doing her best not to make a noise, she lit the
stove, went to milk the goat (all the livestock she had was this one
dirty-white goat with twisted horns), fetched water and boiled it in
15   three iron pots: one for me, one for herself, and one for the goat. She
fetched potatoes from the cellar, picking out the littlest for the goat,
little ones for herself and egg-sized ones for me. There were no big
ones, because her garden was sandy, had not been manured since
the war, and she always planted with potatoes, potatoes, and pota-
20   toes again, so that it wouldn't grow big ones.

    I scarcely heard her about her morning tasks. I slept late, woke
up in the wintry daylight, stretched a bit, and stuck my head out
from under my blanket and my sheepskin. These, together with the
prisoner's jerkin round my legs and a sack stuffed with straw
25   underneath me, kept me warm in bed even on nights when the cold
wind rattled our wobbly windows from the north. When I heard the
discreet noises on the other side of the screen I spoke to her, slowly
and deliberately:

    "Good morning, Matryona Vasilyevna!"
30   And every time the same good-natured words came to me from
behind the screen. They began with a warm, throaty gurgle, the sort
of sound grandmothers make in fairy tales.

    "M-m-m . . . same to you too!"

    And after a little while, "Your breakfast's ready for you now."
35   She didn't announce what was for breakfast, but it was easy to
guess: taters in their jackets or tatty soup (as everybody in the village called it), or barley gruel (no other grain could be bought in
Torfoprodukt that year, and even the barley you had to fight for,
because it was the cheapest and people bought it up by the sack to
40   fatten their pigs on it). It wasn't always salted as it should be, it was

---

[4]Vissarion Grigoryevich Belinsky (1811–1848), Russian literary critic who
emphasized social and political ideas; Fedor Ivanovich Panferov
(1896–1960), socialist-realist writer popular in the 1920s, best known for his
novel *The Iron Flood*.

often slightly burnt, it furred the palate and the gums, and it gave me heartburn.

But Matryona wasn't to blame: there was no butter in Torfoprodukt either, margarine was desperately short, and only
5   mixed cooking fat was plentiful, and when I got to know it, I saw the Russian stove was not convenient for cooking: the cook cannot see the pots and they are not heated evenly all round. I suppose the stove came down to our ancestors from the Stone Age, because you can stoke it up once before daylight, and food and water, mash and
10   swill will keep warm in it all day long. And it keeps you warm while you sleep.

I ate everything that was cooked for me without demur, patiently putting aside anything uncalled-for that I came across: a hair, a bit of peat, a cockroach's leg. I hadn't the heart to find fault with
15   Matryona. After all, she had warned me herself.

"We aren't clever, we can't cook—I don't know how we shall suit. . . ."

"Thank you," I said quite sincerely.

"What for? For what is your own?" she answered, disarming
20   me with a radiant smile. And, with a guileless look of her faded blue eyes, she would ask, "And what shall I cook you for just now?"

For just now meant for supper. I ate twice a day, like at the front. What could I order for just now? It would have to be one of the same old things, taters or tater soup.
25   I resigned myself to it, because I had learned by now not to look for the meaning of life in food. More important to me was the smile on her roundish face, which I tried in vain to catch when at last I had earned enough to buy a camera. As soon as she saw the cold eye of the lens upon her, Matryona assumed a strained or else
30   an exaggeratedly severe expression.

Just once I did manage to get a snap of her looking through the window into the street and smiling at something.

Matryona had a lot of worries that winter. Her neighbors put it into her head to try and get a pension. She was all alone in the
35   world, and when she began to be seriously ill she had been dismissed from the kolkhoz as well. Injustices had piled up, one on top of another. She was ill, but was not regarded as a disabled person. She had worked for a quarter of a century in the kolkhoz, but it was a kolkhoz and not a factory, so she was not entitled to a pension for
40   herself. She could only try and get one for her husband, for the loss of her breadwinner. But she had had no husband for twelve years now, not since the beginning of the war, and it wasn't easy to obtain all the particulars from different places about his length of service and how much he had earned. What a bother it was getting those

forms through! Getting somebody to certify that he'd earned, say,
three hundred rubles a month; that she lived alone and nobody
helped her; what year she was born in. Then all this had to be taken
to the Pension Office. And taken somewhere else to get all the mis-
5   takes corrected. And taken back again. Then you had to find out
whether they would give you a pension.

To make it all more difficult the Pension Office was twelve
miles east of Talnovo, the Rural Council Offices six miles to the
west, the Factory District Council an hour's walk to the north. They
10   made her run around from office to office for two months on end, to
get an *i* dotted or a *t* crossed. Every trip took a day. She goes down
to the Rural District Council—and the secretary isn't there today.
Secretaries of rural councils often aren't here today. So come again
tomorrow. Tomorrow the secretary is in, but he hasn't got his rub-
15   ber stamp. So come again the next day. And the day after that back
she goes yet again, because all her papers are pinned together and
some cockeyed clerk has signed the wrong one.

"They shove me around, Ignatich," she used to complain to me
after these fruitless excursions. "Worn out with it I am."
20   But she soon brightened up. I found that she had a sure means
of putting herself in a good humor. She worked. She would grab a
shovel and go off to pull potatoes. Or she would tuck a sack under
her arm and go after peat. Or take a wicker basket and look for
berries deep in the woods. When she'd been bending her back to
25   bushes instead of office desks for a while, and her shoulders were
aching from a heavy load, Matryona would come back cheerful, at
peace with the world and smiling her nice smile.

"I'm on to a good thing now, Ignatich. I know where to go for
it (peat she meant), a lovely place it is."   •
30   "But surely my peat is enough, Matryona Vasilyevna? There's
a whole truckload of it."

"Pooh! Your peat! As much again, and then as much again, that
might be enough. When winter gets really stiff and the wind's bat-
tling at the windows, it blows the heat out of the house faster than
35   you can make the stove up. Last year we got heaps and heaps of it.
I'd have had three loads in by now. But they're out to catch us.
They've summoned one woman from our village already."

That's how it was. The frightening breath of winter was already
in the air. There were forests all round, and no fuel to be had any-
40   where. Excavators roared away in the bogs, but there was no peat
on sale to the villagers. It was delivered, free, to the bosses and to
the people round the bosses, and teachers, doctors, and workers got
a load each. The people of Talnovo were not supposed to get any
peat, and they weren't supposed to ask about it. The chairman of
45   the kolkhoz walked about the village looking people in the eye

while he gave his orders or stood chatting and talked about anything you liked except fuel. He was stocked up. Who said anything
about winter coming?

5   So just as in the old days they used to steal the squire's wood,
now they pinched peat from the trust. The women went in parties
of five or ten so that they would be less frightened. They went in the
daytime. The peat cut during the summer had been stacked up all
over the place to dry. That's the good thing about peat, it can't be
carted off as soon as it is cut. It lies around drying till autumn, or, if
10   the roads are bad, till the snow starts falling. This was when the
women used to come and take it. The could get six peats in a sack if
it was damp, or ten if it was dry. A sackful weighed about half a
hundredweight and it sometimes had to be carried over two miles.
This was enough to make the stove up once. There were two hun-
15   dred days in the winter. The Russian stove had to be lit in the mornings, and the "Dutch"[5] stove in the evenings.

"Why beat about the bush?" said Matryona angrily to someone
invisible. "Since there've been no more horses, what you can't have
around yourself you haven't got. My back never heals up. Winter
20   you're pulling sledges, summer it's bundles on your back, it's God's
truth I'm telling you."

The women went more than once in a day. On good days
Matryona brought six sacks home. She piled my peat where it could
be seen and hid her own under the passageway, boarding up the
25   hole every night.

"If they don't just happen to think of it, the devils will never
find it in their born days," said Matryona smiling and wiping the
sweat from her brow.

What could the peat trust do? Its establishment didn't run to a
30   watchman for every bog. I suppose they had to show a rich haul in
their returns, and then write off so much for crumbling, so much
washed away by the rain. Sometimes they would take it into their
heads to put out patrols and try to catch the women as they came
into the village. The women would drop their sacks and scatter. Or
35   somebody would inform and there would be a house-to-house
search. They would draw up a report on the stolen peat and threat-
en a court action. The women would stop fetching it for a while, but
the approach of winter drove them out with sledges in the middle
of the night.

40   When I had seen a little more of Matryona I noticed that, apart from
cooking and looking after the house, she had quite a lot of other jobs

---

[5]A cheap small stove (probably made from an oil barrel) that provided heat
with less fuel than the big Russian stove.

to do every day. She kept all her jobs, and the proper times for them, in her head and always knew when she woke up in the morning how her day would be occupied. Apart from fetching peat and stumps which the tractors unearthed in the bogs, apart from the
5   cranberries which she put to soak in big jars for the winter ("Give your teeth an edge, Ignatich," she used to say when she offered me some), apart from digging potatoes and all the coming and going to do with her pension, she had to get hay from somewhere for her one and only dirty-white goat.

10   "Why don't you keep a cow, Matryona?"
Matryona stood there in her grubby apron, by the opening in the kitchen screen, facing my table, and explained to me.
"Oh, Ignatich, there's enough milk from the goat for me. And if I started keeping a cow she'd eat me out of house and home in no
15   time. You can't cut the grass by the railway track, because it belongs to the railway, and you can't cut any in the woods, because it belongs to the foresters, and they won't let me have any at the kolkhoz because I'm not a member any more, they reckon. And those who are members have to work there every day till the white
20   flies swarm and make their own hay when there's snow on the ground—what's the good of grass like that? In the old days they used to be sweating to get the hay in at midsummer, between the end of June and the end of July, while the grass was sweet and juicy."

25   So it meant a lot of work for Matryona to gather enough hay for one skinny little goat. She took her sickle and a sack and went off early in the morning to places where she knew there was grass growing—round the edges of fields, on the roadside, on hummocks in the bog. When she had stuffed her sack with heavy fresh grass
30   she dragged it home and spread it out in her yard to dry. From a sackful of grass she got one forkload of dry hay.

The farm had a new chairman, sent down from the town not long ago, and the first thing he did was to cut down the garden plots for those who were not fit to work. He left Matryona a third of
35   an acre of sand—when there was over a thousand square yards just lying idle on the other side of the fence. Yet when they were short of working hands, when the women dug in their heels and wouldn't budge, the chairman's wife would come to see Matryona. She was from the town as well, a determined woman whose short gray coat
40   and intimidating glare gave her a somewhat military appearance. She walked into the house without so much as a good morning and looked sternly at Matryona. Matryona was uneasy.
"Well now, Comrade Vasilyevna," said the chairman's wife, drawing out her words. "You will have to help the kolkhoz! You
45   will have to go and help cart manure out tomorrow!"

A little smile of forgiveness wrinkled Matryona's face—as though she understood the embarrassment which the chairman's wife must feel at not being able to pay her for her work.

"Well—er," she droned. "I'm not well, of course, and I'm not attached to you any more . . . ," then she hurried to correct herself, "What time should I come then?"

"And bring your own fork!" the chairman's wife instructed her. Her stiff skirt crackled as she walked away.

"Think of that!" grumbled Matryona as the door closed. "Bring your own fork! They've got neither forks nor shovels at the kolkhoz. And I don't have a man who'll put a handle on for me!"

She went on thinking about it out loud all evening.

"What's the good of talking, Ignatich. I must help, of course. Only the way they work it's all a waste of time—don't know whether they're coming or going. The women stand propped up on their shovels and waiting for the factory whistle to blow twelve o'clock. Or else they get on to adding up who's earned what and who's turned up for work and who hasn't. Now what I call work, there isn't a sound out of anybody, only—oh dear, dear—dinner time's soon rolled round—what, getting dark already."

In the morning she went off with her fork.

But it wasn't just the kolkhoz—any distant relative, or just a neighbor could come to Matryona of an evening and say, "Come and give me a hand tomorrow, Matryona. We'll finish pulling the potatoes."

Matryona couldn't say no. She gave up what she should be doing next and went to help her neighbor, and when she came back she would say without a trace of envy, "Ah, you should see the size of her potatoes, Ignatich! It was a joy to dig them up. I didn't want to leave the allotment, God's truth I didn't."

Needless to say, not a garden could be plowed without Matryona's help. The women of Talnovo had got it neatly worked out that it was a longer and harder job for one woman to dig her garden with a spade than for six of them to put themselves in harness and plow six gardens. So they sent for Matryona to help them.

"Well—did you pay her?" I asked sometimes.

"She won't take money. You have to try and hide it on her when she's not looking."

Matryona had yet another troublesome chore when her turn came to feed the herdsmen. One of them was a hefty deaf mute, the other a boy who was never without a cigaret in his drooling mouth. Matryona's turn came round only every six weeks, but it put her to great expense. She went to the shop to buy canned fish and was lavish with sugar and butter, things she never ate herself. It seems that the housewives showed off in this way, trying to outdo one another in feeding the herdsmen.

"You've got to be careful with tailors and herdsmen," Matryona explained. "They'll spread your name all round the village if something doesn't suit them."

5 And every now and then attacks of serious illness broke in on this life that was already crammed with troubles. Matryona would be off her feet for a day or two, lying flat out on the stove. She didn't complain and didn't groan, but she hardly stirred either. On these days, Masha, Matryona's closest friend from her earliest

10 years, would come to look after the goat and light the stove. Matryona herself ate nothing, drank nothing, asked for nothing. To call in the doctor from the clinic at the settlement would have seemed strange in Talnovo and would have given the neighbors something to talk about—what does she think she is, a lady? They

15 did call her in once, and she arrived in a real temper and told Matryona to come down to the clinic when she was on her feet again. Matryona went, although she didn't really want to; they took specimens and sent them off to the district hospital—and that's the last anybody heard about it. Matryona was partly to blame herself.

20 But there was work waiting to be done, and Matryona soon started getting up again, moving slowly at first and then as briskly as ever.

"You never saw me in the old days, Ignatich. I'd lift any sack you liked, I didn't think a hundredweight was too heavy. My father-

25 in-law used to say, 'Matryona, you'll break your back.' And my brother-in-law didn't have to come and help me lift on the cart. Our horse was a warhorse, a big strong one."

"What do you mean, a warhorse?"

"They took ours for the war and gave us this one instead—he'd

30 been wounded. But he turned out a bit spirited. Once he bolted with the sledge right into the lake, the men folk hopped out of the way, but I grabbed the bridle, as true as I'm here, and stopped him. Full of oats that horse was. They liked to feed their horses well in our village. If a horse feels his oats he doesn't know what heavy means."

35 But Matryona was a long way from being fearless. She was afraid of fire, afraid of "the lightning," and most of all she was for some reason afraid of trains.

"When I had to go to Cherusti,[6] the train came up from Nechaevka way with its great big eyes popping out and the rails

40 humming away—put me in a regular fever. My knees started knocking. God's truth I'm telling you!" Matryona raised her shoulders as though she surprised herself.

---

[6]About 100 miles east of Moscow and some 250 miles northwest of Nechaevka.

"Maybe it's because they won't give people tickets, Matryona Vasilyevna?"

"At the window? They try to shove only first-class tickets on to you. And the train was starting to move. We dashed about all over
5   the place. 'Give us tickets for pity's sake.'"

"The men folk had climbed on top of the carriages. Then we found a door that wasn't locked and shoved straight in without tickets—and all the carriages were all empty, they were empty, you could stretch out on the seat if you wanted to. Why they wouldn't
10   give us tickets, the hardhearted parasites, I don't know. . . ."

Still, before winter came, Matryona's affairs were in a better state than ever before. They started paying her at last a pension of eighty rubles. Besides this she got just over one hundred from the school and me.
15   Some of her neighbors began to be envious.

"Hm! Matryona can live forever now! If she had any more money, she wouldn't know what to do with it at her age."

Matryona had some new felt boots made. She bought a new jerkin. And she had an overcoat made out of the worn-out railway-
20   man's greatcoat given to her by the engine driver from Cherusti who had married Kira, her foster daughter. The hump-backed village tailor put a padded lining under the cloth and it made a marvelous coat, such as Matryona had never worn before in all her sixty years.
25   In the middle of winter Matryona sewed two hundred rubles into the lining of this coat for her funeral. This made her quite cheerful.

"Now my mind's a bit easier, Ignatich."

December went by, January went by—and in those two months Matryona's illness held off. She started going over to Masha's house
30   more often in the evening, to sit chewing sunflower seeds with her. She herself didn't invite guests in the evening out of consideration for my work. Once, on the feast of the Epiphany, I came back from school and found a party going on and was introduced to Matryona's three sisters, who called her "nan-nan" or "nanny"
35   because she was the oldest. Until then not much had been heard of the sisters in our cottage—perhaps they were afraid that Matryona might ask them for help.

But one ominous event cast a shadow on the holiday for Matryona. She went to the church three miles away for the blessing
40   of the water and put her pot down among the others. When the blessing was over, the women went rushing and jostling to get their pots back again. There were a lot of women in front of Matryona and when she got there her pot was missing, and no vessel had been left behind. The pot had vanished as though the devil had run off with it.

Matryona went round the worshipers asking them, "Have any of you girls accidentally mistook somebody else's holy water? In a pot?"

Nobody owned up. There had been some boys there, and boys
5   got up to mischief sometimes. Matryona came home sad.

No one could say that Matryona was a devout believer. If anything, she was a heathen, and her strongest beliefs were superstitious: you mustn't go into the garden on the feast of St. John or there would be no harvest next year. A blizzard meant that somebody had ·
10   hanged himself. If you pinched your foot in the door, you could expect a guest. All the time I lived with her I didn't once see her say her prayers or even cross herself. But, whatever job she was doing, she began with a "God bless us," and she never failed to say "God bless you," when I set out for school. Perhaps she did say her
15   prayers, but on the quiet, either because she was shy or because she · didn't want to embarrass me. There were icons[7] on the walls. Ordinary days they were left in darkness, but for the vigil of a great feast, or on the morning of a holiday, Matryona would light the little lamp.
20   She had fewer sins on her conscience than her gammy-legged cat. The cat did kill mice.

Now that her life was running more smoothly, Matryona started listening more carefully to my radio. (I had, of course, installed a speaker, or as Matryona called it, a peeker.)[8]
25   When they announced on the radio that some new machine had been invented, I heard Matryona grumbling out in the kitchen, "New ones all the time, nothing but new ones. People don't want to work with the old ones any more, where are we going to store them all?"

There was a program about the seeding of clouds from airplanes. Matryona, listening up on the stove, shook her head, "Oh, dear, dear, dear, they'll do away with one of the two—summer or
30   winter."

Once Shalyapin[9] was singing Russian folk songs. Matryona stood listening for a long time before she gave her emphatic verdict, "Queer singing, not our sort of singing."

"You can't mean that, Matryona Vasilyevna—just listen to
35   him."

---

[7]Religious images or portraits, usually painted on wood; a small lamp was set in front to illuminate them.

[8]The translator is imitating Solzhenitsyn's wordplay. In the original, the narrator calls the speaker *razvedka* (a military term, literally "scout"); Matryona calls it *rozetka* (an electric plug).

[9]Feodor Ivanovich Shalyapin (or Chaliapin, 1873–1938), was a Russian operatic bass with an international reputation as a great singer and actor; he included popular Russian music in his song recitals.

She listened a bit longer and pursed her lips, "No, it's wrong. It isn't our sort of tune, and he's tricky with his voice."

She made up for this another time. They were broadcasting some of Glinka's[10] songs. After half a dozen of these drawing-room
5 ballads, Matryona suddenly came from behind the screen clutching her apron, with a flush on her face and a film of tears over her dim eyes.

"That's our sort of singing," she said in a whisper.

2

10 So Matryona and I got used to each other and took each other for granted. She never pestered me with questions about myself. I don't know whether she was lacking in normal female curiosity or just tactful, but she never once asked if I had been married. All the Talnovo women kept at her to find out about me. Her answer was,
15 "You want to know—you ask him. All I know is he's from distant parts."

And when I got round to telling her that I had spent a lot of time in prison, she said nothing but just nodded, as though she had already suspected it.

20 And I thought of Matryona only as the helpless old woman she was now and didn't try to rake up her past, didn't even suspect that there was anything to be found there.

I knew that Matryona had got married before the Revolution and had come to live in the house I now shared with her, and she
25 had gone "to the stove" immediately. (She had no mother-in-law and no older sister-in-law, so it was her job to put the pots in the oven on the very first morning of her married life.) I knew that she had had six children and that they had all died very young, so that there were never two of them alive at once. Then there was a sort of
30 foster daughter, Kira. Matryona's husband had not come back from the last war. She received no notification of his death. Men from the village who had served in the same company said that he might have been taken prisoner, or he might have been killed and his body not found. In the eight years that had gone by since the war
35 Matryona had decided that he was not alive. It was a good thing that she thought so. If he was still alive he was probably in Brazil or Australia and married again. The village of Talnovo and the Russian language would be fading from his memory.

---

[10]Mikhail Ivanovich Glinka (1804–1857), a Russian composer who was instrumental in developing a "Russian" style of music, including the two operas *A Life for the Czar* and *Ruslan and Ludmila*.

One day when I got back from school, I found a guest in the house.
A tall, dark man, with his hat on his lap, was sitting on a chair which
Matryona had moved up to the Dutch stove in the middle of the
room. His face was completely surrounded by bushy black hair
5 with hardly a trace of gray in it. His thick black moustache ran into
his full black beard, so that his mouth could hardly be seen. Black
side-whiskers merged with the black locks which hung down from
his crown, leaving only the tips of his ears visible; his broad black
eyebrows met in a wide double span. But the front of his head as far
10 as the crown was a spacious bald dome. His whole appearance
made an impression of wisdom and dignity. He sat squarely on his
chair, with his hands folded on his stick, and his stick resting verti-
cally on the floor, in an attitude of patient expectation, and he obviously hadn't much to say to Matryona, who was busy behind the
15 screen.

When I came in, he eased his majestic head round toward me
and suddenly addressed me, "Schoolmaster, I can't see you very
well. My son goes to your school. Grigoryev, Antoshka."

There was no need for him to say any more. However strongly
20 inclined I felt to help this worthy old man, I knew and dismissed in
advance all the pointless things he was going to say. Antoshka
Grigoryev was a plump, red-faced lad in 8-D who looked like a cat
that's swallowed the cream. He seemed to think that he came to
school for a rest and sat at his desk with a lazy smile on his face.
25 Needless to say, he never did his homework. But the worst of it was
that he had been put up into the next class from year to year because
our district, and indeed the whole region and the neighboring
region were famous for the high percentage of passes they obtained;
the school had to make an effort to keep its record up. So Antoshka
30 had got it clear in his mind that however much the teachers threatened him they would promote him in the end, and there was no
need for him to learn anything. He just laughed at us. There he sat
in the eighth class, and he hadn't even mastered his decimals and
didn't know one triangle from another. In the first two terms of the
35 school year I had kept him firmly below the passing line and the
same treatment awaited him in the third.

But now this half-blind old man, who should have been
Antoshka's grandfather rather than his father, had come to humble
himself before me—how could I tell him that the school had been
40 deceiving him for years, and that I couldn't go on deceiving him,
because I didn't want to ruin the whole class, to become a liar and
a fake, to start despising my work and my profession.

For the time being I patiently explained that his son had been
very slack, that he told lies at school and at home, that his record
45 book must be checked frequently, and that we must both take him

severely in hand.

"Severe as you like, Schoolmaster," he assured me, "I beat him every week now. And I've got a heavy hand."

While we were talking I remembered that Matryona had once
5   interceded for Antoshka Grigoryev, but I hadn't asked what relation of hers he was and I had refused to do what she wanted. Matryona was standing in the kitchen doorway like a mute suppliant on this occasion too. When Faddey Mironovich left, saying that he would call on me to see how things were going, I asked her, "I can't make
10 out what relation this Antoshka is to you, Matryona Vasilyevna."

"My brother-in-law's son," said Matryona shortly, and went out to milk the goat.

When I'd worked it out, I realized that this determined old man with the black hair was the brother of the missing husband.

15   The long evening went by, and Matryona didn't bring up the subject again. But late at night, when I had stopped thinking about the old man and was working in a silence broken only by the rustling of the cockroaches and the heavy tick of the wall-clock, Matryona suddenly spoke from her dark corner, "You know,
20 Ignatich, I nearly married him once."

I had forgotten that Matryona was in the room. I hadn't heard a sound from her—and suddenly her voice came out of the darkness, as agitated as if the old man were still trying to win her.

I could see that Matryona had been thinking about nothing else
25 all evening.

She got up from her wretched rag bed and walked slowly toward me, as though she were following her own words. I sat back in my chair and caught my first glimpse of a quite different Matryona.

30   There was no overhead light in our big room with its forest of rubber plants. The table lamp cast a ring of light round my exercise books, and when I tore my eyes from it the rest of the room seemed to be half-dark and faintly tinged with pink. I thought I could see the same pinkish glow in her usually sallow cheeks.

35   "He was the first one who came courting me, before Efim did— he was his brother—the older one—I was nineteen and Faddey was twenty-three. They lived in this very same house. Their house it was. Their father built it."

I looked round the room automatically. Instead of the old gray
40 house rotting under the faded green skin of wallpaper where the mice had their playground, I suddenly saw new timbers, freshly trimmed, not yet discolored, and caught the cheerful smell of pine tar.

"Well, and what happened then?"

"That summer we went to sit in the woods together," she whis-
45 pered. "There used to be a woods where the stable yard is now.

They chopped it down. I was just going to marry him, Ignatich. Then the German war started. They took Faddey into the army."

She let fall these few words—and suddenly the blue and white and yellow July of the year 1914 burst into flower before my eyes:
5 the sky still peaceful, the floating clouds, the people sweating to get the ripe corn in. I imagined them side by side, the black-haired Hercules with a scythe over his shoulder, and the red-faced girl clasping a sheaf. And there was singing out under the open sky, such songs as nobody can sing nowadays, with all the machines in
10 the fields.

"He went to the war—and vanished. For three years I kept to myself and waited. Never a sign of life did he give."

Matryona's round face looked out at me from an elderly threadbare headscarf. As she stood there in the gentle reflected light
15 from my lamp, her face seemed to lose its slovenly workday wrinkles, and she was a scared young girl again with a frightening decision to make.

Yes . . . I could see it. The trees shed their leaves, the snow fell and melted. They plowed and sowed and reaped again. Again the
20 trees shed their leaves, and the snow fell. There was a revolution. Then another revolution. And the whole world was turned upside down.

"Their mother died and Efim came to court me. 'You wanted to come to our house,' he says, 'so come.' He was a year younger than
25 me, Efim was. It's a saying with us—sensible girls get married after Michaelmas,[11] and silly ones at midsummer. They were shorthanded. I got married. . . . The wedding was on St. Peter's day, and then about St. Nicholas' day in the winter he came back—Faddey, I mean, from being a prisoner in Hungary."

30 I said nothing.

She turned toward the door as though somebody were standing there. "He stood there at the door. What a scream I let out! I wanted to throw myself at his feet! . . . but I couldn't. 'If it wasn't my own brother,' he says, 'I'd take my ax to the both of you.'"

35 I shuddered. Matryona's despair, or her terror, conjured up a vivid picture of him standing in the dark doorway and raising his ax to her.

But she quieted down and went on with her story in a singsong voice, leaning on a chairback. "Oh dear, dear me, the poor dear
40 man! There were so many girls in the village—but he wouldn't marry. I'll look for one with the same name as you, a second Matryona, he said. And that's what he did—fetched himself a Matryona from Lipovka. They built themselves a house of their

---

[11]September 29; *St. Peter's Day*: June 29; *St. Nicholas's Day*: December 6.

own and they're still living in it. You pass their place every day on your way to school."

So that was it. I realized that I had seen the other Matryona quite often. I didn't like her. She was always coming to my
5 Matryona to complain about her husband—he beat her, he was stingy, he was working her to death. She would weep and weep, and her voice always had a tearful note in it. As it turned out, my Matryona had nothing to regret, with Faddey beating his Matryona every day of his life and being so tightfisted.

10 "Mine never beat me once," said Matryona of Efim. "He'd pitch into another man in the street, but me he never hit once. Well, there was one time—I quarreled with my sister-in-law and he cracked me on the forehead with a spoon. I jumped up from the table and shouted at them, 'Hope it sticks in your gullets, you idle
15 lot of beggars, hope you choke!' I said. And off I went into the woods. He never touched me any more."

Faddey didn't seem to have any cause for regret either. The other Matryona had borne him six children (my Antoshka was one of them, the littlest, the runt) and they all lived, whereas the chil-
20 dren of Matryona and Efim had died, every one of them, before they reached the age of three months, without any illness.

"One daughter, Elena, was born and was alive when they washed her, and then she died right after. . . . My wedding was on St. Peter's day, and it was St. Peter's day I buried my sixth,
25 Alexander."

The whole village decided that there was a curse on Matryona.

Matryona still nodded emphatic belief when she talked about it. "There was a *course* on me. They took me to a woman who used to be a nun to get cured, she set me off coughing and waited for the
30 *course*[12] to jump out of me like a frog. Only nothing jumped out."

And the years had run by like running water. In 1941 they did-n't take Faddey into the army because of his poor sight, but they took Efim. And what had happened to the elder brother in the First World War happened to the younger in the Second—he vanished
35 without a trace. Only he never came back at all. The once noisy cot-tage was deserted, it grew old and rotten, and Matryona, all alone in the world, grew old in it.

So she begged from the other Matryona, the cruelly beaten Matryona, a child of her womb (or was it a drop of Faddey's
40 blood?), the youngest daughter, Kira.

For ten years she brought the girl up in her own house, in place of the children who had not lived. Then, not long before I arrived,

---

[12]*Curse/course* reflects word play in the Russian original, where a similar misuse of language indicates Matryona's lack of formal education.

she had married her off to a young engine driver from Cherusti. The only help she got from anywhere came in dribs and drabs from Cherusti: a bit of sugar from time to time, or some of the fat when they killed a pig.

5 Sick and suffering, and feeling that death was not far off, Matryona had made known her will: the top room, which was a separate frame joined by tie beams to the rest of the house, should go to Kira when she died.[13] She said nothing about the house itself. Her three sisters had their eyes on it too.

10 That evening Matryona opened her heart to me. And, as often happens, no sooner were the hidden springs of her life revealed to me than I saw them in motion.

Kira arrived from Cherusti. Old Faddey was very worried. To get and keep a plot of land in Cherusti the young couple had to put
15 up some sort of building. Matryona's top room would do very well. There was nothing else they could put up, because there was no timber to be had anywhere. It wasn't Kira herself so much, and it wasn't her husband, but old Faddey who was consumed with eagerness for them to get their hands on the plot at Cherusti.

20 He became a frequent visitor, laying down the law to Matryona and insisting that she should hand over the top room right away, before she died. On these occasions I saw a different Faddey. He was no longer an old man propped up by a stick, whom a push or a harsh word would bowl over. Although he was slightly bent by
25 backache, he was still a fine figure; in his sixties he had kept the vigorous black hair of a young man; he was hot and urgent.

Matryona had not slept for two nights. It wasn't easy for her to make up her mind. She didn't grudge them the top room, which was standing there idle, any more than she ever grudged her labor
30 or her belongings. And the top room was willed to Kira in any case. But the thought of breaking up the roof she had lived under for forty years was torture to her. Even I, a mere lodger, found it painful to think of them stripping away boards and wrenching out beams. For Matryona it was the end of everything.

35 But the people who were so insistent knew that she would let them break up her house before she died.

So Faddey and his sons and sons-in-law came along one February morning, the blows of five axes were heard and boards creaked and cracked as they were wrenched out. Faddey's eyes
40 twinkled busily. Although his back wasn't quite straight yet, he scrambled nimbly up under the rafters and bustled about down below, shouting at his assistants. He and his father had built this house when he was a lad, a long time ago. The top room had been

---

[13]Lumber was scarce and valuable, and old houses well built.

put up for him, the oldest son, to move into with his bride. And now he was furiously taking it apart, board by board, to carry it out of somebody else's yard.

5 After numbering the beam ends and the ceiling boards, they dismantled the top room and the storeroom underneath it. The living room and what was left of the landing they boarded up with a thin wall of deal. They did nothing about the cracks in the walls. It was plain to see that they were wreckers, not builders, and that they did not expect Matryona to be living there very long.

10 While the men were busy wrecking, the women were getting the drink ready for moving day—vodka would cost too much. Kira brought forty pounds of sugar from the Moscow region, and Matryona carried the sugar and some bottles to the distiller under cover of night.

15 The timbers were carried out and stacked in front of the gates, and the engine-driver son-in-law went off to Cherusti for the tractor.

But the very same day a blizzard, or "a blower," as Matryona once called it, began. It howled and whirled for two days and nights
20 and buried the road under enormous drifts. Then, no sooner had they made the road passable and a couple of trucks had gone by, that it got suddenly warmer. Within a day everything was thawing out, damp mist hung in the air and rivulets gurgled as they burrowed into the snow, and you could get stuck up to the top of your
25 jackboots.

Two weeks passed before the tractor could get at the dismantled top room. All this time Matryona went around like someone lost. What particularly upset her was that her three sisters came, with one voice called her a fool for giving the top room away, said
30 they didn't want to see her any more, and went off. At about the same time the lame cat strayed and was seen no more. It was just one thing after another. This was another blow to Matryona.

At last the frost got a grip on the slushy road. A sunny day came along, and everybody felt more cheerful. Matryona had had a
35 lucky dream the night before. In the morning she heard that I wanted to take a photograph of somebody at an old-fashioned handloom. (There were looms still standing in two cottages in the village; they wove coarse rugs on them.) She smiled shyly and said, "You just wait a day or two, Ignatich, I'll just send off the top room there
40 and I'll put my loom up, I've still got it, you know, and then you can snap me. Honest to God!"

She was obviously attracted by the idea of posing in an old-fashioned setting. The red frosty sun tinged the window of the curtailed passageway with a faint pink, and this reflected light warmed
45 Matryona's face. People who are at ease with their consciences

always have nice faces.

Coming back from school before dusk I saw some movement near our house. A big new tractor-drawn sledge was already fully loaded, and there was no room for a lot of the timbers, so old
5 Faddey's family and the helpers they had called in had nearly finished knocking together another home-made sledge. They were all working like madmen, in the frenzy that comes upon people when there is a smell of good money in the air or when they are looking forward to some treat. They were shouting at one another and argu-
10 ing.

They could not agree on whether the sledges should be hauled separately or both together. One of Faddey's sons (the lame one) and the engine-driver son-in-law reasoned that the sledges couldn't both be taken at once because the tractor wouldn't be able to pull
15 them. The man in charge of the tractor, a hefty fat-faced fellow who was very sure of himself, said hoarsely that he knew best, he was the driver, and he would take both at once. His motives were obvious: according to the agreement, the engine driver was paying him for the removal of the upper room, not for the number of trips he
20 had to make. He could never have made two trips in a night—twenty-five kilometers each way, and one return journey. And by morning he had to get the tractor back in the garage from which he had sneaked it out for this job on the side.

Old Faddey was impatient to get the top room moved that day,
25 and at a nod from him his lads gave in. To the stout sledge in front they hitched the one they had knocked together in a hurry.

Matryona was running about among the men, fussing and helping them to heave the beams on the sledge. Suddenly I noticed that she was wearing my jacket and had dirtied the sleeves on the
30 frozen mud round the beams. I was annoyed and told her so. That jacket held memories for me: it had kept me warm in the bad years.

This was the first time that I was ever angry with Matryona Vasilyevna.

Matryona was taken aback. "Oh dear, dear me," she said. "My
35 poor head. I picked it up in a rush, you see, and never thought about it being yours. I'm sorry, Ignatich."

And she took it off and hung it up to dry.

The loading was finished, and all the men who had been working, about ten of them, clattered past my table and dived under the
40 curtain into the kitchen. I could hear the muffled rattle of glasses and, from time to time, the clink of a bottle, the voices got louder and louder, the boasting more reckless. The biggest braggart was the tractor driver. The stink of hooch floated in to me. But they didn't go on drinking long. It was getting dark and they had to hurry.
45 They began to leave. The tractor driver came out first, looking

pleased with himself and fierce. The engine-driver son-in-law, Faddey's lame son, and one of his nephews was going to Cherusti. The others went off home. Faddey was flourishing his stick, trying to overtake somebody and put him right about something. The lame son paused at my table to light up and suddenly started telling me how he loved Aunt Matryona, and that he had got married not long ago, and his wife had just had a son. Then they shouted for him and he went out. The tractor set up a roar outside.

After all the others had gone, Matryona dashed out from behind the screen. She looked after them, anxiously shaking her head. She had put on her jacket and her headscarf. As she was going through the door, she said to me, "Why ever couldn't they hire two? If one tractor had cracked up, the other would have pulled them. What'll happen now, God only knows!"

She ran out after the others.

After the boozing and the arguments and all the coming and going, it was quieter than ever in the deserted cottage, and very chilly because the door had been opened so many times. I got into my jacket and sat down to mark exercise books. The noise of the tractor died away in the distance.

An hour went by. And another. And a third. Matryona still hadn't come back, but I wasn't surprised. When she had seen the sledge off, she must have gone round to her friend Masha.

Another hour went by. And yet another. Darkness, and with it a deep silence had descended on the village. I couldn't understand at the time why it was so quiet. Later, I found out that it was because all evening not a single train had gone along the line five hundred yards from the house. No sound was coming from my radio, and I noticed that the mice were wilder than ever. Their scampering and scratching and squeaking behind the wallpaper was getting noisier and more defiant all the time.

I woke up. It was one o'clock in the morning, and Matryona still hadn't come home.

Suddenly I heard several people talking loudly. They were still a long way off, but something told me that they were coming to our house. And sure enough, I heard soon afterward a heavy knock at the gate. A commanding voice, strange to me, yelled out an order to open up. I went out into the pitch darkness with a torch. The whole village was asleep, there was no light in the windows, and the snow had started melting in the last week so that it gave no reflected light. I turned the catch and let them in. Four men in greatcoats went on toward the house. It's a very unpleasant thing to be visited at night by noisy people in greatcoats.

When we got into the light though, I saw that two of them were wearing railway uniforms. The older of the two, a fat man with the same sort of face as the tractor driver, asked, "Where's the woman of the house?"

"I don't know."

"This is the place the tractor with a sledge came from?"

5   "This is it."

"Had they been drinking before they left?"

All four of them were looking around, screwing up their eyes in the dim light from the table lamp. I realized that they had either made an arrest or wanted to make one.

10   "What's happened then?"

"Answer the question!"

"But . . ."

"Were they drunk when they went out?"

"Were they drinking here?"

15   Had there been a murder? Or hadn't they been able to move the top room? The men in greatcoats had me off balance. But one thing was certain: Matryona could do time for making hooch.

I stepped back to stand between them and the kitchen door. "I honestly didn't notice. I didn't see anything." (I really hadn't seen

20   anything—only heard.) I made what was supposed to be a helpless gesture, drawing attention to the state of the cottage: a table lamp shining peacefully on books and exercises, a crowd of frightened rubber plants, the austere couch of a recluse, not a sign of debauchery.

25   They had already seen for themselves, to their annoyance, that there had been no drinking in that room. They turned to leave, telling each other this wasn't where the drinking had been then, but it would be a good thing to put in that it was. I saw them out and tried to discover what had happened. It was only at the gate that

30   one of them growled. "They've all been cut to bits. Can't find all the pieces."

"That's a mere detail. The nine o'clock express nearly went off the rails. That would have been something." And they walked briskly away.

35   I went back to the hut in a daze. Who were "they"? What did "all of them" mean? And where was Matryona?

I moved the curtain aside and went into the kitchen. The stink of hooch rose and hit me. It was a deserted battlefield: a huddle of stools and benches, empty bottles lying around, one bottle half-full,

40   glasses, the remains of pickled herring, onion, and sliced fat pork.

Everything was deathly still. Just cockroaches creeping unperturbed about the field of battle.

They had said something about the nine o'clock express. Why? Perhaps I should have shown them all this? I began to wonder

45   whether I had done right. But what a damnable way to behave—

keeping their explanations for official persons only.

Suddenly the small gate creaked. I hurried out on the landing. "Matryona Vasilyevna?"

The yard door opened, and Matryona's friend Masha came in,
5   swaying and wringing her hands. "Matryona—our Matryona, Ignatich—"

I sat her down, and through her tears she told me the story.

The approach to the crossing was a steep rise. There was no barrier. The tractor and the first sledge went over, but the towrope
10   broke and the second sledge, the homemade one, got stuck on the crossing and started falling apart—the wood Faddey had given them to make the second sledge was no good. They towed the first sledge out of the way and went back for the second. They were fixing the towrope—the tractor driver and Faddey's lame son, and
15   Matryona (heaven knows what brought her there) were with them, between the tractor and the sledge. What help did she think she could be to the men? She was forever meddling in men's work. Hadn't a bolting horse nearly tipped her into the lake once, through a hole in the ice? Why did she have to go to the damned crossing?
20   She had handed over the top room and owed nothing to anybody. The engine driver kept a lookout in case the train from Cherusti rushed up on them. Its headlamps would be visible a long way off. But two engines coupled together came from the other direction, from our station, backing without lights. Why they were without
25   lights nobody knows. When an engine is backing, coal dust blows into the driver's eyes from the tender and he can't see very well. The two engines flew into them and crushed the three people between the tractor and the sledge to pulp. The tractor was wrecked, the sledge was matchwood, the rails were buckled, and
30   both engines turned over.

"But how was it they didn't hear the engines coming?"

"The tractor engine was making such a din."

"What about the bodies?"

"They won't let anybody in. They've roped them off."
35   "What was that somebody was telling me about the express?"

"The nine o'clock express goes through our station at a good clip and on to the crossing. But the two drivers weren't hurt when their engines crashed, they jumped out and ran back along the line waving their hands and they managed to stop the train. The
40   nephew was hurt by a beam as well. He's hiding at Klavka's now so that they won't know he was at the crossing. If they find out they'll drag him in as a witness. . . . 'Don't know lies up, and do know gets tied up.' Kira's husband didn't get a scratch. He tried to hang himself, they had to cut him down. It's all because of me, he
45   says, my aunty's killed and my brother. Now he's gone and given

himself up. But the madhouse is where he'll be going, not prison. Oh, Matryona, my dearest Matryona. . . ."

Matryona was gone. Someone close to me had been killed. And on her last day I had scolded her for wearing my jacket.

The lovingly drawn red and yellow woman in the book advertisement smiled happily on.

5 Old Masha sat there weeping a little longer. The she got up to go. And suddenly she asked me, "Ignatich, you remember, Matryona had a gray shawl. She meant it to go to my Tanya when she died, didn't she?"

She looked at me hopefully in the half-darkness—surely I had-
10 n't forgotten?

No, I remembered. "She said so, yes."

"Well, listen, maybe you could let me take it with me now. The family will be swarming in tomorrow and I'll never get it then." And she gave me another hopeful, imploring look. She had been
15 Matryona's friend for half a century, the only one in the village who truly loved her.

No doubt she was right.

"Of course—take it."

She opened the chest, took out the shawl, tucked it under her
20 coat and went out. The mice had gone mad. They were running furiously up and down the walls, and you could almost see the green wallpaper rippling and rolling over their backs.

In the morning I had to go to school. The time was three o'clock. The only thing to do was to lock up and go to bed.

25 Lock up, because Matryona would not be coming.

I lay down, leaving the light on. The mice were squeaking, almost moaning, racing and running. My mind was weary and wandering, and I couldn't rid myself of an uneasy feeling that an invisible Matryona was flitting about and saying good-bye to her
30 home.

And suddenly I imagined Faddey standing there, young and black-haired, in the dark patch by the door, with his ax uplifted. "If it wasn't my own brother, I'd chop the both of you to bits."

The threat had lain around for forty years, like an old broad
35 sword in a corner, and in the end it had struck its blow.

3

When it was light the women went to the crossing and brought back all that was left of Matryona on a hand sledge with a dirty sack
40 over it. They threw off the sack to wash her. There was just a mess . . . no feet, only half a body, no left hand. One woman said, "The Lord has left her her right hand. She'll be able to say her

prayers where she's going."

Then the whole crowd of rubber plants were carried out of the cottage—these plants that Matryona had loved so much that once when smoke woke her up in the night she didn't rush to save her
5   house but to tip the plants onto the floor in case they were suffocated. The women swept the floor clean. They hung a wide towel of old homespun over Matryona's dim mirror. They took down the jolly posters. They moved my table out of the way. Under the icons, near the windows, they stood a rough unadorned coffin on a row of
10   stools.

In the coffin lay Matryona. Her body, mangled and lifeless, was covered with a clean sheet. Her head was swathed in a white kerchief. Her face was almost undamaged, peaceful, more alive than dead.
15   The villagers came to pay their last respects. The women even brought their small children to take a look at the dead. And if anyone raised a lament, all the women, even those who had looked in out of idle curiosity, always joined in, wailing where they stood by the door or the wall, as though they were providing a choral accom-
20   paniment. The men stood stiff and silent with their caps off.

The formal lamentation had to be performed by the women of Matryona's family. I observed that the lament followed a coldly calculated, age-old ritual. The more distant relatives went up to the coffin for a short while and made low wailing noises over it. Those
25   who considered themselves closer kin to the dead woman began their lament in the doorway and when they got as far as the coffin, bowed down and roared out their grief right in the face of the departed. Every lamenter made up her own melody. And expressed her own thoughts and feelings.
30   I realized that a lament for the dead is not just a lament, but a kind of politics. Matryona's three sisters swooped, took possession of the cottage, the goat, and the stove, locked up the chest, ripped the two hundred rubles for the funeral out of the coat lining, and drummed it into everybody who came that only they were near rel-
35   atives. Their lament over the coffin went like this, "*Oh, nanny, nanny! Oh nan-nan!* All we had in the world was you! You could have lived in peace and quiet, you could. And we should always have been kind and loving to you. Now your top room's been the death of you. Finished you off, it has, the cursed thing! Oh, why did
40   you have to take it down? Why didn't you listen to us?"

Thus the sisters' laments were indictments of Matryona's husband's family: they shouldn't have made her take the top room down. (There was an underlying meaning, too: you've taken the top room, all right, but we won't let you have the house itself!)
45   Matryona's husband's family, her sisters-in-law, Efim and

Faddey's sisters, and the various nieces lamented like this, "*Oh poor auntie, poor auntie! Why didn't you take better care of yourself! Now they're angry with us for sure. Our own dear Matryona you were, and it's your own fault! The top room had nothing to do with it. Oh*
5   *why did you go where death was waiting for you? Nobody asked you to go there. And what a way to die! Oh why didn't you listen to us?*" (Their answer to the others showed through these laments: we are not to blame for her death, and the house we'll talk about later.)

10   But the "second" Matryona, a coarse, broad-faced woman, the substitute Matryona whom Faddey had married so long ago for the sake of her name, got out of step with family policy, wailing and sobbing over the coffin in her simplicity, "*Oh my poor dear sister! You won't be angry with me, will you now? Oh-oh-oh! How we used to*
15   *talk and talk, you and me! Forgive a poor miserable woman! You've gone to be with your dear mother, and you'll come for me some day, for sure! Oh-oh-oh-oh!* . . ."

At every "oh-oh-oh" it was as though she were giving up the ghost. She writhed and gasped, with her breast against the side of
20   the coffin. When her lament went beyond the ritual prescription, the women, as though acknowledging its success, all started saying, "Come away now, come away."

Matryona came away, but back she went again, sobbing with even greater abandon. Then an ancient woman came out of a corner,
25   put her hand on Matryona's shoulder, and said, "There are two riddles in this world: how I was born, I don't remember, how I shall die, I don't know."

And Matryona fell silent at once, and all the others were silent, so that there was an unbroken hush.

30   But the old woman herself, who was much older than all the other old women there and didn't seem to belong to Matryona at all, after a while started wailing, "Oh, my poor sick Matryona! Oh my poor Vasilyevna! Oh what a weary thing it is to be seeing you into your grave!"

35   There was one who didn't follow the ritual, but wept straightforwardly, in the fashion of our age, which has had plenty of practice at it. This was Matryona's unfortunate foster daughter, Kira, from Cherusti, for whom the top room had been taken down and moved. Her ringlets were pitifully out of curl. Her eyes looked red
40   and bloodshot. She didn't notice that her headscarf was slipping off out in the frosty air and that her arm hadn't found the sleeve of her coat. She walked in a stupor from her foster mother's coffin in one house to her brother's in another. They were afraid she would lose her mind, because her husband had to go on trial as well.

45   It looked as if her husband was doubly at fault: not only had he

been moving the top room, but as an engine driver, he knew the regulations about unprotected crossings and should have gone down to the station to warn them about the tractor. There were a thousand people on the Urals express that night, peacefully sleeping in the
5   upper and lower berths of their dimly lit carriages, and all those lives were nearly cut short. All because of a few greedy people, wanting to get their hands on a plot of land, or not wanting to make a second trip with a tractor.

All because of the top room, which had been under a curse ever
10   since Faddey's hands had started itching to take it down.

The tractor driver was already beyond human justice. And the railway authorities were also at fault, both because a busy crossing was unguarded and because the coupled engines were traveling without lights. That was why they had tried at first to blame it all
15   on the drink, and then to keep the case out of court.

The rails and the track were so twisted and torn that for three days, while the coffins were still in the house, no trains ran—they were diverted onto another line. All Friday, Saturday, and Sunday, from the end of the investigation until the funeral, the work of
20   repairing the line went on day and night. The repair gang was frozen, and they made fires to warm themselves and to light their work at night, using the boards and beams from the second sledge, which were there for the taking, scattered around the crossing.

The first sledge just stood there, undamaged and still loaded, a
25   little way beyond the crossing.

One sledge, tantalizingly ready to be towed away, and the other perhaps still to be plucked from the flames—that was what harrowed the soul of black-bearded Faddey all day Friday and all day Saturday. His daughter was going out of her mind, his son-in-
30   law had a criminal charge hanging over him, in his own house lay the son he had killed, and along the street the woman he had killed and whom he had once loved. But Faddey stood by the coffins, clutching his beard, only for a short time, and went away again. His high forehead was clouded by painful thoughts, but what he was
35   thinking about was how to save the timbers of the top room from the flames and from Matryona's scheming sisters.

Going over the people of Talnovo in my mind, I realized that Faddey was not the only one like that.

Property, the people's property, or my property, is strangely
40   called our "goods." If you lose your goods, people think you disgrace yourself and make yourself look foolish.

Faddey dashed about, never stopping to sit down, from the settlement to the station, from one official to another, there he stood with his bent back, leaning heavily on his stick, and begged them all
45   to take pity on an old man and give him permission to recover the

top room.

Somebody gave permission. And Faddey gathered together his surviving sons, sons-in-law, and nephews, got horses from the kolkhoz and from the other side of the wrecked crossing, by a
5   roundabout way that led through three villages, brought the remnants of the top room to his yard. He finished the job in the early hours of Sunday morning.

On Sunday afternoon they were buried. The two coffins met in the middle of the village, and the relatives argued about which of
10   them should go first. Then they put them side by side on an open sledge, the aunt and the nephew, and carried the dead over the damp snow, with a gloomy February sky above, to the churchyard two villages away. There was an unkind wind, so the priest and the deacon waited inside the church and didn't come out to Talnovo to
15   meet them.

A crowd of people walked slowly behind the coffins, singing in chorus. Outside the village they fell back.

When Sunday came the women were still fussing around the house. An old woman mumbled psalms by the coffin, Matryona's
20   sisters flitted about, popping things into the oven, and the air round the mouth of the stove trembled with the heat of red-hot peats, those Matryona had carried in a sack from a distant bog. They were making unappetizing pies with poor flour.

When the funeral was over and it was already getting on
25   toward evening, they gathered for the wake. Tables were put together to make a long one, which hid the place where the coffin had stood in the morning. To start with, they all stood round the table, and an old man, the husband of a sister-in-law, said the Lord's Prayer. Then they poured everybody a little honey and warm
30   water,[14] just enough to cover the bottom of the bowl. We spooned it up without bread or anything, in memory of the dead. Then we ate something and drank vodka and the conversation became more animated. Before the jelly they all stood up and sang "Eternal remembrance"[15] (they explained to me that it had to be sung before the
35   jelly). There was more drinking. By now they talking louder than ever, and not about Matryona at all. The sister-in-law's husband started boasting, "Did you notice, brother Christians, that they took

---

[14]Traditionally Russians have *kutiia,* a wheat pudding with honey and almonds, at funerals and memorial gatherings; the villagers are too poor to have the main ingredients and their honey and water are symbolic of the *kutiia.*

[15]"Eternal Remembrance" and "Worthy Is She" are dirges, religious hymns sung to honor the dead; the village still follows religious rituals in time of crisis and does not use the civil ceremony proposed by the Soviet government.

the funeral service slowly today? That's because Father Mikhail noticed me. He knows I know the service. Other times, it's saints defend us, homeward wend us, and that's all."

5   At last the supper was over. They all rose again. They sang "Worthy Is She." Then again, with a triple repetition of "Eternal Remembrance." But the voices were hoarse and out of tune, their faces drunken, and nobody put any feeling into this "eternal memory."

    Then most of the guests went away, and only the near relatives were left. They pulled out their cigarets and lit up, there were jokes
10 and laughter. There was some mention of Matryona's husband and his disappearance. The sister-in-law's husband, striking himself on the chest, assured me and the cobbler who was married to one of Matryona's sisters, "He was dead, Efim was dead! What could stop him coming back if he wasn't? If I knew they were going to hang me
15 when I got to the old place, I'd come back just the same!"

    The cobbler nodded in agreement. He was a deserter and had never left the old place. All through the war he was hiding in his mother's cellar.

    The stern and silent old woman who was more ancient than all
20 the ancients was staying the night and sat high up on the stove. She looked down in mute disapproval on the indecently animated youngsters of fifty and sixty.

    But the unhappy foster daughter, who had grown up within these walls, went away behind the kitchen screen to cry.

25   Faddey didn't come to Matryona's wake—perhaps because he was holding a wake for his son. But twice in the next few days he walked angrily into the house for discussions with Matryona's sisters and the deserting cobbler.

    The argument was about the house. Should it go to one of the
30 sisters or to the foster daughter? They were on the verge of taking it to court, but they made peace because they realized that the court would hand over the house to neither side, but to the Rural District Council. A bargain was struck. One sister took the goat, the cobbler and his wife got the house, and to make up Faddey's share, since he
35 had "nursed every bit of timber here in his arms," in addition to the top room which had already been carried away, they let him have the shed which had housed the goat and the whole of the inner fence between the yard and the garden.

    Once again the insatiable old man got the better of sickness and
40 pain and became young and active. Once again he gathered together his surviving sons and sons-in-law, they dismantled the shed and the fence, he hauled the timbers himself, sledge by sledge, and only toward the end did he have Antoshka of 8-D, who didn't slack this time, to help him.

45   They boarded Matryona's house up till the spring, and I moved

in with one of her sisters-in-law, not far away. This sister-in-law on several occasions came out with some recollection of Matryona and made me see the dead woman in a new light. "Efim didn't love her. He used to say, 'I like to dress in an educated way, but she dresses
5 any old way, like they do in the country.' Well then, he thinks, if she doesn't want anything, he might as well drink whatever's to spare. One time I went with him to the town to work, and he got himself a madam there and never wanted to come back to Matryona."

Everything she said about Matryona was disapproving. She
10 was slovenly, she made no effort to get a few thing about her. She wasn't the saving kind. She didn't even keep a pig, because she didn't like fattening them up for some reason. And the silly woman helped other people without pay. (What brought Matryona to mind this time was that the garden needed plowing, and she couldn't
15 find enough helpers to pull the plow.)

Matryona's sister-in-law admitted that she was warmhearted and straightforward, but pitied and despised her for it.

It was only then, after these disapproving comments from her sister-in-law, that a true likeness of Matryona formed before my
20 eyes, and I understood her as I never had when I lived side by side with her.

Of course! Every house in the village kept a pig. But she didn't. What can be easier than fattening a greedy piglet that cares for nothing in the world but food! You warm his swill three times a day, you
25 live for him—then you cut his throat and you have some fat.

But she had none.

She made no effort to get things round her. She didn't struggle and strain to buy things and then care for them more than life itself.

She didn't go all out after fine clothes. Clothes, that beautify
30 what is ugly and evil.

She was misunderstood and abandoned even by her husband. She had lost six children, but not her sociable ways. She was a stranger to her sisters and sisters-in-law, a ridiculous creature who stupidly worked for others without pay. She didn't accumulate
35 property against the day she died. A dirty-white goat, a gammy-legged cat, some rubber plants. . . .

We had all lived side by side with her and had never understood that she was the righteous one without whom, as the proverb says,[16] no village can stand.
40 Nor any city.
Nor our whole land.

---

[16]Genesis 18:23–33, the story of Sodom.

23. *Alexander Solzhenitsyn*

A WORLD SPLIT APART

*[This is the text of an address by Alexander Solzhenitsyn at the after-
noon exercises during the Harvard Commencement on Thursday, June
8th, 1978.]*

I am sincerely happy to be here with you on this occasion and
to become personally acquainted with this old and most prestigious
university. My congratulations and very best wishes to all of today's
graduates.

5 Harvard's motto is Veritas. Many of you have already found
out and others will find out in the course of their lives that truth
eludes us if we do not concentrate with total attention on its pursuit.
And even while it eludes us, the illusion still lingers of knowing it
and leads to many misunderstandings. Also, truth seldom is pleas-
10 ant; it is almost invariably bitter. There is some bitterness in my
speech today, too. But I want to stress that it comes not from an
adversary but from a friend.

Three years ago in the United States I said certain things which
at that time appeared unacceptable. Today, however, many people
15 agree with what I then said. . . .

A WORLD SPLIT APART

The split in today's world is perceptible even to a hasty glance.
Any of our contemporaries readily identifies two world powers, each
of them already capable of entirely destroying the other. However,
understanding of the split often is limited to this political conception,
20 to the illusion that danger may be abolished through successful
diplomatic negotiations or by achieving a balance of armed forces.
The truth is that the split is a much profounder and a more alienating
one, that the rifts are more than one can see at first glance. This deep
manifold split bears the danger of manifold disaster for all of us, in
25 accordance with the ancient truth that a Kingdom—in this case, our
Earth—divided against itself cannot stand.

CONTEMPORARY WORLDS

There is the concept of Third World: thus, we already have
three worlds. Undoubtedly, however, the number is even greater;
we are just too far away to see. Any ancient deeply rooted
30 autonomous culture, especially if it is spread on a wide part of the
Earth's surface, constitutes an autonomous world, full of riddles
and surprises to Western thinking. As a minimum, we must include
in this category China, India, the Muslim world and Africa, if
indeed we accept the approximation of viewing the latter two as

-265-

compact units. For one thousand years Russia belonged to such a
category, although Western thinking systematically committed the
mistake of denying its autonomous character and therefore never
understood it, just as today the West does not understand Russia in
5   Communist captivity. It may be that in the past years Japan has
increasingly become a distant part of the West. I am no judge here;
but as to Israel, for instance, it seems to me that it stands apart from
the Western world in that its state system is fundamentally linked
to religion.

10   How short a time ago, relatively, the small new European
world was easily seizing colonies everywhere, not only without
anticipating any real resistance but also usually despising any possible values in the conquered peoples' approach to life. On the face
of it, it was an overwhelming success, there were no geographic
15   frontiers to it. Western society expanded in a triumph of human
independence and power. And all of a sudden in the twentieth century came the discovery of its fragility. We now see that the conquests proved to be short-lived and precarious, and this in turn
points to defects in the Western view of the world which led to these
20   conquests. Relations with the former colonial world now have
turned into their opposite and the Western world often goes to
extremes of obsequiousness, but it is difficult yet to estimate the
total size of the bill which former colonial countries will present to
the West, and it is difficult to predict whether the surrender not only
25   of its last colonies, but of everything it owns will be sufficient for the
West to foot the bill.

CONVERGENCE

But the blindness of superiority continues in spite of all and
upholds the belief that vast regions everywhere on our planet
should develop and mature to the level of present-day Western sys-
30   tems which in theory are the best and in practice the most attractive.
There is this belief that all those other worlds are only being tem-
porarily prevented by wicked governments or by heavy crises or by
their own barbarity and incomprehension from taking the way of
Western pluralistic democracy and from adopting the Western way
35   of life. Countries are judged on the merit of their progress in this
direction. However, it is a conception which developed out of
Western incomprehension of the essence of other worlds, out of the
mistake of measuring them all with a Western yardstick. The real
picture of our planet's development is quite different.

40   Anguish about our divided world gave birth to the theory of
convergence between leading Western countries and the Soviet
Union. It is a soothing theory which overlooks the fact that these

worlds are not at all developing into similarity; neither one can be
transformed into the other without the use of violence. Besides, convergence inevitably means acceptance of the other side's defects,
too, and this is hardly desirable.

5   If I were today addressing an audience in my country, examining the overall pattern of the world's rifts I would have concentrat-
ed on the East's calamities. But since my forced exile in the West has
now lasted four years and since my audience is a Western one, I
think it may be of greater interest to concentrate on certain aspects
10   of the West in our days, such as I see them.

A DECLINE IN COURAGE

A decline in courage may be the most striking feature which an
outside observer notices in the West in our days. The Western world
has lost its civil courage, both as a whole and separately, in each
country, each government, each political party and of course in the
15   United Nations. Such a decline in courage is particularly noticeable
among the ruling groups and the intellectual elite, causing an
impression of loss of courage by the entire society. Of course there
are many courageous individuals but they have no determining
influence on public life. Political and intellectual bureaucrats show
20   depression, passivity, and perplexity in their actions and in their
statements and even more so in theoretical reflections to explain
how realistic, reasonable as well as intellectually and even morally
warranted it is to base state policies on weakness and cowardice.
And decline in courage is ironically emphasized by occasional
25   explosions of anger and inflexibility on the part of the same bureaucrats when dealing with weak governments and weak countries,
not supported by anyone, or with currents which cannot offer any
resistance. But they get tongue-tied and paralyzed when they deal
with powerful governments and threatening forces, with aggressors
30   and international terrorists.

Should one point out that from ancient times decline in courage
has been considered the beginning of the end?

WELL-BEING

When the modern Western states were created, the following
principle was proclaimed: governments are meant to serve man,
35   and man lives to be free and to pursue happiness. (See, for example,
the American Declaration of Independence.) Now at last during
past decades technical and social progress has permitted the realization of such aspirations; the welfare state. Every citizen has been
granted the desired freedom and material goods in such quantity
40   and of such quality as to guarantee in theory the achievement of

happiness, in the morally inferior sense which has come into being
during those same decades. In the process, however, one psychological detail has been overlooked; the constant desire to have still
more things and a still better life and the struggle to obtain them
5   imprints many Western faces with worry and even depression,
though it is customary to conceal such feelings. Active and tense
competition permeates all human thoughts without opening a way
to free spiritual development. The individual's independence from
many types of state pressure has been guaranteed: the majority of
10 people have been granted well-being to an extent their fathers and
grandfathers could not even dream about; it has become possible to
raise young people according to these ideals, leading them to physical splendor, happiness, possession of material goods, money and
leisure, to an almost unlimited freedom of enjoyment. So who
15 should now renounce all this, why and for what should one risk
one's precious life in defense of common values, and particularly in
such nebulous cases when the security of one's nation must be
defended in a distant country?

Even biology knows that habitual extreme safety and well-
20 being are not advantageous for a living organism. Today, well-being
in the life of Western society has begun to reveal its pernicious
mask.

LEGALISTIC LIFE

Western society has given itself the organization best suited to
its purposes, based, I would say, on the letter of the law. The limits
25 of human rights and righteousness are determined by a system of
laws; such limits are very broad. People in the West have acquired
considerable skill in using, interpreting and manipulating law, even
though laws tend to be too complicated for an average person to
understand without the help of an expert. Any conflict is solved
30 according to the letter of the law and this is considered to be the
supreme solution. If one is right from a legal point of view, nothing
more is required, nobody may mention that one could still not be
entirely right, and urge self-restraint, a willingness to renounce such
legal rights, sacrifice and selfless risk: it would sound simply
35 absurd. One almost never sees voluntary self restraint. Everybody
operates at the extreme limit of those legal frames. An oil company
is legally blameless when it purchases an invention of a new type of
energy in order to prevent its use. A food produce manufacturer is
legally blameless when he poisons his produce to make it last
40 longer: after all, people are free not to buy it.

I have spent all my life under a Communist regime and I will
tell you that a society without any objective legal scale is a terrible

one indeed. But a society with no other scale but the legal one is not quite worthy of man either. A society which is based on the letter of the law and never reaches any higher is taking very scarce advantage of the high level of human possibilities. The letter of the law is
5 too cold and formal to have a beneficial influence on society. Whenever the tissue of life is woven of legalistic relations, there is an atmosphere of moral mediocrity, paralyzing man's noblest impulses.

And it will be simply impossible to stand through the trials of this
10 threatening century with only the support of a legalistic structure.

THE DIRECTION OF FREEDOM

In today's Western society, the inequality has been revealed of freedom for good deeds and freedom for evil deeds. A statesman who wants to achieve something important and highly constructive for his country has to move cautiously and even timidly; there are
15 thousands of hasty and irresponsible critics around him, parliament and the press keep rebuffing him. As he moves ahead, he has to prove that each single step of his is well-founded and absolutely flawless. Actually an outstanding and particularly gifted person who has unusual and unexpected initiatives in mind hardly gets a
20 chance to assert himself; from the very beginning, dozens of traps will be set out for him. Thus mediocrity triumphs with the excuse of restrictions imposed by democracy.

It is feasible and easy everywhere to undermine administrative power and, in fact, it has been drastically weakened in all Western
25 countries. The defense of individual rights has reached such extremes as to make society as a whole defenseless against certain individuals. It is time, in the West, to defend not so much human rights as human obligations.

Destructive and irresponsible freedom has been granted
30 boundless space. Society appears to have little defense against the abyss of human decadence, such as, for example, misuse of liberty for moral violence against young people, motion pictures full of pornography, crime and horror. It is considered to be part of freedom and theoretically counterbalanced by the young people's right
35 not to look or accept. Life organized legalistically has thus shown its inability to defend itself against the corrosion of evil.

And what shall we say about the dark realm of criminality as such? Legal frames (especially in the United States) are broad enough to encourage not only individual freedom but also certain
40 individual crimes. The culprit can go unpunished or obtain undeserved leniency with the support of thousands of public defenders. When a government starts an earnest fight against terrorism, public

opinion immediately accuses it of violating the terrorists' civil
rights. There are many such cases.

Such a tilt of freedom in the direction of evil has come about
gradually but it was evidently born primarily out of a humanistic
5   and benevolent concept according to which there is no evil inherent
to human nature; the world belongs to mankind and all the defects
of life are caused by wrong social systems which must be corrected.
Strangely enough, though the best social conditions have been
achieved in the West, there still is criminality and there even is con-
10   siderably more of it than in the pauper and lawless Soviet society.
(There is a huge number of prisoners in our camps who are termed
criminals, but most of them never committed any crime; they merely tried to defend themselves against a lawless state resorting to
means outside of a legal framework.)

THE DIRECTION OF THE PRESS

15   The press too, of course, enjoys the widest freedom. (I shall be
using the word press to include all media.) But what sort of use
does it make of this freedom?

Here again, the main concern is not to infringe the letter of the
law. There is no moral responsibility for deformation or dispropor-
20   tion. What sort of responsibility does a journalist have to his readers, or to history? If they have misled public opinion or the government by inaccurate information or wrong conclusions, do we know
of any cases of public recognition and rectification of such mistakes
by the same journalist or the same newspaper? No, it does not hap-
25   pen, because it would damage sales. A nation may be the victim of
such a mistake, but the journalist always gets away with it. One
may safely assume that he will start writing the opposite with
renewed self- assurance.

Because instant and credible information has to be given, it
30   becomes necessary to resort to guesswork, rumors, and supposi-
tions to fill in the voids, and none of them will ever be rectified, they
will stay on in the readers' memory. How many hasty, immature,
superficial and misleading judgments are expressed every day, con-
fusing readers, without any verification. The press can both stimu-
35   late public opinion and miseducate it. Thus we may see terrorists
heroized, or secret matter, pertaining to one's nation's defense, publicly revealed, or we may witness shameless intrusion on the priva-
cy of well-known people under the slogan: "everyone is entitled to
know everything." But this is a false slogan, characteristic of a false
40   era: people also have the night not to know, and it is a much more
valuable one. The right not to have their divine souls stuffed with
gossip, nonsense, vain talk. A person who works and leads a mean-

ingful life does not need this excessive burdening flow of information.

Hastiness and superficiality are the psychic disease of the twentieth century and more than anywhere else this disease is reflected in the press. In-depth analysis of a problem is anathema to the press. It stops at sensational formulas.

Such as it is, however, the press has become the greatest power within the Western countries, more powerful than the legislature, the executive, and the judiciary. One would then like to ask: by what law has it been elected and to whom is it responsible? In the Communist East, a journalist is frankly appointed as a state official. But who has granted Western journalists their power, for how long a time and with what prerogatives?

There is yet another surprise for someone coming from the East where the press is rigorously unified: one gradually discovers a common trend of preferences within the Western press as a whole. It is a fashion; there are generally accepted patterns of judgment and there may be common corporate interests, the sum effect being not competition but unification. Enormous freedom exists for the press, but not for the readership because newspapers mostly give enough stress and emphasis to those opinions which do not too openly contradict their own and the general trend.

A FASHION OF THINKING

Without any censorship, in the West fashionable trends of thought and ideas are carefully separated from those which are not fashionable; nothing is forbidden, but what is not fashionable will hardly ever find its way into periodicals or books or be heard in colleges. Legally your researchers are free, but they are conditioned by the fashion of the day. There is no open violence such as in the East; however, a selection dictated by fashion and the need to match mass standards frequently prevents independent-minded people from giving their contribution to public life. There is a dangerous tendency to form a herd, shutting off successful development. I have received letters in America from highly intelligent persons, maybe a teacher in a far-away small college who could do much for the renewal and salvation of his country, but his country cannot hear him because the media are not interested in him. This gives birth to strong mass prejudices, to blindness, which is most dangerous in our dynamic era. There is, for instance, a self-deluding interpretation of the contemporary world situation. It works as a sort of a petrified armor around people's minds. Human voices from 17 countries of Eastern Europe and Eastern Asia cannot pierce it. It will only be broken by the pitiless crowbar of events.

I have mentioned a few traits of Western life which surprise and shock a new arrival to this world. The purpose and scope of this speech will not allow me to continue such a review, to look into the influence of these Western characteristics on important aspects of a
5 nation's life, such as elementary education, advanced education in the humanities and in art.

SOCIALISM

It is almost universally recognized that the West shows all the world a way to successful economic development, even though in the past years it has been strongly disturbed by chaotic inflation.
10 However, many people living in the West are dissatisfied with their own society. They despise it or accuse it of not being up to the level of maturity attained by mankind. A number of such critics turn to socialism, which is a false and dangerous current.

I hope that no one present will suspect me of offering my per-
15 sonal criticism of the Western system to present socialism as an alternative. Having experienced applied socialism, in a country where the alternative has been realized, I certainly will not speak for it. The well-known Soviet mathematician Shafarevich, a member of the Soviet Academy of Science, has written a brilliant book under
20 the title *Socialism;* it is a profound analysis showing that socialism of any type and shade leads to a total destruction of the human spirit and to a leveling of mankind into death. Shafarevich's book was published in France almost two years ago and so far no one has been found to refute it. It will shortly be published in English in the
25 United States.

NOT A MODEL

But should someone ask me whether I would indicate the West such as it is today as a model to my country, frankly I would have to answer negatively. No, I could not recommend your society in its present state as an ideal for the transformation of ours. Through
30 intense suffering our country has now achieved a spiritual development of such intensity that the Western system in its present state of spiritual exhaustion does not look attractive. Even those characteristics of your life which I have just mentioned are extremely saddening.

35 A fact which cannot be disputed is the weakening of human beings in the West while in the East they are becoming firmer and stronger. Six decades for our people and three decades for the people of Eastern Europe; during that time we have been through a spiritual training far in advance of Western experience. Life's com-
40 plexity and mortal weight have produced stronger, deeper, and

more interesting characters than those generated by standardized Western well-being. Therefore if our society were to be transformed into yours, it would mean an improvement in certain aspects but also a change for the worse on some particularly significant scores.

5   It is true, no doubt, that a society cannot remain in an abyss of lawlessness, as is the case in our country. But it is also demeaning for it to elect such mechanical legalistic smoothness as you have. After the suffering of decades of violence and oppression, the human soul longs for things higher, warmer, and purer than those offered by

10 today's mass living habits, introduced by the revolting invasion of publicity, by TV stupor and by the intolerable music.

    All this is visible to observers from all the worlds of our planet. The Western way of life is less and less likely to become the leading model.

15   There are meaningful warnings which history gives a threatened or perishing society. Such are, for instance, the decadence of art, or a lack of great statesmen. There are open and evident warnings, too. The center of your democracy and of your culture is left without electric power for a few hours only, and all of a sudden

20 crowds of American citizens start looting and creating havoc. The smooth surface film must be very thin, then, the social system quite unstable and unhealthy.

    But the fight for our planet, physical and spiritual, a fight of cosmic proportions, is not a vague matter of the future; it has

25 already started. The forces of Evil have begun their decisive offensive, you can feel their pressure, and yet your screens and publications are full of prescribed smiles and raised glasses. What is the joy about?

SHORTSIGHTEDNESS

    Very well-known representatives of your society, such as

30 George Kennan, say: we cannot apply moral criteria to politics. Thus we mix good and evil, right and wrong and make space for the absolute triumph of absolute Evil in the world. On the contrary, only moral criteria can help the West against Communism's well-planned world strategy. There are no other criteria. Practical or

35 occasional considerations of any kind will inevitably be swept away by strategy. After a certain level of the problem has been reached legalistic thinking induces paralysis; it prevents one from seeing the size and meaning of events.

    In spite of the abundance of information, or maybe because of

40 it, the West has difficulties in understanding reality such as it is. There have been naive predictions by some American experts who believed that Angola would become the Soviet Union's Vietnam or

that Cuban expeditions in Africa would best be stopped by special U.S. courtesy to Cuba. Kennan's advice to his own country—to begin unilateral disarmament—belongs to the same category. If you only knew how the youngest of the Moscow Old Square (The Old
5 Square in Moscow—Staraya Ploschad—is the place where the head-quarters of the Central Committee of the CPSU [i.e., Communist Party of the Soviet Union] are located: it is the real name of what in the West is conventionally referred to as "the Kremlin") officials laugh at your political wizards! As to Fidel Castro, he frankly scorns
10 the United States, sending his troops to distant adventures from his country right next to yours.

However, the most cruel mistake occurred with the failure to understand the Vietnam war. Some people sincerely wanted all wars to stop just as soon as possible; others believed that there
15 should be room for national, or communist, self-determination in Vietnam, or in Cambodia, as we see today with particular clarity. But members of the U.S. anti-war movement wound up being involved in the betrayal of far Eastern nations, in a genocide and in the suffering today imposed on 30 million people there. Do those
20 convinced pacifists hear the moans coming from there? Do they understand their responsibility today? Or do they prefer not to hear? The American intelligentsia lost its nerve, and as a consequence thereof danger has come much closer to the United States. But there is no awareness of this. Your shortsighted politicians who
25 signed the hasty Vietnam capitulation seemingly gave America a carefree breathing pause; however, a hundred-fold Vietnam now looms over you. That small Vietnam had been a warning and an occasion to mobilize the nation's courage. But if a full-fledged America suffered a real defeat from a small Communist half-coun-
30 try, how can the West hope to stand firm in the future?

I have had occasion already to say that in the 20th century Western democracy has not won any major war without help and protection from a powerful continental ally whose philosophy and ideology it did not question. In World War II against Hitler, instead
35 of winning that war with its own forces, which would certainly have been sufficient, Western democracy grew and cultivated another enemy who would prove worse and more powerful yet, as Hitler never had so many resources and so many people, nor did he offer any attractive ideas, or have such a large number of support-
40 ers in the West—a potential fifth column—as the Soviet Union. At present, some Western voices already have spoken of obtaining pro-tection from a third power against aggression in the next world con-flict, if there is one; in this case the shield would be China. But I would not wish a doomed alliance with Evil; also, it would grant
45 the United States a respite, but then at a later date China with its bil-

lion people would turn around armed with American weapons. America itself would fall prey to a genocide similar to the one perpetrated in Cambodia in our days.

LOSS OF WILLPOWER

5

And yet—no weapons, no matter how powerful, can help the West until it overcomes its loss of willpower. In a state of psychological weakness, weapons become a burden for the capitulating side. To defend oneself, one must also be ready to die; there is little such readiness in a society raised in the cult of material well-being. Nothing is left, then, but concessions, attempts to gain time, and

10 betrayal. Thus at the shameful Belgrade conference free Western diplomats in their weakness surrendered the line where enslaved members of Helsinki Watch groups are sacrificing their lives.

Western thinking has become conservative: the world situation should stay as it is at any cost. There should be no changes. This

15 debilitating dream of a status quo is the symptom of a society which has come to the end of its development. But one must be blind in order not to see that oceans no longer belong to the West, while land under its domination keeps shrinking. The two so-called world wars (they were by far not on a world scale, not yet) have meant

20 internal self-destruction of the small progressive West which has thus prepared its own end. The next war (which does not have to be an atomic one and I do not believe it will) may well bury Western civilization forever.

Facing such a danger, with such historical values in your past,

25 at such a high level of realization of freedom and apparently of devotion to freedom, how is it possible to lose to such an extent the will to defend oneself?

HUMANISM AND ITS CONSEQUENCES

30

How has this unfavorable relation of forces come about? How did the West decline from its triumphant march to its present sickness? Have there been fatal turns and losses of direction in its development? It does not seem so. The West kept advancing socially in accordance with its proclaimed intentions, with the help of brilliant

35 technological progress. And all of a sudden it found itself in its present state of weakness.

This means that the mistake must be at the root, at the very basis of human thinking in the past centuries. I refer to the prevailing Western view of the world which was first born during the

40 Renaissance and found its political expression from the period of the Enlightenment. It became the basis for government and social science and could be defined as rationalistic humanism or human-

istic autonomy: the proclaimed and enforced autonomy of man
from any higher force above him. It could also be called anthro-
pocentricity, with man seen as the center of everything that exists.

The turn introduced by the Renaissance evidently was
inevitable historically. The Middle Ages had come to a natural end
5   by exhaustion, becoming an intolerable despotic repressing of
man's physical nature in favor of the spiritual one. Then, however,
we turned our backs upon the Sprit and embraced all that is material with excessive and unwarranted zeal. This new way of thinking, which had imposed on us its guidance did not admit the exis-
10   tence of intrinsic evil in man nor did it seek any higher task than the
attainment of happiness on earth. It based modern Western civilization on the dangerous trend to worship man and his material needs.
Everything beyond physical well-being and accumulation of material goods, all other human requirements and characteristics of a
15   subtler and higher nature, were left outside the area of attention of
state and social systems as if human life did not have any superior
sense. That provided access for evil, of which in our days there is a
free and constant flow. Merely freedom does not in the least solve
all the problems of human life and it even adds a number of new
20   ones.

However, in early democracies, as in American democracy at
the time of its birth, all individual human rights were granted
because man is God's creature. That is, freedom was given to the
individual conditionally, in the assumption of his constant religious
25   responsibility. Such was the heritage of the preceding thousand
years. Two hundred or even fifty years ago, it would have seemed
quite impossible, in America, that an individual could be granted
boundless freedom simply for the satisfaction of his instincts or
whims. Subsequently, however, all such limitations were discarded
everywhere in the West, a total liberation occurred from the moral
heritage of Christian centuries with their great reserves of mercy
30   and sacrifice. State systems were becoming increasingly and totally
materialistic. The West ended up by truly enforcing human rights,
sometimes even excessively, but man's sense of responsibility to
God and society grew dimmer and dimmer. In the past decades, the
legalistically selfish aspect of Western approach and thinking has
35   reached its final dimension and the world wound up in a harsh spiritual crisis and a political impasse. All the glorified technological
achievements of progress including the conquest of outer space, do
not redeem the twentieth century's moral poverty which no one
could imagine even as late in the nineteenth century.

AN UNEXPECTED KINSHIP

As humanism in its development became more and more materialistic, it made itself increasingly accessible to speculation and manipulation at first by socialism and then by Communism. So that Karl Marx was able to say in 1844 that "Communism is naturalized humanism."

5   This statement turned out to be not entirely senseless. One does see the same stones in the foundations of a despiritualized humanism and of any type of socialism: endless materialism; freedom from religion and religious responsibility which under Communist's regimes reach the state of anti-religious dictatorship; concentration
10   on social structures, with a seemingly scientific approach. (This is typical of the Enlightenment in the eighteenth century and of Marxism.) Not by coincidence all of Communism's meaningless pledges and oaths are about Man, with a capital M, and his earthly happiness. At first glance it seems an ugly parallel: common traits
15   in the thinking and way of life of today's West and today's East? But such is the logic of materialistic development.

       The interrelationship is such too, that the current of materialism which is most to the left always ends up by being stronger, more attractive and victorious, because it is more consistent.
20   Humanism without its Christian heritage cannot resist such competition. We watch this process in the past centuries and especially in the past decades, on a world scale as the situation becomes increasingly dramatic. Liberalism was inevitably displaced by radicalism, radicalism had to surrender to socialism and socialism could never
25   resist Communism. The Communist regime in the East could stand and grow due to the enthusiastic support from an enormous number of Western intellectuals who felt a kinship and refused to see Communism's crimes. When they no longer could do so, they tried to justify them. In our Eastern countries, Communism has suffered
30   a complete ideological defeat; it is zero and less than zero. But Western intellectuals still look at it with interest and with empathy, and this is precisely what makes it so immensely difficult for the West to withstand the East.

BEFORE THE TURN

35   I am not examining here the case of a world war disaster and the changes which it would produce in society. As long as we wake up every morning under a peaceful sun, we have to lead an everyday life. There is a disaster, however, which has already been under way for quite some time; I am referring to the calamity of a despir-
40   itualized and irreligious humanistic consciousness.

       To such consciousness, man is the touchstone in judging and evaluating everything on Earth. Imperfect man who is never free of pride, self-interest, envy, vanity, and dozens of other defects. We are

now experiencing the consequences of mistakes which had not been noticed at the beginning of the journey. On the way from the Renaissance to our days we have enriched our experience, but we have lost the concept of a Supreme Complete Entity which used to
5 restrain our passions and our irresponsibility. We have placed too much hope in political and social reforms, only to find out that we were being deprived of our most precious possession; our spiritual life. In the East, it is destroyed by the dealings and machinations of the ruling party. In the West, commercial interests tend to suffocate
10 it. This is the real crisis. The split in the world is less terrible than the similarity of the disease plaguing its main sections.

If humanism were right in declaring that man is born to be happy, he would not be born to die. Since his body is doomed to die, his task on Earth evidently must be of a more spiritual nature. It
15 cannot be unrestrained enjoyment of everyday life. It cannot be the search for the best ways to obtain material goods and then cheerfully get the most out of them. It has to be the fulfillment of a permanent, earnest duty so that one's life journey may become an experience of moral growth, so that one may leave life a better
20 human being than one started it. It is imperative to review the table of widespread human values. Its present incorrectness is astounding. It is not possible that assessment of the President Is performance be reduced to the question of how much money one makes or of unlimited availability of gasoline. Only voluntary inspired self-
25 restraint can raise man above the world stream of materialism.

It would be retrogression to attach oneself today to the ossified formulas of the Enlightenment. Social dogmatism leaves us completely helpless in front of the trials of our times.

Even if we are spared destruction by war, our lives will have to
30 change if we want to save life from self-destruction. We cannot avoid revising the fundamental definitions of human life and human society. Is it true that man is above everything? Is there no Superior Spirit above him? Is it right that man's life and society's activities have to be determined by material expansion in the first
35 place? Is it permissible to promote such expansion to the detriment of our spiritual integrity?

If the world has not come to its end, it has approached a major turn in history, equal in importance to the turn from the Middle Ages to the Renaissance. It will exact from us a spiritual upsurge,
40 we shall have to rise to a new height of vision, to a new level of life where our physical nature will not be cursed as in the Middle Ages, but, even more importantly, our spiritual being will not be trampled upon us as in the Modern Era.

This ascension will be similar to climbing onto the next anthro-
45 pologic stage. No one on Earth has any other way left but—upward.

24. GABRIEL GARCIA MARQUEZ

Gabriel Garcia Marquez was born in Columbia, South America in 1928. His most famous work ·is the novel One Hundred Years of Solitude, *written in the literary tradition of "magical realism"—a tradition that treats magical and miraculous events as ordinary, and ordinary events as miraculous. Magical realism originated in the work of Jorges Luis Borges and other Latin American writers, but also can be traced back to the sixteenth-century Spanish novel by Miguel Cervantes,* Don Quixote. *In the spirit of Cervantes, Garcia Marquez unravels the complacent assumptions of the rational, scientific world-view. Garcia Marquez was awarded the Nobel Prize for Literature in 1982.*

DEATH CONSTANT BEYOND LOVE
(1970)

Senator Onésimo Sánchez had six months and eleven days to go before his death when he found the woman of his life. He met her in Rosal del Virrey, an illusory village which by night was the furtive wharf for smugglers' ships, and on the other hand, in broad
5 daylight looked like the most useless inlet on the desert, facing a sea that was arid and without direction and so far from everything no one would have suspected that someone capable of changing the destiny of anyone lived there. Even its name was a kind of joke, because the only rose in that village was being worn by Senator
10 Onésimo Sánchez himself on the same afternoon when he met Laura Farina.

It was an unavoidable stop in the electoral campaign he made every four years. The carnival wagons had arrived in the morning. Then came the trucks with the rented Indians who were carried into
15 the towns in order to enlarge the crowds at public ceremonies. A short time before eleven o'clock, along with the music and rockets and jeeps of the retinue, the ministerial automobile, the color of strawberry soda, arrived. Senator Onésimo Sánchez was placid and weatherless inside the air-conditioned car, but as soon as he opened
20 the door he was shaken by a gust of fire and his shirt of pure silk was soaked in a kind of light-colored soup and he felt many years

older and more alone than ever. In real life he had just turned forty-two, had been graduated from Göttingen[1] with honors as a metallurgical engineer, and was an avid reader, although without much reward, of badly translated Latin classics. He was married to a radi-
5 ant German woman who had given him five children and they were all happy in their home, he the happiest of all until they told him, three months before, that he would be dead forever by next Christmas.

While the preparations for the public rally were being com-
10 pleted, the senator managed to have an hour alone in the house they had set aside for him to rest in. Before he lay down he put in a glass of drinking water the rose he had kept alive all across the desert, lunched on the diet cereals that he took with him so as to avoid the repeated portions of fried goat that were waiting for him during the
15 rest of the day, and he took several analgesic pills before the time prescribed so that he would have the remedy ahead of the pain. Then he put the electric fan close to the hammock and stretched out naked for fifteen minutes in the shadow of the rose, making a great effort at mental distraction so as not to think about death while he
20 dozed. Except for the doctors, no one knew that he had been sentenced to a fixed term, for he had decided to endure his secret all alone, with no change in his life, not because of pride but out of shame.

He felt in full control of his will when he appeared in public
25 again at three in the afternoon, rested and clean, wearing a pair of coarse linen slacks and a floral shirt, and with his soul sustained by the anti-pain pills. Nevertheless, the erosion of death was much more pernicious than he had supposed, for as he went up onto the platform he felt a strange disdain for those who were fighting for
30 the good luck to shake his hand, and he didn't feel sorry as he had at other times for the groups of barefoot Indians who could scarcely bear the hot saltpeter coals of the sterile little square. He silenced the applause with a wave of his hand, almost with rage, and he began to speak without gestures, his eyes fixed on the sea, which
35 was sighing with heat. His measured, deep voice had the quality of calm water, but the speech that had been memorized and ground out so many times had not occurred to him in the nature of telling the truth, but, rather, as the opposite of a fatalistic pronouncement by Marcus Aurelius in the fourth book of his *Meditations*.
40   "We are here for the purpose of defeating nature," he began, against all his convictions. "We will no longer be foundlings in our own country, orphans of God in a realm of thirst and bad climate,

---

[1]A well-known German university.

exiles in our own land. We will be different people, ladies and gentlemen, we will be a great and happy people."

There was a pattern to his circus. As he spoke his aides threw clusters of paper birds into the air and the artificial creatures took
5 on life, flew about the platform of planks, and went out to sea. At the same time, other men took some prop trees with felt leaves out of the wagons and planted them in the saltpeter soil behind the crowd. They finished by setting up a cardboard facade with make-believe houses of red brick that had glass windows, and with it they
10 covered the miserable real-life shacks.

The senator prolonged his speech with two quotations in Latin in order to give the farce more time. He promised rainmaking machines, portable breeders for table animals, the oils of happiness which would make vegetables grow in the saltpeter and clumps of
15 pansies in the window boxes. When he saw that his fictional world was all set up, he pointed to it. "That's the way it will be for us, ladies and gentlemen," he shouted. "Look! That's the way it will be for us."

The audience turned around. An ocean liner made of painted
20 paper was passing behind the houses and it was taller than the tallest houses in the artificial city. Only the senator himself noticed that since it had been set up and taken down and carried from one place to another the superimposed cardboard town had been eaten away by the terrible climate and that it was almost as poor and
25 dusty as Rosal del Virrey.

For the first time in twelve years, Nelson Farina didn't go to greet the senator. He listened to the speech from his hammock amidst the remains of his siesta, under the cool bower of a house of unplaned boards which he had built with the same pharmacist's
30 hands with which he had drawn and quartered his first wife. He had escaped from Devil's Island[2] and appeared in Rosal del Virrey on a ship loaded with innocent macaws, with a beautiful and blasphemous black woman he had found in Paramaribo[3] and by whom he had a daughter. The woman died of natural causes a short while
35 later and she didn't suffer the fate of the other, whose pieces had fertilized her own cauliflower patch, but was buried whole and with her Dutch name in the local cemetery. The daughter had inherited her color and her figure along with her father's yellow and astonished eyes, and he had good reason to imagine that he was
40 rearing the most beautiful woman in the world.

---

[2]A former French penal colony off the coast of French Guiana in northern South America.

[3]Capital of Surinam (formerly Dutch Guiana) and a large port.

Ever since he had met Senator Onésimo Sánchez during his first electoral campaign, Nelson Farina had begged for his help in getting a false identity card which would place him beyond the reach of the law. The senator, in a friendly but firm way, had
5 refused. Nelson Farina never gave up, and for several years, every time he found the chance, he would repeat his request with a different recourse. But this time he stayed in his hammock, condemned to rot alive in that burning den of buccaneers. When he heard the final applause, he lifted his head, and looking over the
10 boards of the fence, he saw the back side of the farce: the props for the buildings, the framework of the trees, the hidden illusionists who were pushing the ocean liner along. He spat without rancor.

"*Merde*," he said. "*C'est le Blacamán de la politique.*"[4]

After the speech, as was customary, the senator took a walk
15 through the streets of the town in the midst of the music and the rockets and was besieged by the townspeople, who told him their troubles. The senator listened to them good-naturedly and he always found some way to console everybody without having to do them any difficult favors. A woman up on the roof of a house with
20 her six youngest children managed to make herself heard over the uproar and the fireworks.

"I'm not asking for much, Senator," she said. "Just a donkey to haul water from Hanged Man's Well."

The senator noticed the six thin children. "What became of
25 your husband?" he asked.

"He went to find his fortune on the island of Aruba," the woman answered good-humoredly, "and what he found was a foreign woman, the kind that put diamonds on their teeth."

The answer brought on a roar of laughter.
30 "All right," the senator decided, "you'll get your donkey."

A short while later an aide of his brought a good pack donkey to the woman's house and on the rump it had a campaign slogan written in indelible paint so that no one would ever forget that it was a gift from the senator.
35 Along the short stretch of street he made other, smaller gestures, and he even gave a spoonful of medicine to a sick man who had had his bed brought to the door of his house so he could see him pass. At the last corner, through the boards of the fence, he saw Nelson Farina in his hammock, looking ashen and gloomy, but
40 nonetheless the senator greeted him, with no show of affection.

---

[4]"Shit. He's the Blacamán of politics." (French. Blacamán is a charlatan and huckster who appears in several stories, including "Blacamán the Good, Vendor of Miracles.")

"Hello, how are you?"

Nelson Farina turned in his hammock and soaked him in the sad amber of his look.

"*Moi, vous savez,*"[5] he said.

His daughter came out into the yard when she heard the greeting. She was wearing a cheap, faded Guajiro Indian robe, her head was decorated with colored bows, and her face was painted as protection against the sun, but even in that state of disrepair it was possible to imagine that there had never been another so beautiful in the whole world. The senator was left breathless. "I'll be damned!" he breathed in surprise. "The Lord does the craziest things!"

That night Nelson Farina dressed his daughter up in her best clothes and sent her to the senator. Two guards armed with rifles who were nodding from the heat in the borrowed house ordered her to wait on the only chair in the vestibule.

The senator was in the next room meeting with the important people of Rosal del Virrey, whom he had gathered together in order to sing for them the truths he had left out of his speeches. They looked so much like all the ones he always met in all the towns in the desert that even the senator himself was sick and tired of that perpetual nightly session. His shirt was soaked with sweat and he was trying to dry it on his body with the hot breeze from an electric fan that was buzzing like a horse fly in the heavy heat of the room.

"We, of course, can't eat paper birds," he said. "You and I know that the day there are trees and flowers in this heap of goat dung, the day there are shad instead of worms in the water holes, that day neither you nor I will have anything to do here, do I make myself clear?"

No one answered. While he was speaking, the senator had torn a sheet off the calendar and fashioned a paper butterfly out of it with his hands. He tossed it with no particular aim into the air current coming from the fan and the butterfly flew about the room and then went out through the half-open door. The senator went on speaking with a control aided by the complicity of death.

"Therefore," he said, "I don't have to repeat to you what you already know too well: that my reelection is a better piece of business for you than it is for me, because I'm fed up with stagnant water and Indian sweat, while you people, on the other hand, make your living from it."

Laura Farina saw the paper butterfly come out. Only she saw it because the guards in the vestibule had fallen asleep on the steps, hugging their rifles. After a few turns, the large lithographed but-

[5]"Oh well, as for me, you know . . ."

terfly unfolded completely, flattened against the wall, and remained stuck there. Laura Farina tried to pull it off with her nails. One of the guards, who woke up with the applause from the next room, noticed her vain attempt.

5   "It won't come off," he said sleepily. "It's painted on the wall."

Laura Farina sat down again when the men began to come out of the meeting. The senator stood in the doorway of the room with his hand on the latch, and he only noticed Laura Farina when the vestibule was empty.

10   "What are you doing here?"

"*C'est de la part de mon pere,*"[6] she said.

The senator understood. He scrutinized the sleeping guards, then he scrutinized Laura Farina, whose unusual beauty was even more demanding than his pain, and he resolved then that death had

15   made his decision for him.

"Come in," he told her.

Laura Farina was struck dumb standing in the doorway to the room: thousands of bank notes were floating in the air, flapping like the butterfly. But the senator turned off the fan and the bills were

20   left without air and alighted on the objects in the room.

"You see," he said, smiling, "even shit can fly."

Laura Farina sat down on a schoolboy's stool. Her skin was smooth and firm, with the same color and the same solar density as crude oil, her hair was the mane of a young mare, and her huge eyes

25   were brighter than the light. The senator followed the thread of her look and finally found the rose, which had been tarnished by the saltpeter.

"It's a rose," he said.

"Yes," she said with a trace of perplexity. "I learned what they

30   were in Riohacha."[7]

The senator sat down on an army cot, talking about roses as he unbuttoned his shirt. On the side where he imagined his heart to be inside his chest he had a corsair's tattoo of a heart pierced by an arrow. He threw the soaked shirt to the floor and asked Laura

35   Farina to help him off with his boots.

She knelt down facing the cot. The senator continued to scrutinize her, thoughtfully, and while he was untying the laces he wondered which one of them would end up with the bad luck of that encounter.

40   "You're just a child," he said.

"Don't you believe it," she said. "I'll be nineteen in April."

---

[6]"My father sent me."

[7]A port on the Guajira Peninsula.

The senator became interested.

"What day?"

"The eleventh," she said.

The senator felt better. "We're both Aries," he said. And smil-
5   ing, he added:

"It's the sign of solitude."

Laura Farina wasn't paying attention because she didn't know
what to do with the boots. The senator, for his part, didn't know
what to do with Laura Farina, because he wasn't used to sudden
10   love affairs and, besides, he knew that the one at hand had its origins in indignity. Just to have some time to think, he held Laura
Farina tightly between his knees, embraced her about the waist, and
lay down on his back on the cot. Then he realized that she was
naked under her dress, for her body gave off the dark fragrance of
15   an animal of the woods, but her heart was frightened and her skin
disturbed by a glacial sweat.

"No one loves us," he sighed.

Laura Farina tried to say something, but there was only enough
air for her to breathe. He laid her down beside him to help her, he
20   put out the light and the room was in the shadow of the rose. She
abandoned herself to the mercies of her fate. The senator caressed
her slowly, seeking her with his hand, barely touching her, but
where he expected to find her, he came across something iron that
was in the way.

25   "What have you got there?"

"A padlock," she said.

"What in hell!" the senator said furiously and asked what he
knew only too well. "Where's the key?"

Laura Farina gave a breath of relief.

30   "My papa has it," she answered. "He told me to tell you to send
one of your people to get it and to send along with him a written
promise that you'll straighten out his situation."

The senator grew tense. "Frog bastard," he murmured indignantly. Then he closed his eyes in order to relax and he met himself
35   in the darkness. *Remember,* he remembered, *that whether it's you or
someone else, it won't be long before you'll be dead and it won't be long
before your name won't even be left.*[8]

He waited for the shudder to pass.

"Tell me one thing," he asked then. "What have you heard
40   about me?"

"Do you want the honest-to-God truth?"

---

[8]A direct translation of a sentence from Marcus Aurelius in the fourth book
of the *Meditations* (IV.6).

"The honest-to-God truth. "

"Well," Laura Farina ventured, "they say you're worse than the rest because you're different."

The senator didn't get upset. He remained silent for a long time with his eyes closed, and when he opened them again he seemed to have returned from his most hidden instincts.

"Oh, what the hell," he decided. "Tell your son of a bitch of a father that I'll straighten out his situation."

"If you want, I can go get the key myself," Laura Farina said.

The senator held her back.

"Forget about the key," he said, "and sleep awhile with me. It's good to be with someone when you're so alone. "

Then she laid his head on her shoulder with her eyes fixed on the rose. The senator held her about the waist, sank his face into woods-animal armpit, and gave in to terror. Six months and eleven days later he would die in that same position, debased and repudiated because of the public scandal with Laura Farina and weeping with rage at dying without her.

25. SEAMUS HEANEY

Seamus Heaney (1939-) was born in Derry, Northern Ireland, and he is most commonly associated with the violent political "Troubles" that have plagued that part of the world, particularly since the late 1960s. Heaney is deeply influenced by W. B. Yeats, and he shares with him an interest in the artist's role in defining the Irish nation; and, like Yeats, Heaney is frequently an ambivalent, even reluctant, spokesperson for Ireland. In "Digging," Heaney struggles with the passivity of writing, his chosen occupation, and he worries that it is hardly respectable alongside the more active lives of his father and grandfather, who were potato farmers and members of the local militia. Finally, however, Heaney resolves that for him, his pen is his spade, and he'll do his digging with it. This resolution to use writing to carry on the family's and the nation's work is a characteristic note in Heaney's poetry.

Another of Heaney's key concerns is the long history, both human and geological, of his home place, the boggy landscapes of Northern Ireland. For Heaney, the bog is a kind of living record of the place's sufferings, and in poems like "Bogland," he connects the difficulties of his own time with the conflicts and warfare of the place's "primitive" ancestors, some of whose bodies are preserved in the spongy earth of the bog.

Heaney won the Nobel Prize for Literature in 1995, and he remains one of Ireland's most vital literary voices.

DIGGING

Between my finger and my thumb
The squat pen rests; snug as a gun.

Under my window, a clean rasping sound
When the spade sinks into gravelly ground:
5 My father, digging. I look down

Till his straining rump among the flowerbeds
Bends low, comes up twenty years away
Stooping in rhythm through potato drills
Where he was digging.

10   The coarse boot nestled on the lug, the shaft
      Against the inside knee was levered firmly.
      He rooted out tall tops, buried the bright edge deep
      To scatter new potatoes that we picked
      Loving their cool hardness in our hands.

15   By God, the old man could handle a spade.
      Just like his old man.

      My grandfather cut more turf in a day
      Than any other man on Toner's bog.
      Once I carried him milk in a bottle
20   Corked sloppily with paper. He straightened up
      To drink it, then fell to right away
      Nicking and slicing neatly, heaving sods
      Over his shoulder, going down and down
      For the good turf. Digging.

25   The cold smell of potato mould, the squelch and slap
      Of soggy peat, the curt cuts of an edge
      Through living roots awaken in my head.
      But I've no spade to follow men like them.

      Between my finger and my thumb
30   The squat pen rests.
      I'll dig with it.

DEATH OF A NATURALIST

      All year the flax-dam festered in the heart
      Of the townland; green and heavy headed
      Flax had rotted there, weighted down by huge sods.
      Daily it sweltered in the punishing sun.
5   Bubbles gargled delicately, bluebottles
      Wove a strong gauze of sound around the smell.
      There were dragon-flies, spotted butterflies,
      But best of all was the warm thick slobber
      Of frogspawn that grew like clotted water
10   In the shade of the banks. Here, every spring
      I would fill jampotfuls of the jellied
      Specks to range on window-sills at home,
      On shelves at school, and wait and watch until
      The fattening dots burst into nimble-

15   Swimming tadpoles. Miss Walls would tell us how
The daddy frog was called a bullfrog
And how he croaked and how the mammy frog
Laid hundreds of little eggs and this was
Frogspawn. You could tell the weather by frogs too
20   For they were yellow in the sun and brown
In rain.

Then one hot day when fields were rank
With cowdung in the grass and angry frogs
Invaded the flax-dam; I ducked through hedges
25   To a coarse croaking that I had not heard
Before. The air was thick with a bass chorus.
Right down the dam gross-bellied frogs were cocked
On sods; their loose necks pulsed like sails. Some hopped:
The slap and plop were obscene threats. Some sat
30   Poised like mud grenades, their blunt heads farting.
I sickened, turned, and ran. The great slime kings
Were gathered there for vengeance and I knew
That if I dipped my hand the spawn would clutch it.

BOGLAND

FOR T. P. FLANAGAN

We have no prairies
To slice a big sun at evening—
Everywhere the eye concedes to
Encroaching horizon,

5   Is wooed into the cyclops' eye
Of a tarn. Our unfenced country
Is bog that keeps crusting
Between the sights of the sun.

They've taken the skeleton
10   Of the Great Irish Elk
Out of the peat, set it up
An astounding crate full of air.

Butter sunk under
More than a hundred years
15   Was recovered salty and white.
The ground itself is kind, black butter

Melting and opening underfoot,
Missing its last definition
By millions of years.
20   They'll never dig coal here,

Only the waterlogged trunks
Of great firs, soft as pulp.
Our pioneers keep striking
Inwards and downwards,
25   Every layer they strip
Seems camped on before.
The bogholes might be Atlantic seepage.
The wet centre is bottomless.

CASUALTY

I

He would drink by himself
And raise a weathered thumb
Towards the high shelf,
Calling another rum
5   And black currant, without
Having to raise his voice,
Or order a quick stout
By a lifting of the eyes
And a discreet dumb-show
10   Of pulling off the top;
At closing time would go
In waders and peaked cap
Into the showery dark,
A dole-kept breadwinner
15   But a natural for work.
I loved his whole manner,
Sure-footed but too sly,
His deadpan sidling tact,
His fisherman's quick eye
20   And turned observant back.

Incomprehensible
To him, my other life.
Sometimes, on his high stool,
Too busy with his knife
25   At a tobacco plug

And not meeting my eye,
In the pause after a slug
He mentioned poetry.
We would be on our own
30   And, always politic
And shy of condescension,
I would manage by some trick
To switch the talk to eels
Or lore of the horse and cart
35   Or the Provisionals.

But my tentative art
His turned back watches too:
He was blown to bits
Out drinking in a curfew
40   Others obeyed, three nights
After they shot dead
The thirteen men in Derry.
PARAS THIRTEEN, the walls said,
BOGSIDE NIL. That Wednesday
45   Everybody held
His breath and trembled.

II

It was a day of cold
Raw silence, wind-blown
Surplice and soutane:
50   Rained-on, flower-laden
Coffin after coffin
Seemed to float from the door
Of the packed cathedral
Like blossoms on slow water.
55   The common funeral
Unrolled its swaddling band,
Lapping, tightening
Till we were braced and bound
Like brothers in a ring.

60   But he would not be held
At home by his own crowd
Whatever threats were phoned,
Whatever black flags waved.
I see him as he turned
65   In that bombed offending place,

Remorse fused with terror
In his still knowable face,
His cornered outfaced stare
Blinding in the flash.

70　He had gone miles away For he drank like a fish
Nightly, naturally
Swimming towards the lure
Of warm lit-up places,
The blurred mesh and murmur
75　Drifting among glasses
In the gregarious smoke.
How culpable was he
That last night when he broke
Our tribe's complicity?
80　'Now you're supposed to be
An educated man,'
I hear him say. 'Puzzle me
The right answer to that one.'

III

I missed his funeral,
85　Those quiet walkers
And sideways talkers
Shoaling out of his lane
To the respectable
Purring of the hearse . . .
90　They move in equal pace
With the habitual
Slow consolation
Of a dawdling engine,
The line lifted, hand
95　Over fist, cold sunshine
On the water, the land
Banked under fog: that morning
When he took me in his boat,
The screw purling, turning
100　Indolent fathoms white,
I tasted freedom with him.
To get out early, haul
Steadily off the bottom,
Dispraise the catch, and smile
105　As you find a rhythm
Working you, slow mile by mile,

Into your proper haunt
Somewhere, well out, beyond . . .

Dawn-sniffing revenant,
110   Plodder through midnight rain,
Question me again.

26. SYLVIA PLATH

Sylvia Plath (1932–63) was a precocious poet who, by the time she entered college, was already published and had written over fifty short stories. She graduated summa cum laude from Smith College (to which she later returned as a teacher) and won a Fulbright scholarship for postgraduate studies at Cambridge University, where she met her husband, fellow poet Ted Hughes. Plath's troubled life's story has, understandably, threatened to overshadow her poetry: her difficult relationship with her father, who died when she was only eight years old; her tempestuous relationship with Hughes; and her multiple (and ultimately successful) suicide attempts were made public in much of her poetry and in her autobiographical novel, The Bell Jar. Plath's poetry is, however, important as more than a window into the writer's personal life; through the use of powerful imagery, unique motifs, and a rich allusiveness, the poetry explores the complexity of intimate human relationships and of internal psychological conflicts. Her poetry can also be read as social commentary on the mid-twentieth-century culture that, Plath suggests, prescribed confining roles for women and punished women like herself, who transgressed these roles.

DADDY

You do not do, you do not do
Any more, black shoe
In which I have lived like a foot
For thirty years, poor and white,
5   Barely daring to breathe or Achoo.

Daddy, I have had to kill you.
You died before I had time—
Marble-heavy, a bag full of God,
Ghastly statue with one grey toe
10   Big as a Frisco seal

And a head in the freakish Atlantic
Where it pours bean green over blue
In the waters off beautiful Nauset.
I used to pray to recover you.
15   Ach, du.

26. Sylvia Plath

In the German tongue, in the Polish town
Scraped flat by the roller
Of wars, wars, wars.
But the name of the town is common.
20   My Polack friend

Says there are a dozen or two.
So I never could tell where you
Put your foot, your root,
I never could talk to you.
25   The tongue stuck in my jaw.

It stuck in a barb wire snare.
Ich, ich, ich, ich,
I could hardly speak.
I thought every German was you.
30   And the language obscene

An engine, an engine
Chuffing me off like a Jew.
A Jew to Dachau, Auschwitz, Belsen.
I began to talk like a Jew.
35   I think I may well be a Jew.

The snows of the Tyrol, the clear beer of Vienna
Are not very pure or true.
With my gypsy ancestress and my weird luck
And my Taroc pack and my Taroc pack
40   I may be a bit of a Jew.

I have always been scared of *you*,
With your Luftwaffe, your gobbledygoo.
And your neat moustache
And your Aryan eye, bright blue.
45   Panzer-man, panzer-man, O You—

Not God but a swastika
So black no sky could squeak through.
Every woman adores a Fascist,
The boot in the face, the brute
50   Brute heart of a brute like you.

You stand at the blackboard, daddy,
In the picture I have of you,
A cleft in your chin instead of your foot

55 But no less a devil for that, no not
Any less the black man who

Bit my pretty red heart in two.
I was ten when they buried you.
At twenty I tried to die
And get back, back, back to you.
60 I thought even the bones would do.

But they pulled me out of the sack,
And they stuck me together with glue.
And then I knew what to do.
I made a model of you,
65 A man in black with a Meinkampf look

And a love of the rack and the screw.
And I said I do, I do.
So daddy, I'm finally through.
The black telephone's off at the root,
70 The voices just can't worm through.

If I've killed one man, I've killed two—
The vampire who said he was you
And drank my blood for a year,
Seven years, if you want to know.
75 Daddy, you can lie back now.

There's a stake in your fat black heart
And the villagers never liked you.
They are dancing and stamping on you.
They always *knew* it was you.
80 Daddy, daddy, you bastard, I'm through.

METAPHORS

I'm a riddle in nine syllables,
An elephant, a ponderous house,
A melon strolling on two tendrils.
O red fruit, ivory, fine timbers!
5 This loaf's big with its yeasty rising.
Money's new-minted in this fat purse.
I'm a means, a stage, a cow in calf
I've eaten a bag of green apples,
Boarded the train there's no getting off.

THE COLOSSUS

I shall never get you put together entirely,
Pieced, glued, and properly jointed.
Mule-bray, pig-grunt and bawdy cackles
Proceed from your great lips.
5   It's worse than a barnyard.

Perhaps you consider yourself an oracle,
Mouthpiece of the dead, or of some god or other.
Thirty years now I have labored
To dredge the silt from your throat.
10   I am none the wiser.

Scaling little ladders with gluepots and pails of Lysol
I crawl like an ant in mourning
Over the weedy acres of your brow
To mend the immense skull-plates and clear
15   The bald, white tumuli of your eyes.

A blue sky out of the Oresteia
Arches above us. O father, all by yourself
You are pithy and historical as the Roman Forum.
I open my lunch on a hill of black cypress.
20   Your fluted bones and acanthine hair are littered

In their old anarchy to the horizon-line.
It would take more than a lightning-stroke
To create such a ruin.
Nights, I squat in the cornucopia
25   Of your left ear, out of the wind,

Counting the red stars and those of plum-color.
The sun rises under the pillar of your tongue.
My hours are married to shadow.
No longer do I listen for the scrape of a keel
30   On the blank stones of the landing.

27. ADRIENNE RICH

*American poet, essayist, and political activist Adrienne Rich (1929–)
is well-known for her commitment to racial and gender equality. Much of
her poetry expresses feminist values through an autobiographical lens; by
writing about her own diverse life experience as a woman, a wife, a mother, and a lesbian, Rich offers poetic comments on and critiques of the twentieth-century female experience from multiple perspectives. Her social
activism began concretely with her vocal opposition to the Vietnam War in
the mid-1960s. Around this time, Rich left behind the formal conventions
of traditional poetry to write experimental, free-verse poems organized
around strong poetic images.*

DIVING INTO THE WRECK

First having read the book of myths,
and loaded the camera
and checked the edge of the knife-blade,
I put on
5   the body-armor of black rubber
the absurd flippers
the grave and awkward mask.
I am having to do this
not like Cousteau with his
10   assiduous team
aboard the sun-flooded schooner
but here alone.

There is a ladder.
The ladder is always there
15   hanging innocently
close to the side of the schooner.
We know what it is for,
we who have used it.
Otherwise it's a piece of maritime floss
20   some sundry equipment.

I go down.
Rung after rung and still
the oxygen immerses me
the blue light
25 the clear atoms
of our human air.
I go down.
My flippers cripple me,
I crawl like an insect down the ladder
30 and there is no one
to tell me when the ocean
will begin.

First the air is blue and then
it is bluer and then green and then
35 black I am blacking out and yet
my mask is powerful
it pumps my blood with power
the sea is another story
the sea is not a question of power
40 I have to learn alone
to turn my body without force
in the deep element.

And now: it is easy to forget
what I came for
45 among so many who have always
lived here
swaying their crenellated fans
between the reefs
and besides
50 you breathe differently down here.

I came to explore the wreck.
The words are purposes.
The words are maps.
I came to see the damage that was done
55 and the treasures that prevail.
I stroke the beam of my lamp
slowly along the flank
of something more permanent
than fish or weed

60 the thing I came for:
the wreck and not the story of the wreck

the thing itself and not the myth
the drowned face always staring
65   toward the sun
the evidence of damage
worn by salt and sway into this threadbare beauty
the ribs of the disaster
curving their assertion
among the tentative haunters.
70

This is the place.
And I am here, the mermaid whose dark hair
streams black, the merman in his armored body
We circle silently
75   about the wreck
we dive into the hold.
I am she: I am he

whose drowned face sleeps with open eyes
whose breasts still bear the stress
80   whose silver, copper, vermeil cargo lies
obscurely inside barrels
half-wedged and left to rot
we are the half-destroyed instruments
that once held to a course
85   the water-eaten log
the fouled compass

We are, I am, you are
by cowardice or courage
the one who find our way
90   back to this scene
carrying a knife, a camera
a book of myths
in which
our names do not appear.   (1972)

AUNT JENNIFER'S TIGERS

Aunt Jennifer's tigers prance across a screen,
Bright topaz denizens of a world of green.
They do not fear the men beneath the tree;
They pace in sleek chivalric certainty.

5 Aunt Jennifer's fingers fluttering through her wool
Find even the ivory needle hard to pull.
The massive weight of Uncle's wedding band
Sits heavily upon Aunt Jennifer's hand.

When Aunt is dead, her terrified hands will lie
10 Still ringed with ordeals she was mastered by.
The tigers in the panel that she made
Will go on prancing, proud and unafraid.

LIVING IN SIN

She had thought the studio would keep itself;
no dust upon the furniture of love.
Half heresy, to wish the taps less vocal,
the panes relieved of grime. A plate of pears,
5 a piano with a Persian shawl, a cat
stalking the picturesque amusing mouse
had risen at his urging.
Not that at five each separate stair would writhe
under the milkman's tramp; that morning light
10 so coldly would delineate the scraps
of last night's cheese and three sepulchral bottles;
that on the kitchen shelf among the saucers
a pair of beetle-eyes would fix her own—
envoy from some village in the moldings . . .
20 Meanwhile, he, with a yawn,
sounded a dozen notes upon the keyboard,
declared it out of tune,
rubbed at his beard, went out for cigarettes;
while she, jeered by the minor demons,
25 pulled back the sheets and made the bed and found
a towel to dust the table-top,
and let the coffee pot boil over on the stove.
By evening she was back in love again,
though not so wholly but throughout the night
30 she woke sometimes to feel the daylight coming
like a relentless milkman up the stairs.

TOWARD THE SOLSTICE

The thirtieth of November.
Snow is starting to fall.
A peculiar silence is spreading
over the fields, the maple grove.
5   It is the thirtieth of May,
rain pours on ancient bushes, runs
down the youngest blade of grass.
I am trying to hold in one steady glance
all the parts of my life.
10   A spring torrent races
on this old slanting roof,
the slanted field below
thickens with winter's first whiteness.
Thistles dried to sticks in last year's wind
15   stand nakedly in the green,
stand sullenly in the slowly whitening,
field.

       My brain glows
more violently, more avidly
20   the quieter, the thicker
the quilt of crystals settles,
the louder, more relentlessly
the torrent beats itself out
on the old boards and shingles.
25   It is the thirtieth of May,
the thirtieth of November,
a beginning or an end,
we are moving into the solstice
and there is so much here
30   I still do not understand.

If I could make sense of how
my life is still tangled
with dead weeds, thistles,
enormous burdocks, burdens
35   slowly shifting under
this first fall of snow,
beaten by this early, racking rain
calling all new life to declare itself strong
or die,
40   if I could know
in what language to address

the spirits that claim a place
beneath these low and simple ceilings,
tenants that neither speak nor stir
45   yet dwell in mute insistence
till I can feel utterly ghosted in this house.

If history is a spider-thread
spun over and over though brushed away
it seems I might some twilight
50   or dawn in the hushed country light
discern its greenness stretching
from molding or doorframe, out
into the empty dooryard
and following it climb
55   the path into the pinewoods,
tracing from tree to tree
in the failing light, in the slowly
lucidifying day
its constant, purposive trail,
60   till I reach whatever cellar hole
filling with snowflakes or lichen,
whatever fallen shack
or unremembered clearing
I am meant to have found
65   and there, under the first or last
star, trusting to instinct
the words would come to mind
I have failed or forgotten to say
year after year, winter
70   after summer, the right rune
to ease the hold of the past
upon the rest of my life
and ease my hold on the past.

If some rite of separation
75   is still unaccomplished
between myself and the long-gone
tenants of this house,
between myself and my childhood,
and the childhood of my children,
80   it is I who have neglected
to perform the needed acts,
set water in corners, light and eucalyptus
in front of mirrors,
or merely pause and listen

85   to my own pulse vibrating
lightly as falling snow,
relentlessly as the rainstorm,
and hear what it has been saying.
It seems I am still waiting
90   for them to make some clear demand
some articulate sound or gesture,
for release to come from anywhere
but from inside myself.

A decade of cutting away
95   dead flesh, cauterizing
old scars ripped open over and over
and still it is not enough.

A decade of performing
the loving humdrum acts
100   of attention to this house
transplanting lilac suckers,
washing panes, scrubbing
wood-smoke from splitting paint,
sweeping stairs, brushing the thread
105   of the spider aside,
and so much yet undone,
a woman's work, the solstice nearing,
and my hand still suspended
as if above a letter
110   I long and dread to close.   (1977)

28. MARGARET ATWOOD

Prolific Canadian poet and novelist Margaret Atwood (1939–), like her contemporary, Adrienne Rich, blends political (especially feminist) involvement with literary achievement. Atwood's writings are particularly interested in the intersection of the personal and the political; in her poetry and fiction, she often explores domestic relationships with an eye to their larger social significance. In so doing, Atwood has mastered multiple literary genres, including science fiction (The Handmaid's Tale) *the historical novel* (Alias: Grace), *and the psychological mystery* (The Blind Assassin, *for which she won the prestigious Booker Prize). In addition to making use of political subject matter, Atwood's writings often reflect on the act and significance of artistic creation itself; they tend to be both introspective and hopeful about the impact of writing on the real world.*

IN THE SECULAR NIGHT

In the secular night you wander around
alone in your house. It's two-thirty.
Everyone has deserted you,
or this is your story;
5   you remember it from being sixteen,
when the others were out somewhere, having a good
        time,
or so you suspected,
and you had to baby-sit.
10   You took a large scoop of vanilla ice-cream
and filled up the glass with grapejuice
and ginger ale, and put on Glenn Miller
with his big-band sound,
and lit a cigarette and blew the smoke up the chimney,
15   and cried for a while because you were not dancing,
and then danced, by yourself, your mouth circled with
        purple.

Now, forty years later, things have changed,
and it's baby lima beans.
20   It's necessary to reserve a secret vice.
This is what comes from forgetting to eat
at the stated mealtimes. You simmer them carefully,

drain, add cream and pepper,
and amble up and down the stairs,

55   scooping them up with your fingers right out of the
            bowl, talking to yourself out loud.
You'd be surprised if you got an answer,
but that part will come later.

There is so much silence between the words,

30   you say. You say, The sensed absence
of God and the sensed presence
amount to much the same thing,
only in reverse.
You say, I have too much white clothing.

35   You start to hum.
Several hundred years ago
this could have been mysticism
or heresy. It isn't now.
Outside there are sirens.

40   Someone's been run over.
The century grinds on.

THIS IS A PHOTOGRAPH OF ME

It was taken some time ago.
At first it seems to be
a smeared
print: blurred lines and grey flecks

5   blended with the paper;

then, as you scan
it, you see in the left-hand corner
a thing that is like a branch: part of a tree
(balsam or spruce) emerging

10   and, to the right, halfway up
what ought to be a gentle
slope, a small frame house.

In the background there is a lake,
and beyond that, some low hills.

15　(The photograph was taken
　　the day after I drowned.
　　I am in the lake, in the center
　　of the picture, just under the surface.

　　It is difficult to say where
20　precisely, or to say
　　how large or small I am:
　　the effect of water
　　on light is a distortion

　　but if you look long enough,
25　eventually
　　you will be able to see me.)

SPELLING

　　My daughter plays on the floor
　　with plastic letters,
　　red, blue & hard yellow,
　　learning how to spell,
5　spelling,
　　how to make spells.

　　I wonder how many women
　　denied themselves daughters,
　　closed themselves in rooms,
10　drew the curtains
　　so they could mainline words.

　　A child is not a poem,
　　a poem is not a child.
　　there is no either/or.
15　However.

　　I return to the story
　　of the woman caught in the war
　　& in labour, her thighs tied
　　together by the enemy
20　so she could not give birth.

Ancestress: the burning witch,
her mouth covered by leather
to strangle words.

A word after a word
25   after a word is power.

At the point where language falls away
from the hot bones, at the point
where the rock breaks open and darkness
flows out of it like blood, at
30   the melting point of granite
when the bones know
they are hollow & the word
splits & doubles & speaks
the truth & the body
35   itself becomes a mouth.

This is a metaphor.

How do you learn to spell?
Blood, sky & the sun,
your own name first,
40   your first naming, your first name,
your first word.

29. SHARON OLDS

Sharon Olds (1942–) was born in California and has lived in New York for many years. An instructor in the Graduate Creative Writing Program at New York University, she was named poet laureate of New York State for the years 1998–2000. Olds is known for her poetic meditations on private life, especially those concerning family and sexual themes. Because of this intimate subject matter, she is sometimes considered to be a "confessional poet," one who collapses the distinction between the speaker of a poem and the poet herself. "On the Subway" expresses broader sociological concerns: it urges the reader to join with the poem's speaker in examining the foundations and consequences of racial prejudice.

ON THE SUBWAY

The boy and I face each other.
His feet are huge, in black sneakers
laced with white in a complex pattern like a
set of intentional scars. We are stuck on
5   opposite sides of the car, a couple of
molecules stuck in a rod of light
rapidly moving through darkness. He has the
casual cold look of a mugger,
alert under hooded lids. He is wearing
10   red, like the inside of the body
exposed. I am wearing dark fur, the
whole skin of an animal taken and
used. I look at his raw face,
he looks at my fur coat, and I don't
15   know if I am in his power—
he could take my coat so easily, my
briefcase, my life—
or if he is in my power, the way I am
living off his life, eating the steak
20   he does not eat, as if I am taking
the food from his mouth. And he is black
and I am white, and without meaning or
trying to I must profit from his darkness,
the way he absorbs the murderous beams of the
25   nation's heart, as black cotton

absorbs the heat of the sun and holds it. There is
no way to know how easy this
white skin makes my life, this
life he could take so easily and
30 break across his knee like a stick the way his
own back is being broken, the
rod of his soul that at birth was dark and
fluid and rich as the heart of a seedling
ready to thrust up into any available light.

30. CYNTHIA OZICK

Cynthia Ozick was born New York in 1928, to Russian Jewish parents. Her literary accomplishments now range over five decades and have been honored by numerous international grants and awards. Many of Ozick's writings, including the story that follows, address themes of Jewish identity. "The Shawl" is a deeply moving account of the experience of the Holocaust, from the perspective of Jewish prisoners. It was first published in 1980 in The New Yorker *but later bound together in a single volume "The Shawl" with a companion piece entitled "Rosa," which traces the later lives of the characters who survive the events of "The Shawl."*

THE SHAWL

Stella, cold, cold, the coldness of hell. How they walked on the roads together, Rosa with Magda curled up between sore breasts, Magda wound up in the shawl. Sometimes Stella carried Magda. But she was jealous of Magda. A thin girl of fourteen, too small,
5   with thin breasts of her own, Stella wanted to be wrapped in a shawl, hidden away, asleep, rocked by the march, a baby, a round infant in arms. Magda took Rosa's nipple, and Rosa never stopped walking, a walking cradle. There was not enough milk; sometimes Magda sucked air; then she screamed. Stella was ravenous. Her
10 knees were tumors on sticks, her elbows chicken bones.
Rosa did not feel hunger; she felt light, not like someone walking but like someone in a faint, in trance, arrested in a fit, someone who is already a floating angel, alert and seeing everything, but in the air, not there, not touching the road. As if teetering on the tips of
15 her fingernails. She looked into Magda's face through a gap in the shawl: a squirrel in a nest, safe, no one could reach her inside the little house of the shawl's windings. The face, very round, a pocket mirror of a face: but it was not Rosa's bleak complexion, dark like cholera, it was another kind of face altogether, eyes blue as air,
20 smooth feathers of hair nearly as yellow as the Star sewn into Rosa's coat. You could think she was one of *their* babies.
Rosa, floating, dreamed of giving Magda away in one of the villages. She could leave the line for a minute and push Magda into the hands of any woman on the side the road. But if she moved out
25 of line they might shoot. And even if she fled the line for half a second and pushed the shawl-bundle at a stranger, would the woman

take it? She might be surprised, or afraid; she might drop the shawl, and Magda would fall out and strike her head and die. The little round head. Such a good child, she gave up screaming, and sucked now only for the taste of the drying nipple itself. The neat grip of
5   the tiny gums. One mite of a tooth tip sticking up in the bottom gum, how shining, an elfin tombstone of white marble gleaming there. Without complaining, Magda relinquished Rosa's teats, first the left, then the right; both were cracked, not a sniff of milk. The duct-crevice extinct, a dead volcano, blind eye, chill hole, so Magda
10 took the corner of the shawl and milked it instead. She sucked and sucked, flooding threads with wetness. The shawl's good flavor, milk of linen.

It was a magic shawl, it could nourish an infant for three days and three nights. Magda did not die, she stayed alive, although very
15 quiet. A peculiar smell, of cinnamon and almonds, lifted out of her mouth. She held her eyes open every moment, forgetting how to blink or nap, and Rosa and sometimes Stella studied their blueness. On the road they raised one burden of a leg after another and studied Magda's face. "Aryan," Stella said, in a voice grown as thin as a
20 string; and Rosa thought how Stella gazed at Magda like a young cannibal. And the time that Stella said "Aryan," it sounded to Rosa as if Stella had really said "Let us devour her."

But Magda lived to walk. She lived that long, but she did not walk very well, partly because she was only fifteen months old, and
25 partly because the spindles of her legs could not hold up her fat belly. It was fat with air, full and round. Rosa gave almost all her food to Magda, Stella gave nothing; Stella was ravenous, a growing child herself, but not growing much. Stella did not menstruate. Rosa did not menstruate. Rosa was ravenous, but also not; she learned
30 from Magda how to drink the taste of a finger in one's mouth. They were in a place without pity, all pity was annihilated in Rosa, she looked at Stella's bones without pity. She was sure that Stella was waiting for Magda to die so she could put her teeth into the little thighs.

35   Rosa knew Magda was going to die very soon; she should have been dead already, but she had been buried away deep inside the magic shawl, mistaken there for the shivering mound of Rosa's breasts; Rosa clung to the shawl as if it covered only herself. No one took it away from her. Magda was mute. She never cried. Rosa hid
40 her in the barracks, under the shawl, but she knew that one day someone would inform; or one day someone, not even Stella, would steal Magda to eat her. When Magda began to walk Rosa knew that Magda was going to die very soon, something would happen. She was afraid to fall asleep; she slept with the weight of her thigh on
45 Magda's body; she was afraid she would smother Magda under her

thigh. The weight of Rosa was becoming less and less; Rosa and Stella were slowly turning into air.

Magda was quiet, but her eyes were horribly alive, like blue tigers. She watched. Sometimes she laughed—it seemed a laugh,
5   but how could it be? Magda had never seen anyone laugh, still, Magda laughed at her shawl when the wind blew its corners, the bad wind with pieces of black in it, that made Stella's and Rosa's eyes tear. Magda's eyes were always clear and tearless. She watched like a tiger. She guarded her shawl. No one could touch it; only Rosa
10   could touch it. Stella was not allowed. The shawl was Magda's own baby, her pet, her little sister. She tangled herself up in it and sucked on one of the corners when she wanted to be very still.

Then Stella took the shawl away and made Magda die.

Afterward Stella said: "I was cold."

15   And afterward she was always cold, always. The cold went into her heart: Rosa saw that Stella's heart was cold. Magda flopped onward with her little pencil legs, scribbling this way and that, in search of the shawl; the pencils faltered at the barracks opening, where the light began. Rosa saw and pursued. But already Magda
20   was in the square outside the barracks, in the jolly light. It was the roll-call arena. Every morning Rosa had to conceal Magda under the shawl against a wall of the barracks and go out and stand in the arena with Stella and hundreds of others, sometimes for hours, and Magda, deserted, was quiet under the shawl, sucking on her corner.
25   Every day Magda was silent, and so she did not die. Rosa saw that today Magda was going to die, and at the same time a fearful joy ran in Rosa's two palms, her fingers were on fire, she was astonished, febrile: Magda, in the sunlight, swaying on her pencil legs, was howling. Ever since the drying up of Rosa's nipples, ever since
30   Magda's last scream on the road, Magda had been devoid of any syllable; Magda was a mute. Rosa believed that something had gone wrong with her vocal cords, with her windpipe, with the cave of her larynx; Magda was defective, without a voice; perhaps she was deaf; there might be something amiss with her intelligence; Magda was
35   dumb. Even the laugh that came when the ash-stippled wind made a clown out of Magda's shawl was only the air-blown showing of her teeth. Even when the lice, head lice and body lice, crazed her so that she became as wild as one of the big rats that plundered the barracks at daybreak looking for carrion, she rubbed and scratched and
40   kicked and bit and rolled without a whimper. But now Magda's mouth was spilling a long viscous rope of clamor.

"Maaaa—"

It was the first noise Magda had ever sent out from her throat since the drying up of Rosa's nipples.

45   "Maaaa . . . aaa!"

Again! Magda was wavering in the perilous sunlight of the arena, scribbling on such pitiful little bent shins. Rosa saw. She saw that Magda was grieving for the loss of her shawl, she saw that Magda was going to die. A tide of commands hammered in Rosa's
5   nipples: Fetch, get, bring! But she did not know which to go after first, Magda or the shawl. If she jumped out into the arena to snatch Magda up, the howling would not stop, because Magda would still not have the shawl; but if she ran back into the barracks to find the shawl, and if she found it, and if she came after Magda holding it
10 and shaking it, then she would get Magda back, Magda would put the shawl in her mouth and turn dumb again.

    Rosa entered the dark. It was easy to discover the shawl. Stella was heaped under it, asleep in her thin bones. Rosa tore the shawl free and flew—she could fly, she was only air—into the arena. The
15 sunheat murmured of another life, of butterflies in summer. The light was placid, mellow. On the other side of the steel fence, far away, there were green meadows speckled with dandelions and deep-colored violets; beyond them, even farther, innocent tiger lilies, tall, lifting their orange bonnets. In the barracks they spoke of
20 "flowers," of "rain": excrement, thick turd-braids, and the slow stinking maroon waterfall that slunk down from the upper bunks, the stink mixed with a bitter fatty floating smoke that greased Rosa's skin. She stood for an instant at the margin of the arena. Sometimes the electricity inside the fence would seem to hum; even
25 Stella said it was only an imagining, but Rosa heard real sounds in the wire; grainy sad voices. The farther she was from the fence, the more clearly the voices crowded at her. The lamenting voices strummed so convincingly, so passionately, it was impossible to suspect them of being phantoms. The voices told her to hold up the
30 shawl, high; the voices told her to shake it, to whip with it, to unfurl it like a flag. Rosa lifted, shook, whipped, unfurled. Far off, very far, Magda leaned across her air-fed belly, reaching out with the rods of her arms. She was high up, elevated, riding someone's shoulder. But the shoulder that carried Magda was not coming toward Rosa
35 and the shawl, it was drifting away, the speck of Magda was moving more and more into the smoky distance. Above the shoulder a helmet glinted. The light tapped the helmet and sparkled it into a goblet. Below the helmet a black body like a domino and a pair of black boots hurled themselves in the direction of the electrified
40 fence. The electric voices began to chatter wildly "Maamaa, maaa-maaa," they all hummed together. How far Magda was from Rosa now, across the whole square, past a dozen barracks, all the way on the other side! She was no bigger than a moth.

    All at once Magda was swimming through the air. The whole
45 of Magda traveled through loftiness. She looked like a butterfly

touching a silver vine. And the moment Magda's feathered round head and her pencil legs and balloonish belly and zigzag arms splashed against the fence, the steel voices went mad in their growling, urging Rosa to run and run to the spot where Magda had fall-
5   en from her flight against the electrified fence; but of course Rosa did not obey them. She only stood, because if she ran they would shoot, and if she tried to pick up the sticks of Magda's body they would shoot, and if she let the wolf's screech ascending now through the ladder of her skeleton break out, they would shoot; so
10   she took Magda's shawl and filled her own mouth with it, stuffed it in and stuffed it in, until she was swallowing up the wolf's screech and tasting the cinnamon and almond depth of Magda's saliva; and Rosa drank Magda's shawl until it dried.

31. MAXINE HONG KINGSTON

Born in Stockton, California, to Chinese parents, Maxine Hong Kingston (1940–) earned Bachelor's and Education degrees from the University of California-Berkeley, where she became active in the anti-Vietnam War movement thriving on campus in the 1960s. After graduating, she taught English and mathematics before relocating her family to Hawaii to escape the increasing political tension in California. While in Hawaii, Kingston continued her career as an educator, becoming a visiting professor at the University of Hawaii at Honolulu. As a writer, Kingston is deeply aware of both her American national identity and her Asian cultural heritage. Her published work is highly concerned with the importance of memory; it explores our connections to the past and the impact of ancestral heritage on our present-day lives. The stories that Kingston tells are often matrilineal; not only are they concerned with the ways in which this heritage is passed from mother to daughter, but they are also, at times, derived from stories that Kingston's own mother told her. "No-Name Woman" is excerpted from Kingston's first published book, The Woman Warrior, *a postmodern and feminist text which blurs generic lines between novel, short story, autobiography, and memoir. Like the text itself, Kingston's characters, by transgressing social and cultural expectations of them, defy conventional categorization, forging their own complex identities out of personal experience and pain.*

NO-NAME WOMAN

"You must not tell anyone," my mother said, "what I am about to tell you. In China your father had a sister who killed herself. She jumped into the family well. We say that your father has all brothers because it is as if she had never been born."

5   "In 1924 just a few days after our village celebrated seventeen hurry-up weddings—to make sure that every young man who went 'out on the road' would responsibly come home—your father and his brothers and your grandfather and his brothers and your aunt's new husband sailed for America, the Gold Mountain. It was
10   your grandfather's last trip. Those lucky enough to get contracts waved goodbye from the decks. They fed and guarded the stowaways and helped them off in Cuba, New York, Bali, Hawaii. 'We'll meet in California next year,' they said. All of them sent money home.

"I remember looking at your aunt one day when she and I were dressing; I had not noticed before that she had such a protruding melon of a stomach. But I did not think, 'She's pregnant,' until she began to look like other pregnant women, her shirt pulling and the
5 white tops of her black pants showing. She could not have been pregnant, you see, because her husband had been gone for years. No one said anything. We did not discuss it. In early summer she was ready to have the child, long after the time when it could have been possible."
10 "The village had also been counting. On the night the baby was to be born the villagers raided our house. Some were crying. Like a great saw, teeth strung with lights, files of people walked zigzag across our land, tearing the rice. Their lanterns doubled in the disturbed black water, which drained away through the broken bunds.
15 As the villagers closed in, we could see that some of them, proba--bly men and women we knew well, wore white masks. The people with long hair hung it over their faces. Women with short hair made it stand up on end. Some had tied white bands around their foreheads, arms, and legs."
20 "At first they threw mud and rocks at the house. Then they threw eggs and began slaughtering our stock. We could hear the animals scream their deaths—the roosters, the pigs, a last great roar from the ox. Familiar wild heads flared in our night windows; the villagers encircled us. Some of the faces stopped to peer at us, their
25 eyes rushing like searchlights. The hands flattened against the panes, framed heads, and left red prints.
"The villagers broke in the front and the back doors at the same time, even though we had not locked the doors against them. Their knives dripped with the blood of our animals. They smeared blood
30 on the doors and walls. One woman swung a chicken, whose throat she had slit, splattering blood in red arcs about her. We stood together in the middle of our house, in the family hall with the pictures and tables of the ancestors around us, and looked straight ahead."
35 "At that time the house had only two wings. When the men came back, we would build two more to enclose our courtyard and a third one to begin a second courtyard. The villagers pushed through both wings, even your grandparents' rooms, to find your aunt's, which was also mine until the men returned. From this room
40 a new wing for one of the younger families would grow. They ripped up her clothes and shoes and broke her combs, grinding them underfoot. They tore her work from the loom. They scattered the cooking fire and rolled the new weaving in it. We could hear them in the kitchen breaking our bowls and banging the pots. They
45 overturned the great waist-high earthenware jugs; duck eggs, pick-

led fruits, vegetables burst out and mixed in acrid torrents. The old
woman from the next field swept a broom through the air and
loosed the spirits-of-the-broom over our heads. 'Pig.' 'Ghost.' 'Pig,'
they sobbed and scolded while they ruined our house.

5   "When they left, they took sugar and oranges to bless themselves. They cut pieces from the dead animals. Some of them took
bowls that were not broken and clothes that were not torn.
Afterward we swept up the rice and sewed it back up into sacks.
But the smells from the spilled preserves lasted. Your aunt gave
10 birth in the pigsty that night. The next morning when I went for the
water, I found her and the baby plugging up the family well."

    "Don't let your father know that I told you. He denies her. Now
that you have started to menstruate, what happened to her could
happen to you. Don't humiliate us. You wouldn't like to be forgot-
15 ten as if you had never been born. The villagers are watchful."

    Whenever she had to warn us about life, my mother told sto-
ries that ran like this one, a story to grow up on. She tested our
strength to establish realities. Those in the emigrant generations
who could not reassert brute survival died young and far from
20 home. Those of us in the first American generations have had to figure out how the invisible world the emigrants built around our
childhoods fit in solid America.

    The emigrants confused the gods by diverting their curses,
misleading them with crooked streets and false names. They must
25 try to confuse their offspring as well, who, I suppose, threaten them
in similar ways—always trying to get things straight, always trying
to name the unspeakable. The Chinese I know hide their names;
sojourners take new names when their lives change and guard their
real names with silence.

30   Chinese-Americans, when you try to understand what things
in you are Chinese, how do you separate what is peculiar to childhood, to poverty, insanities, one family, your mother who marked
your growing with stories, from what is Chinese? What is Chinese
tradition and what is the movies?

35   If I want to learn what clothes my aunt wore, whether flashy or
ordinary, I would have to begin, "Remember Father's drowned-in-
the-well sister?" I cannot ask that. My mother has told me once and
for all the useful parts. She will add nothing unless powered by
Necessity, a riverbank that guides her life. She plants vegetable gar-
40 dens rather than lawns; she carries the odd-shaped tomatoes home
from the fields and eats food left for the gods.

    Whenever we did frivolous things, we used up energy; we flew
high kites. We children came up off the ground over the melting
cones our parents brought home from work and the American
45 movie on New Year's Day—*Oh, You Beautiful Doll* with Betty Grable

one year, and *She Wore a Yellow Ribbon* with John Wayne another
year. After the one carnival ride each, we paid in guilt; our tired
father counted his change on the dark walk home.

Adultery is extravagance. Could people who hatch their own
5   chicks and eat the embryos and the heads for delicacies and boil the
feet in vinegar for party food, leaving only the gravel, eating even
the gizzard lining—could such people engender a prodigal aunt?
To be a woman, to have a daughter in starvation time was a waste
enough. My aunt could not have been the lone romantic who gave
10 up everything for sex. Women in the old China did not choose.
Some man had commanded her to lie with him and be his secret
evil. I wonder whether he masked himself when he joined the raid
on her family.

Perhaps she encountered him in the fields or on the mountain
15 where the daughters-in-law collected fuel. Or perhaps he first
noticed her in the marketplace. He was not a stranger because the
village housed no strangers. She had to have dealings with him
other than sex. Perhaps he worked an adjoining field, or he sold her
the cloth for the dress she sewed and wore. His demand must have
20 surprised, then terrified her. She obeyed him; she always did as she
was told.

When the family found a young man in the next village to be
her husband, she stood tractably beside the best rooster, his proxy,
and promised before they met that she would be his forever. She
25 was lucky that he was her age and she would be the first wife, an
advantage secure now. The night she first saw him, he had sex with
her. Then he left for America. She had almost forgotten what he
looked like. When she tried to envision him, she only saw the black
and white face in the group photograph the men had had taken
30 before leaving.

The other man was not, after all, much different from her husband. They both gave orders. she followed. "If you tell your family,
I'll beat you. I'll kill you. Be here again next week." No one talked
sex, ever. And she might have separated the rapes from the rest of
35 living if only she did not have to buy her oil from him or gather
wood in the same forest. I want her fear to have lasted just as long
as rape lasted so that the fear could have been contained. No
drawn-out fear. But women at sex hazarded birth and hence life-
times. The fear did not stop but permeated everywhere. She told
40 the man, "I think I'm pregnant." He organized the raid against her.

On nights when my mother and father talked about their life
back home, sometimes they mentioned an "outcast table" whose
business they still seemed to be settling, their voices tight. In a com-
mensal tradition, where food is precious, the powerful older people
45 made wrongdoers eat alone. Instead of letting them start separate

new lives like the Japanese, who could become samurais and geishas, the Chinese family, faces averted but eyes glowering sideways, hung on to the offenders and fed them leftovers. My aunt must have lived in the same house as my parents and eaten at an
5   outcast table. My mother spoke about the raid as if she had seen it, when she and my aunt, a daughter-in-law to a different household, should not have been living together at all. Daughters-in-law lived with their husbands' parents, not their own; a synonym for marriage in Chinese is "taking, a daughter-in-law." Her husband's par-
10   ents could have sold her, mortgaged her, stoned her. But they had sent her back to her own mother and father, a mysterious act hinting at disgraces not told me. Perhaps they had thrown her out to deflect the avengers.

She was the only daughter; her four brothers went with her
15   father, husband, and uncles "out on the road" and for some years became western men. When the goods were divided among the family, three of the brothers took land, and the youngest, my father, chose an education. After my grandparents gave their daughter away to her husband's family, they had dispensed all the adventure
20   and all the property. They expected her alone to keep the traditional ways, which her brothers, now among the barbarians, could fumble without detection. The heavy, deep-rooted women were to maintain the past against the flood, safe for returning. But the rare urge west had fixed upon our family, and so my aunt crossed
25   boundaries not delineated in space.

The work of preservation demands that the feelings playing about in one's guts not be turned into action. Just watch their passing like cherry blossoms. But perhaps my aunt, my forerunner, caught in a slow life, let dreams grow and fade and after some
30   months or years went toward what persisted. Fear at the enormities of the forbidden kept her desires delicate, wire and bone. She looked at a man because she liked the way the hair was tucked behind his ears, or she liked the question-mark line of a long torso curving at the shoulder and straight at the hip. For warm eyes or a
35   soft voice or a slow walk—that's all—a few hairs, a line, a brightness, a sound, a pace, she gave up family. She offered us up for a charm that vanished with tiredness, a pigtail that didn't toss when the wind died. Why, the wrong lighting could erase the dearest thing about him.
40   *It could very well have been, however, that my aunt did not take subtle enjoyment of her friend, but, a wild woman, kept rollicking company.* Imagining her free with sex doesn't fit, though. I don't know any women like that, or men either. Unless I see her life branching into mine, she gives me no ancestral help.
45   To sustain her being in love, she often worked at herself in the

mirror, guessing at the colors and shapes that would interest him, changing them frequently in order to hit on the right combination. She wanted him to look back.

On a farm near the sea, a woman who tended her appearance
5   reaped a reputation for eccentricity. All the married women blunt-cut their hair in flaps about their ears or pulled it back in tight buns. No nonsense. Neither style blew easily into heart-catching tangles. And at their weddings they displayed themselves in their long hair for the last time. "It brushed the backs of my knees," my mother
10   tells me. "It was braided, and even so, it brushed the backs of my knees."

At the mirror my aunt combed individuality into her bob. A bun could have been contrived to escape into black streamers blowing in the wind or in quiet wisps about her face, but only the older
15   women in our picture album wear buns. She brushed her hair back from her forehead, tucking the flaps behind her ears. She looped a piece of thread, knotted into a circle between her index fingers and thumbs, and ran the double strand across her forehead. When she closed her fingers as if she were making a pair of shadow geese bite,
20   the string twisted together catching the little hairs. Then she pulled the thread away from her skin, ripping the hairs out neatly, her eyes watering from the needles of pain. Opening her fingers, she cleaned the thread, then rolled it along her hairline and the tops of her eyebrows. My mother did the same to me and my sisters and herself. I
25   used to believe that the expression "caught by the short hairs" meant a captive held with a depilatory string. It especially hurt at the temples, but my mother said we were lucky we didn't have to have our feet bound when we were seven. Sisters used to sit on their beds and cry together, she said, as their mothers or their slaves
30   removed the bandages for a few minutes each night and let the blood gush back into their veins. I hope that the man my aunt loved appreciated a smooth brow, that he wasn't just a tits-and-ass man.

Once my aunt found a freckle on her chin, at a spot that the almanac said predestined her for unhappiness. She dug it out with
35   a hot needle and washed the wound with peroxide.

More attention to her looks than these pullings of hairs and pickings at spots would have caused gossip among the villagers. They owned work clothes and good clothes, and they wore good clothes for feasting the new seasons. But since a woman combing
40   her hair hexes beginnings, my aunt rarely found an occasion to look her best. Women looked like great sea snails—the corded wood, babies, and laundry they carried were the whorls on their backs. The Chinese did not admire a bent back; goddesses and warriors stood straight. Still there must have been a marvelous freeing of
45   beauty when a worker laid down her burden and stretched and

arched.

Such commonplace loveliness, however, was not enough for my aunt. She dreamed of a lover for the fifteen days of New Year's, the time for families to exchange visits, money, and food. She plied
5 her secret comb. And sure enough she cursed the year, the family, the village, and herself.

Even as her hair lured her imminent lover, many other men looked at her. Uncles, cousins, nephews, brothers would have looked, too, had they been home between journeys. Perhaps they
10 had already been restraining their curiosity, and they left, fearful that their glances, like a field of nesting birds, might be startled and caught. Poverty hurt, and that was their first reason for leaving. But another, final reason for leaving the crowded house was the never-said.

15 She may have been unusually beloved, the precious only daughter, spoiled and mirror gazing because of the affection the family lavished on her. When her husband left, they welcomed the chance to take her back from the in-laws; she could live like the little daughter for just a while longer. There are stories that my grand-
20 father was different from other people, "crazy ever since the little Jap bayoneted him in the head." He used to put his naked penis on the dinnertable, laughing. And one day he brought home a baby girl, wrapped up inside his brown western-style greatcoat. He had traded one of his sons, probably my father, the youngest, for her.
25 My grandmother made him trade back. When he finally got a daughter of his own, he doted on her. They must have all loved her, except perhaps my father, the only brother who never went back to China, having once been traded for a girl.

Brothers and sisters, newly men and women, had to efface their
30 sexual color and present plain miens. Disturbing hair and eyes, a smile like no other threatened the ideal of five generations living under one roof. To focus blurs, people shouted face to face and yelled from room to room. The immigrants I know have loud voices, unmodulated to American tones even after years away from the
35 village where they called their friendships out across the fields. I have not been able to stop my mother's screams in public libraries or over telephones. Walking erect (knees straight, toes pointed forward, not pigeon-toed, which is Chinese-feminine) and speaking in an inaudible voice, I have tried to turn myself American-feminine.
40 Chinese communication was loud, public. Only sick people had to whisper. But at the dinner table, where the family members came nearest one another, no one could talk, not the outcasts nor any eaters. Every word that falls from the mouth is a coin lost. Silently they gave and accepted food with both hands. A preoccupied child
45 who took his bowl with one hand got a sideways glare. A complete

moment of total attention is due everyone alike. Children and
lovers have no singularity here, but my aunt used a secret voice, a
separate attentiveness.

She kept the man's name to herself throughout her labor and
5   dying; she did not accuse him that he be punished with her. To save
her inseminator's name she gave silent birth.

He may have been somebody in her own household, but inter-
course with a man outside the family would have been no less
abhorrent. All the village were kinsmen, and the titles shouted in
10 loud country voices never let kinship be forgotten. Any man within visiting distance would have been neutralized as a lover—
"brother, "younger brother," "older brother"—one hundred and fifteen relationship titles. Parents researched birth charts probably not
so much to assure good fortune as to circumvent incest in a popu-
15 lation that has but one hundred surnames. Everybody has eight
million relatives. How useless then sexual mannerisms, how dangerous.

As if it came from an atavism deeper than fear, I used to add
"brother" silently to boys' names. It hexed the boys, who would or
20 would not ask me to dance, and made them less scary and as familiar and deserving of benevolence as girls.

But, of course, I hexed myself also—no dates. I should have
stood up, both arms waving, and shouted out across libraries, "Hey,
you! Love me back." I had no idea, though, how to make attraction
25 selective, how to control its direction and magnitude. If I made
myself American-pretty so that the five or six Chinese boys in the
class fell in love with me, everyone else—the Caucasian, Negro,
and Japanese boys—would too. Sisterliness, dignified and honor-
able, made much more sense.

30 Attraction eludes control so stubbornly that whole societies
designed to organize relationships among people cannot keep
order, not even when they bind people to one another from childhood and raise them together. Among the very poor and the
wealthy, brothers married their adopted sisters, like doves. Our
35 family allowed some romance, paying adult brides' prices and providing dowries so that their sons and daughters could marry
strangers. Marriage promises to turn strangers into friendly relatives—a nation of siblings.

In the village structure, spirits shimmered among the live crea-
40 tures, balanced and held in equilibrium by time and land. But one
human being flaring up into violence could open up a black hole, a
maelstrom that pulled in the sky. The frightened villagers, who
depended on one another to maintain the real, went to my aunt to
show her a personal, physical representation of the break she had
45 made in the "roundness." Misallying couples snapped off the

future, which was to be embodied in true offspring. The villagers punished her for acting as if she could have a private life, secret and apart from them.

If my aunt had betrayed the family at a time of large grain
5   yields and peace, when many boys were born, and wings were being built on many houses, perhaps she might have escaped such severe punishment. But the men—hungry, greedy, tired of planting in dry soil, cuckolded—had had to leave the village in order to send food-money home. There were ghost plagues, bandit plagues, wars
10   with the Japanese, floods. My Chinese brother and sister had died of an unknown sickness. Adultery, perhaps only a mistake during good times, became a crime when the village needed food.

The round moon cakes and round doorways, the round tables of graduated size that fit one roundness inside another, round win-
15   dows and rice bowls—these talismans had lost their power to warn this family of the law: a family must be whole, faithfully keeping the descent line by having sons to feed the old and the dead, who in turn look after the family. The villagers came to show my aunt and her lover-in-hiding a broken house. The villagers were speed-
20   ing up the circling of events because she was too shortsighted to see that her infidelity had already harmed the village, that waves of consequences would return unpredictably, sometimes in disguise, as now, to hurt her. This roundness had to be made coin-sized so that she would see its circumference: punish her at the birth of her
25   baby. Awaken her to the inexorable. People who refused fatalism because they could invent small resources insisted on culpability. Deny accidents and wrest fault from the stars.

After the villagers left, their lanterns now scattering in various directions toward home, the family broke their silence and cursed
30   her. "Aiaa, we're going to die. Death is coming. Death is coming. Look what you've done. You've killed us. Ghost! Dead ghost! Ghost! You've never been born." She ran out into the fields, far enough from the house so that she could no longer hear their voic- es, and pressed herself against the earth, her own land no more.
35   When she felt the birth coming, she thought that she had been hurt. Her body seized together. "They've hurt me too much," she thought. "This is gall, and it will kill me." Her forehead and knees against the earth, her body convulsed and then released her onto her back. The black well of sky and stars went out and out and out
40   forever; her body and her complexity seemed to disappear. She was one of the stars, a bright dot in blackness, without home, without a companion, in eternal cold and silence. An agoraphobia rose in her, speeding higher and higher, bigger and bigger; she would not be able to contain it; there would be no end to fear.
45   Flayed, unprotected against, space, she felt pain return, focus-

ing her body. This pain chilled her—a cold, steady kind of surface pain. Inside, spasmodically, the other pain, the pain of the child, heated her. For hours she lay on the ground, alternately body and space. Sometimes a vision of normal comfort obliterated reality: she
5   saw the family in the evening gambling at the dinner table, the young people massaging their elders' backs. She saw them congratulating one another, high joy on the mornings the rice shoots came up. When these pictures burst, the stars drew yet further apart. Black space opened.
10   She got to her feet to fight better and remembered that old-fashioned women gave birth in their pigsties to fool the jealous pain-dealing gods, who do not snatch piglets. Before the next spasms could stop her, she ran to the pigsty, each step a rushing out into emptiness. She climbed over the fence and knelt in the dirt. It
15   was good to have a fence enclosing her, a tribal person alone.

    Laboring, this woman who had carried her child as a foreign growth that sickened her every day, expelled it at last. She reached down to touch the hot, wet, moving. mass, surely smaller than anything human, and could feet that it was human after all—fingers,
20   toes, nails, nose. She pulled it up on to her belly, and it lay curled there, butt in the air, feet precisely tucked one under the other. She opened her loose shirt and buttoned the child inside. After resting, it squirmed and thrashed and she pushed it up to her breast. It turned its head this way and that until it found her nipple. There, it
25   made little snuffling noises. She clenched her teeth at its preciousness, lovely as a young calf, a piglet, a little dog.

    She may have gone to the pigsty as a last act of responsibility: she would protect this child as, she had protected its father. It would look after her soul, leaving supplies on her grave. But how
30   would this tiny child without family find her grave when there would be no marker for her anywhere, neither in the earth nor the family hall? No one would give her a family hall name. She had taken the child with her into the wastes. At its birth the two of them had felt the same raw pain of separation, a wound that only the
35   family pressing tight could close. A child with no descent line would not soften her life but only trail after her, ghostlike, begging her to give it purpose. At dawn the villagers on their way to the fields would stand around the fence and look.

    Full of milk, the little ghost slept. When it awoke, she hardened
40   her breasts against the milk that crying loosens. Toward morning she picked up the baby and walked to the well.

    Carrying the baby to the well shows loving. Otherwise abandon it. Turn its face into the mud. Mothers who love their children take them along. It was probably a girl; there is some hope of for-
45   giveness for boys.

"Don't tell anyone you had an aunt. Your father does not want
to hear her name. She has never been born." I have believed that sex
was unspeakable and words so strong and fathers so frail that
"aunt" would do my father mysterious harm. I have thought that
5   my family, having settled among immigrants who had also been
their neighbors in the ancestral land, needed to clean their name,
and a wrong word would incite the kinspeople even here. But there
is more to this silence: they want me to participate in her punishment. And I have.
10   In the twenty years since I heard this story I have not asked for
details nor said my aunt's name; I do not know it. People who can
comfort the dead can also chase after them to hurt them further—a
reverse ancestor worship. The real punishment was not the raid
swiftly inflicted by the villagers, but the family's deliberately for-
15   getting her. Her betrayal so maddened them, they saw to it that she
would suffer forever, even after death. Always hungry, always
needing, she would have to beg food from other ghosts, snatch and
steal it from those whose living descendants give them gifts. She
would have to fight the ghosts massed at crossroads for the buns a
20   few thoughtful citizens leave to decoy her away from village and
home so that the ancestral spirits could feast unharassed. At peace,
they could act like gods, not ghosts, their descent lines providing
them with paper suits and dresses, spirit money, paper houses,
paper automobiles, chicken, meat, and rice into eternity—essences
25   delivered up in smoke and flames, steam and incense rising from
each rice bowl. In an attempt to make the Chinese care for people
outside the family, Chairman Mao encourages us now to give our
paper replicas to the spirits of outstanding soldiers and workers, no
matter whose ancestors they may be. My aunt remains forever hun-
30   gry. Goods are not distributed evenly among the dead.
My aunt haunts me—her ghost drawn to me because now, after
fifty years of neglect, I alone devote pages of paper to her, though
not origamied into houses and clothes. I do not think she always
means me well. I am telling on her, and she was a spite suicide,
35   drowning herself in the drinking water. The Chinese are always
very frightened of the drowned one, whose weeping ghost, wet
hair hanging and skin bloated, waits silently by the water to pull
down a substitute.